Acclaim for Ricky Riccardi's

What a Wonderful World

"Riccardi writes about Armstrong with self-evident and infectious love. . . . Written in a generous spirit. . . . Enhances our understanding of just how good Armstrong really was in the postwar years."
—*The Washington Post*

"[An] in-depth study. . . . Riccardi has done his homework. . . . He has immersed himself in Armstrong's papers, his correspondence, his tape-recorded conversations, and has somehow secured countless bootleg recordings of concerts and broadcasts made over a period of decades. From these and other sources, he has drawn a wealth of new information that will change our perspectives on Armstrong's life and legacy."
—*San Francisco Chronicle*

"Many of Armstrong's critics charged that his artistic stature diminished after 1931, 1940, 1952 . . . (pick a year). Riccardi's meticulous research and engaging narrative put that notion to rest. Armstrong's professionalism, toughness, humor and, most of all, the spirit of his music, emanate from the book's pages. This is an invaluable addition to the Armstrong bibliography—and a great read."
—Doug Ramsey, *Arts Journal*

"Riccardi . . . reveals new dimensions in a portrait of a highly familiar pop-culture icon."
—*Milwaukee Journal-Sentinel*

"A valuable account."
—*Newark Star-Ledger*

"This is not only a tale of interest to jazz fans or academics but the climactic portion of the inspiring life story of a man who, against all odds, rose from extreme poverty and discrimination to become, indisputably, one of the stellar figures of the twentieth century. . . . We need this book."
—Dan Morgenstern, director of the Institute of Jazz Studies, Rutgers University

"Riccardi provides a wealth of detail about the music that brought Armstrong his greatest notoriety, from his collaborations with Ella Fitzgerald and Dave Brubeck to his 'Satchmozation' of pop gems like 'Mack the Knife' and 'Hello, Dolly.' . . . [Riccardi's] love for the music is vivid on every page, and he proves adept at expressing the worth of Armstrong's late-career music. . . . The book's richest value is in its extensive utilization of quotes from Pops himself. The man who emerges is warm, funny and generous, but also unafraid to speak from the heart. . . . Shines a clear light on a much-neglected period of a great musician's life."
—*Jazz Times*

"[Riccardi] makes a strong case. . . . Recount[s] in extensive detail the trials and vicissitudes—and the triumphs—of the musicians' later career, beginning with the arrival of bebop in the late 1940s until his death in 1971. . . . You'll find much to like in *What a Wonderful World* about the later years of a genuine jazz icon."
—*Washington Independent Review of Books*

"Riccardi brings a unique bag of qualifications to the task, including unprecedented access to private Armstrong archives and thousands of hours of tape recordings of the man himself. . . . The rich details of the musicmaking, colorful personalities, and Armstrong's life on the road with his beloved All Stars band is priceless." —*The Christian Science Monitor*

"A major work of research and interpretation which for the first time has provided details of the last half of the most colorful and glorious career in the history of jazz." —George Avakian, Producer, *Louis Armstrong Plays W. C. Handy*

"Magical. . . . Deeply and effectively faces the complex question of what it is to be a working artist in the modern world. . . . [Riccardi is] a fine writer. . . . A pleasure to read. . . . Even if you are someone who appreciates Louis Armstrong only casually, you will find in this book a deep, rewarding, honest portrait of a man, an artist, his century."
—*Jazz Lives*

"A well-wrought biography and flowing read. . . . Riccardi defends [Armstrong] with admirable dispassion." —*New Orleans Magazine*

Ricky Riccardi

What a Wonderful World

Ricky Riccardi holds a B.A. in journalism and an M.A. in Jazz History and Research from Rutgers University. He has lectured at the Institute of Jazz Studies, at the National Jazz Museum in Harlem, and at the annual Satchmo SummerFest in New Orleans. He is the author of a popular Armstrong blog (dippermouth.blogspot.com) and is himself a jazz pianist. He is the archivist for the Louis Armstrong House Museum. He lives in New Jersey.

What a
Wonderful World

What a Wonderful World

The Magic of Louis Armstrong's Later Years

Ricky Riccardi

VINTAGE BOOKS

A DIVISION OF RANDOM HOUSE, INC.

NEW YORK

FIRST VINTAGE BOOKS EDITION, JUNE 2012

Frontispiece: Slowing down in Philadelphia in June 1968,
a thinned-down and tired Armstrong managed to still
flash his smile at Jack Bradley's camera. Two months later,
kidney trouble would force Armstrong to spend
nearly a year and a half recovering at home.

The Library of Congress has cataloged the Pantheon edition as follows:
Riccardi, Ricky.
What a wonderful world : the magic of Louis Armstrong's later years / Ricky Riccardi.
p. cm.
Includes bibliographical reference and index.
1. Armstrong, Louis, 1901–1971.
2. Jazz musicians—United States—Biography. I. Title.
ML419.A75R47 2011 781.65092—dc22 [B] 2010046541

Vintage ISBN: 978-0-307-47329-5

Book design by Maggie Hinders
Author photograph © Michael Lionstar

www.vintagebooks.com

Printed in the United States of America
10 9 8 7 6 5 4 3 2 1

For my parents, without whom
I never would have started this book . . .

and for Margaret and Ella, without whom
I never could have finished.

I've been thinking a whole lot of things. Through the years, I've noticed you take, not only critics, you take the man on the street or some cat that think he knows a whole lot about music and records and things, they'll come up and say, "Man, you're doing all right but I remember when you was really blowing that horn." And I'll look at him and say, "Well, solid, Gate," but he don't realize that I'm playing better now than I've ever played in my life.

—LOUIS ARMSTRONG, 1956[1]

Contents

strong's big features with Erskine Tate's orchestra at the Vendome Theatre. The novelty song he scatted was "Heebie Jeebies" and the preacher routine harked back to his childhood in New Orleans, where he won applause for impersonations and sermons at the local church. A 1927 review found among Armstrong's personal scrapbooks read, "Erskine Tate's orchestra at the Vendome Theatre last week was a 'wow.' Louis Armstrong, who is one of [Heebie Jeebies'] pet writers, led the members of the popular orchestra in a 'prayer' with his cornet. During his 'offering' he wore a high silk hat, frocktail coat and smoked glasses. The fans are still giggling over the act as it was far the most amusing one ever seen here."[1] Such a review was not uncommon for Armstrong: "But when Luis [sic] Armstrong sang 'My Baby Knows How,' to Charles Harris, who slipped a wig over his head and played the role of the baby that Luis was singing about, the fans laughed themselves dizzy. The number was the best Tate had offered since Luis 'preached the Gospel' some weeks ago." Yet another described him with admiration: "This talented musician plays, sings and dances."[2]

Louis Armstrong won audiences over with showmanship, laughter, and sublime music, starting as early as 1927. It is the Armstrong of that year who is usually made out to be the serious artist, celebrated for the groundbreaking Hot Five and Hot Seven—recordings that announced the singularity of jazz as a true American art form. So it was no surprise that Christopher Porterfield's 2006 *Time* magazine review of Armstrong's 1920s work exclaimed, "Forget the Satchmo who sang and mugged his way through his later decades, wonderfully entertaining as he was. This is Armstrong the force of nature—exuberant, inspired, irresistible."

The truth is, Louis Armstrong was a force of nature from the time he first picked up his horn as a teenager until the day he died in 1971. Yet the myth of the "two Armstongs" continues: the young serious artist and the old entertainer. In fact, Armstrong had always been a master show-man. Every aspect of his character, including love of entertaining, was formed during his childhood in New Orleans, singing and scatting in a vocal quartet before even learning to play the cornet. When he joined the Fletcher Henderson Orchestra in New York in 1924, Henderson only grudgingly allowed Armstrong's Bert Williams vaudeville routines on stage, fearing they were too rough around the edges for the predominantly upscale audience. This rankled Armstrong for years: "Yeah, but Fletcher didn't dig me like Joe Oliver," Armstrong recalled in a 1960 interview. "He had a million-dollar talent in his band and he never thought enough to let me sing or nothing. He'd go hire a singer, that lived up in Harlem, that night for the recording the next day, who didn't even know the song. And I'd say, 'Well, let me sing.' 'Nooo, NOOOO!' All he had was the trumpet in mind. And that's where he missed the boat. In those days, all Fletcher had to do was keep in his band the things that I'm doing now."[3]

Even at age twenty-four, Armstrong was confident of his "million-dollar talent" to sing and entertain as well as play the trumpet. When he joined Erskine Tate's symphony orchestra in Chicago in 1925, Armstrong's popularity skyrocketed, leading to the vaunted Hot Five recordings for the Okeh label. The Hot Fives and the later Hot Sevens brim with funny bits, though the humorous songs are usually given short shrift.

This dismissal of Armstrong's later years can be traced back to Gunther Schuller's 1967 work *Early Jazz*, which systematically solidified the jazz canon of the 1920s. With a background in classical music, Schuller had no patience for Armstrong's comedic tendencies and instead focused chiefly on his trumpet playing. Subsequent jazz histories followed Schuller's lead, rightfully praising tunes like "West End Blues" and "Potato Head Blues," but at the expense of less serious works such as "Irish Black Bottom" or "That's When I'll Come Back to You." Twenty years later, Schuller followed *Early Jazz* with *The Swing Era*, in which he continued to praise Armstrong's trumpet playing, but grew increasingly weary of his showmanship. By the time he addressed Armstrong's later years, Schuller was despondent. "But the end was not what it should have been," he wrote before suggesting that "as America's unofficial ambassador to the world, this country should have provided him an honorary pension to live out his life in dignity, performing as and when he might, but without the need to scratch out a living as a good-natured buffoon, singing 'Blueberry Hill' and 'What a Wonderful World' night after night."

Schuller was wrong. Armstrong didn't resent singing "Blueberry Hill" every night. When asked in 1968 what single record he would take to a desert island, Armstrong responded, "I'd like to take 'Blueberry Hill,' 'cause right now, it's like 'The Star-Spangled Banner' in America when I sing it."[4] While Armstrong's trumpet playing may have grown less exhibitionistic over the years, his singing, swinging, mugging, clowning, and playing the hell out of his horn were the same in 1955 as they were in 1925.

In a 1956 interview Armstrong discussed his longtime drummer Sid

Catlett, but might subconsciously have been talking about himself. "Take a man like Sid," he said. "He never did get his just praise like he should. He would get a write-up, sometime they'd say, 'Well, he's more show-man now'—showmanship and blah blah. But they ain't figuring out them notes are comin' out the horn. And if you stand up there and play and don't smile or something or show that you're relaxing, then they call you a deadpan or—I don't know."[5] Armstrong knew he was damned if he did and damned if he didn't. In the late sixties, when riding the wave of "Hello, Dolly!," Armstrong was asked about the critics of his style of per-forming. "Aw, I am paid to *entertain* the people," Armstrong responded. "If they want me to come on all strutty and cutting up—if that makes 'em happy, why not?"[6]

Some writers accused Armstrong of coasting in his later years, relying on the same songs every night, mugging excessively, not really playing the horn as he once did. Nothing could be farther from the truth. As Dan Morgenstern has said, this period was in fact the most taxing of Arm-strong's career:

He's out there all the time. He is the master of ceremonies. He is the lead singer. He is the lead player. He's there on everything. He will be sure to close those ensembles with something that demands a little bit in the way of chops and he's there from beginning to end. So that happens at a time in his career when he's already, you know, this is . . . what, 1947? So he's already in his late forties. This is a time when . . . a brass player of his range and using the kind of, not a non-pressure system but the kind of embouchure and technique that he has, which is very taxing. It's almost incredible what he can do, you know, and continued to do.[7]

Armstrong once said, "I never tried to prove nothing, just always wanted to give a good show. My life has been my music; it's always come first, but the music ain't worth nothing if you can't lay it on the public. The main thing is to live for that audience, 'cause what you're there for is to please the people."[8] Armstrong didn't consider the venues he played or the size of the audience; he always gave everything he had. "I don't give a damn how many come in, if it was one or one thousand," he said in 1960. "I ain't goin' play no louder or no softer, and I ain't goin' play no less. I might play a little *more*, but always up to par."[9] According to Humphrey Lyttelton, the

British trumpet player and author, "Those who worked under him would often declare that, if the curtain went up on a show to reveal only a handful of customers in the house, their hearts would sink. They knew that he was about to work them twice as hard." When a reporter once made the mistake of assuming that Armstrong took it easy when confronted with smaller crowds, Armstrong replied indignantly, "You don't take it easy, never! One of those guys might have hitch-hiked three hundred miles to hear your band for the first time. He don't do that to see you take it easy!"[10]

Armstrong lived for his fans, not for the hardened jazz critics who wanted to hear "West End Blues" every night. He was an international figure and the most beloved jazz musician of all time on the strength of his music *and* his personality, by being Armstrong "the artist" *and* Armstrong "the entertainer."

Yet Armstrong's mugging and eye rolling, his joy while entertaining, did embarrass many young black musicians in the 1940s and beyond. Trumpeter Dizzy Gillespie, a master showman himself, referred to Armstrong in a 1949 *DownBeat* article as a "plantation character." Discussing Armstrong's theme song "When It's Sleepy Time Down South," saxophonist Joe Evans, who played with Armstrong for a short period in the early 1940s, said, "Lyrics like 'when old Mammy falls down on her knees' and 'hearing darkies singin' and the banjos ringin'' weren't politically correct among young modern black musicians like me."[11] Miles Davis later wrote about Armstrong and Gillespie, "I hated the way they used to laugh and grin for audiences. I know *why* they did it—to make money and because they were entertainers as well as trumpet players . . . I didn't look at myself as an entertainer like they both did. I wasn't going to do it just so that some non-playing, racist, white motherfucker could write some nice things about me."[12] The thing Davis probably didn't realize is that the "non-playing, racist, white" critics he spoke about gave Armstrong some of his worst reviews during the latter part of his career. What Davis, the other younger musicians, and the critics didn't know was that Louis Armstrong didn't care about pleasing other musicians or good reviews. In the last twenty-five years of his life, there was no other musician or entertainer who made so many people happy all over the world. "They know I'm there in the cause of happiness," Armstrong said of his audiences, "And I don't worry what nobody thinks."[13]

Even if younger blacks were embarrassed by Armstrong's stage demeanor as reinforcing racist stereotypes, his own feelings about racism were otherwise expressed to close friends backstage and in private. A good example of this can be heard on a private tape recording Armstrong made with his friend Benny Hamilton in Portland at the beginning of 1952. The subject matter turned to Josephine Baker. The legendary entertainer and civil rights pioneer made a rare trip to the United States in 1951 and refused to perform in front of segregated audiences. While this was to be applauded, Armstrong didn't think she had gone far enough. "When this gal made all that stink, not only at the Stork Club, but she goes down in Miami and she raise all that hell because the colored people couldn't come to see her act," Armstrong said. "But she don't raise hell so the colored people could come in the place after she leaves. So you know she's vain." He continued:

And if she had talent, she wouldn't raise no hell at all. She wouldn't have to open her mouth. Her ability would speak for itself. See what I mean? And you can take anybody that's inferior and raise a whole lot of goddamn hell for no reason at all. But she's going to come over here and stir up the nation, get all them ofays—people that think a lot of us—against us, because you take a bunch of narrow-minded spades, following up that jive she's pulling—you understand?—then she go back with all that loot and everything and we're over here dangling. I don't dig her.[14]

This passage is key to understanding Armstrong's views on racism. Trumpeter Lester Bowie summed up this side of Armstrong's persona in the 1989 documentary *Satchmo*. "The true revolutionary is one that's not apparent," Bowie said. "I mean the revolutionary that's waving a gun out in the streets is never effective; the police just arrest him. But the police don't ever know about the guy that smiles and drops a little poison in their coffee. Well, Louis, in that sense, was that sort of revolutionary, a true revolutionary."

Armstrong admitted as much in a 1964 *Ebony* profile titled "The Reluctant Millionaire." In it, Armstrong discussed how he hadn't performed in New Orleans in years because they didn't allow an integrated band.

"I can't even play in my own hometown 'cause I've got white cats in the band," he said. "All I'd have to do is take all colored cats down there and I could make a million bucks. But to hell with the money. If we can't play down there like we play everywhere else we go, we don't play. So this is what burns me up everytime some damn fool says something about 'Tomming.' " Armstrong imparted more of what Bowie would call his "revolutionary" philosophy: "I know what it is; they want me to get out and walk up and down the street holding signs," he said. "This is something I'm not gonna do. Not because I don't believe in it. I think if some young cat feels that's his way of helping out, that's what he ought to do. But me, if I'd be out somewhere marching with a sign and some cat hits me in my chops, I'm finished. A trumpet man gets hit in the chops and he's through. If my people don't dig me the way I am, I'm sorry. If they don't go along with me giving my dough instead of marching, well—every cat's entitled to his opinion. But that's the way I figure I can help out and still keep on working. If they let me alone on this score I'll do my part, in my way."[15]

Ebony's stunning profile of Armstrong—complete with a picture of the trumpeter reading LeRoi Jones's *Blues People*—was a follow-up piece to a 1961 article that similarly featured Armstrong discussing racial issues. "I can have lunch with President [Juscelino] Kubitschek in the presidential mansion in Brazil," he said in 1961. "But I can't walk into a hotel dining room in the South and order a steak or a glass of water, as any ordinary white man can do." Armstrong shared stories of the racism he encountered on the road. "Not long ago, when we arrived late at a Midwest hotel to claim our reservations, the desk clerk told us, 'Sorry, we're all filled up,' " he recounted. "[Pianist] Joey Bushkin . . . kept hammering away at the desk clerk, who apparently made the reservation without knowing that Louis Armstrong was a Negro. The clerk finally let us stay. If it weren't for Joey we would have slept in the street. I felt bad. The mattress was soft, the carpeting thick, but I didn't appreciate the joint. To come from a concert where people are cheering you, taking your autograph, and then be given the icy brush by a hotel clerk can hurt real bad." Armstrong also learned to be wary of wealthy white fans as well: "I don't socialize with the top dogs of society after a dance or concert. Even though I'm invited, I don't go. These same society people may go around the corner and lynch a Negro . . . The main thing is I don't want anybody to hug or kiss me. Just treat me like a man."[16]

The *Ebony* articles demonstrated Armstrong's astute awareness of race relations in the United States, yet the jazz community ignored his sentiments. In a 1962 *Playboy* interview, Miles Davis praised Armstrong as a musician but spoke out against the practices of "Uncle Toms" in the jazz world. Duke Ellington read the *Playboy* article and agreed in a somewhat bitter interview in 1964, alongside his writing partner Billy Strayhorn. Ellington said, "[Miles] said if somebody wants to send some good representative down South, send Uncle, er, er, send Louis down there because he'll make everybody happy! Suppose they enjoy it? It interferes with the race problem, you can't sell your race for your personal gain." Strayhorn responded, "He gets, Louis Armstrong gets, a big contract [based on the Uncle Tom thing] and he [Ellington] gets nothing, because he represents the opposite." Ellington said, "It's a matter of dignity, it's a matter of embarrassing the race."[17] The "Uncle Tom" accusations followed Armstrong around throughout the 1950s and 1960s. He addressed them in the 1961 *Ebony* article: "Some folks, even some of my own people, have felt that I've been 'soft' on the race issue. Some have even accused me of being an Uncle Tom, of not being 'aggressive.' How can they say that? I've pioneered in breaking the color line in many Southern states (Georgia, Mississippi, Texas) with mixed bands—Negro and white. I've taken a lot of abuse, put up with a lot of jazz, even been in some pretty dangerous spots through no fault of my own for almost forty years."[18] As late as 1967, Armstrong expounded on the topic with Larry King. "Why, do you know I played ninety-nine *million* hotels I couldn't stay at? And if I had friends blowing at some all-white nightclub or hotel I couldn't get in to see 'em—or them to see me," he said. "One time in Dallas, Texas, some ofay stops me as I enter this hotel where I'm blowing the show—me in a goddamn *tuxedo*, now!—and tells me I got to come round to the back door. As time went on and I made a reputation I had it put in my contracts that I wouldn't *play* no place I couldn't *stay*. I was the first Negro in the business to crack them big white hotels—Oh, yeah! I pioneered, Pops! Nobody much remembers that these days."[19]

A few years after Louis Armstrong died, his widow, Lucille, was asked in a television interview if Louis was ever hurt by the negative way many in the black community portrayed him. "It hurt him greatly, because Louis has been one of the people all of his life," she responded. "He's

never felt or wanted to be anything other than black." She then recounted
her husband's public defamation of President Dwight Eisenhower during
the 1957 Little Rock integration crisis, saying the President had "no guts"
for allowing Arkansas Governor Orval Faubus control that situation. The
interviewer was shocked; it was the first he had heard the story or that
side of Louis. "Oh, you know, I mean, it's a funny thing," Lucille replied.
"Nobody really stopped to really dig Pops, and it's an unfortunate thing.
He felt it deeply, he really did."[20] Armstrong was so aggrieved because he
never forgot what he had had to endure because of the color of his skin.
"You know, some times I sit around the house and think about all the
places me and Lucille have been," he said in 1964. "You name the country
and we've just about been there. We've been wined and dined by all kinds
of royalty. We've had an audience with the Pope. We've even slept in Hitler's bed. But regardless of all that kind of stuff, I've got sense enough to
know that I'm still Louis Armstrong—colored."[21]

This book will reconsider the importance of Louis Armstrong's later years,
the most misunderstood period of the life of a genius. With apologies to
James Brown, from 1947 to 1971, Armstrong was truly the hardest-working
man in show business. He was sometimes criticized for playing the same
songs night after night, but Armstrong had a show that worked, something that had taken him quite some time to perfect. This repetition
allowed him to treat all of his audiences alike, whether he was playing in
front of cognoscenti at the Newport Jazz Festival or in a high-school gymnasium in Hinsdale, Illinois. The blend of pure jazz, pop songs, comedic
duets, and novelty numbers, all delivered by a New Orleans front line of
trumpet, trombone, and clarinet on top of a hard-swinging rhythm section, was unlike anything else in jazz at that time. As Armstrong grew
older, critics—with their need to pigeonhole artists—grew harsher in their
condemnation of his music and stage presence. The negative comments
could sometimes be stunning, as demonstrated in Wilfred Lowe's review
of a live Armstrong performance in 1954: "Armstrong, with his clowning, rolling eyes, suggestive growls and obscene asides . . . drags his choice
of music from the heights of art to the level of blackface buffoonery."[22]
Three years later, Whitney Balliett wrote, "A celebrated figure, Armstrong

has recently begun offering in his public appearances little more than a round of vaudeville antics—clowning, bad jokes—and a steadily narrowing repertory."[23]

Such criticisms still dog perceptions of his later career. Though Armstrong rarely addressed these issues, he had opinions about what he did onstage. Regarding his trumpet playing in his later years, Armstrong declared, "I'm playing better now than I've ever played in my life."[24] And on playing the same songs every night, his succinct rebuttal was, "Well, Beethoven didn't change his too much, did he?"[25] To critics who claimed Armstrong used clowning to win applause, Armstrong rebuked, "Well, it's nice, but you don't get no more hands than you would if you get that note right. The note's what counts—I don't care if you stand on your head."[26]

Armstrong particularly had no tolerance for those who wished he would "go back to the way he used to be" in the 1920s. Most of those critics built an impression of the good old days solely from listening to records; Armstrong lived through them and could tell reality from myth. "What they say about the old days is corny," he said in 1966. "They form their own opinions, they got so many words for things and make everything soooo big—and it turns out a—what you call it—a fictitious story. And when these writers come up so great they know every goddam thing, telling you how you should blow your horn. That's when I want to shoot the son-of-a-bitch. Just because they went to Harvard or Yale, got to make the public realize how superior they are, so what they do to plain old jazz!"[27] And when he was knocked for playing "set" solos in his later years, Armstrong was dumbfounded, as that was exactly how he—and many of his generation—had done it in the 1920s! "I do that song 'Hello, Dolly!' the same way every night 'cause that's the way the people like it. And even back in the old days it was like that—when everybody was supposed to be improvising. Who knows who's improvising? All trumpet players can hear what you play and they can play the same notes. . . . And always, once you got a certain solo that fit in the tune, and that's it, you keep it. Only vary it two or three notes every time you play it—specially if the record was a hit. There's always different people there every night, and they just want to be entertained."[28]

This work will, I hope, shatter the myths and wrongheaded assumptions that have distorted how people view the later years of Armstrong's career. Armstrong's own words, gleaned from dozens of interviews, television appearances, and private tape recordings, will finally tell his side of the story, one that has been unfairly misrepresented for decades. Armstrong understood his importance and often documented events with his reel-to-reel tape recorder, which captured over a thousand hours of audio over the last twenty years of his life. He recorded concerts, interviews, conversations, joke-telling sessions, even selections from his massive record collection.[29] Armstrong recorded frank discussions of race and his feelings on marijuana. When he wrote an important letter to his manager Joe Glaser in 1954, Armstrong spoke the words into his tape recorder to ensure he had a copy in his collection. He would write indexes for his reels and note all the details in his tape catalogs. Today, because of the foresight of Lucille Armstrong, who made sure to save Armstrong's belongings in the years after he died, these tapes—along with other private writings Armstrong composed and saved during his life, thousands of photographs, scrapbooks, sound recordings, and much, much more—are available to researchers at the Louis Armstrong House Museum in Queens, New York. It is through these tapes that Louis got to speak for himself about his life and music, recording it all "for posterity." Armstrong ended one of his most candid tapes in 1970 by addressing an invisible audience he knew would be listening decades after he died: "Well, folks, that was my life, and I enjoyed all of it. Yes I did. I don't feel ashamed at all. My life has always been an open book, so I have nothing to hide."[30] Some of these tapes will be quoted in the ensuing pages, and the results should surprise those who have viewed latter-day Armstrong as nothing more than a commercial Uncle Tom, a mere shadow of his younger self. Armstrong was equally jubilant offstage and on-, but he could display a short temper when he felt wronged, usually involving swaths of blue language that might make some readers blush. Armstrong never erased his tapes, even when they exposed this more explosive side of his personality, perhaps knowing the insight they would provide into a man more complex than his world-famous smile allowed.

Critics who routinely lashed out at Armstrong during his later years may have had the loudest voices, but in no way did they represent the majority. These were the years when Armstrong's popularity peaked, when he was hailed the world over as "Ambassador Satch." In this time, he was the subject of an Edward R. Murrow documentary; was a ubiquitous presence on television, radio, and in the movies; wrote a success-

What a
Wonderful World

Town Hall was filled to its 1,500-seat capacity that Saturday evening, a standing-room-only crowd even though tickets had gone on sale only six days prior. Seven top-flight jazz musicians, almost all of whom had previously played with Armstrong, had been assembled by the evening's music director, Bobby Hackett, to back the trumpeter. Armstrong arrived at Town Hall at six in the evening, joking with the musicians before going over the songs for the performance (he had been too busy to attend rehearsals). At 11:30, emcee Fred Robbins, a popular New York disc jockey, strode out and delivered his monologue: "Louie opens tonight with some of the golden things from his early Okeh days. And in another respect, this concert is unique. That is, we've surrounded Louie with the best jazz musicians attainable, with Jack Teagarden on trombone, Bobby Hackett on trumpet, Sid Catlett on the drums, as well as [drummer] George Wettling, Dick Cary at the piano, Bobby Haggart on bass. And so, from the golden Okeh days, we give you the greatest figure in American jazz, on a one-night stand, playing 'Cornet Chop Suey,' Louie Armstrong!" To thunderous applause, Armstrong appeared on stage and immediately launched into the unaccompanied introduction he originally wrote and copyrighted in January 1924 and later immortalized on wax with his own Hot Five in 1926. It was a gutsy choice of a tune, vaunted and difficult, a precursor to the more modern sounds of jazz that had sprung up in the 1940s. As a way of demonstrating that he wasn't there simply to re-create the past, Armstrong offered a swinging, up-to-date take on the number, creating something entirely fresh and exciting. Even when he touched on the melody, he'd rephrase it in a new, mature way: different from, but no less effective than, the original. Armstrong was accompanied by just the rhythm section on the tune, and they swung relentlessly, drummer Sid Catlett breaking up the time with his superbly placed accents. Armstrong played only fifty-nine seconds of melody before the piano solo. The audience, already electrified, heartily applauded Armstrong's effort, but the trumpeter was just getting started. The centerpiece of "Cornet Chop Suey" was always the stop-time chorus. Armstrong dove right in, using his original solo as a framework, but making enough changes to keep it fresh before his declamatory final ride-out chorus, his playing full of confidence and heat. He replicated the original "Charleston"-type coda before going into a short, improvised closing cadenza, building it up to a dramatic high concert C, held and shaken for all its glory, even higher than the high A that ended the piece in 1926. Tremendous applause filled the hall, including clapping by a beaming Joe Glaser, Armstrong's white manager, punctuated by enthusiastic whistling and an ecstatic Armstrong yelling, laughing, generally signaling approval in his own inimitable way.

Though he most likely did not know it at the time, Louis Armstrong's later years had just begun.

Armstrong's popularity during the swing era has often been undervalued, despite the numerous Decca records of insipid pop tunes, accompanied by his big band, that influenced young musicians of the period. Armstrong broke attendance and box-office records all over the country. History fusses over Benny Goodman's riotous, record-breaking appearance at New York's Paramount Theater in 1937, but there is little mention of Armstrong's performance there just two weeks later, which smashed Goodman's box-office record.[1] Even during the recording ban of World War II, Armstrong remained a top-drawing act, performing popular songs of the day such as "As Time Goes By" and "I've Got a Gal in Kalamazoo." Personnel changes became more frequent in the 1940s, and a lot of young jazz greats passed through his ranks, including Charles Mingus, Kenny Clarke, and Dexter Gordon. And though he didn't make many records during the war, one from 1945, a cover of Cecil Grant's "I Wonder," became an out-and-out hit. According to the *Pittsburgh Courier,* "his platter, 'I Wonder,' had no longer [sic] hit the music stalls before the first pressing of 75,000 of the tune were gobbled up. Now Decca is pressing another 75,000 and expects Louis' recording to hit the million mark."[2]

"I Wonder" was unusual because it was made with a group of studio musicians instead of his big band, but Armstrong soon began to feature the tune live with his larger outfit. At the time, Armstrong had no intention of ditching the big band for small-group playing—a view he expressed to *Metronome* in April 1945, just after "I Wonder" hit the charts.

> Why should I go back? I want to stay up with the times. That's why I surround myself with youngsters. Every once in a while I lay an old-fashioned phrase on 'em, but music's better now than it used to be, it's played better now. Whether it's arranged or improvised, the music of today is way ahead of what it used to be. We've advanced a lot

since the early days. Music should be played all kinds of ways, anyway. Symphonic stuff, beautiful things, everything goes. If there are people who want to omit arrangements, scored backgrounds, omit any kind of music, you tell 'em I said, "Omit those people!"[3]

Clearly Armstrong was comfortable in a big-band setting. Yet decades later, commentators such as James Lincoln Collier and Gunther Schuller asserted that Armstrong was shackled to his band, unable to perform the small-group New Orleans jazz he truly wanted to play. Armstrong had no patience for musical categories. In a 1945 letter to Leonard Feather, he wrote: "To me, as far as I could see it all my life, Jazz and Swing is the same thing . . . In the good old days of Buddy Bolden it was called Rag Time Music . . . Later on in the years it was called Jazz Music—Hot Music—Gut Bucket—and now they've poured a little gravy over it, called it Swing Music . . . No matter how you slice it, it's still the same music."[4]

Not everyone shared Armstrong's views. During the mid-1940s, most jazz critics associated themselves with either "modern" or "old-fashioned" jazz, creating a divide that grew deeper after the bebop of Dizzy Gillespie and Charlie Parker exploded onto the jazz world in 1945. Such music had never been heard on record, and jazz would never be the same. Bebop, originally known as "rebop" and later shortened to "bop," was developed by younger musicians looking to explore more complex chord changes, new harmonies, and difficult unison melodies, often delivered in the fastest of tempos. Bop may have spawned numerous geniuses such as Parker and Gillespie, but it also spawned chaos. From its very first notes, bop was met with either great admiration or fierce revulsion. A war soon broke out between the boppers and the "moldy figs," as followers and performers of traditional jazz were called. All of a sudden, pure, unadulterated New Orleans jazz bands, such as those led by Bunk Johnson and Kid Ory, were popular again, influencing eventual white imitators such as Lu Watters and Turk Murphy. Things heated up in the music press with bop enthusiasts routinely lashing out against the moldy figs. The result was the end of jazz as America's popular music. Boppers were not showmen (with the exception of Gillespie), and after the swing era, most bop was unsuitable for dancing, which turned off a large portion of the jazz audience. For its part, traditional jazz, while boasting a strong legion of fans, would also never again be wildly popular, for its very old-fashionedness. The new era belonged to singers such as Bing Crosby and Frank Sinatra, who stood in front of large orchestras, crooning hits of the day.

Louis Armstrong's initial position on bop was flattering: "Don't you know I'm crazy about that 'Re Bop' stuff? I love to listen to it," he said in *Esquire*'s 1947 *Jazz Book*. "I think it's very, very amusing. One thing, to play 'Re Bop' one has to have mighty good, strong chops from what I've witnessed. I'm one cat that loves all kinds of music."[5] Yet Armstrong's musical world was about to change, as did his stance toward the new music.

On April 29, 1946, Armstrong's big band received a devastating review in *Time* magazine of its engagement at the Aquarium in New York City. "The greatest jazzman of them all, Louis ("Satchmo") Armstrong was back on Broadway. The word spread, the devotees gathered. But jazz purists who went prospecting for his golden trumpet notes had to pan out a lot of wet gravel. Satchmo arrived with one of the biggest (19 pieces), brassiest, and worst bands he ever had—a kind of unintentional satire on everything wrong with big bands: saxophonists who stood up and writhed as they played; a brass section with a nose for noise rather than an ear for melody."[6] A few months later, United Artists announced it would produce a movie that promised to tell the real story of New Orleans in 1917. The movie, simply titled *New Orleans*, would feature Armstrong and a number of other jazz musicians, including Bunk Johnson, Kid Ory, and Billie Holiday. More importantly, it would also feature Armstrong in small-group settings playing the traditional jazz classics of his youth.[7] With a roster of musicians that also included clarinetist Barney Bigard and drummer Zutty Singleton, the film's music was of high order. The soundtrack included a remake of Armstrong's famous 1928 recording of "West End Blues," his breath control still at its peak as he holds the climatic note during the last chorus for all four bars (ten seconds). On "Mahogany Hall Stomp," Armstrong created new variations on his original 1929 solo, and he blew a tremendous chorus at the close of "Basin Street Blues." The actual film turned out to be a forgettable melodrama, but the jazz community could only focus on the sights and sounds of Armstrong playing in a New Orleans setting. This was the music of Armstrong's youth, the music of the Hot Five and Hot Seven era—an era some critics wished Louis would return to.

While filming *New Orleans*, Armstrong took part in a relaxed small-group session for Charles Delaunay's Swing label, based in France.

The results, including terrific interpretations of two standards, "I Want a Little Girl" and "Sugar," were so successful they were released in America on RCA Victor. A month after that session Armstrong recorded for RCA again in a session that provided a clear picture of the crossroads where he stood. It started with two big-band tracks, "Endie" and "The Blues Are Brewin'," both harmless remakes of tunes from the *New Orleans* soundtrack. Later, however, Armstrong fronted a small group with Kid Ory blowing tailgate trombone on numbers such as "Mahogany Hall Stomp" and the first recorded version of "Do You Know What It Means to Miss New Orleans." Once again, the small-group efforts were preferable to those of the big band. Armstrong was very clear in a letter he wrote to Leonard Feather on December 5, 1946. Joe Glaser wanted Feather to help plan a concert at Carnegie Hall the following February. "I understand you and the Boss Mr. Glaser's planning a concert for me and my gang," Armstrong wrote.

> Well I'll tell ya planning concert's alright—but if any an every old Tom Dick & Harry will be interfering I'd just sooner forget about the concert . . . They have all been awfully messy anyway—from what I can gather . . . So if you boys intend on doing the thing—for God's sake—don't have a lot guys whom think they know whats going down—and come to find out—they're no where . . . It really wouldn't be a bad idea to have the seven piece band (the one I used in the picture) in that concert . . . We really did romp . . . Just to give you a sort of rough idea of what went down in the picture . . . Maybe you can find a place for them in the Concert.[8]

Feather liked the idea and wanted to make the whole evening a small-group affair, but Glaser remained skeptical. It was arranged to have Armstrong front a sextet led by clarinetist Edmond Hall for the first half of the concert, but Glaser made sure the second half featured Armstrong's usual big band, along with guest stars Billie Holiday and Sid Catlett, Armstrong's former drummer.

The concert was given on a late Saturday afternoon, at 5:30 p.m.[9] Armstrong performed a strong sampling of the small-band tunes he had made immortal two decades earlier, though listening to it sixty years later, one can hear that it was at times a pretty ragged affair. On "Muskrat Ramble," the band played the wrong chords under Armstrong's solo, causing a clash. And "Dippermouth Blues" and "Mahogany Hall Stomp" are also a little too loose, with occasional missed notes and sloppy execution of the routines. But even with the roughness of the early moments of the concert, one cannot deny Armstrong's enthusiasm. He brought down the house with the hilarious duet with bassist Johnny Williams on "Rockin' Chair" and his re-creations of a New Orleans funeral with the medley of "Flee As a Bird" and "Oh, Didn't He Ramble," two crowd-pleasing routines that would later appear in the All Stars' repertoire. "Black and Blue," the Fats Waller–Andy Razaf classic Armstrong made a racial protest song in 1929, was dusted off and given an emotional performance, the first surviving Armstrong performance of it since the original recording. Armstrong grew more powerful as the small-group session progressed, culminating in a hard-to-top romp on "Ain't Misbehavin'." The highlights of the second half were a duet with Holiday on "Do You Know What It Means to Miss New Orleans" and drummer Catlett's feature on "Mop Mop." Armstrong continued to play with brio, especially on a slow "Back o' Town Blues." Even with the star-filled, jam-packed second half, all the critics and fans could talk about the next day was Armstrong's first-half performance. *Music Business* magazine reported, "So with Bobby Hackett's horn, an 11th-hour substitution for Satchmo's, stolen from rehearsal the day before the concert, Armstrong reaffirmed for the reverent Carnegie audience the artistry that has made him the country's master jazz man and master showman."[10] Dizzy Gillespie was at the concert, and though the press was trying to drum up a war between the boppers and the older New Orleans musicians at the time, Gillespie simply said to *DownBeat* magazine, "Didn't he play wonderfully!"

Also in attendance that night was Ernie Anderson, a longtime Armstrong friend and the producer of Eddie Condon's successful concerts at New York's Town Hall. Anderson knew Armstrong's big band was struggling after Bert Block, the booker at Glaser's Associated Booking Corporation, privately told him that "the fee for the 16-piece band had fallen to $350 for a week night or $500 for a Saturday." Anderson and Bobby Hackett approached Louis with the idea of Armstrong dedicating an entire evening at Town Hall to his old classics with an all-star small group. Armstrong quickly jumped at the proposal, but told him, "I can't do this unless Joe Glaser wants me to."[11]

Armstrong often said that. Joe Glaser, a central figure in Armstrong's life, has always been viewed ambivalently. For sure, he got Armstrong's career back on track in the 1930s, protected him from physical harm, and made sure he had more money than he would ever need. However, Glaser was a man of contradictions. He is often criticized for working Armstrong too hard and for withholding money.

There's a bit of truth to both sides. Glaser was a product of the North Side of Chicago, involved in the city's notorious gangster scene in the 1920s—he served as a henchman for Al Capone—and in charge of the Sunset Café, one of Armstrong's steady gigs. Armstrong recalled a time in the mid-1930s when his career hit rock bottom: he spent over a year in Europe, nursing a tired lip and avoiding mob-related troubles brought on by another manager. When Armstrong returned to the United States early in 1935, he found himself essentially starting from scratch. Glaser wasn't exactly thriving either; a *Chicago Tribune* article from April 9 of that year spelled out Glaser's troubles clearly: "Joe Glaser, former owner of the Sunset Café at 315 East 35th Street, once convicted of the rape of a 14-year-old girl, was reported named in a true bill voted by the grand jury yesterday charging him with receiving stolen property in connection with his effort to reopen the resort. He is a fugitive. The state's attorney's office charges that Glaser was a participant in a conspiracy by which a $2,500 truckload of liquor was stolen and delivered to the Sunset last June."[12]

Despite his shady background and current troubles with the law, Glaser was the only person from Armstrong's past with the proper connections to make his mob troubles disappear and possibly put his career back on track. Armstrong sought Glaser out in Chicago and made his demands clear: "I want you to be my manager . . . You get me the jobs. You collect the money. You pay me one thousand dollars every week free and clear. You pay off the band, the travel and hotel expenses, my income tax, and you take everything that's left.' " Armstrong and Glaser shook hands and their partnership was formed without an official contract ever being signed.[13] "They needed each other and they suited each other perfectly," David Ostwald, tuba player and Armstrong historian, says. "They realized they each had something that they could offer to the other. What Joe Glaser offered was security—and I mean physical security. He could give him physical protection, which was important. Louie's life had been threatened. And also, one can't underestimate the importance, as unfortunate as it is, of a black man at that time having a person accommodate him in a white world."[14]

Some close to Armstrong felt that Glaser took advantage of Armstrong, working him relentlessly and growing rich from it. In July 1970 one such friend, Jack Bradley, sat down with three highly respected trumpeters—Clark Terry, Ray Nance, and Billy Butterfield—and asked if they believed this to be true. To Bradley's surprise, all three men seemed almost envious of Armstrong's deal with Glaser. "The only thing I could say about that situation is that Pops seemed to be very happy with the arrangement he had going with [Glaser]," Terry said. "And I understand, I don't know the exact figures, but I understand whatever his salary was, x amount of dollars [went to him], which was sufficient for him to live like a king, and x amount of dollars for his wife, Lucille, which was enough for her to live independently, as she chose. And the rest, the taxes and all the worries and so forth with keeping up with the government and staying abreast, staying clear of tax problems, was left up to Joe Glaser. Now if he made a million dollars behind that, I understand that it was none of Pops's business in the agreement. And if he didn't make that, Pops expected his salary right on, and I understand it was a very substantial one." Butterfield said, "[Glaser] kept him clean all the time and he never got in any trouble with government and all of that like a lot of other guys." Bradley mentioned that Armstrong believed he never would have made it as big without Glaser, something Bradley did not feel to be true. But Nance responded, "It's possible, because, I'm telling you, you've got to have good management. I don't care how great you are, you've got to have good management. Good management goes hand in hand with success, with talent. Like we all know there's a whole lot of people that are talented but they never get the right management." Terry summed up the viewpoint of Armstrong's fellow musicians: "If it went down the way I heard it went down, it ain't a bad deal. It ain't a bad deal."[15]

Armstrong knew that some members of the black community frowned upon his being controlled by a white manager, but he paid them no mind. "We ain't looked back since we signed up with Joe, whether we work or not," he told fellow entertainer Babe Wallace in 1959. "There you go. 'Oh, that nigger making all that money for a white man.' So I just keep saying,

'You ever see Louis Armstrong look like anybody who needs something?' They say, 'No.' Well, what the hell? Figure that out. You know? There's always some old spade who's going to say some shit."[16]

Armstrong was happy with the arrangement, following advice he received while still a child in New Orleans—advice he wasn't afraid to share with Glaser: "Always keep a white man behind you that'll put his hand on you and say, 'That's my nigger.' "[17] When Armstrong conveyed that story to Wallace, he expounded on it, adding, "I always remember the old hustlers. Because in those days, what they're talking about, a place gets raided, all Mr. Charlie got to say is, 'You got my nigger down there?' 'Yes sir, Mr. Charlie.' 'If you don't turn my nigger loose, I'll come down there and' . . . and you're liable to have fifty thousand dollars in your pocket and you can't get it. They won't even let you use the phone. You understand? . . . See, but what them niggers told me was real shit. And I tell Joe Glaser many times, I say, 'You that white man I've been looking for.' "[18]

Though some have argued that Glaser did indeed harm Armstrong by overworking him, the truth is Armstrong reveled in hard work. It was the only life he knew. When I asked five surviving members of the All Stars—Danny Barcelona, Joe Muranyi, Buddy Catlett, Jewel Brown, and Marty Napoleon—if Glaser was at fault, they all said it couldn't be farther from the truth. Armstrong was only happy when he was constantly working and was known to complain to Glaser if he had too many nights off in a row.

Though Glaser undoubtedly loved Armstrong, and built an entire booking agency off of his talent, he also had a crude, foul-mouthed, racist side that didn't endear him to many. Witnesses heard him call his secretary "bitch" and "cunt." Ernie Anderson remembered Glaser once complaining, "These shines are all alike. They're so lazy. You know that, don't you?"[19] None of this seemed to bother Armstrong, who wrote in 1944: "I always admired Mr. Glaser from the first day I started working for him. He just *impressed* me different than the other Bosses I've worked for. He seemed to understand Colored people so much."[20] Perhaps Armstrong turned a blind eye toward Glaser's character flaws because Glaser was responsible for resurrecting his career in the 1930s. He wouldn't allow anyone—not even his wife Lucille—to criticize Glaser in his presence.

Ernie Anderson knew Armstrong didn't want to put so many men out of work by breaking up the big band, which continued to make recordings for Victor in March 1947. More importantly, he knew Glaser was tough to deal with and would probably slam the door in his face. Taking a risk, he made out a check for $1,000 and gave it to Glaser's secretary.

When Glaser received it, he grew irate, giving Anderson five minutes to explain. "What are you trying to do, you jerk?" Glaser barked. "That's for Louis for one night without the band," Anderson said. He told Glaser that he knew how badly the big band was struggling, earning $350 a night. "If this works as I think it will," he said, "instead of $350 a night for Louis, you'll be getting $2,500 a night." Glaser said nothing more. Never one to refuse money, he agreed. Besides, Glaser knew that keeping the big band afloat was no longer an easy task. The previous summer, he grew very unhappy when he heard that some of Armstrong's men were complaining about a ten-dollar deduction for upkeep of their uniforms. "The boys should be ashamed of complaining," he wrote to the band's musical director, Joe Garland. "As far as work is concerned they have been working more than any band in the business. I took jobs for them regardless of whether the office received commission or not and even went to extremes to see that they are happy at all times." Glaser took this opportunity to make it clear to Garland that the band business was in quite a slump. "Promoters all over are going broke," he wrote. "Bookings are being cancelled at the last minute—I can name at least half a dozen Colored bands that will disband in the next 30 days and at least 20 White bands that will disband so if our men are complaining then all I can say is God Bless them all and my only hope is that they change before it is too late as I assure you they will be very unhappy unless the situation changes in the immediate future."[21] With the situation not about to change any time soon, it was time for Glaser to give Anderson's idea a shot.

Anderson immediately set up the date at New York City's Town Hall for Saturday, May 17, naming Bobby Hackett musical director, in charge of selecting the rest of the group. With the exception of Sid Catlett, all the musicians Hackett brought in were white, starting a trend of integration that all of Armstrong's future small groups would uphold.

Anderson thankfully recorded the performance, and though the sound quality is less than ideal at times, the recording is historic. Armstrong, without his big band, offered some of his most soulful playing of the evening on "Dear Old Southland," dramatically accompanied only by Cary's piano. He also turned in a smoking solo on "Big Butter and Egg

Man," clearly driven to transcendence by Catlett's backbeats. Armstrong took only one break that night, letting Teagarden feature himself on "St. James Infirmary." Otherwise, he continued to blow with a level of inspiration not present in his recent big-band records on renditions of "On the Sunny Side of the Street" and "I Can't Give You Anything but Love" and touching ballad performances of "Pennies from Heaven" and "Save It, Pretty Mama." "Rockin' Chair," a favorite of the Carnegie Hall concert, was featured in arguably its greatest version, with Teagarden playing the role of the "father." The love between the two men is wonderfully in evidence, capturing the audience convulsing in laughter at Armstrong's witty comebacks and scat passages. But just as he got the audience laughing, Armstrong picked up his trumpet for a final, dramatic statement of the melody. The effortless mixture of comedy and serious music seemed to sum up Armstrong's brilliance in a matter of minutes.

When the reviews came in, the Town Hall concert was a hit. British jazz critic Peter Tanner concluded that "Louis Armstrong is still without any shadow of doubt, the greatest virtuoso of the trumpet in the world. His playing had all the freshness and vigor of the early Hot Five and Seven days. He never strove for effects, never played to the gallery; each phrase, each note he played was always just right. Louis has wonderful taste, impeccable musicianship, and a way of making quite banal numbers as, for instance, 'Sweethearts on Parade,' seem like really great music."[22] Other critics were also bowled over by Armstrong. Wilder Hobson wrote that the concert featured "superb hot music, showing this art form at its best."[23]

Less than a month later, Armstrong headed off to RCA's New York studio for a date organized by Leonard Feather, one that might have seemed like a reunion of old friends as Hackett, Teagarden, and clarinetist Peanuts Hucko again joined him from the Town Hall concert. Armstrong debuted an original composition, soon to become a standard, "Someday You'll Be Sorry." He enjoyed talking about the origin of the song, saying: "We was in North Dakota or South Dakota, or somewhere. It was cold and this thing kept runnin' 'cross my mind, like dreamin' a musical comedy. And this 'Someday' was the theme of this show. So, we was asleep. Lucille was sound asleep. But I got up in my pajamas and got me a piece of paper and pencil out. I say, 'I'm gonna lose it if I don't write it down.' And she wakes up and say, 'Are you all right?' I said, 'I'm all right.' But the next day I had it, and we looked at it . . . and everybody liked the tune."[24] Johnny Guarnieri's celeste adds a charm to the delightful performance. The blues were represented by two vocal duets with Teagarden: a mellow "Fifty-Fifty Blues," arranged to sound almost as if it were a leftover big-band performance, and a fierce remake of the 1944 V-Disc "Jack Armstrong Blues," the new version featuring perhaps Armstrong's best extended trumpet solo of the period; it builds higher and higher over sustained chords by the band. Dan Morgenstern has called it "to my ears the most modern Armstrong on record."[25]

Armstrong was now playing with renewed energy, enlivened by the recent work he had done with small groups, and the press took note. "The public has rediscovered Satchmo," *DownBeat* reported in an article titled "Louis Center of New Commotion."[26] However reluctant he remained to "throw eighteen cats out of work," the time had come. Russell "Big Chief" Moore, who had been with Armstrong's big band since 1944, remembered, "We were beginning to see signs of whatever you call it, the handwriting on the wall. All the bands were breaking up. It was an economic situation where big bands were getting out of style. Everybody was making small bands. So that left me without a job and everybody cut out and that broke up the band."[27] Armstrong wouldn't have to worry about making a living anymore, as there was more money to be made with a small group. Glaser gave in; the big band was in its death throes.

The end of Louis Armstrong's days as a big-band leader came during a July run at the Apollo Theater in Harlem. Jack Teagarden had also recently given up his struggling big band and spent much of the early summer freelancing. Having had recent success with Armstrong, Teagarden was on board as a featured artist, sitting in with the band for specialty numbers such as "I Gotta Right to Sing the Blues" and "St. James Infirmary." A newspaper story of July 5, 1947, remarked, "The management of the Apollo is happy that Teagarden consented [to] desert his band for this one week in order to be able to appear with Armstrong."[28] After their week of success at the Apollo, it was clear that Teagarden would have to be a permanent part of Armstrong's new band. Considered by many to be jazz's greatest trombonist, and a fine singer in his own right, Teagarden had admired Armstrong ever since he heard him play on a riverboat even before the trumpeter was well known. He first got the chance to record with his idol in 1929 on the famous integrated "Knockin' a Jug" session for Okeh. "The first time I heard Jack Teagarden on the trombone I got goose pimples all over; in all my experience I had never heard anything so fine," recalled Louis.[29] Teagarden's laid-back demeanor was compatible with Armstrong; the two never let their egos get in the way of their friendship or the music they created. Barney Bigard said, "Louis got along just fine with everyone in the band, but he loved Jack."[30] Teagarden was happy to join Armstrong. His own big band had led him into great debt, so much so that he barely cleared any money in his early days with Armstrong after paying it. Pianist Dick Cary remembered, "He was in such a low state, he used to say to me, 'Dick, if I don't have enough to buy a pint of Four Roses every day I'm going to quit playing.' "[31]

It was imperative that drummer Sid Catlett be in the mix. Legendarily known as "Big Sid," he was versatile, able to sit in with everyone from Armstrong's sextet and Benny Goodman's big band to Charlie Parker and Dizzy Gillespie in their early bebop sessions. While a very large man, Catlett possessed a soft touch behind the traps and had the ability to inspire and swing any band he anchored. Other musicians loved him for his style, his swing, and a showmanship that featured feats of stick twirling and tossing. A veteran of Armstrong's big-band days, he felt right at home in the All Stars. "Louie Armstrong often pronounced him the greatest jazz drummer and hired him on every possible occasion," said Ernie Anderson.[32] Dick Cary, recommended for the Town Hall performance by Bobby Hackett, was chosen to remain as Armstrong's first pianist. As Cary recalled, when they were picking musicians for the band, "Louis said, 'That *little* ofay who played Town Hall would be *pretty* good.' "[33] Cary, also a fine arranger, was essential to making the first edition of the All Stars sound as good as it did. Replacing Hucko on clarinet was Barney Bigard, with whom Armstrong had performed in the movie *New Orleans* and on the small-group sessions Leonard Feather produced for Victor in 1946, as well as on a Johnny Dodds record date from 1927. Born in New Orleans, Bigard studied clarinet early with the famous teacher Lorenzo Tio Jr. After playing with King Oliver in Chicago, he joined Duke Ellington in December 1927 and remained with him until 1942, contributing many classic solos and a number of compositions, including the seminal "Mood Indigo." Bigard later said, "I enjoyed both bands but I enjoyed

Louis's more because I had more freedom in my playing, where Duke, you got to play what you see on the paper plus, what you say freedom, but it wasn't that much freedom. It doesn't give you a chance to even concentrate on really what you want to do because it's so short."[34] The newest face in the band was bassist Morty Corb, a busy studio musician from Los Angeles.

The new small group was set to debut at Billy Berg's, a nightclub in Los Angeles, on August 13, 1947. A *DownBeat* ad from August 1947 finally gave a name to Armstrong's new congregation: "Louis Armstrong and the Esquire All Stars." The *Esquire* sponsorship would soon end, and though some early critics called the band "Louis Armstrong and His Hot Five," "All Stars" stuck and would be the name of every Armstrong small group for the rest of his career. (Eddie Condon joked, "Joe [Glaser] makes it sound like a basketball team.")[35] Two days before the opening, Armstrong and his new band got together for a warm-up. As reported in *Time* magazine, Armstrong confirmed his confidence in the band: "I don't need no rehearsals. I don't go through that and never will. All these cats I'm playing with can blow. We don't need no arrangements. I just say, man, what you going to play? They say 'Musk'at Ramble.' I say follow me, and you got the best arrangement you ever heard."[36]

The jazz world turned out in droves to see the new coming of Louis Armstrong, the greatest jazz musician of their time. People lined up around the building for the chance to get in. Armstrong didn't disappoint the audience, which included musicians such as Hoagy Carmichael, Johnny Mercer, Woody Herman, and Benny Goodman. A later *Down-Beat* story, by John Lucas, stated, "In returning occasionally to small band jazz, he has revealed that he thoroughly understands the value of basic jazz . . . And now that the smaller groups seem on the way back, Armstrong is beginning to lean more and more toward such ensembles. Jazz is never stagnant and neither is Louis."[37]

Time magazine put it even more dramatically:

Louis Armstrong had forsaken the ways of Mammon and come back to jazz. Shorn of his big (19-piece), brassy, ear-splitting commercial band, he was as happy as a five-year-old with his curls cut off. Billy Berg's neon & chromium Los Angeles jazz temple wasn't big enough to hold the faithful who thronged to welcome him back.[38]

In the *Time* article, Armstrong took fresh swipes at the boppers. While he had been supportive earlier on, he no longer was:

> Take them re-bop boys. They're great technicians. Mistakes—that's all re-bop is. . . . Some cats say Old Satch is old-fashioned, not modern enough. Why, man, most of that modern stuff I first heard in 1918. Ain't no music out of date as long as you play it perfect.[39]

Armstrong, probably figuring any publicity was good publicity, must have known that knocking the boppers would keep the spotlight on him and his new group—he wasn't about to stop any time soon. Armstrong stayed in California after the Billy Berg's engagement, performing to a sold-out crowd at one of Gene Norman's "Just Jazz" concerts in Pasadena on September 9.[40] Bassist Morty Corb was still mentioned in advertisements for the band's September engagement at the Rag Doll in Chicago, but he had already been replaced by the time of the Pasadena concert. "My biggest compliment was when Louis said, 'I like your playing. I would like you to go to Europe with me,' " Corb remembered. "I declined—partly because I do not like to fly, but also because I was just starting to get roots in the studios, and that was what I wanted to do."[41] Corb's departure left an opening filled by Arvell Shaw. The youngest member of the band, Shaw had previously played in Armstrong's last big band.

In a 1997 interview, Shaw fondly recalled joining the All Stars. When Armstrong was asked, "Who you gonna get on bass?" he replied, "Well, I have a young kid who can really play. Why not get him?" "We've never heard of him," critics said, to which Armstrong responded, "So what! At one time nobody never heard of me."[42] Shaw would remain with Armstrong, on and off, until his very last gig, summing up his stay with the band this way: "Working with Louis was like working for a head of state. We made at least one around-the-world tour every year. We played for kings, queens, presidents, prime ministers, popes. He was born the grandson of a slave and he rose to become a world figure and a multimillionaire, but during that time he still remained a very human human being."[43]

By the fall of 1947, female vocalist Velma Middleton had also joined the All Stars. Born in St. Louis in 1917, the heavyset Middleton (she weighed nearly 300 pounds) was originally a dancer. A veteran of the bands of Blanche Calloway, Erskine Hawkins, and Jimmie Lunceford, she entered

Armstrong's big band in 1942 and soon assumed a role as Armstrong's comedic foil. The centerpiece of Middleton's routine was a split that always left the audience roaring and the critics screaming "Tasteless!" But her innuendo-filled duets with Armstrong on numbers like "That's My Desire" and "Baby, It's Cold Outside" always brought down the house. "Deeply devoted to Louis, she didn't mind at all acting the foil for all kinds of unflattering (if always good-natured) badinage," wrote Dan Morgenstern. "She was a special pet peeve of the critics, who seemed to take personal offense at seeing a fat black woman do the splits—Velma, all 300 or so pounds of her, could do a mean split and was light on her feet. No one (including herself) would have claimed her to be a great singer, but she was important to the show the All Stars put on and gave Louis some needed rest from the horn."[44] As Trummy Young, Armstrong's trombonist from 1952 to 1964, would say, "They were a fantastic team together. Velma wasn't a great singer or nothing like that, but she certainly was the right foil for Louis. I would have hated to follow them two on stage, man."[45]

On October 17, 1947, Armstrong and the band headed back to Victor's studios to record four more songs. Released under the name "Louis Armstrong and His All Stars," they were the first recordings by Armstrong's working sextet. The Victor session, however, would be Armstrong's last for almost two years. An American Federation of Musicians' strike shut down commercial recording for most of 1948, and Armstrong wouldn't record again until 1949. Still, his live shows were wildly popular. George Hoefer's review of a November concert at the Chicago Opera House (calling the band the "Louis Armstrong Hot Sextet") stated, "The group as a unit is not and does not pretend to be a Dixieland Band, nor does it offer anything new or sensational in music. Satchmo's superb stage presence binds together a showcase of jazz stars into a jazz production that warmed the hearts of nostalgia music lovers. The greatest contribution to jazz that has come out of the revival of Armstrong's small band is the release of the trumpeter from the fetters of a large commercial jump band. Consequently, Louis is playing and singing with more heart and inspiration than he has for years."[46] Hoefer reserved his wrath for Velma Middleton: "This reviewer has yet to feel the humor that is apparently present when an obese person jumps around on a stage."[47]

On November 15, Armstrong appeared at Carnegie Hall, a midnight concert that lasted until 2:30 a.m. Recorded but never released commercially, a good number of tracks survive, capturing the band already in tight form. Again, disc jockey Fred Robbins was the emcee, and in an eloquent speech pronounced the importance of Armstrong:

> He's shaped the entire course of jazz for the past twenty-five years. His influence on countless musicians here and abroad has been unfathomable. It extends all the way through to every instrument, to singers. No one musician has picked up everything, but almost everyone owes a small debt to this gentleman. It's really a thrill to be able to revel in a genius while we have him. Not to be able to talk about him years from now but to appreciate him and enjoy him while he's still able to put that vibrating lip to his golden horn. This is American music, concert-style, and believe me, it's with a very deep bow of reverence that I introduce you to Louie Armstrong.

Armstrong then took the stage, personally introducing the members of the All Stars. One has to put into perspective the star power on stage during those early All Stars shows. Most jazz fans were very familiar with musicians like Teagarden, Bigard, and Catlett, and Armstrong made sure to feature them well. But to Armstrong, each band member was an All Star. According to Arvell Shaw, "With Louis everybody had a featured spot, and he'd tell you: 'Go out there and tear up the house if you can' . . . That's one of the things I admired about him. He gave everybody an equal chance . . . He was always the first one on stage and he worked hard, harder than anybody else. Nothing can top that."[48] At this Carnegie Hall performance, twenty-six complete numbers were played over two sets (not counting theme-song statements). Of the twenty-six, seventeen featured other members of the group. But on each and every one of them except for Teagarden's "Lover," Armstrong played impressive horn; he sang "Rockin' Chair" with Teagarden and "That's My Desire" with Middleton. He turned in blistering solos even on two Teagarden specialties, "Baby Won't You Please Come Home" and "Basin Street Blues," incorporating a quote from the pop song "The Gypsy" in his break on the latter. Armstrong soared on "Back O'Town Blues" and was explosive at the end of "St. Louis Blues." During intermission, Robbins summed up Armstrong's performance by comically announcing, "The smelling salts are just to the right!" According to the *New York Times*, "This jazz concert . . . proved that no jazz musician can blow Louis off the street even now."[49]

Although the All Stars had been in existence for only three months, the show was as tight as one of Catlett's snare drums. These were professional musicians who teamed up to put on an evening of entertainment. The pacing of the show, the contribution of the other musicians, Velma Middleton's split, the comedy routines on tunes like "Rockin' Chair": all were in place by November 1947. Because the performances were so fresh, critics lavished them with superlatives. But it wouldn't take long before some writers began complaining that Armstrong played the same songs and repeated the same routines night after night, a complaint that would dog the All Stars for more than two decades. The All Stars' band book was huge; new material was always being added after recording sessions. Some favorite charts were perennial ("Basin Street Blues," "Struttin' with Some Barbecue"); others became staples through hit records ("Hello, Dolly!" "Mack the Knife"); some lasted only a short time ("That's for Me," "The Dummy Song"). Once you include the features for the other sidemen—which Armstrong almost always played on—there are more than two hundred songs played by the All Stars in their twenty-four-year history, a repertoire larger than those of Thelonious Monk, John Coltrane, and Lester Young during the same period. It cannot be denied that some parts of Armstrong's stage show were set in stone, but what working jazz band didn't rely on a set list of familiar songs night after night? Armstrong knew which songs worked and which songs his audience wanted to hear, and he didn't care about anything else. Trummy Young recalled, "What he played was Louis and nobody else could do it that well. I played the same numbers over and over with him and every night they sounded pretty to me. Because Louis felt it every night. He had one thing he went by—If you're playing it good, it doesn't matter. And also—If you don't feel it, you can't make them feel it. And he was right. There was a lot of logic in what he said. What most people overlook is that Louis was very sincere and very dedicated [in] what he did. He worked hard at making his music sound good all the time."[50]

Armstrong treated his performances not as jam sessions but as shows (sometimes he would thank the audience "on behalf of all the members of the show"), and he worked hard to ensure that they were tight and entertaining. He was a fanatic about tape recording and listening to his own performances. Once, publicist Ernie Anderson introduced Armstrong to recording his shows by taping one of the trumpeter's concerts without his knowledge and playing it back for him later that night. Armstrong was stunned, and the very next day he bought two reel-to-reel recording machines. "From that time on until the end of his life he saw to it that every performance he did was recorded. Then later that night if you happened by Louis's digs you'd hear what he had played that night. He studied those shows."[51] Armstrong studied them to see what worked and what didn't. If a line got a big laugh, he kept it in. If a song received a lukewarm response, it was left out. Armstrong even studied his solos, tinkering with them until they flowed perfectly.

As to the "set" aspects of the All Stars' live performances, this was a band that traveled so much they never had time to rehearse. They played in front of so many new people every night, they always felt compelled to play something familiar, something they knew would work. "If you come out of an 18-hour road trip from one place to another . . . you come out and you hit in front of thousands of people," Dan Morgenstern explains. "And the spotlight goes on, boom! You are far better off knowing exactly what you're going to do and what the routine is."[52] Armstrong's final clarinet player, Joe Muranyi, agreed. "Of course, then there's the old business of 'Well, it's the same show every time,' " Muranyi said. "Well, I guess if you've heard him twenty times, he's going to play all the songs again. I never understand what people get out of music. That's a very deep, profound question. Some maybe get an erection, some get hungry or some want to dance, God only knows. Someone might want to murder, you know. So somebody that heard him fifty times, they might get bored. But if you've got to live through it like me—and God, I wanted to live through it!—I always found beauties in things that were new to me, even if it was '[When It's]Sleepy Time Down South.' The other thing you've got to think about it is 365 one-nighters in a row, you want a sure thing. You can't be worried about how you're going to do this or you do that. It's a show, not a jam session. But he got a lot of criticism for that."[53]

Interestingly, Armstrong told a radio interviewer in 1952 about what he expected from his band. "Whatever we play together, we try to remember that. It's just like an arrangement. I say whatever background and things like that—of course, if a man wants to change his personal solo, that's his business. But I do ask the boys to try to remember what we play together every night, no more than that. See, that's pretty easy. Some nights you feel like you want to change your solo around. As long as it fits right in there, it's all right." Because Armstrong played in big bands from 1924 to 1947, he was familiar with set arrangements, but he enjoyed the freedom of having a small group that could change things whenever needed. "And you can't do that with a big band," Armstrong continued. "You've got to stick to the music at all times. So that makes it nicer, and I think it's better for the individual man. It makes him a better musician. It expands his starts and his improvisations and a whole lot of things. It's much better."[54]

Two weeks after the Carnegie Hall show, Armstrong and the All Stars headed to Boston for a concert at Symphony Hall produced by Ernie Anderson. Anderson recorded it and a few years later released the date as a two-LP set for Decca, *Satchmo at Symphony Hall*. It was one of the best documents of the early All Stars, including arguably the greatest version of "Muskrat Ramble" ever recorded. The Decca record has gone on to become a classic while the Carnegie Hall show is still unreleased. When one listens to both performances, it's amazing to hear the similarities: the choice of material, the pacing, and even the solos (never mind Armstrong; Catlett's solo on "Steak Face" is virtually unchanged from performance to performance). The biggest change from show to show was of course the audience; they were different, and the Boston crowd didn't care if Armstrong played songs from New York. They were there to be entertained, and Armstrong complied brilliantly at both venues.

Looking back at the early All Stars concerts, one gets the impression that a typical show seemed to cover most of the history of jazz up to that point. There are early New Orleans numbers such as "Royal Garden Blues" and "High Society"; songs Armstrong made famous in the 1920s, like "Muskrat Ramble" and "Black and Blue"; swing-era standards such as "Stars Fell on Alabama" and Duke Ellington's "C Jam Blues"; the recent rhythm-and-blues hits "Since I Fell for You" and Frankie Laine's "That's My Desire" (both sung by Velma Middleton); and even a number recorded by beboppers Howard McGhee and Max Roach, "Mop Mop" (sometimes titled "Boff Boff"). Armstrong proved that even though he had what seemed like an old-fashioned Dixieland small group, he was still forward looking. Soloists were propelled by background riffs played as if

CHAPTER TWO

Europe, 1948

ARMSTRONG'S SUCCESS in 1947 not only made headlines across the United States but also reached the jazz press overseas. A newspaper article from December of that year announced, "The superb notes of jazz Louis Armstrong and his all-star crew set into the ears of a packed Carnegie Hall audience a few Saturdays ago were heard around the world, and particularly in Paris, France. As a direct result, Hugues Panassié, the world-famous French jazz critic, is reported staying up all night in an attempt to get the great musician for a planned 'Jazz Festival' which he hopes to stage in February."[1] Panassié, perhaps Armstrong's biggest European fan, was also a passionate moldy fig. Repulsed by bebop, Panassié wanted his proposed jazz festival to feature only the musicians he liked, those who played what he called "the real jazz." In addition to Armstrong, he reached out to Earl "Fatha" Hines. Little did he know he was about to get two for the price of one.

Joe Glaser had already pondered recruiting Hines to play piano for the All Stars.[2] Known as "the father of modern jazz piano," Hines influenced almost every pianist that heard him, though no one could perfectly duplicate his intricate style. His 1920s recordings with Armstrong have attained legendary status, but the two men seemed not to have remained especially close in the ensuing years. Hines led a big band for years, but broke it up in 1946 to start a nightclub in Chicago, El Grotto. Glaser visited Hines at El Grotto and told him, "I'm getting an all-star band together—all bandleaders who have had bands and given them up—to play with Louis Armstrong. It's a good way to bring you together and we might come up with something. You never know."[3] Hines agreed to come along, closing up his struggling club and saying later, "I'm always glad to be anywhere I can make a dollar, as the saying goes!" Glaser had already drawn up a contract before making his offer to Hines. He was originally hired for only six weeks. He stayed with Armstrong four years.[4]

With Earl Hines aboard, the All Stars became one of Armstrong's greatest bands, and as some critics would hail it, one of the greatest jazz bands in the history of music. Armstrong's new All Stars with Fatha Hines debuted at the Roxy Theatre in New York for a four-week engagement. But because pianist Dick Cary had done such a wonderful job with the band, Armstrong didn't want to let him go yet, knowing that as egotistical as he assumed Hines was, he might not last as a sideman for very long. Thus, the Roxy engagement featured the unusual setup of two pianos. "Earl was going to Europe with them, and I was going to stay behind—with pay—and then rejoin them after a couple weeks and we were going to have two pianos, [and] I could never figure how they were going to do that, unless they were just going to invite Earl up to play solos or something," Cary remembered. "Because, he didn't like to play in someone else's band, he never did."[5]

All the same, the Roxy engagement would prove to be Cary's last, because of an encounter with the infamous Pierre Tallerie, by all accounts a villainous figure in Armstrong's later years. Tallerie, better known as "Frenchy," was originally Armstrong's bus driver but eventually became his road manager. To Barney Bigard, he was a "real asshole."[6] "He was a racist, really," says Armstrong's close friend Jack Bradley. "He'd use the word 'nigger.' You know, I don't know how Glaser got some of these people. I suspect they were all his cronies from Chicago . . . They were all gangster related and tough and insensitive to people's needs and didn't know anything about music."[7] "Frenchy was what you might call a company man," according to Dan Morgenstern. "He was Joe Glaser's spy, you know, but everybody knew that. I guess the reason why Joe had him there was that he wanted a disciplinarian, because he knew that Louie from the get-go did not want to be bothered with any nonmusical issues involved in the management of the group."[8] As Armstrong said in 1950, "Joe Glaser formed this band and appointed me leader . . . I don't know what any of the men get. I can't concentrate and play my heart out and pay the musicians off. Can't put my mind on it. I haven't seen a contract in 10 years. Papa Glaser handles all that stuff. I don't need contracts."[9] When it came to "all that stuff," that's where Tallerie would come in. "If anybody wanted a raise, they'd have to go to Joe and they'd go to Joe through Frenchy," Dan Morgenstern said. "If any issues arose on the road, if somebody didn't like their room, or if somebody wanted, you know, whatever, all the millions of little things that come up when a band is on the road and especially when they travel as much as the All Stars, then it was Frenchy [he went to]. He was the road manager, and it was up to him to take care of these things. And he didn't do that in the nicest way. He was a bit of a blowhard."[10]

According to Cary, Frenchy was "one of the slimiest sonofabitches I ever knew. Oh, he was a horrible man. He started more trouble in that band between people. And that was his job, to do it. I mean I got a glimpse of how they do things like that." In an early effort to get Sid Catlett to leave the band, Tallerie purposely started an argument backstage at Billy Berg's between Catlett and Armstrong. "And at one point," Cary recalled, "Sid had Louis around the neck and he was choking him, then he stopped and he was weeping. It was very embarrassing and [Cary's girlfriend] Virginia and I didn't want anybody to know that we were there, so we huddled in the back until they left. That Frenchy was a horrible man."[11]

At the time of the Roxy concerts, Cary was going through a divorce, drinking too much, and suffering from leg cramps that forced him to leave the stage in the middle of performances more than once. Cary ended up going to a doctor, who prescribed some sedatives for the cramps. Still, because the band had been such a hit, Cary felt he deserved a raise, so he went to see Joe Glaser about it. "So I'm sitting in the office there, and Frenchy comes in and he tells Joe Glaser that I'm a drug addict. And that was absolutely false, and I got mad as hell. I told him what I thought of him and I left the office and that was the end of that."[12] The exit of Dick Cary is one of the saddest stories in the history of the All Stars. For all the glitz and glamour of Earl Hines's name, he never did fit the band as well as Cary did. If Hines hadn't been hired for a limited stint, Cary might have remained with Armstrong for years, a better team player.

With Cary out and the Roxy engagement over, it was off to Europe for Panassié's Nice Jazz Festival, where the All Stars arrived to a riotous reception from fans and musicians on February 21. Armstrong played from February 22 through February 28 at the Opéra de Nice, where British trumpeter Humphrey Lyttelton caught Armstrong's performance and vividly recalled how, in a band with such star power, Armstrong showed he was the leader. "When I first saw him at the Nice Jazz Festival, in 1948, he was in command of a sizeable chunk of jazz history—Earl Hines, Sid Catlett, Jack Teagarden, Barney Bigard," Lyttelton wrote. "Each of these was a jazz giant, and two of them had been for some years bandleaders in their own right. I stood right behind the bandstand one night while they played. And more than once I found myself quaking at the ferocity with which he directed the band. If Sid Catlett's drums started to intrude too heavily upon a solo, Louis would turn to him and hiss at him like a snake. And more than once Earl Hines's exuberance was curbed by a sharp 'Cut it boy!' "[13] Fully in charge, Armstrong was awarded a "President's Cup" for his efforts at the festival. Max Jones wrote: "Make no mistake about it, Louis Armstrong is still as great a jazz sensation as he has ever been. In this friendly and almost worshipping atmosphere of jazz fervour, he is in his element, and he is playing stuff which has raised even such old-timers as Sinclair Traill and myself to almost boyish heights of enthusiasm."[14] But not all press notices were positive. The festival was perfect timing for Panassié, who had recently published a biography of Armstrong in 1947. In a negative review of the book, writer Hugh Rees took some shots at Armstrong's recent Nice performances as well as his status in jazz history—"It seems high time for a reassessment of Louis Armstrong's importance"—while writing off the musicians in the old Hot Five as "musical illiterates, unaware it seems of their own incompetence." Rees began planting seeds of negativity that still sprout today:

It was fortunate for Armstrong that, around 1929, he was taken up by a commercially-minded manager. Louis is a natural showman, an adequate if unimaginative trumpeter and an original if sometimes incomprehensible vocalist . . . But a truly great artist can never be satisfied with his achievements. Were Armstrong, as M. Panassié would tell us, "one of the greatest musicians that humanity has known," he would have developed. Instead, his approach has remained the same.

His technique in a world of Gillespies, Hawkins, and Tatums seems childish. Every phrase that he uses he's used a hundred times before so that now they all sound faded . . . After hearing that sad little broadcast from Nice one must face the truth. Louis Armstrong is a bore, whose manner of telling the old, old story has not improved in the least after twenty-odd years of repetition![15]

Rees notwithstanding, the majority of Europe's jazz fans were in awe of Armstrong and remained so when Armstrong arrived in Paris on February 29 to play the Salle Pleyel for the first time since 1934. The air was tense, as there had been an anonymous threat of violence against Armstrong before the concert; the trumpeter was guarded by fifteen police and secret service men on his way to the show. No one made good on the threat, and Armstrong gave a show well received by a crowd of thousands. Armstrong dedicated "Someday" to France and even sang "That's My Desire" in what *DownBeat* called "a completely surrealist pidgin-French version." Years later, much of the concert was released on LP, but it never has been issued on CD. The only sloppy moments on the record are caused chiefly by Hines's unfamiliarity with the material; he begins "Black and Blue" in the wrong key and has to be admonished by Armstrong for setting the tempo too fast on "Muskrat Ramble." After another sold-out Paris concert, Armstrong flew back to the United States on March 4. Joe Glaser was particularly pleased with the money Armstrong earned. "March 2," he said, "the gross was 1,422,748 francs. March 3, a new record, 1,466,404 francs. Bobby-soxers everywhere asking for autographs." Armstrong was proud of the Sèvres vase presented to him by France's president, Vincent Auriol, though he referred to it with characteristic simplicity as "a plate."[16] Years later, he remembered the vase, saying, "Say, they only give out about 50 of them vases in the las' 500 years to people who really done somethin', like Madame Curie and Toscanini, but I'm the first jazz musician that got one, they tell me."[17]

When he returned to the United States, Armstrong was about to step back into the throes of controversy. The boppers had started lambasting him, but not for musical reasons. "I criticized Louis for other things, such as his 'plantation image,' " Dizzy Gillespie later wrote. "We didn't appreciate that about Louis Armstrong, and if anybody asked me about a certain public image of him, handkerchief over his head, grinning in the face of white racism, I never hesitated to say I didn't like it."[18] Armstrong fought back. "I'd never play this bebop because I don't like it," he said to George T. Simon. "Don't get me wrong; I think some of them cats who play it play real good, like Dizzy, especially. But bebop is the easy way out. Instead of holding notes the way they should be held, they just play a lot of little notes . . . It's all just flash. It doesn't come from the heart the way real music should."[19] The more Armstrong vented to Simon, the more upset he got. "Those were real tears in the big, round Armstrong eyes," Simon wrote, "tears of despair, of frustration, tears from a man who had always tried to do what he felt was right, in his relations with people and in relation to his music; tears from a man whom everybody loved, who wanted to harm no one, but who wanted to be free to blow his horn the way he wanted to blow it."[20] A month later the controversy flared, thanks to an article in *DownBeat* quoting Armstrong at a hotel in Nice talking about the music he heard in New Orleans: "The way they phrased so pretty and always on the melody, and none of that out-of-the-world music, that pipe-dream music, that whole modern malice . . . So you get all them weird chords which don't mean nothing, and first people get curious about it just because it's new, but soon they get tired of it because it's really no good and you got no melody to remember and no beat to dance to. So they're all poor again and nobody is working, and that's what that modern malice done for you."[21]

The All Stars saw a spike in popularity in the spring of 1948 when a readers' poll in the *Chicago Defender*, a black newspaper, named Armstrong's group the most popular small combo in the music world. "There has been a switch in positions among the smaller orks with Louis Armstrong displacing Louis Jordan after a week of solid balloting," the article announced. "Louis in moving to the top is seeing his successful concerts in Detroit and St. Louis bear fruit. To see Armstrong keeping so close to a solid trouper like Louis Jordan is hardly surprising when one peeks into the personnel that makes Satchmo's aggregation click. Certainly Sid Catlett, Earl Hines, Jack Teagarden and Barney Buigard [sic] are aces on their respective instruments. They are a good part of what makes Armstrong click."[22] No bop groups placed in the poll. Below Armstrong and Jordan were rhythm-and-blues-derived jazz combos, including groups led by Illinois Jacquet, Arnett Cobb, Eddie "Cleanhead" Vinson, Earl Bostic, and Roy Milton. Most jazz history books give scant attention to these bluesy, swinging, and honking musicians, focusing instead on bop and its offspring.

As successful as the band was, Armstrong now and then would have to step up and assert his leadership, especially with Hines. W. C. Handy's "St. Louis Blues" was a song Armstrong had recorded and played for decades, but when Hines joined the band, "Boogie Woogie on St. Louis Blues" became his own feature, as it was one of his biggest hits of the swing era. It would remain a feature for All Stars pianists until 1955—except for one night, June 4, 1948. A few days before, Hines had owned it as usual, even introducing it at the microphone. But on June 4, at Ciro's in Philadelphia, Armstrong called "St. Louis Blues" not as a feature for Hines but as an instrumental showcase for the band. For four minutes, Armstrong dazzled, delving into a complex solo climaxed by an angry blue note of extraordinary power. Not done yet, Armstrong saved his best for the three rideout choruses, building to a sensational ending that saw him hitting high concert E-flats as if he were a young man again. Shortly thereafter, "St. Louis Blues" went back to being a Hines specialty. Hines may have angered Armstrong during the Ciro's engagement, compelling the trumpeter to fierce competitiveness. Few, including Hines, could match Armstrong's musicality when he was angry. Hines would get his feature back, but Armstrong had made his point.

Armstrong spent 1948 without a record contract; he didn't make a single studio side and was none the poorer for it. A *Holiday* magazine article quoted Glaser as saying the group's annual gross billings averaged $500,000 and that they had a weekly payroll of $3,200 without commissions.[23] Armstrong made it clear that he was decidedly finished with big bands. "We had all that," Armstrong said. "Take this outfit . . . ump . . . Fatha Hines, Big Sid and that Jackson [Teagarden] all had trouble with big groups, lost dough with some of 'em, had a lotta headaches [that weren't] needed. This is better."[24]

CHAPTER THREE

King of the Zulus, 1949

FEBRUARY 21, 1949, was a banner day for Armstrong. That afternoon, he appeared on a radio broadcast of the *Bing Crosby Chesterfield Show* done at the Marine Memorial Theatre in San Francisco. Armstrong and Crosby were old friends from the 1920s; Armstrong had profoundly influenced Crosby's singing (though Armstrong wasn't above stealing a few Crosbyisms from time to time himself). Crosby helped Armstrong land a major part in the 1936 film *Pennies from Heaven*, beginning a professional relationship that lasted through numerous other film, television, and radio appearances. The two had unbeatable chemistry when sharing a stage, and Armstrong always spoke positively about Crosby offstage. During a party at Armstrong's house on New Year's Eve 1952, a friend mentioned seeing Crosby. "Ah, give that buzzard my regards there! Shove him my regards, Daddy. That's my boy, there," Armstrong happily intoned. But when Armstrong's friend Slim Thompson said that Crosby "didn't do much for Negroes," Armstrong responded, "Well, he did as much as he could. You know, sometime there's no opening for them ofays to do something for a spade, you know? He did something in his way. He kept colored help, a spade chauffeur." Later in the same conversation, when Thompson pressed him a bit more, Armstrong said, "Oh man, I like everybody. Oh, man, shit. There ain't nobody in the world who can help you. Like they say, God help the poor but not the poor and lazy."[1]

On this February broadcast, Armstrong and Crosby confirmed their rapport on "Lazy Bones," a Johnny Mercer–Hoagy Carmichael composition that could have been cringe-worthy with lesser talent. Armstrong and Crosby transcend the lyrics completely, establishing the friendly, easygoing patter that was to become the hallmark of all their future duets. Armstrong sings each one of his lines with such an over-the-top delivery, the audience screams with laughter every time he opens his mouth. Later in life, Crosby called Armstrong "a genius. Never be another like him, and never was one before in so many ways—his command of the instrument, his style, the things he could do in addition to playing the trumpet, his singing, the things he sang. They were so infectious. He was probably the most infectious performer I think I've ever seen in addition to being a genius."[2]

On the same day as the Crosby show, the new issue of *Time* magazine hit newsstands, featuring Armstrong on the cover with a quote of his about jazz that would go on to be one of his most famous sayings: "When you got to ask what it is, you never get to know." It was quite a feat for a jazz musician to make the cover of such a prestigious news magazine, Armstrong being the first to do so. But Armstrong had even more exciting news which he couldn't wait to tell *Time*: "There's a thing I've dreamed of all my life and I'll be damned if it don't look like it's about to come true—to be King of the Zulus Parade. After that I'll be ready to die." The Zulu Social Aid and Pleasure Club, a mainstay in New Orleans for decades, had selected Armstrong to be its king at the upcoming Mardi Gras festival. Armstrong might have been thrilled by the notion, but it would be a move that would make younger blacks squirm. As Zulu king, Armstrong would be made up in blackface, except for the area around his eyes and lips, which were painted white. As Thomas Brothers has written, "The first King Zulu wore a lard-can crown, blackface makeup, ragged trousers, and carried a banana-stalk scepter. 'Zulu' was a common racial slur, used right alongside 'nigger,' 'darky,' 'coon,' and 'monkey.' "[3] As *Time* reported, "Among Negro intellectuals, the Zulus and all their doings are considered offensive vestiges of the minstrel-show, Sambo-type Negro. To Armstrong such touchiness seems absurd, and no one who knows easygoing, non-intellectual Louis will doubt his sincerity."[4] Armstrong was sincere because he knew that being King of the Zulus was wickedly double-edged. "From the start, the Zulu ritual was loaded with double-edged symbolism," Brothers writes, adding, "King Zulu is not an African but rather a minstrel parody of an African. His true object of satire is Rex, the white Mardi Gras king. He does everything that Rex does, only upside down . . . Rex is protected by the city police, King Zulu by his comical Zulu police. It is a classic example of carnivalesque release of class tensions with the special twist of African-American signifying."[5] Armstrong might have known and appreciated the subtext involved in being King of the Zulus, but to anyone outside of New Orleans, the sight of Armstrong in full Zulu regalia was disturbing.

In a letter to a friend, Armstrong touted his assumption of the honor just before the actual parade: "The Zulu Social Aid and Pleasure Club was the first colored carnival club to get together in New Orleans. The club has been together for generations and consists of the fellows in my neighborhood. The members were coal-cart drivers, bartenders, waiters, hustlers, etc.—people of all walks of life. Nobody had very much, but they loved each other . . . and put their best foot forward making a real fine thing of the club. I am a lifelong member and it was always my ambition to be elected King of the Zulus some day."[6]

Armstrong was officially crowned King of the Zulus during the intermission of a concert at Booker T. Washington Auditorium on February 27. After playing an appropriate "Where the Blues Were Born in New Orleans," Armstrong performed one of his old Decca big-band hits, "Shoe Shine Boy." He probably hadn't played it in years, but he revived it at a supremely passionate slow tempo, delivering the lyrics as a way of possibly telling his hometown fans that even though he had become so popular, appearing in movies and on the cover of *Time,* he would always remain a humble, hard-working "shoe shine boy."[7] The next night, Armstrong played a concert in Baton Rouge and received a plaque of honorary citizenship and a miniature key to the city from Mayor deLesseps Morrison at City Hall. Morrison asked Armstrong about a quote the trumpeter made in *Time* about how once named King of the Zulus, he'd be "ready to die." Armstrong replied, "Well, I don't want the Lord don't take me literally!"[8]

On Tuesday, March 1, besides the blackface makeup, he wore black-dyed long underwear, a grass skirt, a red velvet tunic with gold sequins, gold shoes, a green velvet cape, and a red-feathered, cardboard crown for the twenty-mile parade. *DownBeat* estimated a crowd of more than two hundred thousand along the route of the parade, as Armstrong's old Hot Five records blared from radios and public-address systems. Throughout his trip on the lead float, Armstrong drank one toast after another of champagne and tossed painted coconuts into the crowd (one hit a new Cadillac!). Armstrong was having a ball, but it was rough going for the other All Stars, especially for Big Sid Catlett and Velma Middleton, whose float eventually collapsed as the day went on.[9] The procession didn't end until five p.m., and as Nick Gagliano wrote, "As Louis dashed for his waiting automobile, the souvenir-hungry crowd descended upon the tinseled float and stripped it of everything."[10] With barely a chance to rest, Armstrong was whisked away to play one more concert at the Booker T. Washington Auditorium that night, though his voice was so shot from celebrating, he had to stick to playing the horn. *Playback* magazine dubbed the concert an "ill-timed event," saying, "Mardi Gras night in New Orleans finds nearly everyone exhausted, or engaged in activities to which they have been committed for months. As a consequence, Louis, king of the trumpet and king of the Zulus, played to a handful of people."[11] Once the concert started, *Playback* reported, "he played as if there had been 5000 persons in the hall. The fast show pieces of the concert gave way to the tunes and tempos reminiscent of the Hot Five. As one spectator said: 'It was a million dollars' worth of music for a two-bit crowd.' "[12]

Armstrong's turn as King of the Zulus was covered in great detail by the media, but once it was over, criticisms predictably rolled in. George C. Adams, a black attorney from Chicago, spoke with the most venom: "I can't imagine a man who has risen to the heights as Louis Armstrong has, who would stoop to such foolishness and thus disgrace all Negroes. It is unbelievable that an internationally famous musician would insult the face which he should dignify. When I consider the depths to which he has descended in being King of the Zulus, I am reminded of a Bible phrase, 'The dog has returned unto his vomit and the sow that was washed has returned unto her wallow.' "[13] An unpublished note written by jazz critic George Hoefer in 1949 contained more of Adams's criticisms. Hoefer wrote, "[Adams] declared that 'Negroes should file an injunction against that club (the Zulus) restraining it from disgracing all intelligent Negroes, not only of New Orleans, but of the entire United States.' Petitions to this

effect are said to be circulating among New Orleans Negro intellectuals."
Hoefer added, though, that not everyone was as ashamed as Adams. "On
the other hand," he wrote, without naming names, "some Negro leaders are not at all perturbed by the Shrove Tuesday doings. They consider
them a broad satire on the extremes of pageantry which afflict the New
Orleans white folks at the beginning of Lent." Armstrong himself was
described by Hoefer as being "somewhat disturbed" about all the criticism he received in the black press regarding his appearance as King of the
Zulus. Armstrong would always view the Zulu parade as one of the highlights of his career, but he did have to deal with some things that unsettled
him on his return to New Orleans: the segregation and racism of his own
hometown. Of one of the New Orleans concerts, Leonard Feather would
later remember, "I went to the concert, and I saw black spectators seated
on the left and the center aisles, while the whites were over on the right
aisle. But on the stage I saw Louis and Jack Teagarden with their arms
around each other radiating interracial brotherhood singing a duet. And I
saw the white officials shaking hands with Louis on stage and congratulat-
ing him and paying tribute to his talent. I saw Louis bursting with pride
when they gave him an honorary citizenship and the keys to the city. But
I also knew that there were hundreds of places to which those keys would
never admit him."[14]

By the summer of 1949, television was slowly becoming a more common-
place luxury in many Americans' homes. After conquering films and radio,
Armstrong was at home in the new medium, too, making an appearance
on a June episode of *Eddie Condon's Floor Show,* the first regular showcase
for live jazz on television. The episode was hosted by pianist Joe Bushkin,
as Condon was ill and in the hospital. Armstrong began the show by
sending the guitarist his best wishes before introducing a special guest,
his adopted son, Clarence Hatfield Armstrong. Clarence was the son of
one of Armstrong's cousins, who died while giving birth. Armstrong, only
fourteen years old at the time, "adopted" Clarence and took care of him
for the rest of his life. A nasty fall at a young age injured Clarence's brain,
leaving him mentally disabled. "That fall hindered Clarence all through
his life," Armstrong recalled. "I had some of the best doctors anyone could
get examine him, and they all agreed that the fall had made him feeble

minded." Because of this, Armstrong took extra-good care of Clarence, always making sure he had, as Michael Cogswell has written, "a place to live, clothes, pocket money, and even companionship."[15] Armstrong spoke with pride as he introduced Clarence: "Ladies and gentlemen, this is really a treat for me and a thrill. I'd like for you to meet my adopted son. He's a youngster that I raised since [he was] about one year old. My cousin died and she left him right with me. It looked like I was the only one that could scrape up a few nickels in the family to keep him moving and keep his jaws jumping! Here he is, he's a grown man now. I want you to say hello to none other than Clarence Armstrong and he wants to say hello to Eddie Condon." Armstrong then pridefully asked Clarence some questions about how he was enjoying New York and such. Clarence gave short yet enthusiastic answers that left no doubts about his mental disability. It's an incredibly sweet moment and it demonstrates the kind of love Armstrong had for Clarence, who died in a Bronx nursing home in 1998.

The Condon broadcast turned out to be something of a sad occasion, though, for it would mark one of the last times Armstrong ever played with Sid Catlett. Armstrong's favorite drummer was in poor health during his tenure with the All Stars, and *DownBeat* announced that he had become so gravely ill with heart and kidney trouble that he would have to leave the band on doctor's orders. He ended up staying in Chicago, passing away backstage at the city's Opera House on Easter Sunday, March 25, 1951. "No one ever had in mind that Sid would die," said Arvell Shaw. "I'll never forget: we left the hotel and got on the bus to go to the job. Louis said, 'Big Sid died.' He didn't say another word; he really was feeling it. The gig that night was the quietest we ever made. Losing Sid was a shock to everybody."[16] Armstrong played with many great drummers during his long and storied career, but he never locked in with anyone else as much as he did with Catlett. All the recordings they made together, from the big-band days to the All Stars, are testaments to one of the greatest partnerships in jazz. Catlett was really the driving force of the early edition of the All Stars, and though many broadcasts exist, it's a shame that that working band only recorded once in the studio. The greatness of the All Stars with Catlett was finally made immortal when Decca released the 1947 Symphony Hall concert later in 1951, an album that still has the ability to awe today, chiefly because of Catlett's exceedingly creative, wonderfully swinging, and always surprising drum work.

As it turns out, Armstrong was probably itching for a change anyway when Catlett grew ill. "He got so he played everythin' except the drums," Armstrong said in 1956. "He played the chicks, he ran with the cats, he played the horses, played the numbers an' when he should have been concentrating on 'proving up his drumming, he just wasn't there. I talked to him 'cause I was very fond of Sid, but he'd come late for rehearsal time after time. He'd arrive just as we was in the middle of our opening number 'Sleepy Time Down South' an' he'd start to tighten up his drums—scrnch, scronch, scraanch—just as we was playin' real pretty."[17] In more reflective times, Armstrong would admit how much he admired Catlett. While listening to recordings of the 1947 Town Hall concert in his Corona, Queens, house, Armstrong took time to talk about Catlett on one of his homemade tape recordings. "Of course, we're all very sad about Big Sid, we all understand that. I must say that this whole reel is dedicated to him because Sid was with us when we made all these tunes, see? And I still think he's the greatest drummer that ever picked up a pair of sticks. And thousands, I'd say millions of people will agree with me, even to listen to these records. The man was a born genius."[18]

Catlett's long-term replacement, William "Cozy" Cole, a veteran of bands led by Benny Carter, Stuff Smith, and Cab Calloway, was no slouch himself. He had worked with Armstrong on a couple of recording sessions, including a V-Disc session of 1944 and the first Victor session after the Town Hall concert in 1947. According to Cole, Joe Glaser called him first to be the All Stars' drummer, but he turned it down because he didn't want to go on the road. When Catlett became ill, Cole was called again and joined this time, with Catlett's blessing. Cole always admired Armstrong's playing, and on his first night, he expected a rehearsal or discussion of what Armstrong wanted, but it wasn't to be. Cole remembered:

So when I went in, the drums were sitting right up front, and Barney and Jack were standing right next to me and so we're about to open and Louis [said], "Hey, Cozy, how you doing?" "All right, Louie," you know, and I figured that some time during that time he'd say, "Well, Cozy, we're going to do this, we're going to play this, we're going to play this." So I asked Barney, I said, "Barney, what are we playing?" I said, "Louie hasn't said anything to me," and Barney said, "Man, don't pay Louie any mind, because Louie ain't going to tell you nothing." So

Louie just looked at me and said, "Cozy, man, we don't have time to just say a lot of things up there. Just cock your ear and straight ahead." And that's what I did for about a couple of weeks until I learned all the tunes, and it was peaches from then on. It was just wonderful, we never rehearsed, and I was with him five years.[19]

Earl Hines was impressed by Cole. "So full of personality, and a good salesman, he was an excellent replacement. He and I soon began to run around and spend a lot of time together. We would rehearse with Arvell Shaw to get the rhythm together, and we ended up with a very good rhythm section that made us stand out."[20] Truth be told, the All Stars' rhythm section took a hit when Catlett left the band. Cole was an exciting soloist, with the ability to build up to a more ferocious climax than Catlett on any of his recorded drum solos with Armstrong, but he didn't have as well-stocked an arsenal of tricks. He mainly swung on the cymbals without any of the creative accents and subtle shadings Catlett provided, lending something of a drier sound to the band. And he didn't exactly hit it off with Armstrong when he first joined the band. Arvell Shaw remembered Cole and Armstrong having great difficulty working together in Cole's early days: "They used to argue continuously about tempo and things."[21]

Armstrong was probably in no mood for disagreements with his own band members, because he was still constantly agitated by the ascendance of bebop. Perhaps working again with the famously antibop Condon again in the summer emboldened him, because soon after, Armstrong's criticisms of the new music gathered steam. In the summer, Armstrong told a luncheon for the Anglo-American Press Association that Bebop "comes from the sticks. Those kids come to a passage they don't dare tackle, so they play a thousand notes to get around it. It's ju-jitsu music. Nothing but squeezing and twisting notes."[22] Armstrong now found himself nostalgically yearning for the music, not of his youth in New Orleans, but of the swing era, just a few years earlier. About swing music he said, "It was nice. It didn't do no harm. You can say that. It didn't do no harm."[23] He continued to make headlines with a Leonard Feather "Blindfold Test." He was far from impressed by Bill Harris's boppish trombone solo on Woody Herman's "Keeper of the Flame," saying, "This thing looks like everybody is trying to kill themselves. That kind of music is liable to start a fight!" Armstrong recognized it as Woody Herman's band and made a telling remark: "I guess musicians would dig this more than the untrained ear." The younger Armstrong would sometimes hit hundreds of high C's just to impress the musicians in the house; but now, more mature, he clearly wasn't into that anymore. He praised music that was made for the public, music made for dancing, such as Benny Goodman's "Sometimes I'm Happy." His highest marks went to Guy Lombardo, whom he praised to much surprise in the February 1949 *Time* cover story. Upon hearing Lombardo's "Always," he said, "Give this son of a gun *eight* stars! Lombardo! These people are keeping music alive—helping to fight them damn beboppers . . . They're my inspirators!"[24] The now legendary *Birth of the Cool* sessions had just taken place, featuring Miles Davis's trumpet with arrangements by the likes of Gil Evans and Gerry Mulligan. By Mulligan's "Jeru" Armstrong was not impressed: "This is all right according to the current trend, but not for no jazz fan. The trumpet just about saved it. Two stars."[25] But Armstrong was not entirely closed minded. About Tadd Dameron's piece "John's Delight" he said, "You wouldn't call this strict bebop . . . This is the best of the bop things I've heard so far; it's more on the order of polished Dixieland. We could play a piece like that." Holding his own generation to the highest standards, he had harsh words for his old friend Kid Ory's recording of "Creole Bo-Bo": "This is all right; nothing much. Two-and-a-half."[26] Armstrong commented to Feather about his younger audiences: "You know, it's gotten to a point where our band goes into places and we find they've lost all respect for the musicians. We played a university date in Seattle and they had to advertise that we wouldn't play bebop. Then we went in there and played 'Tenderly.' And everybody sat down and relaxed." Later, he added, "Maybe the younger people don't appreciate some of the things we're doing. Okay, so we'll play for the old-time people; they've got all the money anyway!"[27]

Armstrong spent the end of summer 1949 at the New York nightclub Bop City, an event that captured the attention of the *Chicago Defender*, erstwhile denouncers of bop. A *Defender* article stated, "Ironically, the site of his return to Broadway will be Bop City, the last existing stronghold of bop in this country. Not only will Armstrong openly defy the bop addicts there, but he is confident he will swing them to swing—and even further back to ragtime."[28] Indeed, Armstrong scored a moral victory when he brought his band into Bop City and promptly broke more box-office records. "They're thinking of changing the name of the joint to Pops' City since Ol' Satchmo's half-century-old chops blew up 30 years of ephemeral jazz memories Thursday," Hal Webmen wrote. "He came out the winner and still king in the territory which has been ascribed to citizens of oo-bla-dee. This crowd, which was estimated at over 2,000 persons, mobbed Bop City to pay tribute to and come away enthralled by the artistry and showmanship of Louis Armstrong."[29] It was the biggest opening night in the history of Bop City and of the venue's previous incarnations. But Armstrong had to face a new criticism: too much clowning. By Armstrong's success at Bop City, George T. Simon, who had waxed hot and cold about Armstrong through the years, wasn't impressed. "At Bop City, he was mugging like mad, putting on the personality, bowing, scraping and generally lowering himself as a human being in the eyes of his worshipers," Simon wrote. "There is no need for a man as great as Louis to have to resort to such behavior."[30] Simon apparently had been blind to Armstrong's stage presence of the past twenty-five years. Armstrong's showmanship in the 1940s was nothing new; now it seemed perversely out of place to jazz critics newly accustomed to the straight-faced boppers (Dizzy Gillespie excluded). Armstrong never strove to change his ways; he wanted only to entertain his audience. But critics no longer expected entertainment from a true jazz musician. "The Armstrong success at Bop City was a great commercial victory for Armstrong and for Dixieland," Simon concluded. "Too bad that it couldn't have been an equally great triumph for music."[31]

If Simon didn't like what he saw and heard at Bop City, he probably became even more distressed when he heard Armstrong's latest recordings. After a two-year absence from recording studios, Armstrong signed a new contract with Decca in 1949. His producer would be Milt Gabler, an old friend who originally ran the fabled Commodore Music Shop in New York City and was now producing records for the likes of Bing Crosby, Louis Jordan, and Billie Holiday. Though a true advocate of jazz, Gabler also knew how to make pop records, which made Joe Glaser happy. "Glaser never asked to see the material," Gabler recalled. "He used to say, 'Give him a Top Ten hit!' That's what he wanted . . . and pop music . . . And the Decca sales organization, they loved Louis, but they also wanted pop tunes, or a plug tune. In those days, you had more than one record of a song when a publisher really worked on it, and as soon as Louis would make a pop tune, his record would go on all the coin machines immediately. And get air play."[32] So it was decided, for popularity's sake, that Armstrong would cover other people's hits, a shrewd commercial gambit. Gabler then proceeded to put the All Stars on hold. Even though they were a popular live attraction, their records for Victor had made no dent on the charts. Armstrong would be backed by studio big bands or by strings, making his records more appealing to that sector of the population averse to trendy, loud, cacophonous music. With the formula in place, Gabler asked Armstrong to play three record dates in September 1949. The first would pair him with a small big band made up of old friends and former associates and conducted by fellow trumpeter Sy Oliver; the next would find him backed by popular arranger Gordon Jenkins's choir of mixed voices; the third would be collaborative with fellow Decca star Billie Holiday. Each of the three sessions represented a kind of record Armstrong would make for Decca over the next decade.

For the September 1 session, Gabler chose two current hits, "Maybe It's Because" and "I'll Keep the Lovelight Burning (in My Heart)," made popular by Dick Haymes and Patti Page, respectively. Conductor Sy Oliver, who also did the arrangements, was best known for his work with the Jimmie Lunceford and Tommy Dorsey big bands. Oliver had once sat in awe in the trumpet section behind Armstrong when Zack Whyte's band backed him in 1928, and he would become a frequent recording partner over the next decade. Armstrong got sympathetic support from Oliver's studio band which included trumpeter Buck Clayton, tenor saxophonist Budd Johnson, and young bassist Joe Benjamin. "I always liked Louis Armstrong," Benjamin later recalled. "You listen as a youngster and all of a sudden you're an adult. And then one day you find yourself in a Decca recording studio with him and find he's one of the nicest people on this earth."[33] "I'll Keep the Lovelight Burning (in My Heart)" is something of a minor classic; it features not only a tremendous trumpet solo but a lovely vocal full of Crosbyisms and ferociously sublime scatting, leading to an "Oh yeah" that would indelibly be associated with Armstrong in the years to come.

On September 6, Armstrong returned to Decca's studio, this time backed by a choir and a studio band of first-rate musicians, arranged and conducted by Gordon Jenkins. Jenkins was primarily known for his signature emotional string writing (though he didn't use any strings for this Armstrong session) and his excellent compositions, including

"Goodbye" and the very popular *Manhattan Tower* suite. Jenkins felt very comfortable around jazz musicians and worshipped Armstrong like an idol. Gabler saw the combination of the two men as a no-miss proposition: "Everyone wanted to work with Gordy, and as you look back, he was making history back then," he remembered. "He's the one who brought background vocals into combination with musicians. The Armstrong sessions really typified that." Jenkins was overwhelmed. "I cracked up," he said. "I walked into the studio, looked over there, saw Louis and broke down. Cried so hard I couldn't even see him. Later that night I came home, and I was so excited I couldn't eat my dinner. Then I started crying again. I took it pretty big."[34]

After a gorgeous cover of Frankie Laine's hit "That Lucky Old Sun," Armstrong was presented with "Blueberry Hill," a song originally performed by "The Singing Cowboy" Gene Autry, and recorded by Glenn Miller in 1941. Effectively backed by the choir, Armstrong sang a whole section of special lyrics created for him by Jenkins. His voice never sounded smoother—you can practically hear him smiling—and the background choir was pure sunshine. The result was one of Armstrong's biggest sellers and a song he would perform almost every night for the rest of his life to huge ovations. "It just got played so much more than anything he'd had," Jenkins said. "He was well known around the world, but he'd never appeared with a chorus before, or with strings, that kind of treatment." Los Angeles disc jockey Chuck Cecil added, "It took Louis out of the jazz idiom and gave him a piece of pop music. I've always thought it not only changed his career but prolonged it. Made him more popular than he'd ever been in his life."[35]

Armstrong now had a popular record on his hands, but jazz critics noticed something else about his session with Jenkins: there was no trumpet playing. The trend continued on his next date for Decca, on September 30, but this session had been planned as a singing date, for Armstrong and Billie Holiday. Armstrong was one of Holiday's primary inspirations as a singer, and though they had appeared in public together before and in the film *New Orleans*, this would be their first—and, as it turned out, only—recording together. The studio band, again arranged and conducted by Sy Oliver, included Billy Kyle on piano, Armstrong's first recording with a man who would play in his band for over a decade. Armstrong and Holiday's first song, "You Can't Lose a Broken Heart," is a charming one, featuring the two at their vocal peaks (Armstrong's entrance is sublime), but there's barely any interaction between the two legends. However, on the second tune recorded that day, the cute "My Sweet Hunk o' Trash," the couple interacted perhaps a little *too* much, Holiday singing straight as Armstrong jokes around her. Holiday assumes the jocularity when Armstrong takes over. During Holiday's closing stop-time section, she sings, "Now when you stay out very late / It sure makes me mad to wait," and Armstrong replies, "How come, baby?" However, he spaces "how come" so closely that, with his natural rasp, he sounds as if he's saying "Fuck 'em, baby!" Columnist Walter Winchell, for one, went apoplectic and demanded the record be pulled. Decca pulled it and issued a new version with a dubbed-in, clearer "how come," but today, most reissues contain the original.[36]

In October of 1949 the All Stars embarked on their first full tour of Europe, playing forty-eight concerts in nine countries over six weeks, a very lucrative tour indeed. *Variety* reported, "Offers from Spain, Portugal, and Egypt had to be turned down for lack of time. Unit's asking price varied between roughly $2,500 and $3,000 per day, depending on situations, with payment in dollars deposited in U.S."[37] Publicist Ernie Anderson went along for the tour and vividly recalled some odd advice Joe Glaser gave his star client before the tour started. "I remember Joe Glaser instructing Louis, 'Whatever you do, don't sing. These are all foreigners. Remember, they don't understand English.' Louis nodded gravely." Armstrong might have nodded in Glaser's presence, but Anderson added, "It should be noted that Louis completely ignored Joe Glaser's instruction not to sing. He opened every concert [by] singing Fats Waller's paean to the racial mood in America, 'Black and Blue.' It was always marvelously received. He sang a lot on every show."[38]

The tour got off to a bang when the band couldn't land in Stockholm because of a crowd estimated by *Time* at forty thousand, with thousands more waiting in line to get tickets for one of Armstrong's three concerts there.[39] "My trip to Europe was something that I shall never forget," Armstrong said. "My *Gawd* how could I . . . Of course the boys in my group thought they'd be well received as far as their music is concerned but they never thought the enthusiasm and great love for their music and people thrilled to meet them in person awaited them . . . And for me—I felt that I'd met a lot of the good, ol hot club fans and the good, ol worshippers and stuff like that . . . But when they'd stand up and cheer and stand in the rain to get autographs after the concert—My My—isn't that the Cat's whiskers? . . . Tee Hee . . ."[40]

The tour continued in hectic fashion, with multiple concerts sometimes taking place in multiple cities in the course of a single day. After Holland, Belgium, and Switzerland, the band headed to Italy for ten days, arriving first in Milan, where Armstrong heard a young Italian singer named Ray Martino. Impressed by him, Armstrong asked Martino to join the band for the rest of the trip, and the two men remained in touch for years after. Armstrong particularly loved Martino's rendition of an Italian song called "Luna," playing it for his friend the producer George Avakian when Avakian visited Armstrong's home in 1953. At the Louis Armstrong House Museum, a private tape exists of Armstrong in his home playing along with the tune. Though the record is about as far from hot jazz as possible, Armstrong always loved a good melody, and he responds by performing a gorgeous obbligato to Martino's Italian vocal, as well as a heartfelt solo. When Martino was played this tape years later, he cried.

From Milan, the band headed to Trieste, where they played a benefit for United States troops, the first by a U.S. group since World War II. Arvell Shaw remembered Armstrong's problems with drummer Cole coming to a head at Trieste:

> Anyway, we were in Trieste, and just before the curtain went up—you know, we were on stage, we had these white, beautiful tuxedos. And we were standing there and none of the Italian stagehands couldn't speak a word of English and they were waiting for the signal. And all of a sudden, Louie looked back [at] Cozy, he said, "Man, for chrissakes, try to keep tempo for one time!" And then Cozy said, "What are you talking about, 'one time'? I'm the best drummer," you know . . . and the argument got hot and the Italian stagehands are waiting for the curtain to go up. And all of a sudden Louie put his trumpet down and ran, grabbed Cozy, and pulled him off the drums, and they started rolling over the stage, swinging and fighting!"[41]

According to Shaw, Armstrong and Cole went at it for a while until the Italian stagehands, believing this to be the start of the show, began to raise the curtain! Armstrong and Cole realized what was happening, let each other go, and managed to be at their instruments smiling as the emcee introduced them. "They went through the whole first set," Shaw said, slapping his hands together, "and it started all over again!" Listening to the Trieste concert today, one hears no animosity on the bandstand, and indeed, the reception the band receives is overwhelmingly enthusiastic. Fortunately for the group, time heals all wounds, and soon enough Armstrong and Cole learned to put their shaky start together in the past. Armstrong always seemed to enjoy Cole's playing, Cole never had a bad word to say about Armstrong, and the two men kept in touch cordially after Cole eventually left the band years later.

In Rome, for Armstrong and his wife Lucille, a special audience with Pope Pius XII was the high point of the European tour. "Of course our meeting the Pope—that I shall never forget," Armstrong said. "He's such a fine man . . . Speaks everybody's language . . . And talk about anything you wish to talk about . . . He thought it real great that we played for the people of Rome and they enjoyed it well . . . He has a very pleasant smile. He gave us a medal each that's blessed by him."[42] Naturally, Armstrong couldn't resist being Armstrong. Ernie Anderson, who went along with the Armstrongs for this summit meeting, remembered Armstrong lighting a joint on his way to his papal audience. And while waiting for the Pope with Lucille and Anderson in a small room, Armstrong broke the silence by announcing, "I've got to shit."[43] Once the Pope arrived, he engaged Armstrong in a conversation legendary for more than sixty years. "He asked me, he said, 'You got any children?' I said, 'Well, no, Daddy, but we're still wailing!' He said, 'But I'm going to pray for you, I'm going to pray for you!' "[44] Once the Pope left, Armstrong proceeded to the bathroom to do his business, but not before running out and calling to his wife, "Lucille, Lucille, come in here and see the Pope's toilet."[45]

Also while in Rome, Armstrong and the band took time to appear in an Italian film, *Botta e Risposta,* performing "That's My Desire" with Middleton and "Struttin' with Some Barbecue." Earl Hines even got to feature "Boogie Woogie on St. Louis Blues." Hines must have been gratified by this, for he was feeling a little bitter about all the attention Armstrong was receiving. "When we were traveling in Europe, I was a little upset that he had so little time for us," Hines said years later. "I naturally remembered the years when we used to run around and hang out together. But later I found out that it wasn't *his* fault. He was a giant of jazz, a great personality, and he set a wonderful example and did wonderful things in Europe."[46]

After Italy, the band still had to play Paris, where they had been a hit in 1948, stopping at Nice along the way. Of the European concerts, Armstrong said, "They all were just too beautiful to mention with just a few words."[47] It was a remarkably successful tour, though a grueling one. Because of high demand, the number of concerts originally scheduled had to be doubled during the trip. The band had only one day off the entire six weeks. Armstrong loved Europe and said he wanted to tour there yearly, but he also made it clear that he could never permanently reside there, because "the musical times be slipping by you and then when you realized it—sure 'nuff—you'll find you're ten years behind the time." That was why Armstrong kept up such a grueling pace. "That's one reason I'm glad I am able to make those hard one night stands . . . And make 'em very happily I do . . . Then too—I get a chance to keep my chops up by blowing nightly . . . The more I blow the longer they'll go," he wrote.[48] Armstrong concluded this *Holiday* article by saying, "To all the countries that we played or passed through . . . I voice the opinion of my entire group and I'll speak for them in saying for them as well as my wife Lucille and myself . . . We are more than grateful to you for being so very kind to us and appreciating our music and our efforts the way you did." But when *Time* asked him how this European tour compared to the one he did in 1934, he said, "I didn't have my thermometer, but they was both a bitch."[49]

CHAPTER FOUR

Decca Days, 1950–1951

WHILE ARMSTRONG and the All Stars were in Europe, the trumpeter's latest Decca recordings were released back home. The public might have been pleased by them (Armstrong had deftly performed "Blueberry Hill" for a Bing Crosby radio show in January 1950), but some jazz critics demurred: they were put off by Armstrong's jocularity and choice of pop tunes; they wanted re-creations of his instrumental jazz classics of the 1920s. Two collectors, John Davis and Gray Clarke, wrote a piece around this time "wondering whether, after all, [Armstrong] is of any significance at all in jazz!"[1] Disc jockey Frenchy Sartell grew apoplectic when confronted with Armstrong's pop records for Decca. "My blood is boiling, my ire is aroused. How dare they do it to my favourite jazz 'great'? How dare they bury him in commercialism?" Sartell asked. He seemed to think Armstrong was forced at gunpoint to record these pop songs for Decca, writing: "I've heard 'Pops' play and sing plenty of commercial numbers, but they've been materially suited to his inimitable style, and he has always been able to give his own feeling to them. Take Armstrong, put him in front of another orchestra leader's ensemble, give him a current pop tune and you'll find it's a very different story. If you don't let Louis have his own say, it's like tying his hands behind his back. Armstrong MUST create his own atmosphere. He's not a man who can be told what to do and how to do it."[2]

If Armstrong ever did truly go "commercial," he did so while he was still a child in New Orleans. Before he played the trumpet, he sang with a vocal quartet whose theme song was a popular tune of the day, "My Brazilian Beauty." On the subject of singing—which he always called his "first hustle"—Armstrong received valuable lessons from the Karnofskys, a Jewish family he worked for as a youth in his hometown, who taught him how to sing pretty numbers such as "Russian Lullaby."[3] When he finally began fiddling around with a cornet, Armstrong later wrote, "After blowing into it a while I realized I could play 'Home Sweet Home'—then here come the Blues."[4] A popular song that everyone knew and the gritty music that formed part of the basis for jazz: nothing else could have fore-shadowed Armstrong's career so clearly.

Armstrong began his life as a working musician while still a teenager, performing primarily jazz and blues in New Orleans, though he still listened to all sorts of different music. "I had Caruso records too, and Henry Burr, Galli-Curci, Tetrazzini—they were all my favorites," he said. "Then there was the Irish tenor, McCormack—beautiful phrasing."[5] Armstrong's love of opera would later play a heavy influence on his trumpet playing (he went as far as quoting snippets of *Rigoletto, Pagliacci,* and other operas in his playing). In the 1920s, Armstrong played dance sets with King Oliver, recorded Tin Pan Alley tunes with Fletcher Henderson and was featured on the Intermezzo from *Cavalleria Rusticana* and Noël Coward's "Poor Little Rich Girl" with Erskine Tate. In the late 1920s, Okeh records began feeding him a steady stream of pop songs, including "Star Dust," "Georgia on My Mind," "Body and Soul," "I Got Rhythm," and many other entries in the Great American Songbook, a pattern soon continued by Victor ("I've Got the World on a String," "I Gotta Right to Sing the Blues") and Decca ("I'm in the Mood for Love," "Pennies from Heaven," and many more). Thus, for critics to start attacking Armstrong for recording "commercial" music in the fifties and sixties shows just how ignorant those writers were about Armstrong's entire career. From the day he was born until the day he died, Louis Armstrong performed—and listened to—all kinds of music. Thus, by the late sixties, when Armstrong was recording songs like the Lovin' Spoonful's "Daydream" and John Lennon's "Give

Peace a Chance," he was just recording the popular songs of the day, something he had really never stopped doing since he first picked up a horn in New Orleans. The sound of music kept changing through the decades, but Armstrong always remained himself. Unlike the jazz purists who just wanted him to go on remaking New Orleans warhorses, Armstrong realized that any kind of music could be transformed into jazz if played from the heart. The fact that Armstrong recorded so many so-called "commercial" tunes in his later years is consistent with the rest of his career.

Armstrong reflected on this subject in a 1966 interview with Richard Meryman. "I guess it's possible there's people who wish I'd just play like the old days in Chicago . . . Those records aren't why I'm popular today. More people know me since 'Hello, Dolly!' than *ever*. And all my biggest hits are things like 'Mack the Knife' and 'Blueberry Hill.' " Armstrong made it clear that though these were "commercial" songs, he still found something in them to connect with. "But all songs display my life somewhat, and you got to be thinking and feeling about something as you watch them notes and phrase that music—got to see the life of the song. 'Blueberry Hill,' that could be some chick I ain't seen for twenty years— which chick, who cares? . . . And I think of that, even if the songs *is* so commercified."[6] In September 1952 a disc jockey, in the midst of interviewing Armstrong, introduced a recording of one of Armstrong's Decca performances as "commercial." Armstrong was none too pleased, as can be gleaned from the following exchange:

DEEJAY: It's a commercial approach but at the same time, I believe this is the first, shall I say, commercial record I've ever had on *International Jazz Club.*

LOUIS: Could I interrupt there? What is the meaning of "commercial," and why do you use that expression, "commercial"?

DEEJAY: Well, I use it in the sense that it is perhaps designed to sell records rather than not to sell them. It's not purely aesthetic.

LOUIS: Yeah, but sometimes that hurts a tune when they use that phrase. You take a guy that wants to be hip to the tip and he say, "That guy's commercial," you know, you're about calling that guy a dirty name, in a way of saying. Why don't you say just "a good musician" or "a good swing man" or "someone that plays music, period"? A musician ain't supposed to just play one type of music. When they ask me, say, "Why do you play, 'Cold, Cold, Heart,' why do you play this?" I play anything where I come from.

DEEJAY: Let me say then that it's not jazz in the accepted word or meaning which I use when I play jazz on the *International Jazz Club*. Let me put it that way.

LOUIS: Well, what makes you say that? Take tunes like "St. James Infirmary," which goes down in history, everybody okays that as one of *the* numbers. Well, that's an ordinary tune like this "I Laughed at Love," it just was made Negroid and torrid. You see what I mean? So now if you just analyze "I Laughed at Love," there ain't nothing can outswing it.

DEEJAY: Oh, it's a great, it's a great swing thing. I like it!

LOUIS: Well, that alone, look at nothing but swing lead. That's your key right there. That's jazz, don't care what you're playing. *Cavalleria Rusticana*. If you're expressing yourself and you can make that foot move, just pat lightly, you're swinging. So just because it's a late number, they call it commercial.

After the record was played, Armstrong said, "Every tune's hot until you make it otherwise, Pops—don't let anyone use that 'commercial' on you. That word 'commercial,' that ruined a lot of tunes, you'd be surprised."[7]

Decca—and Armstrong—paid the backward-looking critics no mind, and continued making more pop records in the early fifties. France provided the inspiration for two tunes recorded on June 26, 1950, that would become staples of Armstrong's concert repertoire. The first one was "La Vie en Rose," co-written by the legendary "Little Sparrow," Edith Piaf, whose Columbia recording of the song sold over a million copies. Continuing Decca's trend of having Armstrong cover other singers' hits, Armstrong turned it into one of his best-loved performances, one that is used to set the mood in many romantic movies and television shows to this day. His vocal is one of the most passionate of his career, the quality of his voice captured brilliantly by Decca's engineers, while the closing trumpet solo is as majestic as they come in the Armstrong canon. "Of the countless cover versions," Piaf's Columbia producer George Avakian would later write, "Louis' was easily the best and he never stopped singing it."[8] The flip side of "La Vie en Rose" was "C'est Si Bon," already a hit record by the enormously popular French singer Yves Montand. Backed by a dynamic Sy Oliver arrangement, Armstrong spends the first half of the record singing it, giving it a spin in his usual, inimitable style. But then he picks up the trumpet and blows a full chorus, displaying staggering power and intensity. It's one of Armstrong's best solos of the period, but most hardened jazz critics didn't pick up on it because they were put off by the commercial nature of the session. Armstrong remembered going to a hotel bar shortly after the record was released. "There was a guy sitting down there, glass full of whisky," he said. "He comes over and says, 'Man, that "C'est Si Bon" was gone! But I want to know one thing: who played the solo for you?' He said, 'You're an old cat, man, somebody must have played it for you.' So a chick jumped up and said, 'Who COULD play it for him? Get away from there!' She run him away!"[9]

Decca struck gold again in July 1951 when Armstrong recorded what would become one of his best-known records, "A Kiss to Build a Dream On." Written by the formidable team of Bert Kalmar, Harry Ruby, and Oscar Hammerstein II, the song was cut from the 1934 Marx Brothers movie *A Night at the Opera*. It had lain dormant until Armstrong attempted it for *The Strip*, a film released in 1951, leading Milt Gabler to sense a potential hit. After rejecting a version done with the All Stars in April, Gabler gave the song to Sy Oliver to arrange for the July session. The result was a home run. Armstrong's vocal is the definition of warmth, with trombonist Cutty Cutshall providing a thoughtful obbligato behind the vocal. After a short setup by pianist Billy Kyle, Armstrong, Cutshall, and clarinetist Milt Yaner play sixteen bars instrumentally in the best New Orleans style, drummer Bunny Shawker providing tremendous punch in the rhythm section. Armstrong returns one more time vocally, changing up the phrasing and, overall, sounding like he's in love with the song. The public felt the love and responded by making the record another hit. In January 1952, *Jet* magazine reported, "Currently kicking on all fours is Louis 'Satchmo' Armstrong's disking of 'A Kiss to Build a Dream On,' the best-selling platter of his lengthy career. 'Kiss' has sold well over 400,000 copies, surpassing even his 'Lucky Old Sun' which hit the 300,000 sales mark over a year ago."[10]

The hit status of "A Kiss to Build a Dream On" might have been helped by its flip side, "I Get Ideas." This song was adapted from an Argentine tango, "Adios Muchachos," popularized by Carlos Gardel among others and with English lyrics, was a big hit for American crooner Tony Martin. Like most of his Decca pop covers, it seemed like an unlikely choice for a Louis Armstrong performance, but in the end it was another winner. The lazy yet lovely introduction is very atmospheric, enhanced by Armstrong's tender, straight, muted reading of the melody. Armstrong's vocal—without a trace of gravel—is full of all sorts of wicked insinuations. When he picks up the trumpet, the tenderness of the first half of the record is traded for raw passion, Armstrong's playing at its most rhapsodic. Armstrong reprises the vocal but ends the record by laughing to himself. Obviously having fun, he might have also been laughing because he knew the song he just recorded was about to become another hit.

Armstrong performed his two new hits on Bing Crosby's radio show in November 1951. The mere mention of his "little arrangement" of "I Get Ideas" drew a huge ovation from the audience. Throughout his vocal, the audience erupts in periodic laughter, not laughing at Armstrong as much as sounding like they're basking in his contagious effervescence. The real laughter, though, came on "A Kiss to Build a Dream On." Armstrong joined in on Crosby's arrangement of the song, which was in a lower key than Armstrong was accustomed to. When Armstrong hits the titular word "on," he sings as low as his voice can possibly go, causing the audience to scream with laughter. From there, the piece turns to shambles, but Armstrong and Crosby, ever the professionals, save it through their quick comedic skills. "So much used to go on, most of our stuff was ad-libbed," Armstrong said in a 1955 interview. "That's how we got so many laughs and things. The time we were singing 'Kiss to Build a Dream On' and I just finished my number, and he made me go up there and sing it with him and we were hamming it up some. Took up all the time doing that number with him!"[11] When Armstrong changed the phrase "Give me your lips for just a moment" to "Give me your chops for just a moment," the audience laughed so hard, he had to retain the lyric change for the rest of his career. Completely ignoring the jazz critics, the "commercial" Louis Armstrong was making great music and entertaining his audiences at the same time—just as he had always done for his entire career.

.   .   .

Armstrong may have spent most of his time in the studios recording pop songs, but Decca occasionally managed to showcase the All Stars from time to time. In April 1950, the All Stars visited Decca studios with the sole purpose of recording many of the numbers they were now playing on a nightly basis, numbers they were already familiar and comfortable with. The resulting music was issued on two 10-inch LPs titled *New Orleans Days* and *Jazz Concert*. These two recordings offer a strong account of the Armstrong band featuring Teagarden, Hines, and Cozy Cole, the high-lights being a hot Armstrong solo on "Panama," a hilarious parody version of "Twelfth Street Rag," and Armstrong's first recording of "My Bucket's Got a Hole in It," a traditional New Orleans eight-bar blues.[12] Another gem was titled "New Orleans Function," a two-part piece that served as Armstrong's re-creation of the funerals he played and marched in as a child. The whole routine would form a popular segment in Armstrong's live shows.

But the one bona fide classic to come out of these sessions is a complete surprise: "That's for Me," a song written by Richard Rodgers and Oscar Hammerstein II for the movie *State Fair*. The All Stars had been playing it live for a while, tightening it with each passing performance before per-fecting it for Decca. It's a sublimely tender performance, centered around a touching Armstrong vocal that shows off the tenor range of his voice; he struggles a bit to sing some of the high notes, but it all adds up to the charm of the record. He clearly loves the melody, not infusing it with even a single scat syllable or a "mama." Armstrong's trumpet solo is a master-piece of improvisation, enhanced by surprising double-timed runs and slippery rhythmic phrasing. The song would be featured in Armstrong's live performances for only a short period after the record was released, but Armstrong never forgot it. In a 1968 interview for the BBC radio program *Be My Guest*, Armstrong spoke about the inspiration for his recording that song: his fourth wife, Lucille. Though the song wasn't written until 1945, its sentiment reminded Louis of the time he met her. "Every time I look at Lucille dancing," Armstrong said of their Cotton Club days together when they first met, "she had that little step where they'd raise their hand and hit about three steps in front and everything, that tune that I loved so well dawned on me. It's on one of my records." And at this point, the sixty-seven-year-old Armstrong began singing "That's for Me" completely a capella. He sings only a couple of lines, beautifully, and when he finishes he says, "That was for Lucille."

Decca also attempted to cash in on the popularity of the All Stars by recording one of their concerts at the Pasadena Civic Auditorium in January 1951. By this point, a little of the luster had worn off Armstrong's sextet, and some critics had begun complaining that they played the same songs every night. While Armstrong did offer some repeat material—he knew what his audiences wanted to hear—he changed his sets more often than he was given credit for. Four nights before the Pasadena show, he performed twenty-five songs at a concert in Vancouver, Canada. Decca recorded eighteen songs in Pasadena. Between the two concerts, only eight songs were repeated, while the order of both shows was completely different, demonstrating just how large the band's book of tunes was, especially when considering the high number of tunes not played at either show. The Pasadena concert also includes Armstrong's first recorded performance of "Indiana." "He always opened with 'Indiana' and closed with his theme, 'Sleepy Time Down South,' but the rest of the program he would change to suit the audience," said Lucille Armstrong. "His mind worked so fast. He could hear gnats walking on cotton."[13] The Pasadena program flows beautifully as many high points are reached: a touching version of Louis's own composition "Someday," taken at a slower-than-usual tempo; two Earl Hines compositions, "My Monday Date" and "You Can Depend on Me," the latter featuring one of Louis's most heartfelt vocals; some scathing trumpet work on "That's a Plenty"; the horseplay between Armstrong and Velma Middleton on "Baby, It's Cold Outside," and Velma's own features; individual showcases for the other musicians, such as "Honeysuckle Rose" for Hines and wondrous versions of "Body and Soul" and "Star Dust" by Teagarden. Decca successfully captured a great night of music by a band that had many.

Of all the recordings Decca made with Armstrong in 1950 and 1951, perhaps the best session they produced was a once-in-a-lifetime matching of Armstrong with Louis Jordan. Jordan was a saxophonist who began in the jazz big bands of musicians such as Chick Webb, but when he went off on his own to front a tight little combo, his career took off. Jordan, who backed Armstrong in a big band on one of the trumpeter's 1932 Victor sessions, owed a huge debt of gratitude to Armstrong, as his frequent use of comedy on numbers like "Caldonia," "Beware," and "Beans and Cornbread" had won him his biggest audiences. Jordan's combos, featuring a small horn section pounding out riffs over a driving shuffle rhythm, would become the hottest act in rhythm-and-blues and would serve as a prototype for the early rock-and-roll bands of the 1950s.

Jordan recalled that he and Armstrong had tried to get together in a recording studio five or six times before this date, but since they were both on the road all the time, it was hard getting them in the same place at the same time, even though they were both booked by Joe Glaser. However, when Armstrong arrived at the studio for their August 1950 session, he was having serious trouble getting his lip in shape. "His lip had busted on him, had busted all—all the way down," Jordan recalled. Still, Armstrong was adamant about getting through the date, telling Jordan, "We going to record today."

> And he said, "Let's go down here to Chock Full o' Nuts and get a sandwich and some coffee and we see if we can find some fruit." I said, "What about this fruit?" He said, "Well," he says, "I found that if we—if we can get some white grapes and we eat them and rest awhile, probably my voice will clear," because he was hoarse. He was real hoarse. And he says, "And I—I'm going to make it anyhow." I said, "Oh, don't worry about it." He said, "I'm going to—I'm going to make it." So we—we were supposed to record, start recording, at seven o'clock. We didn't start until ten-thirty or ten-forty-five, and we were through in ten minutes because . . . we'd talked it over and he looked at the music and we knew what we were going to do, but we had to wait on his lip. So finally he said, "Let's go." And we went on and played it. He even . . . played those high C's and things with his lip busted. So he was magnificent.[14]

Jordan wasn't kidding. On the first song of the date, a humorous song called "Life Is So Peculiar," Armstrong takes a short trumpet solo on which he plays at least ten high concert B-flats (written as high C's for trumpet) and nails an almost-boppish unison break with Jordan. The other song recorded that date was "I'll Be Glad When You're Dead, You Rascal You," which Armstrong had performed since 1931, but this was the version to end all versions. Armstrong and Jordan's exuberant chemistry is contagious during the vocal choruses, while Armstrong's trumpet lead at the end is freakishly powerful, a showcase for his strength and endurance as he not only hits high notes but holds them for an almost inhuman length, fully conquering his lip problems. Unfortunately it was the only time the two men ever had the opportunity to record together, something Jordan's wife, Martha, blamed on Joe Glaser. "Louis would have loved to have recorded again with Louis Armstrong but Joe Glaser seemed to veto the idea," she said. "I'm certain that it wasn't anything to do with Pops himself, because Louis and I loved Pops and he was always great with us. Joe Glaser somehow saw Louis Jordan as a threat to Louis Armstrong, which was absolute nonsense."[15]

Actually, Glaser might have been onto something. Jordan's outfit proved so popular over time, it had begun taking some of the black audience away from Armstrong in the 1940s. Armstrong might have had hit records and a popular stage act, but watching his black fans desert him disturbed him greatly. Jack Bradley remembered Armstrong telling him about a road trip that took him through Texas. "He was playing one-nighters somewhere, and in the same town Louie Jordan had his band. And all the [black] people went to see him and hardly any went to see Louie. And that really upset him a lot, 'cause he told me about it. But you know, it was obviously a black community, and Louie was considered by the blacks as well to be an Uncle Tom. But he said, 'My own people didn't come.' "[16]

Though he had become a tremendous draw among white audiences, Armstrong still was no stranger to racism. At the end of 1951, he began work on the MGM film *Glory Alley,* in which he had a featured role as an actor, not just a musician, something he was proud of. While being interviewed by *DownBeat,* he showed writer Don Freeman his script (all of his lines circled in red) and said, "Here, look, I got a nice part," adding, "It's a real acting part, Pops." But when asked if he was planning on becoming a full-time actor, Armstrong joked, "No, Pops, Clark Gable doesn't have to worry."[17] His main job was to smile and mug throughout the film, showing that Hollywood still hadn't come very far in figuring out what to do with his acting talents since the demeaning roles he played two decades earlier—something that could not have endeared him to younger black audiences, who were beginning to grow uncomfortable with Armstrong's public persona.

What they didn't understand was that Armstrong might have been the happiest man in show business while onstage, but offstage he demanded respect. Soon after the filming ended, Armstrong was backstage at a gig in Portland, talking with his friend Benny Hamilton while his tape recorder was rolling, catching a tale of the wrath of Armstrong scorned. "This ofay, he was nothing but a call boy—he called, like, the extras and everything," Armstrong told Hamilton. "Then he'll come to the stars' dressing rooms, let them know when they want them for the camera. And he was hanging around on the set all the time, you know what I mean? He'll come up, 'Mr. [Gilbert] Roland, Mr. [Ralph] Meeker, Miss [Leslie] Caron,' and everything, and then he'll come to my dressing room and a whole lot of bullshit. 'Satchmo! You better come on out there, they'll send [for] Harry James.' " Armstrong didn't appreciate the joke and didn't appreciate that he didn't get treated as the film's other stars did. "I said, 'Listen, you cock-sucker, if they wanted Harry James, they would have had him in front. In the first place, he ain't going to play what I play out there.' " When asked why, Armstrong replied, "'Cause he can't."[18]

Armstrong wasn't finished: "You tell MGM to shove that picture up their ass," he said to the call boy. "And he left me alone," he told Hamilton. "I said, 'I ain't no movie star, no how.' I said, 'Why you hand me that shit? 'Cause I'm colored?' " Armstrong then stuttered, mimicking the call boy's response. "Bullshit! And they left me alone. All the bigwigs was out there, too, and I met them. 'Shove your picture up your ass,' I told them. Then I got along with them. I mean, for no reason at all they had to hand me that shit. I mean, why should I? I just sooner do these one-nighters, play for people who appreciate it."[19] Armstrong then read a very appreciative letter from the film's producer, Dore Schary. After commenting on how nice Schary's words were, Armstrong said, "It ain't the big white people that hand you that crap, it's the poor motherfuckers. You try to be a gentleman, they won't let you, that's all."[20]

Perhaps Armstrong's backstage stance against MGM would have endeared him to his black critics, but it never became public knowledge. However, a recording Armstrong made in November 1951 did get widespread attention and only continued to hurt his standing in the black community. Armstrong had continued making records with Gordon Jenkins for Decca, cashing in on the success of their first collaboration on "Blueberry Hill" and "That Lucky Old Sun." This time, Jenkins brought along his famed string section to help remake Armstrong's theme song, "When It's Sleepy Time Down South," his first full studio version since an instrumental version recorded for Decca with his big band in 1941. As if to offset the instrumental nature of the earlier performance, Jenkins's remake focuses on singing, Armstrong contributing a beautifully affecting vocal that shows off his entire range. He goes from a basso-profundo low C up to a high concert E when he returns from the trumpet solo: seventeen pitches in the course of one song. It may have been gravelly, but his voice was always in tune throughout its extended range.

The only problem with the record came in the lyrics, which contained the word "darkies." Written in 1931 by African-Americans Leon and Otis René and Clarence Muse, the song reeked of an earlier era when an offensive word such as "darkies" could actually be passed off into popular music. Armstrong never stopped using "When It's Sleepy Time Down South" as his theme song, though he usually treated it as a short instrumental. When he sang it during a Soundies short film in 1942, "darkies" was there, as well as a 1948 live version from the Nice jazz festival; but he sang it so infrequently for so many years, it never stirred any waves. But when Decca released the record in early 1952, it was met with a huge backlash from the black press. "The name of trumpet player Louis Armstrong joined the list of the 'We Ain't Ready' people in show business when it became known that he has made a new recording for Decca Records in which he sings the radical epithet 'd——s' in referring to colored people," James L. Hicks wrote in the *Baltimore Afro-American*. "Decca, the firm which released the recording, told *Afro* on Thursday that Armstrong's use of the word in the song is 'regrettable' and not in line with Decca's policy, but claimed that its use was not 'intentional' but was a 'slip-up' on the part of both the firm and Mr. Armstrong." Armstrong didn't comment in the article—he was filming scenes for *Glory Alley*—but Joe Glaser was asked if he felt it was appropriate to have him record such an offensive song. According to Hicks, Glaser appeared angry and said, "That's so silly. I don't govern Louis' words. I don't know what you are talking about. If you want to know anything about that, write me a letter." Mike Connors, Decca's promotion manager, was also contacted. "He said he was sure Armstrong sang the words 'without thinking' and that he was also sure that 'it slipped through' the Decca Company without being noticed."[21]

This notion is hard to believe, especially with noted liberal Gordon Jenkins conducting the band and producer Milt Gabler, the man who recorded Billie Holiday's "Strange Fruit," in the control room. Also, it's interesting to note that the song as originally written featured the word "darkies" *twice,* but on this 1951 remake Armstrong changed it the first time to "folks." Was this his idea? Jenkins's? Gabler's? Whatever, one utterance was enough, and the song was not allowed to be played on any major New York radio stations because of their policy to not air any material with offensive words. Representatives from many major stations, including NBC, CBS, WNBC, WOR, WINS, WCBS, WNEW, WGN, and WJZ, all said they would never air anything with that word. "Harlem's own radio station, WLIB, said through its manager Jack Kuney: 'We are absolutely, actually violently against the use of offensive words on our programs and you can make it stronger than that," according to the *Afro-American* article.[22]

To calm the hysteria, Armstrong reentered the studio to overdub the word "people" instead of "darkies." In live performances, he used "folks," and this is how he would sing it for the next twenty years (though he forgot at first, still singing "darkies" at a February 1952 concert, one of the first times he had sung the song publicly in years). A few months later, while giving an interview in Hawaii, Armstrong finally spoke on the whole "Sleepy Time" matter. "We made all those records for generations of 'Sleepy Time,' and just when I made a real beautiful one with Gordon Jenkins, here comes the colored papers making me change the words to 'folks down there,' " Armstrong said, breaking into laughter before adding, "It's a shame, isn't it?"[23] Armstrong was definitely hurt by the attack. Barney Bigard remembered Armstrong's unwillingness to change the lyrics at first and how, when he returned to the studio, he said, "What do you want me to call those black sons-of-bitches this morning?"[24] The following year, while hanging out with George Avakian at his home, Armstrong offered this telling appraisal of the way he felt he was treated by his people: "That's why they say a bunch of niggers is like a barrel of crabs. Because as soon as one gets to the top, all of those motherfuckers reach up there and grab him and pull him right back down. That's what they do."[25]

Though "darkies" was officially a taboo word, Armstrong might have felt bad changing it since the song was written by black friends specifically with him in mind. As Ernie Anderson remembered, "Louis was very proud of his new hit and told Glaser that he didn't want to change it in any way. He said he didn't care a damn about pickets. Finally Joe Glaser got Louis Armstrong to agree to discuss the matter with an emissary from the NAACP. The emissary turned out to be a very slick, well tailored young black who looked and sounded like he must be right out of Harvard Business School . . . The young black tried to explain that the record was demeaning to blacks. Louis replied quite forcefully, 'Two niggers wrote it!' When he heard this line the young Harvard cat visibly wilted."[26]

Armstrong would continue to proudly use "When It's Sleepy Time Down South" as his theme song for the rest of his career. As he said in a later interview, "The people who are there come there to hear what we swing. From the moment we hit 'Pale moon shining,' you know, the theme song, everybody sits right there and relax. And from that first note on, the warmth is there."[27] During an Armed Forces Radio Service interview from Frankfurt in the fall of 1952, Armstrong was asked to name the one song he received the most requests for. "Don't care where we go, they like my theme song," he answered. "There's something about that theme song and I express it in my story. And I can play that for the audience, that's our opening number anyway. And the first thing we open with is 'Sleepy Time' and I don't care where we playing, they understand that and they appreciate that number." When asked if it was his overall favorite song, Armstrong responded, "Yeah, it is, because I, being from the South, I know the life, and the words live. You know, cats in the sunshine, they lazy, layin' up against the tree and all that stuff there. That's all in that song and it's facts. And the music is pretty. You remember the record we made with Gordon Jenkins? You know what I mean? Well, he visualized music and scenes and things in music the same as I do. It's a funny thing how our minds run together when it comes to different things in a song."[28]

For some of Armstrong's critics, though, the song itself—and Armstrong's singing of the word "darkies" on the first version—was more ammunition for their beliefs that he was nothing more than an old Uncle Tom.

CHAPTER FIVE

Personnel Changes, 1951–1952

AS THE "Sleepy Time Down South" controversy raged at the beginning of 1952, the All Stars were about to undergo a transformation. Armstrong appeared in the film *Glory Alley* not with the band but with only trombonist Jack Teagarden, who had left the All Stars four months earlier. After a string of one-nighters in August 1951, Teagarden had played his final date as a member of the All Stars on September 6, 1951. Constant touring had got to him. He left Armstrong on good terms, thankful for the years of employment and the boost to his career, though a clearly sad and puzzled Armstrong would say that Teagarden "won't make any money that way, away from us. I don't think Jack really wanted to leave. It isn't like him to do that. Sometimes people don't do the things they really want to do."[1] All the same, Teagarden couldn't have been happier going back to his wife, Addie, and his son. He had joined the band in 1947 in debt, picking up the pieces in the wake of his big band's failure. Now he was more acclaimed as a musician than ever. He would soon start his own group, Jack Teagarden and His All Stars, which he led until his death. Months after Teagarden left, Armstrong was still disconsolate: "What really bothers me, Pops, is losing Jack. That Teagarden, man, he's like my brother."[2] Even in 1958, when Teagarden had been out of the band for seven years, Armstrong was asked to name his favorite musician and responded, "You mean the cat I like to play with the best. Easy. It's Jack Teagarden, Pops."[3] The two would go on to make a few memorable film and television appearances together (including a legendary "Rockin' Chair" captured live at the Newport Jazz Festival in Bert Stern's *Jazz on a Summer's Day*), but Teagarden's departure from the band would signal the end of one of the great partnerships in jazz.

Meantime, he was replaced by Russ Phillips, a trombonist from the Midwest who had worked with trumpeter Wingy Manone as well as in the nonjazz bands of Del Courtney and Tiny Hill. In the late 1940s, he settled in Denver, where he first met Armstrong. The All Stars were there in 1949 when Teagarden succumbed to pneumonia and had to return to California. Phillips was playing with a similar combo of his own, so he filled in for Teagarden and must have impressed the maestro. According to his son, Russ Jr., Phillips heard that when Teagarden left, it was Armstrong himself who remembered his playing, saying, "Get the fat white cat from Denver!"[4] About working with the All Stars, Phillips was ecstatic in 1952: "I think it's a great kick to play with a jazz group such as this, fine gentlemen, and to be able to play with fine musicians, I think it would be a kick to anybody."[5] Phillips added "Coquette" to the band's repertoire, but also performed Teagarden's feature of "Baby Won't You Please Come Home" and took on Teagarden's vocal duties on "Rockin' Chair."

On July 6, 1951, after an engagement at the Blue Note in Chicago, Arvell Shaw also left the band to study music in Switzerland (he would marry Swiss journalist and photographer Madeleine Bérard). He spent a full year immersed in arranging, voice, theory, harmony, and even piano lessons. Leaving the All Stars had been a difficult decision, as Shaw related to Armstrong in a letter he wrote from Switzerland the following year. "Pops, that was the hardest thing I ever did was to make up my mind to leave home and the band to study," Shaw wrote. "But in the long run, I don't think I will regret it." He also hinted that a chief reason for his decision to go abroad was that blacks in America at the time were denied proper respect as legitimate musicians. "Now-a-days, you have to know so much, especially being an Arabian [i.e., black] to make a living," he wrote. "I knew so little and with such a long way to go, I hope, with this background, there is nothing they can say, especially after having played with you." Shaw concluded touchingly, "You gave me my start and I will always appreciate it."[6]

Shaw would eventually return to the All Stars, but for now, he was replaced by Dale "Deacon" Jones, a veteran of Teagarden's big band. Born in Nebraska in 1902, Jones already had been in the music business for thirty years when he joined the All Stars. "I haven't been to Europe and I haven't been to South America yet but I've been everywhere else," he said in 1952. Jones added a unique feature to the band with his vocal on the Bert Williams–associated song "Nobody." Jones wasn't much of a soloist, but Armstrong loved his showmanship, and privately told friends that his addition elevated the quality of the band.[7] With regards to the All Stars, Jones said in 1952, "I'm enjoying myself right now more than I ever have in the last thirty years, playing with this group."[8]

Shaw's and Teagarden's departures might have been amicable, but the same couldn't be said of Earl Hines's. Whereas Teagarden was willing to take a backseat to Armstrong, Hines considered himself just as much of a star and started yearning to become a leader again. "I didn't think I was greater than Louis, and I didn't think I had as much experience as he had, so far as going around the world was concerned, but I thought what I had contributed to the music business entitled me to more consideration than they offered," Hines said of the new contract he was offered in 1951. "I had had a contract with 75 percent publicity and a good salary, but now they wanted to list me merely as a sideman. I thought they should have kept me with 75 percent publicity, but they were not going to, so that was my reason for leaving."[9] It was during the long vacation the All Stars had lined up while Armstrong filmed *Glory Alley* that Hines decided to make his move; he quit the band in Richmond, Virginia. He later wrote, "I think [Armstrong] never really understood why I left." Armstrong was furious and didn't hide his frustration: "I don't give a damn. Hines and his ego, ego, ego! If he wanted to go, the hell with him. He's good, sure, but we don't need him . . . Earl Hines and his big ideas. Well, we can get along without Mr. Earl Hines."[10] Hines also learned that it might have been unwise to cross Joe Glaser. "I had pretty tough dealing after that, maybe because Joe Glaser thought I shouldn't have left," he said years later. "They gave me a rough way to go. It never was pinpointed. I never knew why it was so hard to get engagements, even with other booking agencies. It was hard to break into some of the elite clubs, places where the agencies had, you might say, franchises on the clubs. Yes, it was pretty rough for me for a while."[11]

Now that the All Stars had lost half its members in the span of four months or so, many critics averred that it no longer lived up to its name. But while the band had been star-studded, it never cohered as did later incarnations. Armstrong would spend most of the next couple of years rebuilding, but when he finally got the pieces to fit together just right, the All Stars entered their golden era.

For a two-week gig at the Oasis in Los Angeles beginning on December 18, 1951,[12] Armstrong turned to Chicago stalwart Joe Sullivan, of whom Armstrong simply said, "Pops plays fine piano."[13] While Phillips and Jones were no match for Teagarden and Shaw as musicians, Sullivan was another matter altogether: he was a highly talented pianist, who added his "Little Rock Getaway" to the All Stars' repertoire as well as an exciting, stride-filled solo version of "I Found a New Baby." The downside to Sullivan, though, was that he was a heavy drinker, and that he played in an old style that didn't exactly fit the All Stars' swing. Recordings survive of only three performances of the Phillips-Jones-Sullivan All Stars, and they are some of the weakest entries in the Armstrong discography. Jones kept solid time as a bassist, but many a solo disintegrated before its conclusion. Phillips was Teagarden Lite; he played many of the same features and had a somewhat similar style, but any other comparisons of their achievements in the band would be misguided. For his part, Sullivan never attempted to change his monotonous oompah backing, setting the group's rhythm section twenty years backward. Sloppy moments also abound; on "Steak Face" from a concert at Kitsilano High School in Vancouver, Sullivan forgot to modulate his piano solo from F to D-flat, so when the horns enter, a nasty clash occurs. The very next evening, Sullivan and Jones combined to play some wrong changes during the bridge to "Blueberry Hill." And even on something as simple as "Back o' Town Blues," Sullivan got lost for at least half of it, changing chords at all the wrong times.

Though the All Stars were floundering now and then, most of the time they still put on a great show. Armstrong was going through a period of particularly strong trumpet playing, and at times it sounds as if he's compensating for the rest of the band with his fiercely strong lead. The Vancouver dates are particularly interesting because the All Stars were performing in front of a riotous crowd of high-school kids eager to scream and shriek their approval at every turn—they even go crazy for Jones's Bert Williams routine on "Nobody." Armstrong may still have sent many of his crowds into bedlam, but he could not have liked the sloppy playing, especially from Sullivan, whose features and solos were all spot-on but whose accompaniments were a disaster, even worse than Hines's, who, too, had not been a good listener.

Sullivan was replaced on February 25, 1952, by Marty Napoleon, who came from a strong jazz background: his brother Teddy was also a fine jazz pianist, and his uncle was trumpeter Phil Napoleon of the famed Original Memphis Five. By the time he joined Armstrong, Napoleon, who started playing professionally in 1940, at the age of nineteen, had played with the bands of Bob Astor, Joe Venuti, Charlie Barnet, and Gene Krupa.[14] He had been playing with the Big Four with Buddy Rich, a group that was booked by Joe Glaser, when he joined Armstrong, though originally he turned Glaser's offer down because he had promised his wife he wouldn't spend any more time on the road. Napoleon remembers, "So [Glaser] says, 'Come up and see me, we'll talk.' I said, 'Okay.' So I went up to see him and we talked and he talked me into it. He was the kind of guy who always made you an offer you couldn't refuse. That's what happened, so I went for a year."[15] Napoleon soon began featuring a turbo-charged version of "St. Louis Blues" that never failed to stop the show. After such heavy hitters as Earl Hines and Joe Sullivan, Napoleon might have seemed like a lesser choice, but in my opinion he was the most exciting pianist the All Stars ever had.

It didn't take long before Napoleon realized he was working for Glaser, not Armstrong, but he never saw any reason to tarnish Glaser, as some have. "I have black friends that say, 'You know, Joe Glaser made all that money, he became a millionaire with Louie, sending him on those one-nighters,' " he says. "I said, 'Wait a minute, wait a minute! Joe Glaser made Louie a millionaire. What's the matter with you guys? Louie didn't make Joe Glaser a millionaire. If Joe Glaser hadn't said "Louie, I'm going to book you," he would still be in New Orleans playing in some honky tonk joint.' "[16]

Napoleon also noticed firsthand how Armstrong's audiences were changing. "We played a ballroom in Lubbock, Texas," he remembered. "We were there Sunday and Monday. Sunday night was an all-black audience; Monday night, all-white . . . Sunday night, maybe 250 people, 300 people; Monday night, white people, 1,200 people." Napoleon asked road manager Pierre "Frenchy" Tallerie why the blacks didn't show up. "He says, 'Don't you know they don't like him?' I said, 'What do you mean? Who doesn't like him?' He says, 'The black people don't like Louie 'cause he's an Uncle Tom. He rolls his eyes, he sweats, he comes with the handkerchief, he laughs, he shows his teeth, he carries on. He's like an Uncle Tom.' And the blacks despised him because they were trying to elevate themselves, you know? They'd say, 'He's degrading us.' " Napoleon was outraged at such thinking. "I said, 'But how about the way musicians revere him? And say the guy's a genius? The way he plays? So he's not educated. So what? People still love him!' "[17]

The new version of the All Stars was heard to great advantage at the Municipal Auditorium in New Orleans in May of 1952, a thrilling evening of music whose recording sadly remains unreleased. "Indiana," the standard opener (after "When It's Sleepy Time Down South"), allowed Armstrong the opportunity to warm up his chops every night on something familiar. Critics would later chastise Armstrong for playing a set solo on the tune, but the truth is he improvised many different variations on "Indiana" into the mid-fifties, and some of these were captured on tape. Charting the progress of "Indiana" is fascinating, as one can hear Armstrong continually toying with ideas, sticking with certain motifs for a number of months before discarding them for something new. He approached his solos like a great composer, studying them each night in his hotel room, listening fastidiously and making changes as he saw fit. When he finally emerged with something of a set solo in 1956—five years after the tune first appeared in an All Stars show—it was a dynamic, adventurous outing, full of bravura high notes, skipping, fleet-fingered phrases, and even a humorous quote of "I Cover the Waterfront." But even when he perfected it, critics still griped, much to his chagrin. "I also remember when Leonard Feather criticised him in print," Ernie Anderson recalled. "The complaint was that Louis had once more opened a concert with 'Back Home Again in Indiana.' Louis never responded to the critic directly but he turned to me and said, thoughtfully, 'When I improvise something, I don't forget it! If it's good, of course I remember it. Every note! That's why I play it again. Nearly everything I ever play I improvised at some time or other. Why that third chorus of "Indiana" is a masterpiece, man!' He had been listening to that concert on his tapes. He spoke as though someone else had played that third chorus that Leonard Feather obviously hadn't listened to."[18] Armstrong was rightfully proud of that solo, but in 1952 it was still a work-in-progress.

Armstrong, clearly eager to please his hometown fans, blows with incredible force on many New Orleans classics, including "Struttin' with Some Barbecue," "Muskrat Ramble," and "Way Down Yonder in New Orleans." Yet the highlight of the evening had nothing to do with music. During the intermission, Armstrong was honored by some local politicians and even given the keys to the city by Myra Menville, secretary of the New Orleans Jazz Club. Asked to say a few words, Armstrong stopped the show by deciding to tell a bawdy joke: "This waitress, in this restaurant, you know," he began. "It's about this fella, every time you look around, he's ordering a hamburger. So the waitress said the next time he come off the job and come in this restaurant, she's going to scratch hamburger off the list. And the minute the fellow sit down, she say, 'Good afternoon, sir. I just scratched what you like.'" The audience immediately began convulsing with laughter (Menville can be heard saying, "That's wonderful!"), but Armstrong hadn't even gotten to the punch line: "So the young man said, 'That's all right, miss—just wash your hands and bring me a hamburger!'" Armstrong's joke was greeted with over thirty seconds of laughter.[19]

Armstrong returned to New York in late August for a month-long engagement at the Paramount, sharing the bill with Gordon Jenkins. "Oh, I loved that man," Napoleon says of Jenkins. "He was great. Well, we did the Paramount Theater, he was on the stage with us. And he wrote an arrangement on 'When the Saints Go Marching In' where we closed the show with that. And I swear, one day we came off the stage and you had the elevator that used to take us downstairs to the dressing rooms and Gordon had tears in his eyes, man. And I said, 'Gordy, what's going on?' And he said, 'Man, that's the most exciting ending I've ever heard of on a show, playing with a band on stage.' It was fantastic, just great. And he was just a great guy."[20] Drummer Nick Fatool remembered the extent of Jenkins's hero worship, saying, "Back at the Paramount, he'd stand in the wings holding Louis's handkerchiefs. And hell, Satch would sweat and spit into those things, you know. But Gordy said just holding those handkerchiefs revived him, like an electric shock. It was his way to get back."[21]

Arvell Shaw returned to the band late in the summer of 1952, after clarinetist Barney Bigard, the other original member of the All Stars, left in early August. "I started getting sick of the traveling and of always being on the move," Bigard later wrote, "so I gave my notice in to that 'fat-bellied' Frenchy and went home to take a long rest. I really did rest most of the time. It was good to be off the road for a while."[22] He was replaced by Bob McCracken, a native of Dallas who was boyhood friends with Jack Teagarden. Through the years, he played with the likes of Joe Venuti, Wingy Manone, Frankie Trumbauer, Bud Freeman, Jimmy McPartland, and Benny Goodman, and he recorded as early as 1927. "I didn't think he was a great player," Napoleon says of McCracken. "When he did his clarinet solo featured spot in the show, he would practice, all the time we were in the dressing room, he would practice a four-bar introduction to play for his solo. And the minute he got on stage, when he was introduced and he started to play, he would always crack. He'd always make a mistake on it . . . Why don't the guy play something else for crying out loud or just ad-lib something? He wasn't a very good ad-lib player."[23]

McCracken entered the band around the same time another change was made. On September 10, during the Paramount engagement, James Osbourne "Trummy" Young replaced Russ Phillips. Armstrong had run into Young during a tour of Hawaii earlier that year, jamming with Young's band, which featured a fresh-out-of-high-school drummer, Danny Barcelona. Armstrong was always a fan of Young's playing. In a 1948 letter to one of his friends, he wrote, "I've received a letter from the Philippines Island. And they said that Trummy Young is over there Singing and blowing up a Storm. He's one of my favorite musicians."[24] Armstrong had asked Young to join the All Stars in Hawaii, but Young couldn't at the time. Nevertheless, Young more or less became part of Armstrong's entourage during the trip, appearing with him every time Armstrong did an interview, as tapes at the Louis Armstrong House Museum bear out. "The first time I heard Louie play, oh, I just didn't believe it," Young said during the trip. "I didn't think things like that happen. It was so beautiful. And, gee, I had just started playing trombone so I bought every record I could find of his and I just tried to copy them note-for-note on the trombone. Couldn't make them all, but I made a few that I could copy and they helped me out a lot."[25] Young eventually turned the leadership of his band over to Barcelona and was an All Star by the fall.

Young had an impressive pedigree, having played in the big bands of

Earl Hines and Jimmie Lunceford and recorded with Dizzy Gillespie and Charlie Parker. But previous experience paled in comparison with his employment by Armstrong. "Louis wasn't only a great musician," he said. "Louis was a great showman on top of it. So there isn't nothing wrong with using showmanship out there along with your music, a combination, and this is what Louis had. This is one of the things that made him so great. He could play one of the greatest choruses you ever heard in your life, and after he got through, he could give some little mannerisms that was greater than the chorus, you know. So he'd shoot you down one way or the other."[26]

Because of the company he kept, Young didn't consider himself a Dixieland player, but his excitable style jibed with the ensembles. After the exquisite virtuosity of Teagarden, Young offered something different: loud, roaring, all swing. But because he was less well known to many critics, they dismissed his robust style for cluttering the ensembles, as they heard it. But the roar of Young's trombone often generated tremendous excitement, and as Dan Morgenstern points out, "When Pops was a bit tired, Trummy's relentless energy often saved the day, and he was a team player first and foremost."[27] Young also sang a lot with Armstrong, inheriting Teagarden's old part on "Rockin' Chair" and bringing in his old hits from the Lunceford days, "T'ain't What You Do" and "Margie." On the latter, Young would occasionally indulge in some showmanship, playing the slide with one of his feet. As a great trombonist, a charming singer, and an unpredictable showman, Young was a triple threat in the All Stars. Morgenstern adds, "Trummy became the backbone of the All Stars, Louis's closest friend in the band, and a 12-year iron traveling man. He took critical licks for supposedly having simplified his style for Louis, but that was a mishearing; always a blustery player, Trummy saw his role in the All Stars as chief instrumental supporter of the leader, and if he got a bit raucous at times, it was all for the cause."[28]

On September 24, new personnel in tow, the All Stars embarked on yet another tour of Europe. Now an old hand at this, Armstrong said of the trip: "It's just like going back to New Orleans." Of the European jazz fans: "They go to jazz concerts there like we go to football games . . . The Europeans are familiar with every riff you play and you can't jive 'em. Jazz and longhairs are treated the same—and if they like your riff, they'll 'bravo' you to death."[29] The music on this tour would also be broadcast by Radio Free Europe in such Communist countries as Czechoslovakia, Poland, and Hungary. Here was Armstrong breaking through the Iron Curtain with his brand of jazz.

The trip started off inauspiciously with a concert in Eskilstuna, Sweden, that featured a subpar sound system. According to Gösta Hägglöf, "The usually good-humoured Louis lost his temper, but finally resigned himself and played the concert. 'I can't let my audience down,' he said."[30] A few days later, on September 29, recording equipment caught daring versions of "On the Sunny Side of the Street" and "High Society." McCracken more than passed the test on the New Orleans clarinet showpiece, while "Sunny Side" was stretched out to seven minutes and forty seconds to accomplish its stirring achievement.[31]

Armstrong signed many autographs during the Scandinavian leg of the tour, greeted as he was by throngs. *DownBeat* reported:

> Seldom has anything been seen like the riotous reception accorded to Louis Armstrong on his first visit since 1949. Incredible prices were offered in a black market for tickets to Satchmo's concert at the Royal Hall in Stockholm (capacity almost 5,000). Scores of fans lined up all night outside the hall to await the opening of the box office. A dozen people were reported to have fainted in the crowds that tried to break a police cordon in Oslo, Norway. In Gothenburg police had to chase the more fervent fans off the roof of the Cirkus Hall. In four shows at the huge KB Hall in Copenhagen, Denmark, Armstrong played to more than 18,000 frenzied customers.[32]

When the tour landed in Germany, Armstrong met up with his old friend Franz Schuritz. Twenty years earlier, Schuritz had invented a lip cream called Ansatz Crème, of which Armstrong said, "If you don't use salve on your lip, it will split like a pig's foot. This Ansatz Crème is the greatest salve in the world. I'd be dead without. Before World War II I told Joe Glaser, my manager, to buy $250 worth of it. He said 'Are you crazy,' and I said, 'Man, I can read between the lines. There's trouble coming. Now buy it, dammit.' When I say dammit, I get service. He bought the stuff and now he's more sold on it than I am. He wants to buy it for America and call it Louis Armstrong Salve. They'll be using it for generations."[33]

But the salve was not always balm for Armstrong's chops. Many broadcasts survive from this tour, capturing him playing erratically. In the Stockholm and Belgium concerts, he is in peak form; in Switzerland and Italy he struggles mightily. Armstrong was rapidly gaining weight, and this, together with the relentless pace of the tour, may have deleteriously affected his chops. Regardless, audiences were never unsatisfied; Armstrong always gave his all, singing more if he needed to compensate for sore chops. The tour ended in Paris, where Art Buchwald spent time with Armstrong and asked him how the trip had gone. "It was just great," Armstrong said. "I wasn't cutting for the money. The cats were there, that's all I cared about." Buchwald also asked him how his autobiography was coming along. "I'm up to 1922," he said. "I can't get time to write. Between my wife and that horn I got all the work I can cut out." Finally, the humorist asked the trumpet player why he wasn't going to stay in Europe any longer. Armstrong's answer was simple: "I go where Mr. Glaser sends me. He's king in my country."[34]

The next tour Mr. Glaser would book for Armstrong would be far more explosive than anything he had encountered on his visitations to Europe.

ABOVE Louis with two charter members of the All Stars, drummer Big Sid Catlett and trombonist Jack Teagarden, at Billy Berg's in Los Angeles

LEFT Louis and his manager Joe Glaser. Note the placement of Glaser's hand on Armstrong's shoulder, echoing a piece of advice Armstrong received in New Orleans: "Always keep a white man behind you that'll put his hand on you and say, 'That's my nigger.'"

Louis, center, in blackface as King of the Zulus at Mardi Gras in New Orleans, 1949. Sid Catlett is to the right of Armstrong, while Velma Middleton is to the left, on the top of the float.

The All Stars in Brussels in 1949. From left to right: road manager Pierre "Frenchy" Tallerie, Cozy Cole, Barney Bigard, Doc Pugh, Velma Middleton, Earl Hines, Lucille Armstrong, Jack Teagarden, unknown, and Arvell Shaw

ABOVE Louis, his wife Lucille
Armstrong, and publicist
Ernie Anderson outside of
Castel Gandolfo, Italy, where
they visited Pope Pius XII
in 1949

RIGHT Publicity photo for Louis's
appearance at a March of Dimes
benefit in Honolulu, Hawaii,
in January 1954. Armstrong's
performance at this event helped
lessen the fine charged against
Lucille Armstrong after she
was charged with possession
of marijuana.

Armstrong recording a song for the album *Louis Armstrong Plays W. C. Handy* for Columbia Records in 1954

Louis and Velma Middleton recording "Honeysuckle Rose" for the 1955 album *Satch Plays Fats*

From left to right: George Avakian, Edmond Hall, Lotte Lenya, Arvell Shaw, Armstrong, Trummy Young, Billy Kyle, and Barrett Deems. Photo taken September 28, 1955, the day Louis first recorded "Mack the Knife" for Columbia at Avakian's suggestion. The record became one of his biggest hits.

Louis considered this photograph, taken by Milan Schijatschky at the Chez Paree in Chicago, to be his favorite. He had hundreds of miniature copies made, which he affixed to letters, cards, and his reel-to-reel tape boxes.

Armstrong extolling the virtues of his favored laxative, Swiss Kriss, to an unidentified fan in the 1950s

Edmond Hall, Louis, and Trummy Young perform to a crowd estimated at more than 100,000 in Accra, Ghana, while members of Edward R. Murrow's camera crew film the event for the 1957 theatrical documentary *Satchmo the Great.*

Swiss photographer Milan Schijatschky captured three sides of Louis at a typical one-nighter at a high school gymnasium in Hinsdale, Illinois, on March 20, 1957. Warming up in a locker room, patiently signing autographs for young fans offstage, and having the time of his life onstage with his All Stars.

Louis with drummer Danny Barcelona, who devoted thirteen years of his life to performing with the All Stars

With a nun after recovering from a heart attack in Spoleto, Italy, 1959

CHAPTER SIX

The King of Jazz Meets the King of Swing, 1953

IN EARLY 1953, Barney Bigard received a phone call. "I had been rest-ing for a period of six or seven months," he remembered, "working the Hollywood studio scene, when the phone rang one day and it was Glaser's office. They wanted to know if I would consider coming back with Louis. I guess by then I had had my share of sitting around, so I told them yes." When Bigard returned in mid-February, he found Armstrong still play-ing "When It's Sleepy Time Down South" as his theme and "Indiana" as his opener. "Nothing had changed," he said, but added, "In a way I was glad to be back with the old gang. One thing was that I noticed we had made a whole lot of new fans."[1] Armstrong's steadily growing fan base was partly attributable to his popular recordings for Decca. So it came as no surprise that his first two Decca sessions in 1953 stuck to the win-ning formula: covering hits of the day, including Hank Williams's "Your Cheatin' Heart." Much of the credit for the success of that record must go to Sy Oliver's arrangement, which, in contrast to the stiff, countri-fied two-beat of the original, struts and nods to Jimmie Lunceford–style swing and to "Yes Indeed" for churchlike soul. As pianist Marty Napo-leon described the session: "[Joe Glaser] gave me a lead sheet on 'Your Cheatin' Heart' . . . and . . . said, 'Run this over with Louie, 'cause we're going to record it with Sy Oliver.' So I played it over myself and I said, 'My

God, what kind of song is this?' It was like a flat, hillbilly song, you know what I mean? And then Sy came in with this arrangement, and that thing was swinging like crazy. It was magnificent, man! It was wonderful."[2]

That session proved to be Napoleon's last for a while; he was replaced by Armstrong's old friend Joe Bushkin just in time for one of the biggest debacles of Armstrong's career: an All Stars tour of the United States paired with Benny Goodman. The idea for the tour came from concert promoter, record producer, and jazz impresario Norman Granz, who was working with famed record producer John Hammond at Mercury Records at the time. Hammond, Goodman's brother-in-law, had asked Granz to consider a Goodman engagement. Granz had responded, "Well, if the conditions are right, sure, that's my business." Granz met Goodman at the Colony, an upscale restaurant in New York City, wearing tennis shoes and carrying a Jazz at the Philharmonic program featuring some of the musicians he represented, among them Teddy Wilson, Gene Krupa, Lester Young, Ella Fitzgerald, and Coleman Hawkins. Goodman looked at the program and said, "You expect me to play with this circus?" Insulted, Granz responded, "Benny, Lester Young plays better saxophone than you play clarinet. Coleman Hawkins would blow you out of the room. Ella sings better than anything you can play. So, go fuck yourself, and forget the tour."[3]

Hammond was not deterred, insisting that Granz work things out with Goodman, though he told him, "Listen, I talked to Benny, and he doesn't like you." Goodman was willing to do a tour, but not by himself. Granz proposed Louis Armstrong and Goodman approved. Granz, however, would not stay on Goodman's good side. For a Goodman and Armstrong concert at Carnegie Hall, Granz raised the usual two-dollar ticket price to five. An irate Goodman called Hammond, who told Granz, "Benny is furious. He doesn't want to play, because he thinks you're trying to destroy him by charging high prices." Granz replied, "Look, I got a contract. He's getting paid even if not a single person comes in. And if I want to charge a hundred dollars a ticket, that's my business. So he's going to have to accept it." "Well," Granz recalled, "the concert sold out, like, in two minutes. And that bugged Benny because now he felt he didn't need Louis."[4]

What Goodman didn't know was that Armstrong had his own bones to pick with him. The concert tour had been arranged by New Year's Eve 1952, when Armstrong threw a party for his friends that was recorded.

Three days earlier, Armstrong's former bandleader Fletcher Henderson had died at age fifty-five. In the 1930s, Henderson's arrangements had provided the sound that propelled the Goodman band to unprecedented heights of popularity and led to Goodman's being crowned "the King of Swing." When Henderson died, Armstrong had sent a floral arrangement in the shape of a piano and attended the funeral, though he was late. "I wouldn't miss it for the world," he said at the New Year's Eve party. "Fletcher's my man. He did have me for the first time in the big band era. You've got to appreciate." Minutes later, someone mentioned Benny Goodman's presence at Henderson's funeral. Apparently, Goodman had read a few telegrams of condolence before vanishing. Armstrong didn't think that was right, and was amazed when Hammond told him at the funeral that Goodman had said he had no idea if Trummy Young was any good even though Young had played and recorded with Goodman in 1945. "I mean, [Goodman] just don't know nobody, he's overrated all his life. The man's been spoiled all his life." Venting some more, he continued: "Shit, he didn't remember, we got a goddamn tour. I don't care if I ever play with the sonofabitch."[5]

With both camps bitter, the tour was set to commence in April 1953. Goodman scheduled a rehearsal for his big band, which included many of the musicians who had played with him in the 1930s—Teddy Wilson, Gene Krupa, Ziggy Elman, Helen Ward, Georgie Auld—two days before the first concert in New Haven, Connecticut, on April 15. During the rehearsal, Armstrong and the All Stars showed up blowing "When the Saints Go Marching In," accompanied by a large entourage. Goodman didn't take kindly to Armstrong's appearance. "Louis was, of course, a gregarious man, so everybody greeted him and there was bedlam for about twenty minutes," Hammond wrote. "Benny took it as long as he could, then asked Louis if he would mind sending his entourage out so the rehearsal could continue. Louis took offense. He considered himself a co-star, although actually Goodman was the boss."[6]

Goodman was determined to prove as much, prima donna that he was. "That character kept us sitting around there for three hours while he carried on rehearsing his own band," Barney Bigard remembered. According to Goodman's guitarist Steve Jordan, "Louis's feelings were so hurt he actually started to cry. Georgie Auld went over and patted him on the back, and Louis said, 'That son of a bitch! When he was a little boy in short pants, I used to let him sit in with my band to learn how to play, and now he lets me hang around and wait like I'm nobody.' "[7] Armstrong wasn't about to wait much longer. Barney Bigard recalled the occasion:

> I went to Louis and said, "What's with this guy? When is he going to get to our bit so we can get out of here?" "You know, Pops," said Louis, "I'm thinking the same damned thing that you're thinking." So Louis went up on the stage and got a hold of Benny not physically speaking though, and started calling him everything but "the child of God." He was cussing him up and down, but good. It tickled me when Louis told him, "I remember you in Chicago when you were sitting under Jimmie Noone, trying to learn something. Now your head's got fat." So Louis just stormed out of there in a big hurry and we went right along with him."[8]

According to Goodman trumpeter Al Stewart, Goodman ended the rehearsal by saying, "OK boys, tomorrow morning at Carnegie Hall, 9 o'clock." Armstrong grumbled, "Only place I'm gonna be tomorrow at 9 o'clock is bed." The following day, Armstrong and the All Stars refused to show up at Goodman's next rehearsal. When Armstrong eventually showed up later in the day, he told Goodman outright that he wasn't going to play with the clarinetist's band. A frustrated Goodman complained, "Jesus Christ, let's get this goddamn show on the road." Armstrong sat down, looked at Goodman, and said, "Man, I been trying to get this show on the road for two days now. But it seem like some asshole done snuck in here somewhere."[9]

Armstrong and Goodman also fought over who would go on first. "So, Benny insisted that he close the show, and Louis open the show," Granz said, but he knew this wasn't the right format. "You have to turn it around," he said. "The big band, and then Louis does what he does, and then Benny might want to jam a number with Louis. That would have been the format. But Benny refused to play."[10] Armstrong opened their first joint show in New Haven, but he stayed onstage for fully an hour and twenty minutes instead of the forty he had agreed to play. When it was Goodman's turn on, there was nothing he could do to win the audience back. "When he put Louis on first he could hardly get on afterwards,"

Trummy Young said.[11] Upon concluding his set, Goodman called out to Armstrong to join him in a duet. Armstrong did not comply.

The next night, Goodman and Armstrong were scheduled to play at the Newark Mosque. In an effort to make peace, Goodman invited Armstrong to meet him at the venue a little early so they could settle their differences. Armstrong didn't, and as showtime neared, he still was nowhere in sight. "Benny was backstage, fuming," Granz remembered. " 'What's going on?' I said, 'Listen, I don't know what happened to Louis, but you're going to have to go on.' He said, 'I'm not going to open the show.' I said, 'There is no show. You're going to have to go out there.' You know, he took a big bottle of scotch, and . . . if you've ever been backstage . . . there are usually body-length mirrors before you go out, so the singer can fix her hair or whatever. He took that bottle and threw it against the mirror, and shattered the glass everywhere. And he went on." It turned out that Armstrong had been hiding in his car outside the whole time. He asked Granz, "Is he on?" When Granz replied in the affirmative, Armstrong prepared to close the show. Meanwhile, "Benny was so angry, he lost himself," Granz remembered. "He was taking all the choruses, calling numbers wrong. Everything was a disaster."[12] Armstrong may have pulled a fast one by forcing Goodman to open for him, but he was still unhappy enough to complain to Joe Glaser about how Goodman was treating him. That was all Glaser needed to hear. According to Georgie Auld, Glaser "laced into Benny the next night at the Mosque Theater. 'Where do you come off? Who the fuck do you think you are? When this man lands in Europe there are 35,000 people waiting for him. Can you do that? How dare you tell him what to do! He's a legend! He's bigger than you!' He screamed and screamed at him."[13]

Next on the schedule were two dates at Carnegie Hall. Backstage, Armstrong and Goodman went at it again, this time about Armstrong's showmanship. Goodman had been confounded by audience reaction to Armstrong's clowning with Middleton; they loved it. "That guy ain't doing nothing but clowning out there," Goodman fumed. "That's not music, you know!" Goodman was not amused by Middleton's splits, and asked Armstrong to remove it from the act. Armstrong would do nothing of the kind and instead encouraged Middleton: "You go ahead and do it, honey."[14] She performed her routine at both concerts. The reviews of Armstrong's playing and of some of his comedic turns, so despised by Goodman, were glowing. *The New York Times* intoned: "He also had his strut, his wonderful hoarse voice and his usual high spirits. He and his crew put on a show that was as much comedy act as music: some of it, between us, is cornball showmanship. But he can still blow that horn, and his All Stars have the know-how to keep up with him."[15] Goodman and Armstrong had finally agreed to take turns at Carnegie Hall: Goodman played the first half of the 8:30 show; at the midnight show, Armstrong opened with eleven straight numbers. He would return for another long set after Goodman's. Howard Taubman of the *Times* reported that the audience was rapturous: "Clapping, stamping and roaring with joy, there were moments when it seemed as though the sound barrier would be broken."[16] According to Hammond, "In both [concerts], Benny played atrociously . . . According to the Saturday papers it appeared that Goodman had returned in all his glory. Those of us in the audience who knew better . . . recognized that his performance was less than glorious."[17]

One such person was Bobby Hackett. "Oh, did he sound terrible!" Hackett said of Goodman. "Just couldn't do anything. It was embarrassing. Jesus, if I'd been able to do so I'd have stopped the show already. He sounded like someone first learning the instrument—you know, practicing." Armstrong knew Goodman was flailing so he went in for the kill. "And then Pops came on and shook that place," Hackett continued. "Oh, I never heard him play like that. . . . Was he angry? He was out to get Benny Goodman." This was even true backstage. When a dazed Goodman brushed off fellow clarinetist Peanuts Hucko, Armstrong saw the slight and called Goodman on it. "You no-good mother, who do you think you are, to hurt a kid like that?" Armstrong shouted. "You're nothin'!"[18]

Though the following evening's performance in Providence, Rhode Island, was his smoothest so far, Goodman started looking for a way out. Before a performance at Boston's Symphony Hall, Granz received a phone call from Joe Glaser telling him Goodman was canceling the tour because of a bad back. A disbelieving Granz rounded up a few members of Goodman's band. "I said, 'Tell me what happened.' " As one of the musicians would have it, Goodman had called a meeting of the band and said, "Listen, I'm going to feign that I've got a bad back. The tour will be cancelled, and we'll go out alone in another tour."[19] Other rumors quickly swirled: Goodman had suffered a nervous breakdown; *DownBeat* reported that he had had two heart attacks in Boston. "Pops came close to killing him without touching him, just playing," Hackett remembered.[20] Goodman abandoned the tour and fired Hammond. Granz refused to panic. "I went to Glaser and I said, 'Look, I'm going to keep the tour. I'm going to keep the band. It will be a big band, and it will be Gene Krupa's band. It's going to be a Gene Krupa tour.' Gene was happy. He got paid. And I said, 'Don't cancel any of the halls that we got.' And we made the whole tour."[21]

Through the years, different accounts of the Armstrong-Goodman debacle have been proposed, but perhaps the most scathing can be heard on an undated private tape held at the Louis Armstrong House Museum. It records a conversation among Armstrong, his wife Lucille, and an unknown friend. The subject of Goodman comes up and Armstrong pulls no punches. Armstrong begins by relating how Joe Glaser once suggested that Armstrong join Goodman for a finale. "Joe Glaser said to me, 'Go on out there, Benny Goodman might need you' . . . Need who? Kiss my ass. Shit. I thought you knew show business. Scared to hurt Benny Goodman's feelings. Hurt *my* feelings—I'm there, too." Armstrong recalled a conversation with Goodman: "This sonbitch tells me, 'Well, you know, I'm so forgetful, I forget that you're on the bill with me.' I say, 'Goddamn! How forgetful can a cocksucker get? All that horn I'm playing, you kidding?' I say, 'Hell with me, respect that trumpet, that's all.' Right, motherfucker, never bothered me, just respect the horn. The world does, right? So you respect it."

Vis-à-vis a finale, Armstrong had once had an idea: he and the All Stars would play their set; the curtain would then rise to reveal the Goodman orchestra, and Armstrong would join them for two or three of his hits. That was how Armstrong and Gordon Jenkins ended their joint appearances at New York's Paramount Theatre in 1952, and it always electrified the audience. When he told this to Goodman, Goodman replied, according to Armstrong, "I have contracts to do all the staging here." In his retelling, Armstrong vents exasperation, "Oh, man, shit." When his friend asks, "Benny Goodman said that to you?" Armstrong responds, "Yeah, that cocksucker! I said, 'Well, that's nice, Daddy. You take those contracts and shove them right up your ass.' "[22]

Armstrong never fully forgave Goodman for his impertinence. "The best that can be said is that Benny believed he was the boss," Hackett said. "And Pops didn't take that, as you know. Benny tried it on him, and Pops was so mad at that guy, man. I don't remember all the details but Lucille told me when Benny was up in New Jersey he wanted Louis to come and have dinner with him, wanted them to try and make contact of some kind with each other. Louis wouldn't go, said to her: 'Are you crazy? I don't want to have dinner with that motherfucker.' "[23]

During the summer of 1953, after the aborted tour, Armstrong found time to appear in the film *The Glenn Miller Story*, a bowdlerized Hollywood dramatization of the bandleader's life, starring Jimmy Stewart, who would say that "during the shoot, I had the best jazz teacher in all America: Louis Armstrong. That incredible man really is jazz personified."[24] In the film, Armstrong appeared in a nightclub scene, performing "Basin Street Blues." Marty Napoleon was back on piano, though he appeared not to have had much say in the matter. "In 1953, I saw Joe Glaser in New York City. I met him on the street and he said, 'You're coming back to the band.' I said, 'What!?' He says, 'Yes, and we're going to go to California and we're going to make a movie.' I said, 'Really? That's great!' He said, 'Well, they wanted just Louie, Teddy Wilson, and Gene Krupa, and Teddy Wilson wanted one thousand dollars day and I said forget about him, we're getting Marty Napoleon.' I said, 'Am I getting a thousand?' He says, 'No, no!' I said, 'Hey, if I'm going to replace him, you can give me some part of that, right?' Of course, I didn't get that."[25]

Arvell Shaw remembered the fun the band had on the set. "We did our part in three days," he said. "On the set with Gene Krupa and Louie and . . . Ben Pollack, it was like a circus on the stage. And the director said, 'My goodness, I didn't know Louie was this type of guy!' 'Cause Louie was sharp, man—the jokes were coming a mile a minute. The band was on the stage—you know, it takes time to set up the sets and get the smoke in for the nightclub scene—we were supposed to be in Connie's Inn. And man, the jugs were flying and Gene Krupa was telling jokes and by the time they shot the scene, man, the band was stoned out of their skull and all the cast, the cameraman was stoned, Louie got everybody stoned!"[26] "Basin Street Blues" is notable because it had been a trombone feature for the All Stars since their inception, though Armstrong always managed to take a brilliant short solo. "Basin Street Blues" would soon become an Armstrong feature, as well as one of his most popular live performances.

The Glenn Miller Story reveals an Armstrong who had by then ballooned. He addressed his weight with a new product he had begun to take: a laxative called Swiss Kriss. Armstrong always had a laxative fixation. His mother had instilled in her kids that they be "physic-minded." Armstrong was a fan of Pluto Water, which came in big glass bottles—difficult for travel. Still, this didn't stop him from drinking three bottles a day and encouraging his friends to try it. Napoleon, who was given Pluto Water early in his tenure with the All Stars, could only say, "Thank God I had the day off!" But in 1952, Lucille Armstrong read two books written by a self-proclaimed food scientist, Gayelord Hauser, that changed her husband's life forever. One was titled *Be Happier, Be Healthier,* and the other was *Diet Does It: Incorporating the Gayelord Hauser Cook Book.* With his lack of medical credentials, some dismissed Hauser's works as bogus. But he did have followers galore, so his books were best-sellers. Hauser championed the wonders of wheat germ and yogurt, among other foods, but also of laxatives. Soon he was promoting a product from Switzerland, Swiss Kriss. As Armstrong recalled, "Then here come this book—a health book written by Gayelord Hauser. When I read down to the part where he recommended some 'herbs'—herbal laxatives—I said to myself, 'Herbs—hmmm, these herbs reminds me of the same as what my mother picked down by the tracks in New Orleans.' Right away I went to the health store and bought myself a box of Swiss Kriss and took a big tablespoonful—make sure it worked me the same as other laxatives. Yes it did. Wow! I said to myself, yes indeed, this is what I need from now on—and forsake all others."[27]

Armstrong would recommend Swiss Kriss to anyone and everyone he met. "Joey Bushkin took my place once in the band and Louie gave him this packet of Swiss Kriss," Napoleon said. "And it looks just like marijuana, you know, they're like tea leaves. Joey thought it was marijuana so he smoked it! And he was two days in the toilet. He said, 'He almost killed me! I didn't know what it was, he didn't tell me what it was' . . . So he thought he was helping him; he almost killed him!"[28]

In October 1953, Armstrong entered the Decca studios yet again, but now with Tutti Camarata and his powerhouse big band, the Commanders. His chops in outstanding condition, the session featured some of Armstrong's best trumpet work of the decade, energized as he was by Camarata's tight and strong unit, powered by the drums of the band's co-leader, Ed Grady. Two Christmas songs started things off, "Zat You, Santa Claus" and "Cool Yule," each more or less a novelty, but Armstrong imbued them with tremendous enthusiasm and good humor. From there, the session went from strength to strength. There was the extraordinary remake of an Armstrong composition, "Someday (You'll Be Sorry)." Originally recorded as a ballad in 1947 and played at a relaxed pace in concerts through the years, the new version swings hard. Camarata wrote a brassy chart, completely obliterating the song's gentility. Armstrong's muted opening trumpet reading of the melody is fairly straight, but after the vocal he comes back to improvise and plays out the rest of the track, playing the melody an octave higher and hitting high C's with ease.

The next song recorded was Billy Reid's "The Gypsy," made famous by the Ink Spots and well known in jazz circles as a tune recorded by Charlie Parker, strung out on drugs, at the "breakdown session" of July 29, 1946. It would become one of Armstrong's favorite showpieces. He had featured the song with his big band; a July 2, 1946, live version survives, with a vocal by Leslie Scott, and even though Armstrong didn't play on it, he clearly liked the melody, quoting it on "Save It, Pretty Mama" at the historic Town Hall concert of 1947 as well as on some versions of "Basin Street Blues" from the same period. Of "The Gypsy," Milt Gabler recalled: "Louis loved the song . . . He loved the lyric content, and he loved the tune of it, and he just loved to play it. And he came in; he said he wanted to record it. So we recorded it. That's all. It . . . was good for him wherever he worked, but it wasn't a hit single record for him. And Louis liked to make hits because it makes anybody feel good when you get on stage and people yell for a song, you know. You know . . . you've done something. But he knew—he loved to sing and he loved to do ballads, and the sadder the song the better." Armstrong's solo on the Decca record is yet another stirring improvisation, rich with invention. Armstrong assessed his performance: "Well, you know, that record I think is one of my finest."[29]

The session closed with "I Can't Afford to Miss This Dream"—taken at a relatively slow pace—a piece Armstrong recorded as a favor to a friend, Lillian Friedlander. On one of Armstrong's private home recordings made on December 31, 1952, Armstrong can be heard asking Friedlander to sing her composition, and tells her that he plans to record it. "You really like it that much?" Friedlander gushes, "I love you!"[30] The session's arrangement features a charming Armstrong vocal and a trumpet solo that, in only twelve bars, tells a passionate, dramatic story as it builds to a climax.

By the fall of 1953, the All Stars began fielding an entirely new rhythm section as Arvell Shaw, Marty Napoleon, and Cozy Cole each left the band. Shaw had left again in July, replaced this time by "the Judge," Milt Hinton, one of the most beloved figures in jazz history. After a fifteen-year stint with Cab Calloway, Hinton became one of the top studio musicians in New York City in the 1950s and 1960s, recording with everyone from Billie Holiday and Woody Herman to Tony Bennett and Frank Sinatra to Bobby Darin and Barbra Streisand. It is estimated that Hinton has appeared on more records than anyone else in history, yet, sadly, he never did a studio recording with the All Stars. On live broadcasts from Hinton's tenure in the band, his big sound, sense of humor and powerful swing proved ideal.[31] Cole was replaced by the relatively unknown Kenny John, then performing with Marty Napoleon's trumpeter uncle, Phil Napoleon (who was booked by Joe Glaser). John had first performed at the age of three and was touring by ten. "Well, Kenny's been around," Armstrong told an interviewer. "He's just a kid. About twenty-five, he looks like he's sixteen. He's played with Raymond Scott. You know, he plays some hard music."[32] Milt Hinton described him as "a short, thin, pale, blond kid who'd been fairly successful as an actor in Hollywood and was also a good drummer. But he had some serious problems. He'd gotten his way most of his life and that's probably why he'd fallen into some bad habits which were destroying him."[33] Barney Bigard summed him up as "a real young guy who drank plenty, but could play good drums."[34]

Napoleon's replacement was Billy Kyle, who had worked on a number of Armstrong's Decca sessions. Kyle was best known for his stint in bassist John Kirby's small group in the 1930s, but he became primarily a studio musician in the late 1940s and even spent three years in the early fifties as the pianist for Broadway's *Guys and Dolls*.[35] Kyle's piano style was extremely elegant and nimble, of the Earl Hines school; his solos swung and his accompanying skills were perfect for the band. A talented arranger, Kyle also sketched many of the informal arrangements the band played and soon after joining became the band's official music director. And on stage, Kyle was a valuable asset. Not possessed of Hines's ego, he never tried to show anyone up on the bandstand. "In my opinion, Billy Kyle was the best piano player Louis ever had," wrote Bigard. "I think he was perfectly suited to the All Stars."[36]

With the new personnel in place, the reconstituted group made a hugely successful tour of Japan at the end of 1953. *DownBeat* wrote, "Initial reports on Louis Armstrong's tour of Japan indicate that Pops is getting his biggest reception ever from the jubilant Japanese. Joe Glaser cabled back that it was the most fabulous greeting Louis has ever received—even exceeding the European one. Receiving the largest guarantee of anyone who had ever visited Japan, Louis earned an average of $2,500 a night against 50 percent of the gross."[37] Of the tour, Armstrong himself said, "Japan—how many people would think the Japanese would dig our music the way they did? Why, all the trumpet players in Japan gave a dinner for me. Took my shoes off, you know, and sit down at this funny table and have a big meal—nothin' but the trumpets."[38]

According to George Pitts in the *Pittsburgh Courier*, Armstrong had to work hard at first to win the Japanese public over. "Louis and his combo were playing before an extremely non-emotional Japanese audience on his recent tour of Japan," Pitts wrote. "Noticing no response from the listeners, Satchmo asked why. When informed that the Japanese were naturally a passive people, Satch really began to blow. One Japanese began patting his foot; another clapped his hands. Soon practically everyone in the auditorium joined beats with the rhythmical rovings of the jazz-time group. To which Louis coyly remarked, 'Cats is cats anywhere.' "[39]

Such a line might have been good for a few laughs, but upon his return to the United States, the laughter in Armstrong's life came to a crashing halt. Within a few weeks, he would be contemplating his desire to ever pick up his trumpet in public again.

lently or knowingly' importing narcotics in violation of a section of the code dealing with smuggling."[3]

Though the incident made national news, its coverage was reduced to small items in a number of newspapers and magazines, probably because it dealt with Armstrong's wife instead of the trumpeter himself. If Louis had been busted, it probably would have been front-page news, but anyone who followed Armstrong's career closely could have guessed the marijuana in question belonged not to Lucille but rather to her husband. Armstrong had been smoking marijuana almost daily since the 1920s and occasionally celebrated it in song titles such as "Muggles" in 1928 and "Song of the Vipers" in 1934. In 1930, Armstrong was busted for smoking it in California, but he escaped from that controversy relatively unscathed. "From that time until this, my public and I haven't had anything but the greatest love and respect for each other," Armstrong said in 1954.[4]

But in 1930, Armstrong's reputation was still on the rise with the general public. At the start of 1954, he was at the peak of his popularity and was already being touted as an "Ambassador of Goodwill" due to his tremendous popularity overseas. His arrest for possession of narcotics could have had quite a damning effect on his career. In fact, it had an almost immediate negative effect on the remainder of his stay in Hawaii. According to Milt Hinton, Armstrong and the other All Stars were searched thoroughly after Lucille was arrested. "Even though Louis and the guys were clean, they got held for hours," Hinton later wrote. "I saw Louis the next day and he was absolutely furious, ranting and raving about being stopped and how badly he'd been treated. 'I spread good will for my country all over the world and they want to put me in jail,' he yelled."[5] Armstrong spent his evenings in Honolulu performing at the Brown Derby, a nightclub run by Lee E. Sartain and his wife, Joann. When news spread about Lucille's arrest, the Sartains tried to cancel the rest of Armstrong's engagement as well as the March of Dimes benefit. Armstrong personally fought to be allowed to perform at the event, as is clear in a letter he wrote soon afterward to Joe Glaser. "Joann Sartain actually refused to let us play the March of Dimes benefit. The day before the benefit, I got Joann in the corner and I demanded that she call those people up and give them the go sign for us to appear. She said she'd talk it over with Frenchy. I said, 'No! You okay the benefit and *then* talk it over with Frenchy.' Because Frenchy might have agreed with her."[6] Armstrong was allowed to play the benefit, telling the press, "I wouldn't miss it for the world." Four thousand people showed up, and according to writer Richard Gima, "Perhaps the biggest hit with the audience was the King of Jazz Louis Armstrong and his band. Introduced by Jimmy Walker, master of ceremonies, Ol' Satchmo, who said he possesses a 'sawmill voice,' sang and played for almost an hour."[7]

Meanwhile, Lucille had to spend the entire next day in court, which was not easy for Louis to watch. "While his wife faced the court, her husband sat in the front row of the spectators' section, looking glum," a local report read. Lucille, on the advice of her lawyer, Hiram L. Fong, pleaded guilty. "Mrs. Armstrong did not have conscious possession of the marijuana," Fong told the press. "I advised her she had a chance for an acquittal in a trial, but she agreed it would be better for herself and the Government in the matter of expense if she pleaded guilty to a technical violation."[8] In the end, Judge Jon Wiig only fined Lucille $200, but he also gave her a break, which Armstrong was eager to report to Glaser: "Anyway . . . he told her he'd take one hundred dollars from her two-hundred-dollar fine because her husband was so kind to play such a real wonderful concert for those kids, who were all so very happy over the whole affair, you dig?"[9]

Lucille Armstrong's ordeal was over, but the drama in Louis's life hadn't quite finished. The Sartains still claimed their business was hurt by the negative publicity over Lucille's arrest and they wanted Armstrong barred from playing in Hawaii.[10] As the *Honolulu Star-Bulletin* reported, "Lee E. Sartain, owner of the Brown Derby, where Armstrong and his group appeared, said the argument originated between himself and Armstrong over a dispute involving money payments under their contract and 'bad publicity' caused by the arrest of Mrs. Armstrong for smuggling $5 worth of marihuana into Hawaii. 'We went to the union more or less as a mediator,' Mr. Sartain explained. 'And he [Armstrong] flipped his lid.' "[11]

Sartain wasn't kidding. The blurb in the *Honolulu Star-Bulletin* didn't go into any details, but Armstrong was happy to share the specifics five days later in a letter to Joe Glaser. "This woman [Joann Sartain] threatened Lucille something terrible the night before we went to the union, even all during the trial." Armstrong was upset because while Lucille's case was over, Sartain wouldn't let it go, even though, according to Louis, it "didn't have any bearings on the [new] case whatsoever. I made this point very clear to the [union] president, which he absolutely ignored . . . I asked him to have Mr. and Mrs. Sartain produce the nightly receipts from the

night we opened since he claims he lost money, which everybody ignored."
Tired of being mistreated, Armstrong's temper flared up. "The president
kept on slinging mud at Lucille 'cause she's colored, I'm sure, until I got so
mad, I stood up and asked Mrs. Sartain, 'Have you ever been a prostitute?'
And before she realized it, she said, 'Yes!' " Armstrong couldn't contain
his laughter when he read this portion of his letter into his reel-to-reel tape
recorder, adding, "And that did settle it."[12]

This was too much for union president I. B. Peterson to handle. The
local papers reported: "During the meeting, the association's officials
'asked for' Louie's card denoting him an honorary member of the local
union, and got it."[13] Once again, Armstrong fills in the details: "Pres flew
up and told me to turn in my Honolulu card. I threw it at him and told
him to wipe his ass with it. P.S. His ego was more hurt when he saw the
card I threw at him was not theirs, it was an honorary card from the Japanese local and union!"

At that point, Armstrong had had enough. "That's when I took Lucille
by the hand and said, 'Come on, let's get out of here.' As we were leaving,
I could hear the president apologizing to Mrs. Sartain. When they passed
their decision I told them, including Frenchy—who was as yellow and
scared as a rat—the decision is unfair and Frenchy lied on you just like
a scared lackey-dog. I said, 'To hell with all you bastards!' Mrs. Sartain,
her husband and Frenchy sitting there like three crackers. When I passed
that fast one on Mrs. Sartain by quickly making her admit she's a whore,
I immediately turned to the president and said, 'You see, she is no better
than my wife,' and walked out on all of them."

With the ordeal over, Armstrong was upset about being barred from
playing in Hawaii, because his fans had showed him nothing but support during his week there, which included receiving an honor from the
Honolulu Hot Jazz Society on his final night in town. "My fans, look how
nice they were to Lucille and I," Armstrong told Glaser. "Even the gent,
the narcotic agent who arrested her, he acted like he didn't want to make
a statement the day of her trial. There she was standing there in front of
the judge along with her lawyer, the D.A. and all the rest. She looking like
a million dollars to me. I'm very proud of her, most much. More so now
than I've ever been during our 11 years of marriage."[14]

When Armstrong left Hawaii, he was grateful that Lucille was exoner-
ated and that his Hawaiian fans stuck by him. But this brush with the law

had been a little too close for comfort. On January 10, Louis and the All Stars arrived in San Francisco, where they played a week-long engagement at the Club Hangover. On the evening of January 16, Louis, alone in his hotel room, composed a letter to Joe Glaser. When he was finished typing the letter, Armstrong read its contents out loud into his reel-to-reel tape recorder, making sure to have a copy of his words for his private record. In the letter, whose contents have never been published till now, Armstrong told Glaser his side of Lucille's arrest, as well as the ensuing trial, as quoted above. He also vented about Frenchy Tallerie, who was quick to side against him in his turmoil. "What a man. What a man you trust," Armstrong said of Tallerie disgustedly. With the preliminaries out of the way, Armstrong's tone turned gravely serious as he made an important request to his manager:

> Now, if there is one thing you must realize, and it's very important—and I'm going to get serious with you for one moment—I don't know how long do I have to go through this shit, being around deceitful, connivin' and dogass people such as Frenchy and all the shit that you just think I can't live without. But I feel that's the way you want it, and since I have to tough it out, I will, even if I die trying. But I will tell you this—and from here on down to the end of this letter, you must read very careful—I have never been as serious with you, Mr. Glaser, as I am about to get right now. You must immediately gather all the friends that you know of, just—whatever you got to do about it, I mean, I'm going to leave it up to you, you know who to get. I don't care who you get, I mean, you have your way about things. But there's one thing I ask of you and that is, Mr. Glaser, you must see to it that I have special permission to smoke all the reefers that I want to when I want or I will just have to put this horn down, that's all. It can be done. Nothing impossible, man.

Armstrong threatening to put his horn down for good is the ultimate example of his using his leverage against Glaser. His devotion to Glaser knew no bounds, but he also knew that without him, Glaser's business would take a serious blow, so he wasn't afraid to remind him that he was a pretty special performer, one that Glaser couldn't live without. "Do you ever stop to think what I have to go through to keep that note—which thrills millions all over the world—right up there where it belongs? Do you ever stop to realize that? No one else boasts it. No one in the universe. They don't have the courage, they don't have—well, I don't know, they just don't do it. Now, there's not another man in the whole world can boast it. Do you realize that?" Armstrong wasn't kidding; he was going through a period of particularly strong blowing, as evidenced by a broadcast from the Club Hangover from the very same evening Armstrong composed this letter. On that broadcast, the All Stars swung like never before on "When the Saints Go Marching In." Armstrong even felt good enough to call "West End Blues," a song that in its landmark 1928 performance, to some, epitomized young Armstrong. But more than just music, Armstrong also knew about the happiness he brought his fans all over the world. Later in the letter, Armstrong added, "What colored or white, if only a few, are doing as much for humanity's sake as I am?"

Armstrong then made it clear that marijuana—or any other drug—didn't have anything to do with his greatness as a musician. "Of course, it's not the reefers in the manner, but since I do like to have a little drag or so—I don't drink and have never once thought of using a needle, freezing my nose, as the users express it. To each his own, quite naturally. Not even have I ever smoked hop. None of that crap. But I can gladly vouch for a nice, fat stick of gage, which relaxes my nerves, if I have any. When I am through with my work, I'm no clown, I'm no criminal. I tend to my own business." To Armstrong, life as a black musician in the United States wasn't easy; the marijuana was a way to take the edge off, to relax and let all of his troubles drift away. To Armstrong, it was a medicine, and he didn't understand why it was illegal. Incidents like what happened in Hawaii only made the dangers of smoking it that much clearer. He told Glaser, "A hard-working salary man such as myself, I have to go through the whole world with this horn, making millions happy, and at the same time ducking and dodging cops, dicks, immigration, stool pigeons, so forth—why? 'Cause they say it's against the law?" Armstrong added, "Why shouldn't I have something with me that relaxes my nerves, concentrate on ideas of importance for my horn, my happiness, yours, Lucille's, the public, there's a lot more reasons . . . I can't afford to be . . . tense, fearing that any minute I'm going to be arrested, brought to jail for a silly little minor thing like marijuana."

Armstrong was particularly upset over what Lucille had to go through in Hawaii. "Can you imagine anyone giving Lucille all of those headaches and grief over a mere small pittance such as gage, something that grows out in the backyard among the chickens and so forth? I just won't carry on with such fear over nothing and I don't intend to ever stop smoking it, not as long as it grows. And there is no one on this earth that can ever stop it all from growing. No one but Jesus—and he wouldn't dare. Because he feels the same way that I do about it." As long as it remained illegal, Armstrong feared that scenes like what happened in Hawaii would continue to repeat themselves. "I'm telling you just like the fellow who told his wife, when she caught him in bed naked with another woman," Armstrong continued. "He told her, 'Honey, when you set a trap for me and bait it with cunt, you will catch me every time.' Just like this incident; it happened once or twice, it will happen again. And that, my friend, is what you shouldn't want to happen."

Armstrong once again felt the need to remind Glaser of his talent. "Just a little freshen-up in your memory: you have within Louis Armstrong a million-dollar attraction. Whether you [and] Frenchy think so or not, I should always be vain enough, if you want to put it thataway, I should always believe that I am. I came from a long ways and I notice through my travels the love and warmth of a million people can't be wrong." Armstrong then reiterated his threat to retire. "I think it a better idea to put the horn down and pitch shit with the chickens after all. It's just Lucille and I. It just isn't worth being kicked in the ass by jerks, especially because we're colored people." As he continued, Armstrong made it clear to Glaser that many who smoke marijuana could go "forever" without thinking about lighting up, but he just wanted insurance against any future "pressure." If Glaser could use his connections to get Armstrong a permit to smoke it—"Nothing impossible where you're concerned, you know that"—Armstrong would be forever grateful and continue performing.

"So get me that paper, man!" Armstrong insisted. "And stipulate all over the world, I must not be humiliated again, ever, as long as I'm blowing trumpet for you. Europe should be easier because they always call me the 'Ambassador of Goodwill.' Most of these guys who are giving us musicians a hard way fail to realize that their teenage children, straight on down to the little babies, like Satchmo's horn. Not only like it, they *love* Satchmo's horn and respect it. They don't give a damn what I smoke." Armstrong then lightened the mood, saying, "I really don't feel like I'm asking too much. I'm not asking y'all to buy marijuana for me. Just keep it straight so I can buy it." Armstrong then jokingly quoted what he figured Glaser's reaction to be: "No, no, not that!" he said with a laugh, "I've given you heart failure enough just talking about it! If I should feel that I'd like a few drags, it's just got to be all right, that's all. Because gage ain't nothing but medicine. Everyone that's in [J. Edgar] Hoover's regiment knows gage is not habit-forming, or dope. It's a damn shame as much as I try to live just to make the whole world happy, they have never been able to prove marijuana as a narcotic."

Nearing the close of his missive, Armstrong brought up the issue of guns. "I'm not so particular about having a permit to carry a gun. All I want is a permit to carry that *good shit*. But if all of those bullshittin' guys such as some of the cats around New York are permitted to carry guns, why in the hell the law should not only let me have a permit, but they should buy my gage for me! That's a joke, son. One can die quickly from a gun. A man carry a gun, he'll shoot it; yes he will, especially if he gets mad enough. Gage, just the opposite, you dig? You'll stay present, no one could make you mad. So dig that. Regards to the staff. As ever, your boy, Louis Satchmo Armstrong."

This letter to Glaser is one of the most stunning documents Armstrong ever composed. Not only is it fascinating because it allows Armstrong to discuss why marijuana means so much to him, but it's also important in illustrating how Armstrong could manipulate Glaser into getting whatever he wanted, something that should surprise those who believe Armstrong to be the subservient one in his relationship with the man he always called "Mr. Glaser." Armstrong was confident in his talents and knew what he brought to the table and wasn't afraid to use that as ammunition to get what he needed from his manager.

Of course, the aftermath of this letter is unknown; Armstrong never referenced it again, and there is no record of how Glaser reacted. Whether or not he was able to use his connections to get Armstrong a "permit" to smoke marijuana is unknown, but the fact remains that Armstrong continued to smoke it until near the end of his life, and there was never another incident of him getting in trouble because of it. Glaser might have pulled some strings, but that doesn't mean he ever learned to live with Armstrong's marijuana use. "Joe, all those years he managed Louie, was scared to death Louie would get busted and he'd lose the goose that lay the golden egg," recalled Jack Bradley. "Oh, that was the only thing Louie stood up against Joe Glaser: smoking pot. He said, 'Joe, I'll do anything for you . . . I'll work anywhere and do anything but I won't give that up 'cause that's too important.' " To Bradley, Swiss Kriss and marijuana were "very definitely tied in. They both looked the same and both are natural herbs and Louie loved them both probably equally. He took them both daily before he'd go to bed at night no matter how much he was drinking or smoking or eating. He'd take a double dose of Swiss Kriss . . . and that way, when he got up in the morning, first thing he'd do is go to the bathroom and spend a half-hour there. And he'd usually light up a bomber, which is a joint about the size of a pencil, and sit on the toilet . . . and get high and leave it all behind him. This was his motto for Swiss Kriss: 'Leave it all behind you.' "[15]

With the smoke cleared around Louis and Lucille's marijuana incident, it was business as usual for the All Stars. Bassist Hinton was astounded by the band's schedule, which he found "unbelievable. We were on the move constantly. We never seemed to play any single place more than once or twice . . . There were always places for Pops to play."[16] Hinton, along with Young's brash trombone and John's powerful drumming, had helped drive the band to new heights of swing. After somewhat of a rebuilding phase, the All Stars were starting really to lock in again, but only a week after the Club Hangover broadcasts, Hinton left the band, realizing there was more money to be made, as well as far less traveling to do, by staying in New York and working as a studio musician. Arvell Shaw would be called back yet again.

During a Basin Street engagement in early 1954, Armstrong's old pal Zutty Singleton sat in with the All Stars, the first time he had played with his old friend since the 1946 Victor session of tunes from the film *New Orleans*. Singleton was hardly in prime form. Armstrong summed up Singleton's performance in a privately recorded conversation with his secretary/mistress Lucille "Sweets" Preston. "Wasn't that terrible?" Armstrong asked. Singleton apparently had asked to join the All Stars, but Armstrong told Preston, "Time has marched on. He'll never get in that thing." Proof of Armstrong as his own boss is confirmed by his telling Preston, "There are two restrictions on musicians and two musicians that I ain't never supposed to play with again. And I made that very clear to Joe Glaser. And I don't think he'll go over my will or my demand when he sees that I'm serious. And that's Earl Hines and Zutty Singleton."[17] Backward-looking jazz fans might have been thrilled by a reunion of Armstrong and two mainstays of the 1920s, but those days were long gone.

On April 5, 1954, Decca reteamed Armstrong with Gordon Jenkins, who now went all out with a studio big band, strings and a choir. Milt Gabler remembered some of the vicissitudes of the session:

> I remember a session in '54 with Gordon Jenkins, a normal call to do four songs with orchestra and chorus in three hours at our Pythian Temple studio in New York. Everyone was on time except no Louis Armstrong. Louis had never been late before, so we rehearsed the orchestra and chorus. We rehearsed all of the songs, and still no Louis. I called Joe Glaser, and he was out. Two and a half hours late and straight from the dentist, Louis comes to the studio, full of remorse and with jaws full of Novocain. He could hardly talk. I asked him if he could work the next day, but Pops had other commitments. I told Gordon to start running the songs down with Louis. Maybe his jaws would loosen up.[18]

Not only did Armstrong's jaws loosen, but as Gabler recalled, "We finished the four sides with only an hour of overtime."[19] "Trees" is insipid material, a Joyce Kilmer poem set to a banal melody, but the Armstrong-Jenkins team pulls it off, with Armstrong infusing the vocal with much more emotion than the material deserves, while Jenkins's arrangement allows the strings to humorously quote a series of licks associated with Armstrong's trumpet playing. Armstrong blew with tremendous force on "Bye and Bye," a New Orleans gospel-cum-jazz tune Jenkins saddled with a very good big-band arrangement that opens with arguably Armstrong's greatest trumpet cadenza of the 1950s. The final recording, though, would prove to be one of Armstrong's most controversial. For a few years there had been a cease-fire in the war between Armstrong and the boppers. In 1950, Armstrong wrote, "I have been quoted as saying this and that about Bop, etc, and they've given me hell to boot . . . But any time we would run across each other, there would always be a lot of warmth amongst us . . . Ya Dig? . . . And the public, they'd think,—My Gawd those guys pan each other so bad—they really must be enemies . . . Shucks, Pay it no mind . . . We musicians have always loved each other."[20]

But on July 18, 1952, Dizzy Gillespie had recorded a piece for Dee Gee titled "Pops' Confessin'." The song featured singer Joe Carroll performing in a devastating impersonation of Armstrong's vocal style while Gillespie parodied Armstrong's glissando-filled trumpet work. By now Gillespie was a friend of Armstrong's, and the piece was intended as affectionate satire. Armstrong responded by having Jenkins rewrite "The Whiffenpoof Song," an old Rudy Vallee and Bing Crosby hit, and the result was called "The Boppenpoof Song." "I wrote some parody lyrics and the original publishers just went to pieces, they were so unhappy with it," Jenkins recalled. "At the time I was doing real well; otherwise I couldn't have gotten away with it. They insisted on not paying me, which was fine; I just wanted to make the record, get it played, and not get sued. They finally agreed to it. The song was an absolute standout, the kind you hit maybe once in fifty years. Louis wasn't that crazy about the bop scene, nor was I, and we had a little fun with it."[21]

At one point, Armstrong sings, "Dixieland music, they condemn / But every wrong note that they play is a gem!" Armstrong closes with some wild scatting before punctuating the end with a triumphant "Bebop!" Reviews were mixed, but Ralph J. Gleason, for one, put the song's humor in perspective. "There's been too little humor in jazz in recent years," he wrote in the *San Francisco Chronicle*. "The young musicians have been so busy dedicating their talents to finding new paths and shaking off tradition, they have neglected to laugh. Louis Armstrong, by all odds the greatest individual musician produced by the traditional jazz culture, is a comic too and that's one of his strongest assets. Decca has just released a single disc of Louis singing a parody of 'The Whiffenpoof Song' which I urge everybody who loves jazz and loves Louis and wants a good laugh to buy immediately."[22] Armstrong began playing it during his live performances, donning a red beret and sunglasses, lampooning bop fashion.

The All Stars continued touring the United States in the spring of 1954[23] but without Kenny John. Armstrong could no longer tolerate his drinking nor his intrusive drumming, badmouthing John in private conversation, especially after an offstage altercation with the young drummer. On the aforementioned 1954 private tape on which Armstrong bashed Zutty

Singleton, Armstrong can be heard to say about John: "I told him, 'You're playing too fast, man . . . I caught up with him, still salty about what I said. I said, 'Well, fuck you. I'm the leader, man.' Shit, and all backstage, we was getting ready to tie asses. I said, 'I'm the leader and I'll go down with this fucking ship 'cause I'm playing right and you got to play it right.' And everybody told him he was too fast. He's got a nervous foot. He can't play a slow tempo to save his life. I haven't seen one tempo yet that he didn't finish up faster. I dig all them drummers. They're all nuts motherfuckers. All of them nuts."[24] John was out before the end of May. As Dan Morgenstern put it, John "was a bit of a jerk, you know—it was a personality thing . . . In order to be a functioning member of that group you had to have a certain attitude. You had to be a good team player, and I don't think Kenny worked out that way."[25]

About to embark on a tour of forty one-night stands, Armstrong needed a drummer, and he chose Barrett Deems. Once billed as the "World's Fastest Drummer," Deems—or "Deemus," as friends called him—had played with Paul Whiteman, Clyde McCoy, and jazz greats such as Joe Venuti, Red Norvo, Charlie Barnet, and Muggsy Spanier before joining the All Stars.

While he had many critics, he was a favorite of many musicians, including drummer Tony Williams, Louis himself, and Barney Bigard, who in 1980 wrote, "[Deems] was a little crazy. Crazy in a nice way. He was really a real nervous guy. He stayed with the band for a good while, and he's still a hell of a drummer."[26] For Armstrong, better a crazy drummer than an erratic alcoholic. As with the rest of the band, the ceaseless traveling could wear Deems down, but he could still joke about it on a 1954 radio show: "Traveling with Louie is a lot of fun. I get my kicks. It's better to play with Louie than anyone else, but I'm afraid I'm going to be the richest corpse in the cemetery!"[27] His eccentric style and powerful beat suited the band, and as Morgenstern remarks, he "never deserved the flack he got from critics eager to pick on the only ofay in the All Stars—he did a fine job for Louis, who didn't want any namby-pamby drumming."[28] With Deems onboard, Armstrong said, "My current aggregation . . . is about the greatest. Without them, I don't know what I'd do."[29] With them, he was about to record arguably the greatest album of his career.

CHAPTER EIGHT

Columbia Masterpieces, 1954–1955

ARMSTRONG HAD BEEN a longtime friend of Columbia Records executive George Avakian, who, while still a student at Yale, broke into the music world by discovering some unissued Armstrong recordings from the 1920s. In the ensuing years, Avakian had become a major producer, responsible for what is generally regarded as the first-ever jazz "album" (a group of 78s of new music informed by a common theme), as well as the head of the popular-music department at Columbia, but he still oversaw Columbia reissues such as the multi-volume *Louis Armstrong Story*. Those sets sold spectacularly, but now Avakian wanted to make an album with Armstrong's current band, an album of tunes composed by W. C. Handy, "the Father of the Blues."

Armstrong, however, had been recording exclusively for Decca since 1949. When Avakian asked Joe Glaser when the Decca contract would end, Glaser simply responded, "Ask me again in a year and a half." Avakian told Columbia president Jim Conkling about his idea and Conkling came up with a solution: "Our Armstrong reissues from the Okeh label have done really well," he said. "They were made on a flat-payment contract. Tell Glaser that if he can get a release for Louis to make this one album now, we'll guarantee that when we can sign Louis to a term contract, we'll include a clause for royalties on the Okehs." Glaser, never one to turn down more money, gave the project a green light. Naturally, Armstrong was more than eager to oblige, saying, "No problem getting Mr. Handy's music ready!" Avakian selected the Handy tunes and Armstrong and the All Stars rehearsed much of the material on the road during a string of forty straight one-nighters. Avakian sent Armstrong only eleven songs, because he wanted the band to stretch the material out. One Sunday afternoon, Armstrong called Avakian: "I'm laying over in Chicago next month for a few days. Line up the studio and I'll be ready."[1]

The result was *Louis Armstrong Plays W. C. Handy*, arguably the greatest album Armstrong ever recorded. Armstrong and the All Stars played with consummate authority, but the unsung hero of the album would be Avakian himself. Avakian took his job as record producer very seriously; he was always passionate about making the best possible album, even if he had to resort to heavy editing and tape splicing—anathema to some producers who decry these practices as violations of the supposed natural spontaneity and authenticity of jazz as improvised music. Avakian says he had approval from all of his artists to edit and splice because they themselves concurred that he had their best interests in mind. "I hate it when people get into the files at Columbia as they do now and then and come up with the terrific discovery that there were three takes used in something," Avakian said in 2007. "That doesn't matter! What matters is you've got to get the right performance that's right for the artist."[2] Session reels exist containing all the material that didn't make it onto the final album, including some fascinating rehearsals and alternate takes. Thanks to the generosity of Avakian and David Ostwald, a New York tuba player and Armstrong historian who helped Avakian prepare Sony's 1997 reissue, which featured theretofore unheard performances, I have been fortunate to study two and a half hours of surviving session tapes. They offer insight into how one of Louis Armstrong's greatest albums took shape and how professional Armstrong and the All Stars were in the recording studio.

While Avakian knew Armstrong, he had had scant interaction with the All Stars, but was quickly impressed by their work ethic. "A joy and a pleasure," Avakian says of working with Armstrong's group. "See, they were all nice people. They were fun to work with, they were very responsive, cooperative with everything. Especially Trummy, because [he] was like Louie's other half, you might say. I never saw two musicians lock into each other the way those two did." Avakian also met the group's newest member, Barrett Deems, at this session for the first time. "I always thought he had a screw loose somewhere because he had a wild look to him and he was always mumbling to himself and muttering and so forth," he recalls. "I never said anything to Louie like, 'Hey, is this guy slightly off his head or something?' Then, when I got to know him, I realized this is just the way he is. He's kind of an introverted person, mumbles to himself, but he's a very solid drummer. And Louie said of him, 'He's the best drummer I've ever worked with.' I didn't want to say, 'Wait, what about Sidney Catlett? What about Zutty?' But then I realized what he meant. He was rock solid. He hit the tempo properly and stayed there."[3]

But, excepting Armstrong, perhaps the most valuable musician of the date was Billy Kyle. "I never realized how important he was until I worked with him in the studio," Avakian says of the pianist. "Kyle was the one who knew what everybody else was going to do. He would be the first one to suggest things like a key change, which I like because I'm always suggesting key changes . . . He was like an assistant arranger, and he was very quick with any problems Velma had. Apparently they had a very good rapport." Indeed, after listening to the session tapes, one might conclude that Kyle deserved an arranger's credit. He's always in charge, rehearsing the band, conceiving introductions, even giving the players harmony notes to play. As for Middleton, who had done a few Decca sessions with Armstrong, she was very nearly a co-star on the album, sharing vocals with Armstrong on four tracks. "Velma was a good singer," Avakian says. "People would say to me, 'Gee, why did you use her?' I finally came up with the right answer. I said, 'Because Velma was family.' Louie hired her, he loved her, she was an asset to the group, so she was family. She was not a bad singer, either. I mean, she's perfectly adequate. And Louie never had a better singer with the group anyway."[4]

The band arrived in Columbia's Chicago studio on July 12, 1954, with basic sheet-music versions of the Handy tunes, as well as simple sketches written out by Kyle. The group would rehearse the tunes, and when they were ready for a take, Avakian would begin recording. First up was "Aunt Hagar's Blues," a Handy composition from 1920. Armstrong was playing off the sheet music, unaccompanied, when Avakian started rolling. After two beats, Armstrong, who was supposed to start, missed on his first attempt. He stops and cheekily says, " 'Aunt Hagar's,' take two!" "Yeah,"

Avakian responds, in keeping with Armstrong's relaxed mood, as some members of the band chuckle lightly in the background. When he misses it again, Armstrong's on it, saying, " 'Aunt Hagar's,' take three," breaking up. This relaxed scene was common during the sessions, but Armstrong never let up in his playing for a minute. Once a routine was settled for "Hesitating Blues," Armstrong and the band decided to do a rehearsal take with no intention of it being released. Nevertheless, Avakian let the tapes roll and caught a performance that was simply brilliant. It couldn't be issued because Middleton used the opening choruses to go over her lyrics, singing them softly in the background, but Armstrong plays like a man possessed, especially in his obbligato to Middleton's vocal. Avakian included this take on the 1997 reissue of the album, writing, "It remains a truly impressive stone-cold 'first-timing' of a song they'd never played before."[5]

After a swinging romp through "Ole Miss Blues," Armstrong turned in one of his finest blues solos ever on the next tune to be recorded, "Beale Street Blues." The surviving session tape begins with Armstrong embold-ening his fellow musicians, "Now if we can knock this on the nose, we're straight." As some of the other members continue carrying on a quiet con-versation, Armstrong addresses them, "Y'all still talking. They're waiting on you." All business, Armstrong contributed some exceptional playing, needing only a couple of insert takes to straighten out the ending. At this point Armstrong had four tunes in the can, but he was playing at white heat and had breezed through the last couple of tunes in only a few takes.

Avakian then suggested a fifth, "Loveless Love," Handy's reworking of "Careless Love," a tune Armstrong had accompanied Bessie Smith on in one of their 1925 recording sessions. Avakian decided to do something that, even more than fifty-five years later, remains a mystery to him: he let the tape run nonstop. He captured more than thirty minutes of Armstrong and the All Stars rehearsing, polishing, and perfecting "Loveless Love." On the tape Armstrong wonders whether the key is right for Middleton or whether there should be a modulation. Middleton says she wouldn't mind a change but wants to make sure it's okay with Armstrong. "Well, I can jive in anything, you know what I mean," Armstrong replies. "I want you to hit yours on the nose." But then he changes his mind: "No, that's too low for Velma." Accordingly, Kyle modulates the tune and it sounds much better. Armstrong's trumpet playing is so fierce on the first take as to move Avakian to remark over his control-room microphone, "I hate to think what's going to happen when you get warmed up on this tune!" Armstrong laughs, but is quickly back in command, making sure that everyone is comfortable with the arrangement. Armstrong contributed two more excellent solos on "Loveless Love," and for the master, Avakian edited the best parts together. When one listens to all of the trumpet playing done by Armstrong on "Loveless Love," one can only be astonished by the sheer amount of creativity Armstrong displayed for one tune. All of the takes are different, confirming that Armstrong was still a formidable improviser, and contradicting the critical charge that he played only "set" solos with the All Stars.

Again, with the final tune, "Long Gone John (from Bowling Green)," Avakian let the tapes roll and caught more than a half-hour of rehearsal and performances. Armstrong is heard reading through the lyrics, cracking up in response to the humor of some, provoking Young to say, "It's going to be a killer." Clearly, the All Stars had never played the tune prior to the session, for Kyle plays the melody in a bunch of different keys, trying to find the one best for Middleton. "How many have we knocked off so far?" Bigard asks, seemingly ready to call it a day. "This will be the sixth one if we can knock it," Armstrong responds. Avakian asks, "When's the last time you made six in [one evening]?" "Man," Armstrong says, "it's been years since that shit. It's wonderful." Back to work, Armstrong wonders about an introduction for "Long Gone." He comes up with an idea, singing an over-the-top trombone part and saying, "Why don't you put one of those hokum vamps on it?" Kyle begins running over harmonies with Young and Bigard, again calling out specific notes for them to play. Armstrong, enticing his closest friend in the band, asks Avakian, "Hey, George, you don't think it's too long for Trummy to play two choruses?" "No, no," Avakian says, "I'd like to have them." More tinkering and rehearsals followed, including a couple of breakdown takes, but in the end the All Stars—with the help of a choir of studio guests—waxed perhaps the most infectiously fun song of the entire album.

And so one of the most productive evenings of Louis Armstrong's entire career came to an end. Six songs—more than half the album—were finished. The next day, Armstrong and the All Stars were at it again, starting with Handy's first blues composition, "The Memphis Blues." One of the shortest tracks on the album, it was almost all vocal save two stunning blues choruses played at the end. In the first run-through Bigard is lost in the mix, something that was becoming a problem. "Barney, we can use a little more of you in the last ensemble," Avakian tells the clarinetist. "You're being overshadowed by Trummy." The result is a fine performance, but a bona fide classic was to come: Handy's most famous composition, "St. Louis Blues." Avakian wanted the musicians to stretch out, but got more than even he expected. In 2008, he told me: "I did not expect what Pops gave me on that tune."[6] On the session tapes, there are a few false starts, but once the band got going it did not stop rocking for nearly nine minutes. The highlights are bountiful: two and a half minutes or so of brilliant instrumental playing at the start; Middleton's vocal, with new lines about Armstrong himself and a decisive obbligato by the trumpeter; Armstrong's impromptu quotation of a solo he had played on a 1924 record by the Red Onion Jazz Babies, "Terrible Blues"; Armstrong's hilarious new lyrics, decidedly not in Handy's original; Bigard's thrilling solo, in the wake of Avakian's exhortation during the recording of "The Memphis Blues"; one of the raunchiest solos of Trummy Young's career with Armstrong (he growls, roars, snarls through two choruses, with mighty backing by the rhythm section); and, finally, two majestic rideout choruses, Armstrong leading the way, consistently pounding home high concert D-flats with a tone of breathtaking fullness.

As soon as the take ended, Armstrong was compelled to yell: "Wailin'!" amidst laughter and other verbal acknowledgments that these musicians knew they had just achieved something special. As good as the performance was, it had yet to be perfected; Avakian did not think it sufficiently polished. Still, over the control-room microphone he can be heard to say: "Louie, that was really a bitch!" The band breaks up laughing as everyone chants: "Wail! Wail!" When Shaw and Deems request a playback, Avakian implores, "Everybody relax for eight minutes and fifty seconds." The surviving session tape then ends abruptly, but Armstrong and the All Stars reprised the song later, tightening it up here and there, completing the album's momentous opening number. Even Barney Bigard would claim "St. Louis Blues"—a hallmark of Armstrong's later years, perhaps even of his career—as his favorite recording with the All Stars.[7]

The last tune recorded that day was "Atlanta Blues," Handy's reworking of an old chestnut, "Make Me a Pallet on the Floor"—taken at the fastest tempo on the album. The group nailed the first take except for a botched ending, and Bigard's attempt to pull a fast one. Bigard was supposed to play an obbligato behind Armstrong's first chorus, but he was nearly inaudible on the first and each subsequent take, hoping for more takes to push the session into overtime. Avakian was onto him and, at the end of what would be the final take, told the musicians that everything was fine and they could go home. A surprised Bigard asked if he had been close enough to the microphone and Avakian lied, responding that he was. But Armstrong knew something had been fishy with Bigard, so he talked to Avakian about it. "Pops, I was onto him all the way," Avakian said, "but I didn't want to embarrass him in front of the guys. We'll wait till you're in New York. Come to the studio and I'll overdub you with earphones, blowing against your own voice."[8] In the end, "Atlanta Blues" stood out for its overdubbed duet between Armstrong and Armstrong!

The third and final session would prove to be an easy one; nine of the eleven planned tunes had already been recorded. The song "Chantez Les Bas" had inspired Avakian to propose the idea of a Handy album. He had heard Katherine Handy singing it on a 1944 record with James P. Johnson and had always thought it would be a natural for Armstrong. The song featured a minor theme, something Armstrong always excelled at, while the eight-bar blowing strain was reminiscent of "My Bucket's Got a Hole In It," but here the band opts for a lowdown, stomping medium tempo. On the first take, Armstrong had some trouble while singing the melody, but he remedied that between takes by consulting the sheet music. As for the music itself, it found the musicians simply playing at their peak. Armstrong dug in deeply, spurred on by Young's trombone to a final chorus that consisted of repeated glisses to high concert E-flats. On the master take, Young pushed Armstrong to take an extra chorus at the end, one of the album's most thrilling moments. Asked to name his favorite performance from the record, Armstrong responded, "Well, I liked the 'Chantez Les Bas,' that's a Creole tune, and there was an incident I liked about the tune. When we was getting ready to play the last chorus—I mean, we were swinging in the last chorus, and everybody was getting ready to go out, and it got so good that Trummy, he wouldn't stop—we had to go back again and play an extra chorus. He just kept on blowing."[9] "I got carried away, that's all!" Young said with a laugh during a radio interview from the period. "I got carried away too," Armstrong responded.[10]

"Yellow Dog Blues" went off without a hitch. Its only alternate take on the session reels is complete and rivals the album version, a relaxed affair for Armstrong's singing, though it again features intense trumpet playing. With both songs out of the way, Armstrong decided to offer Trummy Young a present: he asked him to sing and play his old Jimmie Lunceford hit "'Tain't What You Do." After a swinging run-through take, Avakian, blinded by Armstrong's star power, asks the trumpeter, "Louie, do you ever talk to Trummy during this vocal? You know, jive in between his lines?" "No," Armstrong responds, "I don't want to interfere with that." He wants his trombonist to shine in the spotlight. Young jokes, "What he says to me, you can't put it on wax, anyway!" To much laughter, Armstrong refers to his leaving Decca to record this album for Columbia: "He's worrying about the contract. I said there ain't no contract. We're like a band without a country, man. We're trying to get a contract!" Playing along, Avakian announces the next take as "Audition, take one."

Listening to how this masterpiece of an album was put together in the studio is an illuminating experience. Armstrong is very serious about his playing and very humble about compliments, but he's also quick with a joke to strike the right ambience. Middleton is clearly in awe of him, and Kyle's importance to the arrangements and sketches cannot be underestimated. For the most part Bigard sounds bored, which, unfortunately, was not about to change anytime soon. Avakian did a masterful job in the control room, and with the final editing he crafted an album that led Armstrong to remark to his new producer, "I can't remember when I felt this good about making a record."[11] Years later, Trummy Young said about the sessions, "Yes, I'll never forget that. That stands out more than any other recording session. Louis was so inspired on this date, and he inspired all of us. I'm sure the band played better than they ever had before or ever after. All you have to do is listen to that album."[12]

In the December 4, 1954, issue of *DownBeat*, Nat Hentoff gave the recording five stars and noted, "This LP is one of the greatest recordings not only of the year, but of jazz history. After years of wandering in a Decca desert (with very few oases) Louis finally had a full-ranged shot at the kind of material he loves, along with the kind of freedom that George Avakian provides at a jazz date." Hentoff realized that Avakian deserved a lot of credit for the success of the album, writing, "This album is an accomplishment Avakian can well be self-congratulatory about. By arranging this session and supervising it with this much unobtrusive skill and taste, Avakian, too—as well as W. C. Handy and Louis—has made a lasting contribution to recorded jazz."[13]

A few months later, after Armstrong listened to some playbacks with Handy himself and did the overdubbing on "Atlanta Blues," he remarked to Leonard Feather, "Man, a cat came in from Columbia and said we gotta make some more of these. It was an album of W. C. Handy's blues. Mr. Handy came in too and listened to all the records. They're perfect—they're my tops, I think." And proving that he still refused to be pigeonholed, Armstrong told Feather, "I wouldn't call them Dixieland—to me that's only just a little better than bop. *Jazz* music—that's the way we express ourselves."[14]

Soon after, Armstrong participated in another of Feather's "Blindfold Tests." He was still uncomfortable with most modern jazz, including Shorty Rogers's "Morpo," of which he said, "It's not a matter of being old-timey, but, shucks, we can get *too* damn modern, you know?"[15] Of Charlie Parker's "She Rote," he complained about the alto saxophonist's embellishments of the melody: "The saxophone player on this—nothing but variations!"[16] But of the cool jazz of Chet Baker on "Imagination," he said, "Sure is a perfect record; the tone is beautiful, but what puzzled me is how he can get in such a low register."[17] Armstrong positively reviewed Clifford Brown for his furious attack on "Cherokee": "Let's lay about four [stars out of five] on him," Armstrong said, "because a trumpet player's got to get a rating, regardless . . . that's the toughest of all instruments." By this point it should have come as no surprise that Armstrong was crazy about Guy Lombardo; he gave his recording of "Undecided" five and a half stars. Armstrong once told Murray Kempton, "They ask me my favorite band and I tell them Guy Lombardo. They say you don't really mean that. And I say you asked me, didn't you."[18]

After the Handy album, the All Stars spent the rest of the summer of 1954 on the road, playing fifty-three one-nighters in a row at one point, before settling into a record-breaking two-month engagement at New York's Basin Street. Surviving broadcasts show Armstrong and the band in prime form, but during this engagement Armstrong received one of the most scathing reviews of his career by Wilfred Lowe in England's *Jazz Journal*: "Armstrong, with his clowning, rolling eyes, suggestive growls and obscene asides, and his childish tantrums—(remember the Benny Goodman affair?)—his puerile utterances, drags his choice of music from the heights of art to the level of black-face buffoonery," Lowe wrote. "His concerts seldom rise above the plane of a coon carnival, complete with comedy splits and other vulgarities."[19]

Of his trumpet playing, Lowe wrote, "His phrasing is par excellence, but technically—well, there are dozens of jazz men, traditionalists, too, who can leave him frozen. There's nothing extraordinary about his range—a point which is always offered in his favor; the 'warm vibrato' in the upper range sounds more like a strenuous battle to reach the notes—there's nothing that sounds effortless. And his inventiveness—his solos today seem to consist of three or four notes, well phrased and blown like mad." He concluded:

> The time has come for us to hand Louis Armstrong his cap and bells and to force his abdication before he can pull jazz music even further into the slime. Let us, by all means, treasure the memory of Louis when he was great. He has played his part. Now he must be allowed to either bow gracefully out or be forcibly ejected. We owe it to the pioneers as well as the future of jazz music to ensure that Armstrong does no more harm. Place the crown on a head more worthy; clothe Louis in more fitting apparel—that of a jazz jester.[20]

The review appeared at an inauspicious time, for Armstrong's autobiography was about to be published that fall. In the writing of it, Armstrong had not gotten past 1922, but Prentice Hall decided to release it as *Satchmo: My Life in New Orleans*. Armstrong had typed the manuscript himself, and after comparing Armstrong's own version to the published one, Dan Morgenstern wrote, "Though substantial editing was done, it was mostly a matter of changing Armstrong's three-dot style to conventionally punctuated sentence structure. The words are essentially Armstrong's own, and nothing of importance he did not write has been put in his mouth."[21] Whitney Balliett, for one, was disappointed to see Armstrong's idiosyncratic writing style not represented in the book. "Perhaps if the publisher had let the manuscript alone—Louis has a written style, typographically and otherwise, that makes E. E. Cummings's seem like ladyfingers on a spree—and not hoked it up with grammar and sentences that its author could never have written, [Armstrong's] personality might have come closer to the surface." Balliett, of course, couldn't resist taking some digs at the present-day Armstrong: "Now, of course, Louis, who was born on July 4, 1900, is past [his] peak; his trumpet-playing is only rarely evocative of the clarity and surge it possessed twenty years ago, and his singing, although still capable of making one's skin travel, has become bearish in comparison with the delicate, quarreled instrument it once was." But he concluded on a positive note: "He has also become, in his way, as noble a figure as we ever allow any creative person in this country to be."[22]

On September 5, during his long engagement at Basin Street, Armstrong starred in an episode of the CBS television show *You Are There* titled "The Emergence of Jazz." In the show, Armstrong played King Oliver while Bobby Hackett played Nick LaRocca, the leader of the Original Dixieland Jazz Band, the first jazz group to ever appear on record. Armstrong was given a touching speech to deliver about how blacks and whites were now playing jazz together. However, CBS feared the South's reaction to an integrated group, and took appropriate, if unseemly, measures: Hackett was kept offscreen and Barrett Deems was forced to wear blackface. As Deems told it, "They told Louie, 'You gotta use another black drummer.' And Louie said, 'No, that's my drummer.' So finally Joe Glaser and him figured out something. They said, 'We'll make him use blackup.' So we put the blackup on . . . and Louie said, 'Boy, you look great!' " After the show, Deems couldn't entirely remove the blackface. "We ended up in California with black makeup," he said. "So when I got to the airport, all of the black cats that I knew out there, they said, 'Welcome to the race!' "[23]

Meanwhile Decca all but ignored the W. C. Handy masterpiece and—to cash in on the latest hits—continued making records with the trumpeter. In August 1954, Armstrong had covered a popular tune called "Skokiaan," playing a trumpet solo of earth-shaking force. He would later sing dopey new lyrics to "Muskrat Ramble," as the McGuire Sisters had recently had a hit with their vocal version. By the dawn of 1955, Decca was paying closer attention to the emerging sounds of rock and roll, and with good reason: producer Milt Gabler was the man behind Bill Haley's historic recording of "Rock Around the Clock," released on Decca in April 1954. So the record company gave Armstrong two early rock ballads, "Sincerely" and "Pledging My Love," to record in January. Armstrong does his best with them, but neither is an ideal fit. Decca also teamed Armstrong with Bing Crosby's son Gary for a forgettable cover of "Ko Ko Mo," a novelty hit by the Crew Cuts, performed complete with a 1950s "ooh-wah" chorus by Jud Conlon's Rhythmaires (though Armstrong had more success performing it live with Velma Middleton).

Decca made up for its lack of judgment by recording an entire evening of the All Stars, live at Hollywood's Crescendo Club, one of the finest live accounts of the band, capturing every side of Armstrong's persona: from jazz genius ("Indiana" and "Basin Street Blues") to pop singer ("The Gypsy" and "C'Est Si Bon") to comedian ("Me and Brother Bill" and a duet with Middleton, "Don't Fence Me In"). But as great as the Crescendo Club recordings are, Decca was clearly losing its grip on Armstrong's studio recordings, eager as it was for Glaser-driven commercial success, however vapid the music. Timeless music, such as the Columbia W. C. Handy album, was not part of its Armstrong marketing plan.

Armstrong was now appearing on the tube more frequently than ever. On April 17, he was on Ed Sullivan's *Toast of the Town,* broadcasting live from the Sands Hotel in Las Vegas to boot. On the show he appeared with opera star Robert Merrill, which Armstrong remembered fondly: Merrill sang "Honeysuckle Rose" and Armstrong "Vesti la giubba" from *Pagliacci* after his own fashion ("Ridi, Pagliaccio, come and dig little Satchmo!"). As entertaining as his appearance on the Sullivan show was, Armstrong had likely enjoyed something that happened earlier in the day more. "They had rehearsals before the show, the afternoon of the show," Jack Bradley remembered. "And Louie, like he did with everything, when rehearsal began, he talked to Robert Merrill. He said, 'You've got to try some of this shit. It's Swiss Kriss and it will cure cancer and cure everything and you'll love it. I take it every day.' So to be nice, he took some. And after the rehearsal, [Merrill's] in his dressing room, warming up. He hit a high C and shit his pants. You can imagine how Louie loved it. Anything to do with shitting and Swiss Kriss, he loved."[24]

Nine days later Armstrong was scheduled to return to Columbia's studios to record an album featuring "Honeysuckle Rose," among other songs by Fats Waller—an album again conceived by George Avakian. It would feature the All Stars renditions of nine songs by Waller, a legendary stride pianist, rakish composer, and old friend of Armstrong's. Armstrong had recorded five of the nine in the late twenties and early thirties, and while some of the earlier versions weren't surpassed this time around, there are enough great moments on this disc to make it an essential part of Armstrong's later discography. As accomplished as the finished product was, though, George Avakian still has regrets about it. "The Fats Waller album was not as well prepared, possibly because [Armstrong] was not as excited about the music," he says. "Mr. Handy meant something to him as a symbol. And Fats Waller meant a drinking buddy to him!" Avakian also proposed that some of Waller's lesser-known works be recorded. "There were a couple of other songs we could have done," he said. "I looked for any obscure Fats Waller songs that Fats had never done. One of them was 'Clorinda,' which Bix Beiderbecke did on a very early session. When I mentioned it, Louie knew it. How do you like that? He even sang it back to me. And he said, 'No, but I can't do that, that's Bix's song, that's Bix's song.' Just like all his life, Louie refused to record 'Singin' the Blues' because it's Bix's song. I think we might have done 'Willow Tree,' and I can't remember the rest. We talked about it, but we never got serious about it. Louie was so busy I decided nine tracks will do."[25]

Avakian was kind enough to share the session tapes for this album with me, though they have none of the long rehearsals or studio discussions of the Handy session tapes. All the same, they capture Armstrong's seriousness of purpose and drive. On the first run-through of "Honeysuckle Rose," Armstrong plays the melody an octave higher than written, a stunning bit that never made it onto the final album. Avakian had his work cut out for him in the editing room: Armstrong's solos were a burden of riches. The high point is arguably a touching version of "Blue Turning Grey Over You," clearly a stronger performance than Armstrong's first recorded version from 1930. "Keeping Out of Mischief Now" also surpasses its 1932 rendition, featuring as it does a medium tempo allowing for irresistible swing. There is a masterful "Black and Blue" as well as a roaring "Ain't Misbehavin'," the song Armstrong brought the house down with on Broadway in 1929. He had recorded it numerous times, but while his singing on the 1955 version hardly compares with that of 1929, his playing—indeed, the playing of the entire band, especially Young—swings with tremendous power. Avakian is justly proud of the album and of especially "two fantastic tracks. I mean, that 'Black and Blue' he did and 'Blue Turning Grey,' which was Lucille's [Armstrong's] favorite song. In both cases, I think he topped the original records."[26]

But it cannot be denied that Bigard proved a drawback on the album, even if he sounds competent. Deems had to switch his style of playing from heavy, swinging patterns behind Young's trombone roars to quiet cymbal playing behind Bigard's liquid solos because Bigard was not projecting sufficiently. Listening to the complete session tapes (nearly three hours of continuous takes), one must conclude that Bigard did not acquit himself well throughout the album's three sessions. He sounds out of gas, when not sloppy, even squeaking a few times. Avakian probably had Bigard in mind when he wrote to Joe Glaser a few weeks after the sessions: "The results are very good although the sidemen were not tremendous by any means and I had to do a great deal of splicing and editing to produce really good tapes. Louis himself was, as always, truly wonderful. The album is one that we can all be very proud of."[27]

Bigard hit rock bottom during a broadcast from Basin Street in July 1955—possibly his lowest moment with the All Stars—on a messy, poorly performed "Rose Room" feature. He meandered aimlessly, as if he were simply going through the motions. "When you listen to Barney's features, I mean, they're basically, totally empty of any musical content," Dan Morgenstern says. "They're just exercises and they're displays . . . That was one thing that became annoying if you followed the All Stars."[28] Clearly, Bigard's heart wasn't in it anymore and in September of 1955, he quit the band. "It had gotten harder because Louis was always getting more and more popular," Bigard wrote. "That meant we had to work twice as hard to satisfy the people. It was getting to be a drag again, on the road for months on end, and so I decided that I would quit once and for all."[29] Bigard would be replaced by a native of Louisiana and a master of the New Orleans clarinet idiom, Edmond Hall. After playing with New Orleans bands led by the likes of trumpeters Kid Thomas Valentine and Lee Collins, Hall headed for the North in the late twenties and was in great demand for the next two decades, working with Claude Hopkins, Lucky Millinder, Zutty Singleton, Joe Sullivan, Red Allen, Teddy Wilson, and Eddie Condon. Hall brought the All Stars more fire, power, and swing than Bigard could muster; his uniquely dirty tone was a godsend to the group's ferocious front line. "His hot, swinging approach added bite and energy to the All Stars' music," wrote Dan Morgenstern. "To these ears, Hall was the greatest clarinet the band ever had."[30] Armstrong immediately agreed. "The new clarinet man arrived last night (Thursday)," Armstrong wrote on September 8, 1955, in a letter to Joe Glaser. "He spent the night out at the club with us . . . You sure did send a good man this time . . . Yea—Edman [sic] Hall is one of the very best, there is, on the Clarinet . . . A man whom I've always admired as a great musician, from the very first time I heard him, until, this very day . . . I personally, think that he will lift up the band a hundred percent."[31]

The All Stars never sounded better, now that they were on the verge of becoming more popular than ever.

CHAPTER NINE

Ambassador Satch, 1955–1956

BY LATE SEPTEMBER 1955, with the All Stars in top form, good news was in the offing for the many fans of *Louis Armstrong Plays W. C. Handy* and *Satch Plays Fats*: George Avakian would oversee Armstrong's recordings over the course of the next year. Joe Glaser was more than pleased with Avakian's work. After *Satch Plays Fats* was finished in May 1955, he had written to the producer: "It's wonderful to know the record date was a good one and assure you I appreciate your kind efforts in my behalf."[1] Avakian and Glaser spent much of the summer in friendly correspondence about music, baseball, and, of course, Armstrong. In one of his letters, dated September 19, Avakian wrote: "If possible . . . I would like to have Louis record the Kurt Weill 'Moritat' ('Ballad of Mack the Knife'), which we were not able to record in Hollywood. I realize it will be next to impossible to do so because Louis will have so many things to do in the three days before he leaves for Europe, but I will save some time late at night in our 30th Street Studio in case one session is possible. This number is all arranged, and I have the score and complete parts in my office. It would, of course, be a hit in Europe because of its great familiarity to European audiences."[2]

On September 28, 1955, two days before the All Stars departed for a three-month tour of Europe, Avakian got his wish and recorded Armstrong singing and playing a tune that would become one of the biggest hits of his career. The previous year, Kurt Weill and Bertolt Brecht's *Threepenny Opera* (original title: *Die Dreigroschenoper*) had a revival in New York. The musical play featured Brecht and Weill's murder ballad, "Die Moritat von Mackie Messer," which Columbia had already recorded as a honky-tonk piece replete with banjo. Marc Blitzstein's English version retitled it "Mack the Knife," and Avakian thought it could make a catchy pop song, but everybody he showed it to—including Erroll Garner, Dave Brubeck, Gerry Mulligan, and John Lewis—said, "George, what can I do with eight bars over and over, from a German opera yet? And how about those lyrics, man?" One of the musicians Avakian offered it to was Dixieland trombonist Turk Murphy. Murphy said he'd do it, and wanted to write an arrangement for Armstrong at no extra charge. "Brilliant me!" Avakian remembered. "I had never thought of Louis Armstrong."[3] Murphy and Avakian recorded a quick run-through and played it for Armstrong while the trumpeter was appearing in San Francisco. "So we played the acetate for Louie and showed him the arrangement," Avakian says. "And Louie's reaction was marvelous. He broke into a big smile as he listened to the lyrics and he said, 'Hey, I'll record that. I knew cats like that in New Orleans. They'd stick a knife in you as fast as say hello.'"[4]

Murphy wrote the arrangement, which was given to Armstrong's valet, Doc Pugh, before the session. But on the day of the session, Pugh lost it, so Murphy had to be summoned to the studio with a duplicate. Armstrong sang "Mack the Knife" with gusto, and once again Avakian had Armstrong overdub himself playing a trumpet obbligato behind the vocal. At the same session, Avakian came upon the idea of pairing Armstrong with Lotte Lenya, Weill's widow and a theater legend in her own right. There was one problem, however, as Avakian recalls: "Lenya just had no sense of jazz rhythm," he says. "I couldn't believe it." Rehearsal tapes exist of Armstrong, the gutbucket crooner with the gravel voice, teaching the future Tony Award–winning performer how to phrase properly. "It's horrible," Avakian says of the rehearsal. "I never wanted anybody to hear it."[5] As painful as it was to Avakian, the recording is nonetheless fascinating: one hears Lenya struggling mightily with a half-note rest, as Armstrong patiently coaches her through it. Lenya herself was immortalized in the song by Armstrong when he listed her as among Mack's victims, an inclusion to appear in future versions by Bobby Darin and Frank Sinatra, among others. The day after the session, Armstrong and the band embarked on a tour of Europe, but throughout the trip, they couldn't play "Mack the Knife" because Doc Pugh had lost the arrangement yet again!

This European tour would be different from Armstrong's previous overseas ventures. Avakian was going to produce live recordings from across the continent; he even convinced newsman Edward R. Murrow to follow the band, filming pieces for his television program *See It Now*. More than before, reporters saw jazz in ambassadorial terms: its proliferation might improve relations among countries. "America's secret weapon is a blue note in a minor key," Felix Belair Jr. wrote in the *New York Times*. "Right now its most effective ambassador is Louis (Satchmo) Armstrong. A telling propaganda line is the hopped-up tempo of a Dixieland band heard on the Voice of America in far-off Tangier."[6]

The tour covered ten nations including Germany, Belgium, Switzerland, Sweden, France, Italy, and (for the first time) Spain. Again, everywhere he went, Armstrong was mobbed by adoring fans. Gösta Hägglöf hoped to meet Armstrong at his hotel in Sweden for an autograph during the early Scandinavian leg of the tour. Hägglöf wasn't alone; about fifty other people were waiting. Hägglöf marveled at how Armstrong signed autographs for everyone. "Still scribbling, he and the crowd entered the hotel, but the hotel personnel asked the gathered fans to leave," Hägglöf remembered. "They did—together with Satchmo who saw to it that everybody got their autographs outside with the recipient's name correctly spelled, before going back to the hotel for a well earned rest after three wonderful concerts. I have learnt that this was typical of Louis Armstrong and how he cared for his fans."[7]

After Scandinavia, the All Stars flew to Germany on October 16, where they were met by fans who carried their excitement a bit too far. In Hamburg, the loudspeaker system at Ernst Merck Halle was not functioning properly, provoking the seven thousand fans in attendance to start throwing objects onstage and breaking furniture. In the riot that ensued, ten people were injured and fifteen arrested.[8] Armstrong downplayed the incident: "I was supposed to play two concerts that night, but they broke up the chairs—they got tired of applaudin' with their hands and started applaudin' with the chairs. And they still wouldn't go—the police tried to get them out to clear the hall for the next concert. But they refused to go. Then the police turned the fire hose on them. The hall was a mess." It wasn't Armstrong's only brush with violence during the trip. "The same thing happened in Roubaix, France," he said. "And in Lyons, too. They started throwin' things at the local band when they came back to take over."[9]

Armstrong was surprised by the number of jazz fans from Communist countries who had slipped in to hear him. "Now, them boys that slipped over the Iron Curtain to take in the concert," he said. "In the Hot Club in Berlin these boys were there, and one of them said, 'We slipped over the Iron Curtain to hear our Louis,' and they said, 'We don't know how we gonna get back.' And I never heard of 'em since, but that's what they did."[10]

In Paris, the trumpeter gave a lengthy interview to *U.S. News & World Report.* When asked if jazz was the same in Europe as it was in America, Armstrong said, "It's the same all over the world. I always say a note's a note in any language, if you hit it on the nose—if you hit it."[11] The interview also let Armstrong express informative views on his music. Asked why he preferred the six-piece All Stars to a big orchestra, he said, "I don't prefer it—the public does. They feel with a small combination they will get every individual's soul better than fifteen men sitting up there playing what one guy wrote. Probably he didn't know nothin' about music—he just studied it at college from a score, and you're playing what he thinks. But six men, they play what comes out of each of them, personally." Still averse to categorization, he bristled when questioned about playing "Dixie." "Any kind," he said. "I play music—you call it what you want."[12]

The interview revealed that Armstrong imagined his music as important to the improvement of foreign relations. Asked if he was being paid in any way by the U.S. State Department, he said, "No sir, not a penny. They're talking about that . . . Just think, if they sent this combo around to a big stadium where thousands of people could hear it—I think it would do a lot of good. But who am I to suggest things like that?" As to whether hot jazz could end the cold war, he remarked: "Well, not knowin' about politics—but I know that hot jazz can do a whole lot for a lot of fans that don't care so much for that. If it's left to people that's peaceful with music, there wouldn't be no wars. Wouldn't be none. It comes from people that probably don't care so much about jazz, but, I mean, music has done a whole lot for friendships, and everything."[13]

The All Stars traveled to Milan in December, where Armstrong had one of his biggest thrills of the trip. "We was playin' up at the Odeon—that's a concert hall about two blocks from La Scala, the opera house—and after my concert I had to get in the cab and go over to La Scala and get pictures taken standin' beside all these great men like Verdi and Wagner and—their statues, you know—and right between 'em—that's what the Italians requested."[14] It was also in Milan that Armstrong caught up with Avakian to record some tunes for an album to be titled *Ambassador Satch*. Avakian wanted to give the album the feel of a live date, but most of the recordings took place in either a studio or an abandoned movie theater in Milan. "We did three concerts that day, with intermission included," Armstrong said of that December date. "And 1:00 that night, we begin to record that *Ambassador Satch*. And at 5:00 in the morning, we're wailing 'West End Blues.' See what I mean? And 'Tiger Rag,' you ain't never heard 'Tiger Rag' in your life like them cats, the longer they played it. But that's what I'm talking about. If you didn't feel good, you couldn't do that. You can't force those things."[15] Armstrong was in heroic form that evening, all the more remarkable for having already done three concerts. He was justifiably proud of the remake of "West End Blues"—the pure round sound of his horn was much in evidence—and his raw power was breathtaking. It isn't quite revolutionary but it is a remarkably moving performance.

In addition to a free-wheeling "Tiger Rag," the All Stars cut excellent versions of concert staples such as "Clarinet Marmalade," "Royal Garden Blues," and "Someday You'll Be Sorry," as well as three songs Armstrong hadn't played in years: "You Can Depend on Me," "Lonesome Road," and "That's a Plenty." While all three had their moments, they were not issued on the original album. Altogether, more than seventy minutes of audio survive from the Milan session, all of it capturing the new edition of the All Stars in peak form.

As Armstrong prepared to leave Europe on December 29, Avakian planned to talk to Glaser about signing Armstrong to an exclusive contract with Columbia. On that day, Avakian wrote to Goddard Lieberson, the head of the entire record division, recounting a phone conversation he had with Glaser. "Glaser said that he appreciated the fact that we had done so much for Armstrong, but he had so many offers from all the major companies that he had to take a realistic view and he felt that it would take a $50,000 advance to land Armstrong." It was a lot of money, but he told Lieberson, "In any case I feel that to make a large advance to get Armstrong would be a worth while investment because Armstrong is certain to emerge in the immediate as well as long-range future as one of the very few great jazz musicians of all time. I think that any money invested in him now is better spent than it would be for any other purpose that I can think of off hand."[16] Avakian's confidence was fueled by the fact that Armstrong's "Mack the Knife" had become an explosive hit while the trumpeter was overseas.

"Opening night at the Fontainebleau in Miami," Avakian wrote about Armstrong's return to the United States, "Louis fielded requests for his hit with charm and 'come back tomorrow, folks, and we'll lay it on you!' That evening, he took the band down to the hotel coffee shop, armed with five dollars worth of dimes and a stack of blank music paper. They fed the jukebox over and over, copying their own parts . . . and that's how Louis Armstrong got to play his multi-million seller-to-be for the first time in public."[17] The record continued to climb the charts, even if some reviews frowned on the song's lyrics. One in *Gramophone* discussed "Mack's" "unnecessarily long, and in places, revolting lyric that might easily incite impressionable teenagers to violence (and has had that effect in America, I understand)."[18]

As grueling as the European tour had been, the band would have no respite. As Barrett Deems remembered, "And then, after the tour is over, Joe Glaser meets us [at the airport and says], 'Now, we'll relax.' I said, 'That's great, I'll go home and see my wife.' He said, 'But you've got to be at MGM studios in 36 hours, seven in the morning.' I said, 'What's this?' He said, 'You're going to work.' So I called my wife and told her, 'Can't come through.' She said, 'Well, let me know when you get to Chicago sometime. Wear a red flower so I can recognize you!' "[19] Armstrong and the All Stars found themselves in Hollywood, recording their scenes for an MGM musical remake of *The Philadelphia Story* to be called *High Society*. The movie featured Bing Crosby, Frank Sinatra, and Grace Kelly in roles made famous by Cary Grant, Jimmy Stewart, and Katharine Hepburn. Armstrong played himself, getting a few chances to blow with the All Stars, and also acting as something of a one-man Greek chorus, expounding the film's plot musically during the opening "High Society Calypso," and appearing now and then to comment on events taking place. His musical duet with Crosby, "Now You Has Jazz," is a classic, but perhaps the most beautiful number is Crosby's rendition of Cole Porter's "I Love You, Samantha," with spine-tingling backing by Armstrong.

"It was a pleasure to be in the picture," Bing Crosby said. "Chuck Walters's a very fine director with great taste and sophistication. And a marvelous cast, all people I knew and people I admired, Sinatra, Louis, Celeste Holm, Grace Kelly. It was just a breeze, really."[20] Johnny Green, the film's musical director, also had fond memories of the making of the film. "You talk about one big happy family, that's what it was," Green remembered. "And such a variety of personalities. You know, Sinatra and Crosby about as different as two guys can be—you know, that easygoing Crosby and the frenetic Sinatra. And then Louis, you know, is kind of the wise grandfather of the whole thing . . . Louis's influence on that fun element—you know, he's the greatest laugher in the whole world, with that laugh of his, you know, and his sense of humor and his sense of fellowship and play and so on. It was an incredible experience."[21]

High Society was also notable for prominently featuring the All Stars performing and even acting a bit. On a private tape, Armstrong told a hilarious story about Trummy Young hamming it up in front of the camera for "High Society Calypso." "That's in the beginning of the picture," he says, "and you talk about a bunch of cats—you know your boys, how they can ham up a thing! And they're all trying to steal that scene. Trummy Young mugged so much, folks, I'm telling you, even when the director was explaining the scene, he was mugging listening!" Armstrong cracks himself up at the memory and says, "Oh, we had the greatest laughs, everybody trying to steal scenes."[22]

While in Los Angeles filming *High Society,* Armstrong and the All Stars headed back into the Columbia studios to record another session for George Avakian. Avakian had a batch of recordings made during the European tour ready for release, including live performances at a Netherlands concert, as well as some from the after-hours movie-theater session in Milan. He dubbed in fake applause to make the tracks come to "life," as it were, and would do the same for two Los Angeles performances, "Twelfth Street Rag" and "All of Me." The latter, usually a feature for Velma Middleton, is extraordinary for Armstrong's performance, especially his singing.

Avakian assembled a total of ten tracks from the three sessions for

Ambassador Satch, arguably the definitive album featuring Armstrong as trumpeter in the mid-fifties. With the exception of "All of Me," on which he sings, and two other tracks, on which he scats, *Ambassador Satch* features the trumpeter front and center, unlike previous albums on which Armstrong more or less equally divided his singing and playing. Its version of "Muskrat Ramble" might be Armstrong's greatest and gives a clean instance of the powerhouse swing of the Armstrong-Hall-Young All Stars. The Armstrong solo had been sculpted over the years into a monument of swinging phrases and clever quotes, and on this version of "Muskrat Ramble" one climax is topped by yet another as the performance reaches its conclusion. As Arvell Shaw witnessed: "Louis Armstrong and Trummy Young, those two guys . . . and Edmond Hall, that band, they could play louder than a nine man brass section of big band, you know? And it wasn't loud unpleasant, it was loud, it was just power, because those guys, they, they lived their . . . profession, and they trained for it."[23]

When the album came out, interviewer Joe Jeru commented to Armstrong how much he had enjoyed the trumpeter's Decca recording from the Crescendo Club. Armstrong was clear about his own preference: "Okay, but you can get a later album than that—*Ambassador Satch* that I made in Milano, Italy, just coming out here. It's better than the Crescendo. Dig that."[24] Though Armstrong may have been proud of his album, the reviews were mixed. *DownBeat* said, "Of Louis' three albums for Columbia in the last two years, this is the least satisfying. A large part of the reason is his band, whose weaknesses are more open-ended on stage than in a more controlled studio context. Trombonist Trummy Young's playing has become increasingly coarsened. The rhythm section is stiff, largely because of the unremitting heaviness of drummer Barrett Deems, who has not loosened up since joining Louis." About the All Stars, the review adds, "The unit never sustains one whole number in irresistible collective flight."[25] This would not be the last time the All Stars would get blasted in print. Once the "big" names—Teagarden, Hines, and Catlett—had departed, most critics focused on the diminished star power of the band rather than on the quality of the music produced. Armstrong, however, demurred. He told Sinclair Traill:

Oh yeah, that first group of All Stars was a good one all right, but I think the group I have now is the best of 'em all. It seems to me this band gets more appreciation now than the other All Stars. Some of the other Stars got so they was prima donnas and didn't want to play with the other fellows. They wouldn't play as a team but was like a basket ball side with everybody trying to make the basket. They was great musicians, but after a while they played as if their heart ain't in what they was doin'. A fella would take a solo but no-one would pay him no attention—just gaze here, look around there. And the audience would see things like that—I don't praise that kind of work y' know. Then, you get cliques in a band. Want to play that way and this way, full of that New Orleans fogeyism. I was taught to watch that kind of thing as a youngster and always to give my mind to my music before anything else. The All Stars now ain't like that and the audience appreciate the spirit in the band. As musicians they ain't any better, but a lot of people say these boys seem like they're real glad to be up there swingin' with me.[26]

As much as Armstrong enjoyed recording pop tunes, he remained proud of his working group and wanted to record the material he was playing nightly with the All Stars. "I used to go to this company that I record with, one of them there, and I used to tell them, 'Well, man, why don't you turn us loose in the studio here and let us wail?' " Armstrong recounted in July 1956. "They'd say, 'Well, that's a good idea.' And I'd say, 'It's a very good idea. If them people listen to our concerts and give us thunderous applause over these tunes we play, you know they would like to have it in their files. So why don't you just record these things, the same as we're on the stage?' 'That's nice, but we've got a few pop tunes here I think is going to be on the Hit Parade' blah blah blah." Armstrong knew the pop tunes were harming his reputation: "And that's when you look around, people are wondering, 'What happened to Louie Armstrong?' So here come another fellow, say, 'Well, you just tear out, man.' So that's why you got *Handy* albums, and oh, you got *Ambassador Satch*, you got the *Crescendo*, and they're all a-wailin'."[27]

On the day Avakian had summoned the All Stars to the studio to spruce up *Ambassador Satch*, he had them record a new rendition of "The Faithful Hussar," a song the All Stars had picked up in Germany and rocked mightily in Milan. The tune was a nineteenth-century German folk song, but Avakian saw the promise of another pop hit. Using the pseudonym "Dots Morrow," Avakian wrote silly lyrics for "The Faithful Hussar," turning it into a novelty, "Six Foot Four." Avakian's version never took off (though "The Faithful Hussar" remained for years in the All Stars' repertoire); but, as it turned out, it would play a part in the beginning of the end of Armstrong's recording relationship with Columbia. Armstrong's career had undoubtedly been boosted by his association with the label, with all signs pointing to a long and fruitful relationship. However, nothing was ever as it seemed when it came to Joe Glaser.

In one of his letters to Avakian, Glaser bragged that Armstrong was now making between $5,000 and $6,000 a night. Considering records, films, magazine features, and all else, Louis Armstrong's popularity was at an all-time high. As a result, Glaser was hesitant to saddle Armstrong with anything resembling a long-term contract: as popular as Armstrong was now, he might be even more so in years to come. A long-term contract would leave Glaser no recourse to demand more money.

Glaser, being Glaser, was never straight with Columbia about his thinking. Instead, he complained until Columbia threw up its hands. Glaser grew annoyed over a flap concerning "The Faithful Hussar" and "Six Foot Four." "The Faithful Hussar" was a public-domain composition in Germany, so Avakian planned on releasing it as such. Because he wrote the lyrics to "Six Foot Four," he intended to publish it through April Music. Glaser wanted his own ASCAP firm, International Music, to publish the two songs, listing Armstrong as composer of "Hussar" and Armstrong and Avakian as co-composers of "Six Foot Four." "We are notifying ASCAP to this effect," Glaser wrote, "that the Copyrights reside with International Music, and ask that you revise your records accordingly."[28]

Glaser was used to getting what he wanted, but Avakian refused to let him get away with anything. According to Avakian, Glaser had already approved an agreement and changed his mind after consulting his lawyer, Oscar Cohen. "I gave Joe some mild but firm hell about how he always brags that his word is so good, and here he was not only going back on his word but also his signature," Avakian wrote to his bosses at Columbia. "He simply repeated, 'It's a bad deal and Decca wouldn't never hold me to it,' so I told him I would cancel the record at once." Avakian said he'd agree to give Armstrong the copyright of the instrumental, but not of "Six

Foot Four," as that was entirely his own idea. "I am glad you concur with me that we should call Joe's bluff and withhold the record until he gets some sense," Avakian wrote.[29]

The next day, Glaser repeated to Avakian his complaint that Columbia had done nothing special for Armstrong compared to Decca—even though Columbia had produced one of Armstrong's biggest hits, Avakian had arranged for Murrow's *See It Now* segment on the trumpeter, and Armstrong had earned more than $22,000 from his Columbia recordings and $13,000 in advances—and, as a result of all this, was being featured in major magazines such as *Time* and *Newsweek*.[30]

Avakian dared Glaser to have "his accountant break out some directly comparable figures of Decca vs. Columbia over an equal period of time, and that was how we left it."[31] Avakian wrote to tell him Columbia was withholding "Six Foot Four." Glaser refused to give in, writing back immediately, "Under the situation that prevails, I have no alternative but to advise you and your associates that we will forget about recording Louis Armstrong in the future with Columbia Records."[32] Avakian stood firm and wrote to his higher-ups: "By now you know that Joe Glaser is running his last bluff on Louis Armstrong and I have called him in the nicest way I could, leaving him a chance to back down if he gets some sense . . . Unfortunately I think Joe will save face by cutting Louis' throat; i.e., keeping Louis off Columbia, which is as ridiculous a thing as Glaser ever will have done because I think he knows perfectly well that Louis badly wants to, and should be, with Columbia." Avakian now wanted Armstrong's name off both "The Faithful Hussar" and "Six Foot Four." "I hate to pull the rules on Louis, but Glaser is begging for it," Avakian wrote. "Too bad Louis is the one who is going to get badly hurt on this."[33] Convinced that Columbia's numbers would look better than Decca's and that Glaser would change his mind, all Avakian could do was wait for Glaser's accountant David Gold to report back.

As soon as the numbers came back, Glaser wrote to Avakian: "Even though you insist we received more from Columbia, the fact remains that comparatively we received considerably more from Decca, especially on our worldwide distribution. I deeply regret the fact that unless you want to give me the same terms on Louis Armstrong's music, songs, etc. that I have obtained from Decca and Victor in the past, as I advised you in my recent letter, I am not interested in any contract with Columbia."[34]

Glaser wasn't bluffing after all. Columbia offered Armstrong a lucrative deal, the terms of which Avakian proposed to his bosses: "Length of contract: 5 years' exclusivity for $250,000 advance (including talent cost of sessions), to be spread over 10 years. (I believe we gave in on our wish to make it 7 years, and I know we gave in on the idea of $200,000 for 5 years plus option for $50,000 for 2 more years.) . . . Minimum sides: 36 per year, costs deducted from advance. We also told Joe we would record as much more as was felt would be worthwhile, as we were anxious to build catalog. We said we would shoot for 48."[35]

Still Glaser would not make up his mind. Avakian kept pressing forward with ideas for Armstrong, including turning Murrow's *See It Now* piece into a full-blown feature-length film. Murrow and his producer Fred Friendly wanted more footage and planned to shoot Armstrong in Australia in April, but plans fell through. Armstrong, however, had another, more ambitious tour lined up: his first visit to London since the early 1930s. And Avakian planned on doing some recording during the tour, even though Glaser hadn't signed a contract yet.

By now Avakian was confident that things would work his way: "It is sufficiently certain that we will have a deal [by May 7]."[36] Meanwhile, for his part, Murrow made a proposal to Glaser, which Glaser related to Avakian in a letter: "I had a long meeting with Ed Murrow this morning and I am now in the process of trying to arrange Louis' dates so that he can be in Africa immediately after his English tour where Ed Murrow will photograph him."[37]

The idea of the African visit was a good one, but Armstrong had to get through the United Kingdom first. He was ready. "Man, Old Satch is raring to blow," Armstrong said at the start of the tour.[38] After a stroll through Soho with Lucille, Armstrong, along with the All Stars (now with Jack Lesberg on bass), was slated to play in London at the Empress Hall, a massive exhibition space no longer in use; it once could accommodate ten thousand people. Ten shows were scheduled, Armstrong sharing the bill with vocalist Ella Logan, one-legged tap dancer "Peg Leg" Bates, and Vic Lewis and his orchestra. The fans grew impatient with the opening acts. Ella Logan fared worst; as the *Daily Mirror* told it, they booed her seven-song set and chanted, "Where's Louis?" The other acts shortened their sets in response, according to London newspapers.

This engagement is notable as an instance when Armstrong took criticism to heart. In the *Evening Standard* on May 5, 1956, Kenneth Allsop wrote a review with the headline "Genius is rationed." "A great deal of wrapping had to be peeled off—introductory music by British Vic Lewis's band, a one-legged tap dancer and singer Ella Logan—before the pearl in the parcel was reached. And even then, although the Armstrong All-Stars played for an hour, there seemed to be more all-stars than Armstrong," Allsop wrote. And traditional jazz expert James Asman added in the *Record Mirror*, "A young enthusiast near my seat was, I could see out of the corner of my eye, gripping the side of his chair and muttering, 'This isn't New Orleans jazz! What's happened to Louis?' " Asman concluded, "The magic of Louis remained, but it was the magic of a superb showman and personality rather than that of a top rank jazz musician."[39]

Armstrong was listening. An Associated Press story later reported, "A few of Britain's highly informed jazz fans told him very plainly that he was coasting, that he was letting the rest of the band do too much playing, that the people were dishing out their shillings to hear him. 'That did it,' said Louis. 'Them cats put it to me. I couldn't let 'em down. Maybe I'll blow my teeth out, but I decided to blow more.' At his next performance he included six old New Orleans classics which require a lot of effort and bruised his lips until they looked like beaten beef steak."[40]

The major London newspapers covered Armstrong's stay daily, many focusing on his use of Swiss Kriss, now an indelible part of the Satchmo persona. It was also then that Armstrong uttered what would become one of his best-known quotes. Asked, "What do you think of folk music?" Armstrong replied, "Folk music. Why, Daddy, I don't know no other kind of music but folk music—I ain't never heard a hoss [horse] sing a song."[41] An ado ensued when twenty-five-year-old Princess Margaret attended a show at Empress Hall. "Louis (Satchmo) Armstrong broke all rules of theatrical protocol before Princess Margaret tonight. And the princess apparently loved it," Eddy Gilmore wrote in an Associated Press story picked up by newspapers the world over. " 'We've got one of our special fans in the house,' growled the gravel-voiced American trumpeter, 'and we're really gonna lay this one on for the princess.' A gasp went over the huge audience in Empress Hall. Professional performers are not supposed to refer to members of the royal family when playing before them. 'Yes, sir' said Satchmo, as the princess grinned and hugged her knees, 'we gonna blow 'em down with one of those old good ones from New Orleans—"Mahogany Hall

Stomp.'" The princess applauded with marked enthusiasm."[42] Another AP story in the *New York Times* added, "Princess Margaret began applauding with the first tune, 'Sleepy Time Down South.' Then she started to beat her feet up and down in full view of hundreds when an old New Orleans clarinetist, Edmond Hall, began to improvise on 'Clarinet Marmalade.' She applauded enthusiastically and Mr. Hall played 'High Society' as an encore."[43]

Though he was making headlines and appearing before sold-out, screaming houses, Armstrong met criticism in London, mainly from the New Orleans revival camp but also from those of the modern school who found him hopelessly out of date. In a *Sunday Times* story titled "Jazz In Turmoil: The Flight from 'Uncle Tom,'" Iain Lang wrote about Armstrong's diminishing influence on young American jazz musicians in the previous fifteen years because of his Uncle Tom–isms. But British trumpeter Humphrey Lyttelton, always one of Armstrong's staunchest supporters, came to his defense. During a May 13 performance, Lyttelton appeared on stage with a homemade crown, placing it on Armstrong and announcing, "On behalf of all British jazz musicians I would like to crown Louis Armstrong undisputed King of Jazz."

After London, Armstrong traveled the British Isles, with Lyttelton's band joining him for the Scottish leg of the tour. (Photos exist of Armstrong with a set of bagpipes.) When the tour was over, Lyttelton recounted his feelings in a column titled "Satchmo Post-Mortems." "I heard him at Nice in 1948 and in Paris last year," Lyttelton wrote. "And, considering the time allotted to him, I thought he did us better in London than at either of the previous places. I do not comprehend the criticisms about showmanship. For years, our local critics, professional and armchair, have derided British bands for their stolidness, their stiff, inhibited behavior onstage. Along comes an American group with an entirely appropriate brand of showmanship and up go the noses in the air!" Lyttelton grew even more emphatic: "As I sat in the audience at Birmingham, I was never more ashamed at having been associated with the New Orleans Revival," he wrote. "If all that we have done is to nurture a generation of jazz fans who are so ignorant as to dismiss the greatest jazz when it is laid on their doorsteps, then we deserve a heretic's fate."[44]

Armstrong then embarked on what was the most important journey of his life: a two-day trip to the Gold Coast of Africa, a British colony about to become the independent nation of Ghana. This visit was the brainchild of Edward R. Murrow, who had produced separate segments on both Armstrong and the Gold Coast for his *See It Now* television program in 1955. Murrow had wanted to go back to the Gold Coast for a follow-up special but wanted a good reason. Since he was already filming Armstrong's tour of Great Britain, it only made sense to combine the two subjects and send the trumpeter to the land of his ancestors.

Murrow wouldn't visit the Gold Coast himself; instead he sent a four-man camera crew led by Gene de Poris and Charles Mack. Because of the last-minute nature of the tour and the short amount of time allotted (Louis would arrive at nine a.m. on Thursday, May 24, and depart at noon on Saturday, May 26), it promised to be a hectic fifty-one hours, with frequent tests of will between de Poris and James Moxon, the director of the Department of Information Services and the man in charge of making Armstrong's visit a successful one. Moxon planned for Armstrong to perform an outdoor concert in the evening, but de Poris wanted it changed to the afternoon so there would be better lighting. "James said that this occasion meant too much to the people of the Gold Coast to be subordinated to purely commercial considerations," recalled Robert Raymond, a member of the Department of Information Services in the Gold Coast, who later wrote in detail about this trip. " 'In Africa,' James kept saying, 'Armstrong is more than a band leader, he is a symbol.' "[45] However, a threat from de Poris to cancel the whole affair led Moxon to switch the concert to the afternoon.

De Poris grew increasingly frantic as Armstrong's arrival approached and there still weren't any fans to welcome him at the airport. "We gotta get our welcome shots before they arrive!" he complained. "Where are these goddam fans?"[46] De Poris's frustration was for naught, as soon enough of a crowd gathered, including thirteen African bands and entertainer Ajax Bukana, dressed in tails, a top hat, and minstrel makeup. Upon his arrival, the bands joined forces to play a traditional song, "Sly Mongoose," which they transformed into a new anthem, "All for You, Louis." Others chanted, *"Na nue, nanue akwba"* ("Here is the man . . . yes sir, the man").[47] Armstrong, Trummy Young, and Edmond Hall picked up their instruments and soon figured out the song. "The crowd suddenly swarmed over the fence into the prohibited tarmac area, and the two cultures met with explosive zest," Raymond wrote. "The Americans, now with the tune between their teeth, blew as hard as anyone, led by Armstrong's swinging, driving trumpet. As the animated mass of players and singing people moved across the tarmac, gathering strength and impetus all the time, the noise and the clamour rose to the skies in the greatest paean of welcome Accra had ever known."[48]

Armstrong and the All Stars had been going nonstop since their British tour and wouldn't have much time for rest in Africa. Armstrong told the press how thrilled he was to be there. "I can stand it," he said of the crowds of people who mobbed him at the airport. "After all, my ancestors came from here and I still have African blood in me."[49] Louis and Lucille then had lunch with Premier Kwame Nkrumah. *Time* magazine reported, "The conversation: almost solely Swiss Kriss, a herbal laxative that Louis discovered from reading Gayelord (yoghurt and molasses) Hauser, and recommended insistently to the Prime Minister and all his Cabinet. He dallied so long over his Benedictine and brandy that he was late for his afternoon concert."[50]

This concert would prove historic. "To afford workers the opportunity of seeing and hearing Satchmo," George Padmore reported, "the Prime Minister declared Empire Day, which Dr. Nkrumah has abolished in the Gold Coast since coming to power in 1951, a half holiday. All government departments and private firms were closed."[51] Originally, Raymond and Moxon weren't sure of the kind of crowd Armstrong would attract, but as they reached the concert stage at the Old Polo Ground, they were shocked. "The entire area of the Old Polo Ground was covered with people," Raymond wrote. "The police later estimated it at seventy thousand. It was an overwhelming, almost frightening sight. There they were, packed solid for hundreds of yards in every direction, pushing and talking animatedly, waiting for the show to start." Before a note had been played, the police were worried. "My God, this is going to be a riot!" a white police superintendent was heard to exclaim. "We can't possibly control this crowd."[52] While Armstrong was late from his lunch with Nkrumah, a barrier separating the excited fans from the bandstand collapsed. De Poris wondered if the concert could even go on in such circumstances.

Armstrong finally arrived and hopped onstage, exclaiming "Greetings, all you cats!" to the delirious fans. After the usual theme statement of "When It's Sleepy Time Down South," Armstrong lit into a roaring version of "Ole Miss." All remained calm until Barrett Deems took an extended drum solo toward the end of the performance. "The afternoon went crazy," Raymond wrote. "The crowd surged wildly, and hurled hats and shirts into the air. Several boys leaped the barrier in front of the stand, or what was left of it, and began to jive wildly below Armstrong. As Deems smashed and battered his drums, the noise and shouting grew deafening." At the onset of this bedlam, the police superintendent ran onstage, telling Armstrong, "Stop! Stop! You must stop! They'll go mad!"[53] Armstrong then called a slow number, which calmed the crowd, but the trumpeter did not like some of the violent displays he witnessed. "The police stopped swinging their clubs at people's shins, and fell back to the fence," Raymond wrote. "James and I, standing at the side of the stage, saw that Armstrong looked grim and angry. We thought he must have been annoyed at the demonstration."

The slow blues worked for a few minutes, but once Velma Middleton hit the stage, it was pandemonium all over again. "The police below were forced to charge the crowd again, swinging their clubs fearsomely," Raymond wrote. "Armstrong immediately stopped playing. He looked angrily towards us. We could not have known it, but the scene was painfully reminiscent to Armstrong of an ugly and recent incident in Germany. A first-house audience had been reluctant to make way for the second house, and the German police had thrown them out with great brutality. Armstrong had been extremely upset by this. Now, it clearly seemed to him, violence was again being used, and this time by black men on black men. As the dust clouds thinned, and the police were revealed falling back again, Armstrong stood immobile at the front of the stage, looking down. His face was drawn and irresolute, a lifetime's struggle suddenly etched on it."[54]

To Raymond, the enthusiasm of the crowd was "good-natured," not violent. "And as we watched and listened the vast concourse became one living carpet of happy faces, dusty and sweating, but fiercely proud of that black man up there playing for them and speaking for them, the famous Mr. Satchmo." Nevertheless, the police superintendent did not trust the crowd and ordered his men to push them back. "This time the crowd was reluctant to run," Raymond recalled. "The policemen, at first half-hearted, became rattled, and determined to show their authority. A few sickening blows were heard above the pandemonium. Armstrong stopped playing. He waved an abrupt farewell, and turned from the crowd. His face was stiff with unhappiness." Armstrong was still upset as he headed to Moxon's house for another party. "All my life I tried to get away from this," he said. "Black people getting beat up. Knocked around. Always getting beat up. I saw the white folks do it, who maybe don't know any better. Now the coloured people do it to their own folk. Worse than the Nazis."[55]

Matters proceeded more smoothly as the night progressed, with Louis spending the evening with Lucille enjoying E. T. Mensah's band at the Paramount nightclub. The rest of the All Stars barely got any sleep, jamming with local musicians and being treated like heroes. (Deems, recognized for his earlier drumming, was carried shoulder-high through the markets, causing him to exclaim, "Man, this is real drummin' country!") The next morning, Armstrong and the All Stars met respectful students at a university, a touching moment captured by Murrow's camera crew. From there, it was off to the Achimota School for a display of traditional African drumming and tribal dancing, with Louis, Lucille, and the All Stars front and center. "We spend all our lives going round the world entertaining people, but this is the first time anybody ever entertained us," Armstrong said.[56] About the music he was hearing, Armstrong said, "I've heard it all down here. Every time I listened to these cats beat it out on them tribal drums I kept saying to myself, 'Satch, you're hearing the real stuff.' "[57]

It was then time for Armstrong and the All Stars to play a short set on the tribal lawn. "This was the moment that Ed Murrow must have had in mind when he set the whole affair in motion," Raymond wrote. "Would American Negro jazz make contact with the Africa whose rhythms moved it? Would the music of the Deep South, its African origins overlaid with traces of French and Spanish melody, work songs and anguish, with the gusty flavour of street parades, make any appeal to the African people?"[58]

At first the audience barely reacted, but once Armstrong played "Royal Garden Blues," a lone old man began to dance. Sensing the moment, Lucille Armstrong jumped up and joined him. "She was an odd but significant figure in her crisp New York dress, dancing with the old tribesman in his cotton robe," wrote Raymond. According to him, "This was the turning point. As the American woman and the man of Africa danced, more and more people from around the arena got up and joined in. Soon a hundred African men and women were dancing to music and rhythms that they had never known. They danced in all kinds of ways. Some adapted the tempos of their own dances to suit the music of America. Others hopped, skipped on one leg, or just stood and shook their bodies. The unifying spirit was one of sheer enjoyment."[59]

As Mack and de Poris captured the euphoria on film, something caught Armstrong's eye and caused him to stop playing. He spotted a dancer of the Ewe tribe who he said "danced and sang like my mother." He added, "When I went over to talk to her she even held her head like Mama used to hold hers, and before long I was calling her 'Mama'."[60] Armstrong couldn't hide his delight at this surprise and couldn't wait to tell everyone about it. "Jim, now I know," he told Moxon afterwards. "I just saw a woman out there jiving around, and she reminded me of my mother. She died twenty years ago. I know it now, Jim. I know I came from here, way back. At least my people did. Now I know this is my country, too. I'm coming back here some day." Back in Moxon's bungalow, Armstrong excitedly began to write the story in a series of telegrams for friends back in the United States. He was so exhilarated that, according to Raymond, "the pain and the sadness of the day before was completely blotted out."[61]

That evening, Armstrong and the All Stars performed their standard show at Accra's Opera Cinema to a packed house of two thousand people, including Nkrumah. There, Armstrong played Fats Waller and Andy Razaf's "Black and Blue," as a teary Nkrumah applauded enthusiastically.[62] Armstrong pushed himself hard for his African fans, who responded the most to his comic duets with Velma Middleton. "Weary but beaming, Armstrong mopped his face," Raymond remembered after Louis closed the show with "When It's Sleepy Time Down South." "His silk dinner suit was saturated, and his lips were swollen and raw from three and a half hours of playing." At this point, after Louis, Lucille, and the All Stars received numerous gifts onstage, Armstrong stepped up to the microphone to deliver a speech, the only one of his two-day stay in Ghana. It was typical Armstrong:

Mr. Prime Minister, and all you good people. This evening reminds me of something that happened to me when I was a little boy. My ma sent me down the yard one day to get some water from the pond. I came back quick and said Ma, I can't get water from that pond, there's a big alligator in there. So Ma said, Son, you go right back and get that water. Don't you know that old 'gator is more scared of you than you is of him? And I said Ma, if that old 'gator's more scared of me than I is of him, that water ain't fit to drink!

With that punchline, Armstrong smiled and left the stage. "After a moment's startled silence, the Opera Cinema reverberated to a mighty roar of laughter," Raymond remembered.[63] But just as Armstrong thought he was through for the night, Gene de Poris stopped to tell him they needed to film "Black and Blue" one more time while the audience was still present. Louis agreed to it, but he wasn't pleased. "When they finished they climbed wearily off the stage," Raymond wrote. "Armstrong's face was as grim and angry as it had been at the Old Polo Ground." Doc Pugh was waiting for Armstrong backstage to go through his post-show ritual, which included disrobing, applying lip salve to his swollen lips, and sponging his face and neck with spirits, not saying a word to anyone. As de Poris approached him to discuss the following morning's schedule, Armstrong cut him off with a curt "I'm finished." "The argument was short and conclusive," according to Raymond. "Armstrong had performed prodigies of endurance and performance for the past six months. There was no performer in the business of public entertainment who so consistently gave more of himself. But now he had no more to give. While his men listened silently, Armstrong told de Poris that the All Stars would play no more before they left. 'Jeez, Louis, what about the street parade!' cried de Poris. He began to rage up and down. But Armstrong, in one of his rare moments of anger, cut him down, and left the anguished little American silent."[64]

A crowd of people waited for Louis outside the theater and he wearily waved and smiled at them as he left. Then it was off to Moxon's house, where an exhausted Armstrong relaxed and spent much of the night by himself, listening to his recordings from the 1920s, which Moxon had in his collection. At lunch before departing Armstrong extolled the virtues of Swiss Kriss and gave the heavyset Moxon a lifetime supply. At the Accra airport Armstrong was met by another large crowd and with more bands playing and people singing, "All for you, Louis, all for you." "I'm coming back here, folks," Armstrong shouted to the crowd as he walked onto the plane. "This is my country now. Now I'm sure of it."[65]

With those words, the weary All Stars left for America on Saturday, May 26. (They would have to overcome their fatigue quickly, as they were to perform in Atlantic City on Monday evening, May 28.) De Poris and Mack nervously shipped their footage back to New York, hoping that it was okay. The results were more than okay and provided the backbone of Murrow's documentary, *Satchmo the Great*, released in movie theaters in 1957. It remains the definitive look at Armstrong's "Ambassador Satch" period, though for unknown reasons it has never been issued on home video or DVD in the United States. While Armstrong's life soon returned to normal, he was frequently reminded of his impact in the Gold Coast from the scores of fan letters he continued to receive at his Corona home in the ensuing years. He had especially made his mark on the many African musicians who followed his every step in what was to soon become Ghana. *Time* magazine spoke to one who summed up Armstrong's visit as, "Man, it was just very." Asked "Just very what?" the musician replied, "Just very great."[66]

CHAPTER TEN

Wrath of the Critics, 1956

WHEN ARMSTRONG and the All Stars returned to the United States from their European jaunt (now with Dale Jones back on bass), the group was looking forward to a major engagement at Medinah Hall in Chicago on June 1. The theme of the evening would be "50 Years of Jazz." Helen Hayes was to narrate a history of the music, written by *DownBeat* editor Jack Tracy, with special sets constructed by Domenico Mortellito.[1] Produced by Barry O'Daniels, the event was a benefit for the Chicago chapter of the National Multiple Sclerosis Society.[2] During the first half of the show, Armstrong and the All Stars would alternate with Hayes; during the second the band would do its normal show. Though Glaser still hadn't signed an exclusive deal with Columbia, George Avakian stuck to his plan to record the evening's music, which had been discussed as far back as February. Avakian had even suggested a repertoire he wanted Armstrong to perform. That night, however, Armstrong played many of his usual specialties, numbers that had been released by both Decca and Columbia, so Avakian had no fresh material and decided not to release an album. But in 1980, another producer at Columbia, Michael Brooks, happened to come across the recordings, striking gold. Brooks edited out Hayes's contributions and released the musical portion of the evening on a double-LP set simply titled *Chicago Concert*, capturing Armstrong arguably at his finest in the 1950s. Its sound quality is above average—though here and there Armstrong plays off-mike—and it showcases the band to superb advantage. Here was a representative instance of the joyous enter-tainment the All Stars offered night after night. Armstrong's trumpet soars on "Struttin' with Some Barbecue," "The Faithful Hussar," and "On the Sunny Side of the Street," to name just three of the twenty-six tracks. Perhaps the highlight is a five-minute version of "Bucket's Got a Hole in It," an extended treatment of a staple in which Armstrong turns up the heat on successive encores. "West End Blues" was also performed, a ver-sion rivaling *Ambassador Satch*'s.

Summertime is of course jazz-festival season, and Armstrong played at the third American Jazz Festival at Newport, Rhode Island, in early July. Again Avakian was in tow to record for Columbia, though there still was no contract. George Wein, the festival's impresario, had agreed to pay Armstrong $2,500 for his appearance. But Glaser was notified that Ava-kian had offered to reimburse the festival "and charge one-third of same to Louis' royalty account." Glaser announced that he would not stand for this. "George, I have no intention of allowing you or George Wein to charge Louis Armstrong one single penny of the money that Louis is receiving to play the Festival."[3] Perhaps sensing that the end might be near, Avakian told Glaser two weeks or so before the Newport engage-ment that "Six Foot Four" would be released, with the copyright assigned to International Music, complying with Glaser's demand. It was too late. Five days later, Glaser's response was to request from Avakian the list of tunes that Armstrong had issued through Columbia, for Norman Granz was interested in recording Armstrong for his new label, Verve, but only fresh material. Avakian's dream of an extended, exclusive contract between Armstrong and Columbia Records was dead.

But Columbia still had rights to record one more session, on July 14, the occasion being the first jazz concert ever held at New York's Lewisohn Stadium, where Armstrong and Dave Brubeck would appear. The main event of the evening would be a concert arrangement of W. C. Handy's "St. Louis Blues" with the eighty-two-year-old Handy, now blind, in attendance. The arrangement, by Alfredo Antonini, would be performed by the Stadium Symphony conducted by Leonard Bernstein. Armstrong remembered an apprehensive Bernstein saying to him, "Now when you get to this cadenza, and you get a little nervous, well, just shorten it." Armstrong had no idea what Bernstein meant by "nervous." "I said, 'Okay, daddy.' Well, I warm up at home. I hit the stage, I'm ready. From the first rehearsal on, we wailed. Well, from then on, he got confidence; it don't take long for a person to relax once they hear me go down with the arrangement. After that, he got himself straightened. After the performance he liked to shake my hand off."[4]

The arrangement was a tad ponderous, but Armstrong rarely sounded more majestic; the performance was a rousing success, bringing tears to the eyes of Handy. Avakian released it on *Satchmo the Great*, Armstrong's final Columbia album, the soundtrack of Murrow's Armstrong documentary of the same name. Three days after the New York concert, having come to terms with the end of Armstrong's association with Columbia, Avakian wrote an interoffice memo concerning the contracts with Glaser for the most recent live recordings: "If my assumptions are correct, I suggest that you hold on to what you've got in the form of one of the carbons and ask Glaser to have the other two initialed, because the situation with Armstrong and Glaser is very touchy and once we have everything nailed down, I think we are through, in capital letters and underlined thickly, with Mr. Glaser."[5] Though Avakian tried his best to play hardball with Glaser, Glaser was a man who would settle for only what he wanted, what he felt was best for his client, and nothing less. By Joe Glaser's lights, Armstrong was now simply too popular to be saddled with a long-term contract with any label. He had been stringing Avakian along better to ascertain Armstrong's market value. Henceforth Armstrong would be a free agent, his services going only to the highest bidders in the recording industry. (The rough-and-tumble Glaser did admire Avakian's pluck, however, and once introduced Avakian to a friend as "the only man to have ever hung up on me—and lived!")

The premature ending of Armstrong's partnership with Columbia Records still stands as one of the biggest disappointments of Armstrong's career. The music he made in his two years with the label stands among the best he ever waxed. And Avakian was only getting started; his big plan was to do an album with Armstrong's trumpet fronting Duke Ellington's orchestra, which returned to Columbia in early 1956 and was also represented by Glaser. Avakian had both men's approval and even had begun selecting repertory for the album, dreaming of the sound of Armstrong's trumpet and Ellington's outfit swinging together on pieces such as "Stompy Jones" and "Tight Like This." Glaser continued to play hard to get, putting a ridiculously high price tag on both clients' services. When Glaser put an end to Armstrong's recording for the label, he pulled the plug on this potential summit meeting. According to Avakian, it was the only time he ever saw tears in Armstrong's eyes, but Armstrong told him there was nothing he could do if Glaser already had said no.

Stories like that easily justify the common line of thought that Joe Glaser was simply a villain in Louis Armstrong's career, controlling him like a slave and working him too hard with only one thing in mind—gaining the maximum amount of money at all times—and with no patience for potentially landmark artistic ideas such as the ones Avakian presented if the cash wasn't there. But, the Armstrong-Glaser relationship was a little more complex than it might seem at surface level. Glaser offered Armstrong something very important: freedom to never worry about money, to just concentrate on performing his music. As Armstrong's popularity grew and Armstrong made Glaser more money, he wasn't afraid to spend some of it on himself and his friends. Correspondence survives such as this telegram Armstrong sent Glaser in 1955:

> HAVE BALLED AWHILE SINCE CHECKING AT THE MOULIN ROUGE AND OVER SPORTED MYSELF SO BAD UNTIL MY SALARY FOR THIS ENGAGEMENT WON'T BE HELP AT ALL. LET [ME] HAVE AS MUCH AS YOU CAN IN CASH. TAKE IT OUT DURING MY EUROPEAN TOUR. HURRY DAD. SEND FAST. LOVE—SATCHMO[6]

According to Ernie Anderson, who knew both men well, this was not an uncommon occurrence. "We were on the road one night in Chicago when Louis decided to prove to me once and for all that he could get a fair deal out of Joe Glaser," Anderson wrote. "He told me that he was going to do something that he often did when he thought Joe was taking advantage of him." Armstrong decided to call Glaser—at four o'clock in the morning. "Then I heard Joe's voice," Anderson wrote. "He had just been awakened from a deep sleep. When he recognized Louis's voice on the phone he sounded terrified. 'What's the matter?' He was shouting, but you could hear panic in his voice. Louis was calm as usual. 'Nothing's the matter, Pops. But you know we ran up such a big score over there in Europe that I thought it was time for you to send me a little taste,' Louis was saying. Joe, who had seemed out of control at first, now was trying to placate Louis. 'Yes, of course,' he was saying. 'I'll see what I can do. I'm sure we can fix that up.' The next day Louis had a telegram for $2,500."[7]

Because Armstrong let Glaser have final say over his bookings and matters such as the handling of the Columbia contract, he did so knowing that Glaser would cater to his own demands. A letter to his boss dated August 2, 1955, also spells out the nature of their working relationship vividly. In it, Armstrong agreed to a lucrative overseas tour, but only if Glaser compensated Armstrong's mistress "Sweets" Preston, who Armstrong believed was carrying his baby (she wasn't). Armstrong also wanted payments made on three cars, those of his secretary Velma Ford, his good friend Stuff Crouch, and Lucille's sister and brother-in-law. He wrote slyly to Glaser in his original, rhythmic way of typing: "But Seriously Mr. Glaser there's one thing that's going to be a big *drag*—And that is these Personal bills of mine. Which runs up to $1100.00 per month. I don't care how soon we leave—where we're going. Just if you'll, Personally, Pay these Bills while I am over seas, It's alright with me." Examining such a letter, as well as the aforementioned 1954 letter regarding marijuana, it's clear that Armstrong was just as much in control of Glaser as vice versa. At the close of the letter, Armstrong wrote words Glaser probably knew all too well: "Now that I have made myself very Clear. Book Anywhere—Anytime." As Thomas Brothers has written about this letter, "The anecdote allows Armstrong to say as directly as he can that he has chosen Glaser, not the other way around. No matter to what extent Armstrong may agree to give up business control as a means of coping with a racist society, he will control ultimately the hiring and firing of his manager."[8]

As Armstrong's popularity grew, the negativity of the critiques of him intensified. Reviewing the Lewisohn Stadium show, John S. Wilson, a frequent detractor of Armstrong's in this period, savaged the trumpeter: "Saturday night's audience at Lewisohn Stadium heard the same program that he has played several times in New York. They applauded it enthusiastically, attempted to clap in time with one number and even made a brief attempt to dance in the aisles. Unfortunately, the stimulus for all this was rather shoddy jazz, although it may have had its merits as vaudeville."[9] Wilson concluded: "There is no question of Mr. Armstrong's merits as an entertainer. It is natural that audiences in all countries should be drawn to him, just as the one at Lewisohn Stadium was. But, except for occasional instances, it would be misleading if the antics of Mr. Armstrong and his colleagues were to be accepted as representative of well-played jazz."[10]

In August, Harold Lovette of *Metronome* added the race factor in a scathing attack on Armstrong: "Throughout the entire history of jazz there has been a continuous struggle for acceptance and understanding in addition to the fact that the race angle has kept back its progress. Now 'uncle' Louis adds insult." Lovette's purpose was to put Armstrong's performance history into perspective, but still he could not resist a dig at his trumpet playing: " 'Pops' came along when 'rastus' showmanship was demanded from jazz artists and to some extent it holds true today. I definitely do not condone this type of performance but it is to be understood that Louis is a product of his time. But as trumpet players go at this point, I am of the opinion that Louis is a much better singer." Lovette saved his most biting remark for last: "It is elementary that to understand contemporary jazz you either must be a musician of [a] certain caliber or your appreciation must be developed jazz-wise. Louis has not had the time to do either, he has been too busy being a 'Tom.' "[11]

This came in the wake of a controversy promoted by the black press in early July 1956. A story was sent out to many black papers by the Associated Negro Press titled "Satchmo Plays, Negroes Barred in Indianapolis." The article stated that Armstrong had recently played a public dance in Indianapolis supposedly open to all. But many blacks had been turned away at the door, the justification being, according to the venue's white management, that they were not members of the Indiana Roof Club, which sponsored the event. The article referred to the trumpeter: "[Armstrong] stated that he 'wouldn't hesitate to play before Jim Crow audiences.' Asked that if he had been informed in advance that the ballroom operated on a segregated basis, would he still have appeared, he answered, 'Yes I would have played. I play any place my manager books me.' "[12] Uncle Tom indeed.

But Armstrong never made those remarks, and was forced immediately to issue a rebuttal, which appeared in the black press, as well as in *DownBeat*. According to a *Pittsburgh Courier* article, "a very indignant and a very warm" Armstrong called the paper's office personally to clear up the matter. "Nothing could be further from the truth," Armstrong said. "What are they trying to do? I don't expect these things, so I never question owners of dance halls or my manager about the racial pattern of places I am contracted to play. I certainly didn't expect to run into this kind of business in Indiana. The fella who wrote that story put words in my mouth I never spoke." Armstrong continued, "I have been with Joe Glaser too many years to worry about where I play and for whom. He is as keen on the race question as I am and goes to great lengths to keep the record straight. Somehow I have always been a greater attraction among whites than my own people, a thing which has always disturbed me. I have to love them and what they stand for to love myself. After all, it's no secret what I am. I have my own ideas about racial segregation and have spent half of my life breaking down barriers through positive action and not a lot of words. It's high time that as a race we become more concerned with what a man does, instead of misquotes to make headlines out of what one is supposed to have said. Certainly, I am concerned about what happens to my people, but I am trying to do something about it and not talk for headlines."[13]

In retrospect, it was probably road manager Frenchy Tallerie who was responsible for the contested quote, which contradicted Armstrong's feeling about segregation, which could be viewed in a decision he had just made about performing in New Orleans. The All Stars had played a two-week engagement at the Absinthe House there in February 1955 but that would be their final trip to Armstrong's hometown for quite some time. After the historic *Brown* vs. *Board of Education* decision of 1954 desegregated schools around the country, the notoriously segregated New Orleans rebelled at the end of that year by passing multiple "draconian statutes that further codified longstanding Jim Crow practices," Jonathan Mark Souther wrote. In July 1956, according to Souther, a statute was passed "which barred interracial contact in any form of public accommodations. . . . The segregationist measure even forbade the longstanding practice of black and white musicians sharing the stage in bars and clubs."[14]

This was too much for Armstrong, who had grown disgusted by the city's segregationist policies. The All Stars had been an integrated band from day one, something that Armstrong had always prided himself on. "Ain't nobody gonna call me intolerant," he said when asked about it in May 1956.[15] Now the band found itself under the heel of segregation. Bitter, Armstrong vowed never to return until the city changed its racial stance. In a 1958 interview that reunited him with his old bassist Pops Foster, the topic of segregation came up. Foster said, "I played around New Orleans in mixed bands, for years. It wasn't like today, like it is in New Orleans now." Asked to elaborate, Armstrong jumped in and answered, "Since [1956], in New Orleans, they don't want white and Negro musicians playing together. All I can say is, the people who made those laws, they don't know anything about music. Because in music, it doesn't make any difference. I don't run into much trouble with segregation, 'cause I don't go where I'm not wanted. And—please don't take this out, I'm going to tell this straight—I don't go to New Orleans . . . no more."[16]

Though Armstrong prided himself in his integrated band, there's no doubt that the negative publicity about performing in front of a segregated audience in Indianapolis only served to worsen his standing in the black community. As he himself stated, Armstrong was now a bigger attraction with white audiences. So when he showed up in Indianapolis and saw no blacks in the crowd, he had no reason to assume that segregation was at fault. His audience was changing, and nothing he could do or say could stanch the diminishment of his black fan base.

A few days after the Indianapolis incident, Armstrong sat down for a series of interviews with the Voice of America. The point was to have Armstrong play his favorite records—both his own and those of other musicians—and talk about the music. Armstrong's selections included "Shine" and "Black and Blue," which led to a discussion not only of the titles themselves but of the racial sensitivity of the black community. "Boy, people, you know, especially our people, the Negroes, they'd probably get insulted a little for no reason at all," Armstrong said. He even mentioned the "Sleepy Time Down South" uproar of 1951, saying that in its aftermath, "I'm so glad that my people began to dig that, because they get a little too [offended] over the smallest things and I think it's bad."[17] Armstrong was alluding to a recent incident involving Nat "King" Cole, who had been beaten onstage by four whites during a concert in Birmingham, Alabama. The black press had not warmed to Cole's plight. As Ingrid Monson has written: "Rather than eliciting sympathy from the African American press, Nat Cole, who was not badly hurt, was roundly denounced for having accepted an engagement in a segregated theater to begin with." A cartoon even appeared in a black newspaper depicting "Nat Cole as a minstrel figure smiling and tossing bills and coins into the air while seated on a pile of money." Like Armstrong, Cole claimed that his management made the bookings and he didn't know which venues were segregated, but the *Amsterdam News* remained unconvinced by his explanation: "We've heard that one before from too many colored performers."[18] Some establishments in Harlem even started banning Cole's records.

"Now, can you tell me why those boys up in Harlem, whoever they were that took King Cole's records off the Piccolo just because they think they should take it off?" Armstrong asked. "Well, who are they? I mean, we're the people who bring customers in their place and put 'em on the map and spend our good money in the place and they're the first ones who try to push you down." As a hard-working entertainer, Armstrong took the slight against Cole personally: "You've done struggled all these years to accomplish something on your instrument or something and here comes some raggedy cat, just because, you know, they're all riding on the bandwagon of that race mess and things and he ain't thinking about nothing but to try and pull you back where, if he just leave you alone, you'd do more for him with your instrument. You see what I'm talking about? So, if we just go on and just enjoy this good music and forget about a whole lot of malice and things—I notice the colored newspapers, the minute a little minor thing happen to a musician or one of those actors or something, why, you'd never seen such headlines, when they should take into it and stand by this man . . . We only have a few in our race that's on top in this music game, and I think if we get together and stick by each other, we could have a few more." Armstrong's words would fall on deaf ears for now: his appearance in the Zulu Parade, the "Sleepy Time" fracas, the persistent eye rolling and mugging were not about to be forgiven by the black community or certain white critics. Armstrong's detractors could not have felt more self-righteous when the film *High Society* opened in the summer of 1956, featuring the mugging, eye-rolling persona they were quick to denounce.

Vis-à-vis his denigration, Armstrong was growing testy in the summer of 1956. After a one-nighter, he agreed to do an interview in his hotel room with Joe Jeru and Maynard Johnson, an interview that survives on one of Armstrong's private tapes housed at the Louis Armstrong House Museum. Perhaps he was getting tired of the negative reviews and the "race mess," for when one of the interviewers asks Armstrong about "progressive" music, Armstrong grows petulant: "Well, that's what I'm trying to find: what is progressive music? Now you explain what is progressive music. We were just taught to play *good* music. Now what would be progressive music? A whole lot of stiff arrangements the untrained ear can't understand. What's any more progressive than my 'Blueberry Hill,' 'La Vie en Rose,' 'C'Est Si Bon,' what's any more progressive?"[19] Even as Armstrong speaks, the interviewer sounds flustered. He tries to explain himself, but Armstrong steamrolls right over him, bristling at the notion that his music is old-fashioned.

On the evening of August 15, Armstrong and the All Stars found themselves at the Hollywood Bowl performing at a concert produced by Norman Granz. It was the first time Granz and Armstrong had worked together since the Benny Goodman debacle of 1953. Granz showed off his stable of stars: Ella Fitzgerald, Oscar Peterson, Art Tatum, Roy Eldridge, Illinois Jacquet, Ray Brown, Buddy Rich, and others all performed on the same bill with Armstrong. Armstrong always thrived when competing with other legends, and he responded that night by blowing with fearsome ferocity, especially on transcendent encore versions of "Ole Miss" and "Bucket's Got a Hole in It."

The very next day, moved as he was by the Hollywood Bowl event, Granz found himself recording a full-length album for his Verve label, featuring Armstrong and Fitzgerald together again. The night before, these two legends of jazz singing had performed two numbers: "Undecided," highlighted by scorching trumpet at a demanding tempo, and "You Won't Be Satisfied," a remake of a song from a 1946 Decca session. Granz was Fitzgerald's manager at this time, and would oversee the "Songbook" series just beginning on Verve, which found "the First Lady of Song" tackling dozens of compositions by the Gershwins, Cole Porter, Irving Berlin, Duke Ellington, and others. But while getting the Oscar Peterson Trio and Fitzgerald in was relatively easy, finding free time in Armstrong's schedule was always a challenge.

"The logistics were always difficult, on almost all of Louis's sessions with Ella, because Louis traveled so much," Granz said. "I didn't have that much time. I think literally I might have [had] only a day or two days to do an album, which wasn't Joe's [Glaser's] problem. He simply said, 'Well, he's available June the tenth. You can have him June the tenth.' "[20]

With so little time to record Armstrong, there was even less to prepare.

"There was no preparation whatsoever," Granz said. "Again, those were economic arrangements with Glaser, and I didn't have any rehearsals with Louis or certainly not with Peterson [and his group]. That was all improvised, all 'head' [arrangements]."[21] One thing that had to be worked out was the keys the songs would be played in. Because Fitzgerald had greater range than Armstrong, most songs were played in Armstrong's key or featured quick modulations. Armstrong plays scant trumpet on the date, perhaps from exhaustion caused by his life on the road, but what he does play is great, especially considering his unfamiliarity with the material.

Ella and Louis—featuring a hard-swinging "Can't We Be Friends?" (arguably the best song they ever recorded), a breezy "They Can't Take That Away From Me," touching harmonizing on "Stars Fell on Alabama," a joyous "Cheek to Cheek," and a tender "The Nearness of You"—appeared to tremendous éclat. *DownBeat* gave the record five stars, in a glowing review: "*Ella and Louis* is one of the very, very few albums to have been issued in this era of the LP flood that is sure to endure for decades." The review goes on: "The exaggerated tooth-shaking of the lyrics is minimized by Louis here since the context is musically adult, and the clowning doesn't fit. The material, moreover, is superior to much of the dross (not counting the jazz standards) he usually sings. As a result of the fact that he hasn't sung many of these songs for years, the challenge awakens the whole musician in Louis; and because the melodies and lyrics are fresh to him, there are no pat routines for him to fall into. Hearing him here is a joy; and hearing him interweave horn and voice with Ella is often euphoria."[22]

Armstrong continued to be a constant presence in the news in fall 1956. The jazz press was still at war over his persona and musicianship, even as movie critics raved about his performance in *High Society*, while the September issue of *Look* displayed a photo spread on Armstrong, calling him "Mr. Jazz." And, yes, his fascination with laxatives continued to draw attention. *Ebony* reported: "Anyone who meets Satchmo cannot escape his ardent sales talk. While working on the movie, *High Society*, he tried to convert Bing Crosby, Grace Kelly, and Frank Sinatra. He also sent a copy to President Eisenhower. 'I told the President,' he recalls, grinning, 'to do it the Satchmo way and he'd feel ten years old. He wrote back and said as President he isn't supposed to feel like he's ten years old.' " Around the time Armstrong filmed *The Glenn Miller Story* in 1953, he had weighed

268 pounds, but by mid-1956 he was down to 170, thanks to his diet, based on a teaspoonful of Swiss Kriss nightly, a dose of the antacid Bisma Rex twenty minutes after every meal, and fresh orange juice. "Gas, man, that's what's causing the deaths today," Armstrong was quoted as saying. "You got to get rid of the gas."[23] Soon after, Armstrong even gave a speech on the subject at an unusual venue: "I went down to the Stanford Research Institute and gave 'em a speech on my diet chart. Everybody's been looking for a cure for cancer and nobody's found it yet so they decided to hear about my diet." Stroking his abdomen, Armstrong added, "You got the right diet, you're all right down here. No ulcers, no cancer."[24] Armstrong would give his diet chart to anyone he met. When a young William Kennedy interviewed him in 1956, Armstrong gave him a copy of the chart and wrote on it, "P.S. My slogan. The more you shit, the thinner you'll git. No shit."[25]

Armstrong ended 1956 with one more trip overseas, a one-night stand in London on December 18. He was to play in a charity concert at Royal Festival Hall together with a British symphony orchestra to reprise Armstrong's successful concert version of "St. Louis Blues" at the Lewisohn Stadium concert. Instead of the All Stars, Armstrong would be accompanied by top British jazz musicians, including drummer Jack Parnell and pianist Dill Jones. Joe Glaser wired *Melody Maker* to announce that Armstrong would play the charity concert for free. "Have cancelled Louis's bookings," Glaser wrote, "so that he, his personal valet and I can leave here on December 16 in time to rehearse for the benefit on the 18th. Louis and I accept your kind invitation and consider it an honor to appear for the Lord Mayor of London's Hungarian Relief Fund."[26] Of course, Glaser had Armstrong working right up to the minute they left, performing for three thousand fans at the Mosque in Newark, New Jersey, on December 15.

When Armstrong met Royal Philharmonic Orchestra conductor Norman Del Mar at a rehearsal, though, things did not get off to a good start. Dill Jones remembered:

> We were a little bit self-conscious, naturally, during the rehearsal in the morning with Louis. And there was Mr. Norman Del Mar, the great conductor, a magnificent musician. A rather large, portly man. Norman Del Mar sat down at the piano and played this score of Leonard Bern-

stein's [sic] "St. Louis Blues," and Louis was playing along with him, you see? Anyway, they were halfway through this "St. Louis Blues" when suddenly Mr. Del Mar says, "Stop, please. Stop. Mr. Armstrong," he said, "I perceive at letter H you have here forty-eight bars, and you're playing anything but forty-eight bars, Mr. Armstrong. What's it going to be? Forty-eight or one hundred and forty-eight?" And with that Louis came around the piano. I was sitting . . . right by them and [Armstrong] looked over Norman Del Mar's shoulder and says, "We'll play 'em both, Fats."[27]

Their relationship would not improve. In addition to "St. Louis Blues," symphonic versions of "When It's Sleepy Time Down South," "The Lonesome Road," "Shadrack," and "Nobody Knows the Trouble I've Seen" had been arranged, but regarding "Trouble" Armstrong told Del Mar, "I don't dig you. Something ain't right. At the end of this bar I'm supposed to go home—like this." He blew a quarter-note G loud and clear. "Right? Well, these other cats, why, they're going *bom-bom*," he said, probably referring to two eighth-notes. "They're a *bom* behind, or I'm a bom ahead." Del Mar replied, "I'm sorry. That's the way it's written here. There's no time to reorchestrate it." "Reorchestrate nothin'!" Armstrong came back. "Let's roll it that way—grab it, boys, we're off!" After playing the song, Del Mar complained, "You finished before we did." Armstrong simply smiled and replied, "Don't matter at all, at all."[28]

The night of the concert ran no smoother. The evening began with a speech delivered by Sir Laurence Olivier in which he condescended: "Now listen to this noble character—for that's what he is—play you some rather basic music."[29] Del Mar started the concert by conducting the Royal Philharmonic through Brahms's *Tragic* Overture and Stravinsky's *Firebird* Suite. Armstrong then came onstage to do "St. Louis Blues" and a few more numbers. Robert Musel wrote: "After each number the crew-cut college crowd and the rock-'n'-rollers roared their approval. The mink-and-tails set joined in and soon the joint was jumping."[30]

Decades later, recordings of the evening's performance have turned up, and though the sound quality is far from perfect, Armstrong's brilliance shines. His trumpet never sounded at once more fragile and triumphant than it does on "Lonesome Road." He swings mightily with the British musicians on "Royal Garden Blues" and "Mahogany Hall Stomp," among others. But there is confusion now and then because the band in lieu of the All Stars was unaccustomed to the repertoire. Armstrong is adept at covering up imperfections, as when the drummer forgets to play a four-bar drum tag on "St. Louis Blues." Silence ensues until Armstrong, waiting for the appropriate four bars, storms in with a concluding trumpet phrase that calls everybody home, ending on a sky-high concert F.

While the surviving tapes reveal Armstrong in peak form, playing for an adoring crowd, contemporaneous reports focused on the combustible relationship between Armstrong and a visibly annoyed Del Mar, who eventually began trying to sabotage Armstrong. As Armstrong finished singing "When It's Sleepy Time Down South," Del Mar continued to hold the final note so long as to make it seem that Armstrong had stopped singing prematurely. And toward the end of a short All Stars–like set with the British small group, Armstrong told Del Mar he was not allowed to resume the classical portion of the program "until we finish."[31] As the applause grew louder and longer, Armstrong played a chilling version of "West End Blues," a piece he pulled out only for special occasions. In all, according to one report, "Armstrong did five encores while the Duke of Kent, the Earl and Countess of Harewood, the Hon. Gerald Lascelles and hundreds of others applauded for more." Olivier said, "If anyone came into this Royal Festival Hall with any anti-American feeling, then, Louis, you've blown it away."[32] Indeed, thirty seconds survive of the crowd, in bedlam, chanting, "We want Louis!"

After his five encores, Armstrong's concert segment ended before the concluding items on the program: Del Mar's interpretation of Liszt's Hungarian Rhapsody No. 2, and remarks by the Lord Mayor of London, Sir Cullum Welch. "In the event," Max Jones wrote, "neither of these performances took place. The majority of the people there had come to hear Armstrong. They had heard a lot of him, but not enough. They clapped and stamped and shouted. Minute after minute the uproar continued. At first conductor Del Mar smiled tolerantly. The smile gave way to a pained expression."[33] Del Mar waited a good five minutes for the cheers and applause to die down before giving up and storming off the stage. Afterward, he said, "I terminated the concert because it had ceased to be a concert and had become a shambles." Always the professional, Armstrong was put off by Del Mar's behavior: "The thing the professor should have done was to stop the cats shoutin' and play 'God Save the Queen' or something."

In an effort to calm the crowd, Armstrong returned to the stage for another encore, but was stopped by impresario S. A. Gorlinsky. "He tore the horn out of my hand and said it was too late," Armstrong said.[34] Nevertheless, Armstrong was immensely proud of his achievement that night. According to Max Jones, "Armstrong felt it as a kind of climax to his career. He worked magnificently, quickly gaining in confidence and allowing his natural manner [to] intrude on what had been, up to then, a 'serious' musical evening. The clash was felt more in the matters of show-manship, approach and audience response than in the music itself. Louis with strings has always sounded delightful, and though there were times when he and the orchestra got away from each other, they managed to fin-ish together—more or less. It was a triumph for Louis and he should have been brought back as the customers insisted."[35]

When Armstrong returned to the United States, he had a massive record-ing project awaiting him: a musical "autobiography" he had started before the London trip and one that would last into the New Year. Producer Milt Gabler, who hadn't worked with Armstrong in more than a year, set about re-recording for Decca classic Armstrong from Okeh, Columbia, and Vic-tor. Gabler's thought was that if a motion picture on Armstrong's life were ever produced, its soundtrack would require new, clean recordings. Hav-ing sold Joe Glaser on the idea, he aimed for ideal recording circumstances for Armstrong. Gabler made sure Armstrong was well rested. "I told Joe Glaser that I wanted him to book Louis in New York exclusively for the sessions, and not at Basin Street East (which then was the Armstrong performance venue in New York)," said Gabler. "I wanted the All Stars off in the evening, not from two to five in the afternoon, as customary, with them having to work at night. This way I could book them from seven to ten, when it was a natural thing, giving the guys time enough to have had dinner and get to the studio and be relaxed and not having to think about going to work later."[36]

Still, the idea for *Satchmo: A Musical Autobiography* was a risky one from the start. It found Armstrong re-creating more than forty songs he had originally recorded in the twenties and thirties. Nearly every time Armstrong waxed a record in his youth, it had been greeted as a "masterpiece." But it was now 1956, and although he was still blowing powerful trumpet and singing better than ever to sold-out audiences, it seemed virtually impossible that he would be able to improve upon or even match his earlier achievements.

It was Gabler who chose the songs to be performed. Sy Oliver was brought in to arrange the re-creations of Armstrong's big-band work. The arrangements of the original recordings were copied, as were Louis's original solos, but as Gabler recalled, "Sy was funny; he put the solo notation down on the lead sheet that was in front of Louis on the music stand, and wrote on it, 'Go for yourself.' "[37] Bob Haggart, bassist and arranger for the Bob Crosby big band, handled the new arrangements of the celebrated Hot Five and Hot Seven recordings. Studio musicians were added to Armstrong's All Stars, which now featured a new bass player, Squire Girsback. Girsback became better known as Squire Gersh when, as Dan Morgenstern points out, "Louis shortened his name to something easier to pronounce!"[38] Gersh was born in San Francisco and worked with Lu Watters's band, which specialized in New Orleans revival music, including original arrangements by Jelly Roll Morton and King Oliver, among others. He joined the All Stars in October 1956 and would remain for fifteen months.

With the material in place, the arrangements written, and the musicians picked, recording started in Decca's New York City studios on December 11 with a big-band date arranged by Oliver. The six songs recorded that day are taken mainly at a slow-to-medium tempo, but Armstrong turns each into a classic performance. It was inevitable that critics would compare these versions to their originals to the disadvantage of the former, but to my ears many of the new versions are superior. Highlights of the first day included the trumpet solos on "If I Could Be with You" and "Lazy River" and the vocals on "I Can't Believe That You're in Love with Me." An extended version of "On the Sunny Side of the Street" is arguably Armstrong's greatest since his 1934 original recording. From the passionate two-chorus vocal (Oliver's reed writing sounds like a choir of angels) through the climactic-high-note trumpet solo, the performance is astounding. All six songs are classic late-period Armstrong, harbingers of what was to come. One would be remiss not to mention, among the explosion of highlights, Armstrong's stunning slow version of "When You're Smiling." As Dan Morgenstern wrote, "To swing at this almost static pace takes some doing."[39] Yet after an ebullient vocal (you can hear him smile) he takes off on a trumpet solo that surely ranks as among the very best of his career. He doesn't deviate far from the melody, but the pure sound of his tone in the upper register is breathtaking. "If you compare the 1950's recording of 'When You're Smiling' with the famous one from [1929], I think there's no comparison. They're both magnificent, but that second one is mind-blowing," says critic Gary Giddins in the documentary *The Wonderful World of Louis Armstrong.* "It's the most gorgeous sound on the trumpet I've ever heard." "I don't know who can play that now," says Stanley Crouch in the same documentary. "I mean right now, forty years later, I don't know anybody who can play that. But the sound he got and the intensity and he plays way in the upper register for a long time with great expressiveness, not just high notes . . . it's staggering."

And of course there are: the trumpet work on "That's My Home"; the pleading vocal on "I Surrender Dear"; the wild scatting on "Song of the Islands" and "Hotter Than That"; the powerful blues playing on "Gully Low Blues" and "Knockin' a Jug"; the joyous "You Rascal You"; the daring, almost modernized "Wild Man Blues"; the dazzling, sure-footed closing cadenza on "Exactly Like You"; the trumpet obbligatos behind Velma Middleton's blues songs; the soulful, operatic "Dear Old Southland"; and the scintillating "King of the Zulus," comparable to the sublimity of "When You're Smiling." This part of the *Autobiography* contained some of Armstrong's most inspired blowing of the decade.

Needless to say, not every one of the forty-three songs recorded in little more than a month's time is a masterpiece. Middleton's four vocals were meant to re-create Armstrong's classic recordings with blues singers such as Bessie Smith and Ma Rainey, but her joyful voice did not fit the material. Some of the small-band song recreations are too Dixielandish here and there; and the remake of "Potato Head Blues" fares badly in comparison with the original. What is more, Deems sticks mainly to playing closed hi-hat cymbals and snare drums, most likely at Gabler's suggestion, as many of the early tunes did not feature drums. This imprisons Deems, and as a result, rhythm occasionally suffers (some of Haggart's arrangements survive at the Louis Armstrong House Museum and they clearly state "closed hi-hat" on Deems's part). But these are minor complaints in relation to the overall greatness of the project, an astonishing document of Louis Armstrong's artistry in the 1950s.

When the boxed set was released, while some carped about the insufficiency of the new versions in relation to their originals, for the most part reviews were enthusiastic. "There are mediocre pieces, but the album also contains some of his most durable work," wrote Whitney Balliett. "On tunes like 'Lazy River,' 'Song of the Islands,' 'If I Could Be with You,' and 'I Surrender Dear,' Armstrong plays and sings with a life and ease that at times remind one of his greatest period."[40]

The *Autobiography* is a definitive document of Armstrong's powers as a trumpet player in the 1950s. Armstrong's style had changed over the years. He had played quicker runs in his youth, and his love of opera always had led him to the dramatic glisses and suspended high notes that started creeping into his playing by the 1930s. As he got older, the change in his style can be compared to that of a young baseball pitcher who starts out by throwing nothing but fastballs, but, as he matures and loses a couple of miles off his velocity, begins mixing in curveballs and changeups to get the job done, perhaps to even greater effect. Armstrong was always among the most uninhibited jazz musicians, especially at quick tempos, where his almost free-floating sense of time was preternatural. He had begun practicing this skill in the 1920s, and it would remain constant for the rest of his career. Never one to just tear through eighth-note patterns, Armstrong played with a complete rhythmic freedom over the beat that most of today's jazz musicians would be hard pressed to match. He taught jazz musicians to swing, and even had the rare ability to swing quarter-notes directly on the beat without making it sound stiff.

Also, as he got older, Armstrong became a better technical trumpeter, something pointed out to me by esteemed trumpeter Randy Sandke after listening to some examples from *A Musical Autobiography*.[41] His tone got bigger as he got older, which is clear from a comparison of his 1929 and 1956 versions of "When You're Smiling." His range also improved. On his famous 1929 recording of "I Can't Give You Anything but Love," Armstrong cracks the final high concert E-flat on both takes, barely even producing the pitch. But on the 1956 remake, he hits the high E-flat and *holds* it dramatically. In discussing *Autobiography*, trumpeter Dave Whitney has written, "The years had given Louis more power and maturity to his playing. His work in the upper register was more impressive. (The earlier solos were daring and revolutionary, but sometimes he just skated by)."[42] Wynton Marsalis has called Armstrong's later solos "virtually impossible to learn."[43]

The high form of his trumpet playing and voice on *Autobiography* carried over into Armstrong's next project, *Louis and the Angels,* recorded immediately after the *Autobiography* sessions. Armstrong and Sy Oliver waxed twelve more tracks featuring the trumpeter on a variety of songs with a common theme: angels. A listener gets the opportunity to hear the great man improvise on "Angela Mia" and "I Married an Angel" and charmingly sing tunes like "When Did You Leave Heaven?" and "A Sinner Kissed an Angel." As trumpeter, he takes flight on "Angel" and "The Prisoner's Song." Oliver's studio band for these sessions was augmented by strings, harp, and a choir. The resulting album—not one George Avakian would likely have made at Columbia—was brimming with the kind of material that had most jazz critics at the time (and probably some of today's crop) scratching their heads. But even with younger musicians calling him "Uncle Tom" and older critics deriding his live performances, Armstrong simply shrugged it all off. "As long as they spell my name right and keep it before the public," he would tell his friends. He would often clip negative articles for his scrapbooks, but he rarely complained publicly. But three events the following year, 1957, would provide evidence that Louis Armstrong was not a person to be messed with.

CHAPTER ELEVEN

Showdown, 1957

IN THE MIDDLE of a tour of sixty one-nighters, Louis Armstrong and the All Stars pulled up to the Chilhowee Park Administration Building in Knoxville, Tennessee, on February 19, 1957. Just another gig—or so they thought. The audience was segregated: two thousand whites and one thousand blacks. But it is possible that amidst the routine and rigors of the tour Armstrong didn't even notice at first. He was putting on his typically entertaining show—performing his big hits, including his newest, "Mack the Knife"—when, in the middle of "Back o' Town Blues," he and everyone else heard and felt an explosion. A stick of dynamite had been thrown from a passing car over a ten-foot fence toward the auditorium, creating a four-foot hole two hundred feet away from where Armstrong was playing. The *New York Post* reported, "Police Lt. Ross Sims, cruising in a squad car two miles away, said he felt the blast. A woman who lives a half mile from the scene said the force was great enough to cause a headache."[1] Armstrong responded by joking with the audience, "That's all right, folks, it's just the phone." A few people got up and went outside to see what the trouble was, but Armstrong continued to play. "Man, I'll play anywhere they'll listen," Armstrong said after the show, unaffected.[2] The White Citizens' Council in Knoxville was blamed, as it had recently protested the use of the Chilhowee Park Administration Building for concerts attended by both races, even if segregated. Armstrong was unfazed by the possible racial motivation: "Man, the horn don't know anything about it." He went on touring the South, but deep down a bitterness was seething.

Soon after, journalist David Halberstam spent a few days with the band to get a sense of what it was like to tour with Armstrong. Halberstam wrote kind words about all the All Stars, "but it was Armstrong himself who surprised me. I had gone to Atlanta half prepared to write a twilight-of-career piece about him. It's perfectly true that he paces himself carefully, but the essence of the trumpet is all there, still able to touch a man in almost any mood; and the voice, deep and gravelly, is still expressive, light and flirtatious or deep and sentimental."[3]

Halberstam quoted Trummy Young: "He still projects something special . . . I get a spark playing with him that I never had with any other trumpet man. He gets the feeling for his music over, not only to the audience but to his band as well . . . The guy does it every night, and I think he's got a bigger tone, a lot fuller than before."[4]

Halberstam experienced firsthand the toll these one-nighters took on each member of the band. Barrett Deems told him one morning: "No damn sleep. No sleep the night before, none last night, and none tomorrow. At least we spent the night in Atlanta." Armstrong, though, was the iron man. He was frequently up until four-thirty in the morning tape-recording albums he had brought with him. "These one-nighters aren't so bad," he said.

> You gotta take care of yourself. I play them because I love music. I can make it in New York without trouble. But I don't mind traveling and that's where the audiences are—in the towns and the cities—and that's what I want, the audience. I want to hear that applause. Hell, I made money when I was a kid driving a coal cart in New Orleans, and I've got all I need now. But I'm a musician and I still got to blow. When I get so I can't blow my horn the way I want, then it gets put down for good . . . Now don't get the idea I'm planning to retire. Why should I when I feel the same way about sex as I did when I was a kid? No reason to. But I got to take care of myself. Don't forget a man can blow a horn and still be a civilian.[5]

By now the new music on the scene had firmly taken root: rock and roll. Armstrong was, of course, expected to offer an opinion. "The music will survive, don't worry about that," he told Halberstam. "As long as it's good it'll get by, no matter what they try to do. But this rock and roll stuff they play, that's not music. Anyone with a shrill harsh voice can do that. Don't mean nothing. That's why it sounds so bad—there's nothing to it. Man's not feelin' when he's singin'. Hell, there's nothing to feel."[6] About young rock bands and their fans, Armstrong told a moving story: "Take 'You Made Me Love You.' They won't play something like that. Too slow for them. They gotta have something to pop their eyes out. When we hit Savannah we played 'I'll Never Walk Alone' and the whole house—all Negroes—started singing with us on their own. We ran through two choruses and they kept with us and then later they asked for it again. Most touching damn thing I ever saw. I almost started crying right there on the stage. We really hit something inside each person there."[7]

Armstrong was now approaching what he believed to be his fifty-seventh birthday on July 4, 1957 (after Armstrong died, it was discovered that he had been born on August 4, 1901, not July 4, 1900, making him really a year younger). His birthday was lavishly celebrated at the Newport Jazz Festival. The All Stars and Louis arrived around five p.m., straight from a one-nighter they had played elsewhere in New England. Armstrong was told he'd have to go on at eight and would have to appear with nearly every act on the bill, including such past associates as trumpeter Red Allen, trombonists J. C. Higginbotham and Kid Ory, and even two former All Stars, Cozy Cole and Jack Teagarden. The planned finale would feature Armstrong and Ella Fitzgerald, and then everyone would come out for "Happy Birthday." The whole thing might have looked good on paper, but not to Armstrong, ever the professional: "We haven't rehearsed and I'm not going to go out there and make a fool out of myself."[8] To boot, the All Stars had been glaringly omitted from the evening's events. This was too much for Armstrong, who reasoned, "Maybe a number [or] two [with the other acts], but I go on with my band to close the show—no other way." Sidney Bechet, Armstrong's old musical nemesis, was supposed to have flown in from Europe but was unable to attend. The band could now be accommodated. "We don't do less than an hour," Armstrong insisted. But Velma Middleton was told she wouldn't be performing, because Ella Fitzgerald would be and one female vocalist was enough.[9]

The rest of the scene was keenly remembered by Dan Morgenstern, who retold the events in liner notes for Columbia's *Chicago Concert* release. "Louis has had it by then; and he withdraws behind the tent flap that contains his 'private' area," he wrote. "Soon Velma hears the news, and bursts into tears. Louis, who has fantastic ears, hears her crying. Suddenly he appears from the flap, wearing nothing but a handkerchief tied around his scalp. Shouts and alarums. Women shriek, grown men flinch, and everyone scatters to the winds, Louis's curses in their ears. Like an ancient African king, he smites them with his righteous wrath."[10] Armstrong said, "I'm playing with my band and my singer and none of this other shit."[11]

Critics might have enjoyed knocking Middleton's antics onstage, but to Armstrong she was family, something George Wein might have underestimated. Speaking alone on a private tape recording at the end of 1957, Armstrong seemed to have the Newport affair still on his mind. Of Middleton he said, "You know, she's right there with us. There ain't gonna be no damn All Stars without her. I made that very clear to Glaser. He looked at me like I'm nuts but I said, 'Listen, man, shit, we're on these tours eight months out of the year and you're sitting in the office counting money. No, but [we] work our ass off, you can't split that. You put all the stars with us that you want. Just let them stand out there and sing, we'll play for them. But Velma's one of us."[12]

Armstrong was supposed to be honored at a special Newport society dinner party before playing, but he didn't show up, though Morgenstern reasons, "That it would take the place of his only chance to rest before the performance did not occur to the well-bred planners." At the concert attended by ten thousand fans at Newport's Freebody Park, Armstrong played with only the All Stars, turning in high-octane versions of "Mahogany Hall Stomp" and "Lazy River," dedicating the latter to Glaser. And Middleton performed, as Armstrong had promised. Nobody messed with his All Stars. "The show goes down in style; no one not in the know senses anything wrong," writes Morgenstern. "At the end of Louis's set, a giant birthday cake is wheeled on stage, and Ella and Johnny Mercer sing 'Happy Birthday.' Louis has fine manners; he joins in, backing them up on his horn. As Ella cuts the cake, someone (perhaps the producer himself) whispers to Louis that Ory and the other musicians are waiting to come on stage with him for a jam session finale. 'No one hangs on my coattails,' says Louis, and intones the National Anthem, his band falling in behind him. He doesn't taste his cake. That night, Louis Armstrong didn't eat anything they were dishing out."[13]

The next day, some critics, especially influential columnist Murray Kempton, had a field day bashing Armstrong's behavior. "The 57-year-old master tore the patience of his hosts to shreds Friday night by turning what had been planned as a sentimental birthday party for him into a massive display of the sulks," Kempton wrote. Later, he added: "The expectation had been that, by bringing back Ory, the friend of his earliest, and Miss Fitzgerald, the associate of his latest triumphs, Newport might inspire Armstrong to raise his sights above the well-worn grooves of the program of standard tunes—almost burlesques—he has plowed so incessantly over the last three years. Instead, he drew largely on the repertoire he used at the Roxy last month—the set he has played from Reno to Rome."[14]

That evening Armstrong was decidedly not his usual, laughing, happy-go-lucky self, and Kempton did not know what to make of it. "Armstrong's dismal performance left his hosts with their affection for him undiminished—nothing can destroy it—but recognizing that jazz's greatest son is much more complicated than they had ever thought," he wrote. "The old genial, simple Armstrong is gone, if he ever existed. He has been replaced by an insecure, infrequently happy man, in constant need for reassurance as to his stature, working harder in familiar paths than he needs to, reluctant to learn new things or even to revive all but the most familiar of the old, jealous of his billing and distrustful of his juniors. The mask of the clown is only a mask."[15]

Kempton's Psychology 101 diagnosis of Armstrong anticipated those of James Lincoln Collier and other misguided writers. There is no reason to assume that, ever the professional, a happy showman onstage and friendly offstage, Armstrong should have countenanced others messing with his act. He had worked hard to perfect his All Stars show and was not about to demean it, much less for something far less assured. Had he had time to rehearse the Newport program as presented to him, he might have gone ahead with it, but he did not appreciate that it was being forced on him at the last minute. While the press was merciless, those close to him were more understanding. "He kept his own counsel and nobody could turn him around," said Lucille Armstrong.[16] For his part, Jack Teagarden, who Kempton suggested was hurt by Armstrong's behavior, was moved to comment, "Some of these people seem to be trying to crucify Pops."[17]

Kempton also claimed that Armstrong "snubbed" Ella Fitzgerald, lamenting the missed opportunity to reclaim the magic of their first album together. But Fitzgerald did not seem to have felt that she was slighted, for at the end of July, just a few weeks after the Newport debacle, she and Armstrong recorded a follow-up album for Norman Granz. All of the musicians who had played on the first Armstrong-Fitzgerald collaboration—save drummer Buddy Rich, who was replaced by Louie Bellson—returned for *Ella and Louis Again*, which was eight tracks longer than the original. Unlike most sequels, this one lived up to the achievement of its predecessor, especially on "Let's Call the Whole Thing Off," "Autumn in New York," "Love Is Here to Stay," and a free-wheeling version of "Stompin' at the Savoy," which originally had started as a rehearsal take but became such a loose, joyous performance that Granz issued it on the final album. *Ella and Louis Again* also featured solo tracks by the two stars. Ella's three are above average; Armstrong's four are classics. "Willow Weep for Me" has a solo extraordinary for the slightly burnished tone of Armstrong's trumpet; the vocal-only "Makin' Whoopee" is a crash course in storytelling; and Armstrong's vocal on "I Get a Kick Out of You" swings so hard in the out chorus it challenges all other recordings of the Cole Porter standard, including Frank Sinatra's, for greatness. Armstrong's eight-minute-and-forty-one-second rendition of Porter's "Let's Do It"—his delivery a gem—might very well be the only version of the song to feature every verse Porter wrote. Full of humor, and taken at a dangerously slow tempo, "Let's Do It" is arguably the highlight of his association with Verve—no wonder that the terrific two-CD sampler of his Verve years is titled *Let's Do It*.

The first two Armstrong-and-Fitzgerald pairings on Verve were highly successful; the original *Ella and Louis* rose to number 11 and number 12 on the *Billboard* and the *Cash Box* charts, respectively. For their third (and sadly, final) album, recorded in August 1957, Granz broke from the format of the first two. The Peterson rhythm section was dispensed with, and in its place was Russell Garcia's orchestra, a gigantic ensemble of horns, woodwinds, and strings. Rather than another tour through the Great American Songbook, Armstrong and Fitzgerald undertook the score of George and Ira Gershwin's *Porgy and Bess*. "I loved both of them," Garcia remembered in 2008. "Louis was such a wonderful, nice person. He loved everybody. Nothing could wipe that beautiful, loving smile off his face.

Which is amazing considering what he must have gone through with racism when he was young. When we were recording *Porgy and Bess,* I ran down the orchestra part for the first tune, and Louis said in that rough voice, 'Russ, you're a genius. If I ever get rich I'm going to put you on salary.' " Garcia said that Armstrong and Fitzgerald "were a joy" to work with, but "Louis annoyed her a little bit. When she was singing a beautiful passage, he'd come in with his growling. She'd shoot him a sharp look and go on. It would throw her for a second. But it came off beautifully. Some people call that album 'Whipped Cream and Sandpaper.' "[18] Bassist Ray Brown, who worked on the first two Verve collaborations, agreed, saying, "If Armstrong's voice was the male equivalent of Ella Fitzgerald's voice and had the same range, I don't think it would have been as much fun. I think that the big difference in their styles is what made it work. What one sings is so completely different from what the other sings."[19]

The album, naturally, featured Armstrong singing the original male parts and Fitzgerald the female. Her "I Wants to Stay Here" is a masterpiece; his "There's a Boat Dat's Leavin' Soon for New York" is a romp with an extended trumpet solo. Their duets are just as memorable, especially "Summertime" and "Bess, You Is My Woman Now," arguably their greatest performance together (exquisite "whipped cream and sandpaper" indeed!). The high point of the album, however, is "Oh Bess, Oh Where's My Bess?," a solo performance by Armstrong more emotionally powerful perhaps than anything he had previously recorded. In the notes to *Let's Do It,* Dan Morgenstern writes, " 'Oh Bess, Oh Where's My Bess?' one of the opera's most moving arias, is an Armstrong vocal masterpiece. In theory, it is far beyond his range, but he was a tenor in his youth, and he handles the tessitura splendidly. Or, in plain Nineties English, he sings the shit out of it. He would have made some Porgy on stage!"[20] Granz said, "I think Louie's fantastic as an artist and I thought he had a certain quality . . . When I finished doing something, I would go back and see Ira Gershwin, who's a friend of mine, and Ira and I would play it and Ira was overwhelmed by the poignancy of Louie's voice, the quality when he was singing 'Oh Bess,' I mean, it was to cry, it was marvelous, and I thought Louie would be fantastic for this album which he . . . was."[21]

Porgy and Bess would not be released until 1959, so as to coincide with the motion picture produced by Samuel Goldwyn. When reviews of the album finally appeared, they were among the best of Armstrong's career. Patrick Scott wrote, "Both have sung better before (though not together—this is a big improvement on their earlier collaborations for Verve), but seldom in recent years has either of them, especially Mr. Armstrong, sounded so interested in—or challenged by—the material at hand." Scott added, "And on two numbers—'A Woman Is a Sometime Thing' and 'There's a Boat Dat's Leavin' Soon for New York'—Mr. Armstrong turns in extended trumpet solos which are not only this album's highlights but the best work he has put on record in years."[22] "Indeed, as the tracks progress, you think [Fitzgerald] is cutting Armstrong—only to turn around and believe that Armstrong is cutting her. The truth, of course, is that they are outdoing themselves," wrote *DownBeat*, which gave the album five stars. "As for Armstrong . . . well, this is an Armstrong the younger generation has had little chance to know. Though his voice is one of the most unpromising instruments any man ever chose to work with, what he does with it here is remarkable. Like a Rubinstein saddled with a battered old upright, he overcomes his instrument by sheer force of innate musicianship, and achieves a degree of acting realism that is seldom heard this side of Frank Sinatra or some of Maria Callas' better performances." Armstrong was proud of the work, too. When asked in 1960 to name his favorite records, Armstrong said, "I thought that *Porgy and Bess* I made with Ella was a very good album."[23] During a 1968 BBC radio program, he chose "Bess, You Is My Woman Now" as one of eight records he would bring to a mythical "desert island."

As for Fitzgerald, she recalled: "It never seemed like we were really recording, because he was always so happy. And he came in like it was nothing to it, he's just going to have a ball. And I would always mess up because I'd be so fascinated watching him that I would—sometimes I wouldn't come in on time on my song, you know, because he'd go through the whole motion just like *he* were really singing [it], you know, 'Sing it, Ella,' you know. And . . . he'd be talking and cracking and making jokes . . . you don't know whether you should sing or laugh. But that's the kind of guy he was."[24]

In mid-August 1957, between the making of *Ella and Louis Again* and *Porgy and Bess*, Granz had teamed Armstrong with the big band and strings of Russell Garcia for two albums, *I've Got the World on a String* and *Louis Under the Stars*. Garcia's arrangements were somewhat bland, incongruent with Armstrong's style, unlike Gordon Jenkins's. Armstrong does his best with the material, though when he picks up the trumpet it is clear he was going through a rough patch. Granz, however, was in no position to postpone the sessions, as Armstrong's schedule allowed for little recording time. Granz would later say:

> Normally with a trumpet player you have trouble [with] your lip well you just don't even think of recording, but I think we did Louie, I think it was on the big band date where it was really kind of [a] drag because even the band was sympathetic to Louie. His chops just weren't right and I would like to have canceled it completely but Louie insisted that we could do it if we did it and spaced it and gave him some breaks in between and then had him sing some solos that we might have done instrumentally. That wasn't a problem as far as I was concerned because I enjoyed his singing equally to his playing, so, if he sang a number instead of playing it, it was okay with me and with him too."[25]

Recording for Granz in Los Angeles every day and performing every night with the All Stars in Las Vegas had taken a huge toll on the trumpeter's chops. As Garcia remembered of one of the sessions recorded after an evening of blowing, "The next morning he came in and pointed his trumpet against the wall. He tried to blow through it, but air came out from the sides of his lips. No sound. He'd keep this up, and then all of a sudden—bang, the sound would come, and his lips would be vibrating and he'd be off and doing fine."[26] The 1999 two-CD reissue of this material includes a great number of alternate takes and rehearsals, and one can hear Armstrong struggling, playing air notes here and there while cracking others. When he musters up all his strength and powers over the ensemble on "Stormy Weather," the results are breathtaking. Though in severe pain, Armstrong was not about to concede anything.

Away from the confines of the studio, where he could take as many breaks as needed, Armstrong could not hide his lip troubles during live performances. In the midst of the Garcia sessions, he had to perform with battered lips at a major concert at the Hollywood Bowl. "Doc [Pugh] and Louis didn't know what to do," Ernie Anderson remembered. "The lip was in tatters. They couldn't cancel the concert. Yet that seemed the only logical recourse. If they cancelled they'd have to call Joe Glaser in New York first. Of course Joe didn't know Louis was having lip trouble." Anderson called a Latin-American doctor who, though he barely spoke English, was able to realize how important his client was and how important the show was to him and wrote a prescription for hydrocortisone salve. "It was now about two o'clock in the afternoon," Anderson recalled. "The concert was at eight. At two-thirty I had the ointment and I took it up to Louis. 'What do I do with it?' Louis asked. 'Just rub it on your lip,' I replied. Some people are just more sensitive than others. Louis began very gently to rub the salve onto his lip. 'I feel it,' he cried. 'I really do feel it and it's good stuff.' And then he began rubbing it all over his face." After a break for dinner, Anderson and Pugh returned to the hotel to a startling surprise: Armstrong warming up on the tune "Wyoming." Anderson remembered, "He played a beautiful show that night and got a rave review in the *Los Angeles Times*."[27]

Throughout the summer of 1957 Armstrong persisted with his hectic schedule, traveling the long, hard road night after night as the band continued bringing in more money than ever before. However, this led to a run-in between Armstrong and Frenchy Tallerie. According to a letter Armstrong wrote to Joe Glaser on August 25, 1957, Tallerie was taking advantage of Armstrong. "Why won't Frenchie pay me on one niters according to the raise you gave me? It really doesn't make sense," Armstrong wrote. "My expenses are almost triple and . . . he still gives me the same ole money which is a drag. He short changed me fifty dollars per nite since we left the Sands. All the work that I did at the Hollywood Bowl. He gave me the same old money which isn't right at all. . . I dig him and his way back plays huh. Am way ahead of him. Please Mr. Glaser impress on Mr. Tallerie that a raise is a raise no matter how you slice it. I won't mention the whole thing daddy but since I am the poorest and need the morest." In retrospect, it was humiliating for Armstrong—in the midst of such a grueling stretch—to have to fight for a fifty-dollar raise he was promised, but such were Tallerie's underhanded ways. Armstrong didn't blame Glaser, who was suing one of his former clients, boxer Sugar Ray Robinson, at the time. He ended the letter by writing, "Hope that everything turns out OK with you and your boy Ray Robinson. Some people fail to realize when they have the dearest friend in the world in their corner until after its too late. A big hello to Mother Glaser. An don't let nothing drag ya daddy. You still have ole Satchmo an that's for sure. Your Boy, Satchmo."[28]

On the evening of September 17, everything came to a head: the Knoxville explosion, the Newport fiasco, the grueling one-nighters, the beat-up chops, the need to fight for extra money, as well as a lifetime of racial injustice. That day, Armstrong and the All Stars arrived in Grand Fork, North Dakota, for an evening performance. Earlier he saw on television news about the school desegregation crisis in Little Rock, Arkansas. Governor Orval Faubus used the National Guard to prevent black children from entering the Little Rock Central High School. Armstrong watched the fearful expressions on the children's faces, the vicious heckling of the white crowd, and footage of a white man spitting in the face of a black girl. After the reports from Little Rock, Armstrong met in his hotel room with a student reporter from the University of Arkansas, Larry Lubenow. "The way they are treating my people in the South, the government can go to hell," he said. "It's getting so bad, a colored man hasn't got any country." The rest of the interview found Armstrong calling President Dwight Eisenhower "two-faced" and denouncing him for having "no guts" for allowing Faubus to run the country.[29] Fifty years later, Lubenow told the full story of his interview to journalist David Margolick. Armstrong had called Faubus "a no-good motherfucker" and sung his own version of "The Star-Spangled Banner," with such obscenity-laced lyrics as "Oh say, can you motherfuckers see by the motherfucking early light," until he was hushed by Velma Middleton, who was also in the room. Lubenow realized he had struck gold, but to protect Armstrong he changed "motherfucker" to "uneducated plowboy" with Armstrong's approval in his final copy.[30] Lubenow approached the Associated Press about running the story, but they demurred until he provided proof that Armstrong had spoken so bluntly. Lubenow returned to the hotel the next day and showed Armstrong the story. "That's just fine," he said. "Don't take nothing out of that story. That's just what I said and still say."[31] At the bottom, he wrote "Solid" in big letters, his own unique stamp of approval. Armstrong then continued his diatribe, calling the use of National Guard troops to prevent school integration at Little Rock "a publicity stunt led by the greatest of all publicity hounds." And about performing in the Soviet Union,

Armstrong said he would not: "The people over there ask me what's wrong with my country, what am I supposed to say?"[32]

Armstrong's words were soon in every newspaper and on every newscast in the country. No one could quite believe good ol' Uncle Tom Satchmo, the smiling, grinning Negro, could say such things. Frenchy Tallerie, of all people, took it upon himself to tell the press Armstrong "was sorry he spouted off." Upon hearing Tallerie's remarks, Armstrong called the *Pittsburgh Courier* and said, "As much as I'm trying to do for my people, this road man, Tallerie, whom I've respected for 20 years, although I've suspected him of being prejudiced, has worked with Negro musicians and made his money off them, has proved that he hates Negroes the first time he opened his mouth, and I don't see why Mr. Glaser doesn't remove him from the band." After giving Tallerie hell and temporarily firing him, Armstrong insisted, "I wouldn't take back a thing I've said. I've had a beautiful life over 40 years in music, but I feel the downtrodden situation the same as any other Negro. My parents and family suffered through all of that old South and things are new now, and [no] Tallerie and no prejudiced newspaper can make me change it. What I've said is me. I feel that." He continued, "My people—the Negroes—are not looking for anything—we just want a square shake. But when I see on television and read about a crowd in Arkansas spitting on a little colored girl—I think I have a right to get sore . . . Do you dig me when I still say I have a right to blow my top over injustice?"[33]

At the time of the uproar, the State Department had been trying to organize a tour of Russia for Armstrong, but he now told an interviewer that if he ever did go, "I'll do it on my own." The Associated Press reported, "In Washington the State Department declined to comment on Mr. Armstrong's statements. Officials made no attempt, however, to hide the concern they caused . . . They said Soviet propagandists undoubtedly would seize on Mr. Armstrong's words."[34] The next morning, television cameras met Armstrong at an airport. Asked, "What are you going to tell the Russians when they ask you about the Little Rock incident?" Armstrong responded without a hint of a smile, "It all depends what time they send me over there. I don't think they should send me now until they straighten that mess down South. And for good. I mean not just to blow over. To cut it out . . . Because they've been ignoring the Constitution . . . They're taught it in school, but when they go home their parents tell them different. Say, 'You don't have to abide by it because we've been getting away with it a hundred years. Nobody tells on each other. So don't bother with it.' So, if they ask me what's happening if I go now, I can't tell a lie . . . [That's] the way I feel about it."[35]

This was a defining moment for Louis Armstrong. Criticized for years for being an Uncle Tom and for not supporting his race, he finally spoke out about the injustices his people were facing. He had probably hoped to stir passion about the Little Rock incident and get support from others in the black community. Some did just that. Sam Lacy of the *Baltimore Afro-American* wrote: "If you were shocked by Louis Armstrong's blast at President Eisenhower and the government, what do you think about this laborer? Occupant of this space had long since given up on Satchmo as anything but a toothy throwback to a better-to-be-forgotten era. Maybe I can agree he's not overrated as a musician now. And I guess even his singing will sound better from here on, at least for a while. We ain't prejudiced."[36]

But Armstrong's stance drew more criticism, harsher than usual. "Louis 'Satchmo' Armstrong, justly famous Negro trumpet player and jazz singer, plays what the boys in the trade call a 'gang o' horn. But in politics, it is evident now, he blows sour," a California newspaper editorial read. It continued, "He made a grievous error however, when he put his horn down and blasted President Eisenhower, 'the government,' and various other persons and places for their handling of the Negro problem . . . For Armstrong to charge the President with 'no guts' because he has taken the orderly road is to indulge in pointless insult."[37] Another article used the opportunity to attack Armstrong's stage shows: "At any rate, Satchmo hardly qualifies as an expert on what contributes to the advancement of the colored race; if he did, he would long ago have divorced himself professionally from Velma Middleton, whose tasteless (nay, vulgar) performances with the Armstrong band rate as 'handkerchief-head' with progressives, and do anything but elevate the prestige of the Negro in our society."[38] The *Chicago Defender* reported that "though not organized, there's a growing boycott of records by Louis Armstrong and other Negro artists who criticized the handling of the Little Rock school integration dispute . . . Without making any public announcements, disc jockeys in Memphis, Little Rock, Jackson, Miss., Charleston, S.C., and Nashville indicated they just would not spin any platters made by Negroes."[39] Armstrong did receive support for his remarks from Eartha Kitt, Marian Anderson, and Pearl Bailey, but their records, too, were boycotted.[40]

When Eisenhower finally sent troops to Arkansas a few days after the controversy began, Armstrong commented, "This is the greatest country. Things are looking better than before."[41] He also sent the following telegram to the White House:

MR PRESIDENT. DADDY IF AND WHEN YOU DECIDE TO TAKE THOSE LITTLE NEGRO CHILDREN PERSONALLY INTO CENTRAL HIGH SCHOOL ALONG WITH YOUR MARVVELOUS TROOPS PLEASE TAKE ME ALONG "O GOD IT WOULD BE SUCH A GREAT PLEASURE I ASSURE YOU. MY REGARDS TO BROTHER BROWNWELL[42] AND MAY GOD BLESS YOU PRESIDENT" YOU HAVE A GOOD HEART.
YOU CAN CONTACT ME THROUGH MY PERSONNEL MANAGER MR JOE GLASER 745 FIFTH AVENUE NEW YORK. AM SWISS KRISSLY YOURS LOUIS SATCHMO ARMSTRONG.[43]

Armstrong had changed his position about Eisenhower: "That man has a soul. He has done as much as Lincoln did and more than any other president between them did." And about going to Russia, he now said, "I'll go anytime they want me."[44] Still, Armstrong's September tirade continued to haunt him. Sammy Davis Jr. attacked him. "You cannot voice an opinion about a situation which is basically discrimination, integration, etc.," said Davis, "and then go out and appear before segregated audiences . . . which Louis Armstrong has done for many years." Davis said he agreed with Armstrong's sentiment, but not with his "choice of words." Davis also took Armstrong to task for using the word "darkies" on his 1951 recording of "When It's Sleepy Time Down South."[45] Even Harlem's best-known politician, the Reverend Adam Clayton Powell Jr., claimed Armstrong was embarrassing his race. Four years later, Armstrong would write about his Little Rock comments in *Ebony*: "When I made that statement, Congressman Adam Clayton Powell was interviewed over TV. He was asked about what I said. He told the TV reporter he didn't agree: 'Louis Armstrong isn't up on current events.' Well, I may not be up on current events, but I'm up on head-whipping."[46] Even Nat "King" Cole blasted Armstrong in the press.

This lack of support scarred Armstrong for the rest of his life. In

1972, Lucille Armstrong recalled, "But the press, you know, they inter-viewed Adam Clayton Powell, they interviewed Sammy Davis—and I don't mind calling names because it's on record—they put Pops down because they said he was a musician, he didn't know what he was talking about . . . He felt it deeply, he really did."[47] In 1959, Armstrong expounded on the response from the black community in a private conversation with entertainer Babe Wallace. Though he rarely spoke about the Little Rock incident, he bragged to Wallace that he "caught 'em napping." He then added, "But some spades, you know, all spades are always going to ham it up. 'Nigger, you better stop talking about them white folks!' I said, 'Kiss my ass.' That's what you got to watch. That's what was happening."[48]

What probably hurt Armstrong most was the lack of support he received from musicians. Since the dawn of bebop, younger musicians had lambasted Armstrong for "Tomming" and for his popularity among white audiences. But now, when he had publicly taken a brave position—one they should have agreed with—not a single musician from the jazz world had stepped forward to support him. "Although Charles Mingus gave Orval Faubus a permanent role in jazz history with his 1959 composition, 'Fables of Faubus,' Mingus was one of many boppers and post-boppers who did not bother to stand beside Armstrong when he publicly denounced official racism," wrote Krin Gabbard.[49] "Not one of the younger musicians who had accused him of Tomming in the past publicly came to his defense," add Geoffrey Ward and Ken Burns.[50]

One person who did show unflagging support throughout the con-troversy was Joe Glaser. Pierre Tallerie wrongly tried to get Armstrong to back off his statements, but the trumpeter faced no such opposition from Tallerie's boss, Glaser. More than money or friendship or anything else, Armstrong admired Glaser because he provided one major thing: "Protec-tion. And the [Little Rock] statement I made, I mean, I know Joe's going to back me," Armstrong told Wallace during their private conversation in 1959. "I didn't even write him, I didn't say nothing, he didn't even know I was going to do it. He wasn't going to turn me around. So he couldn't do that, so right there he say, 'Well, whatever he said, he don't waste words, and I'm with him a hundred percent.' That's all I want to hear, what he's got to say." Armstrong added, "Shit, Joe Glaser ain't say nothing yet to discourage me. And when I made that [Little Rock] statement and let-ters come in by the sacksful, he took his time and sorted the good ones from the bad ones. He kept all the bad ones and say, 'You keep the good ones, I'll answer the bad ones.' From the South. You know, there's a lot of diehards. Shit."[51]

Armstrong wasn't kidding about letters from the South. Glaser might have prevented them from reaching his prized client, but that didn't stop newspapers from publishing such incendiary words. The *Herald-Journal* of Spartanburg, South Carolina, did just that with a letter to the editor from reader Alexander T. Goodale. "Reference is made to an Associated Press dispatch printed in the *Herald* which quoted the statements of one loud mouth Negro known as (Satchmo) Louis Armstrong, whose ancestors came to this country from the jungles of Africa," Goodale wrote on September 22. "The inhabitants possessed only the level of intelligence found in a region of primitive ignorance and savage environment. He is indebted to the white race for all he has accomplished and he owes a debt of gratitude to America for the privilege of sharing in the freedom and prosperity he enjoys in the United States . . . I think it is the duty of the press and the officials of both national and state governments to join in righteous indignation until such low specimens are brought before the bar of justice and forced to apologize to the American people—or be given a one-way ticket to Africa where he belongs."[52]

A month after the controversy erupted, Glaser announced that Armstrong would perform at a nonsegregated dance the following March at the University of Arkansas. "I'll go wherever he (Glaser) says," Armstrong said. "The only thing I resent, is that Gov. Faubus will be listening to those beautiful notes that will come from my horn. He doesn't deserve them." Glaser bragged, "Armstrong will play with a mixed band for a mixed audience for a big fat fee."[53] The day after the report appeared, the University of Arkansas backed out of the concert, claiming the school's students had canceled the date. Glaser's response was typical: "Who cares? . . . We don't have to return the contract if we don't want to. The university signed it. But we'll send it back. I have nothing against the boys at the university. We have them hooked if we want to be nasty, but we wouldn't do that to a bunch of nice guys. I think this is the result of Gov. Faubus. He definitely put the pressure on them. It's all pretty silly, but who cares?"[54]

Glaser continued to book Louis overseas in the ensuing years, but Armstrong made sure to stress that those trips had nothing to do with the State Department. Regarding the proposed trip to Russia, Armstrong told Babe

Wallace in 1959 that he had no qualms with the Soviet Union, because he was a musician, not a politician. "I said, 'Well, what do you want me to tell these people when I go over there? It's all right? Bullshit!' How many Russians we jammed with in New York in the good days, all nationalities up in Harlem? . . . And then they ask me, 'Did the state department send you?' And I say, 'You know no state department sent me over here. It's the fans.' " Armstrong also grew tired of being questioned about Soviet leader Nikita Khrushchev, saying, "What the hell, if he's there [at an Armstrong concert], he's likely to appreciate it like everyone else." He knew that an official State Department–sponsored tour would be peppered with these kinds of questions, and that was something he did not want to deal with. "You see, I told them, you want to go through that kind of shit, have [Secretary of State John Foster Dulles] do the talking, we do the blowing, that's all. I ain't going to make no speech for shit."[55]

When the controversy died down, the Uncle Tom image once again supplanted the Armstrong of Little Rock, denouncing injustice. He never could understand it, especially as one of the most influential African-Americans ever. While recovering from a life-threatening illness in 1969, Armstrong reflected on the Little Rock incident. "I think that I have always done great things about uplifting my race, but wasn't appreciated," he wrote. "I am just a musician, and still remember the time, as an American citizen, I spoke up for my people during a big integration riot—Little Rock, remember? I wrote Eisenhower. My first comment, or compliment, whatever you would call it, came from a Negro boy from my hometown New Orleans. The first words that he said to me after reading what I had said in the papers concerning the Little Rock deal—he said as we were sitting down at a table to have a drink. He looked straight at me and said, 'Nigger, you better stop talking about those white people like you did.' Hmmm. I was trying to stop those unnecessary head whippings at the time—that's all."[56]

Louis in Rome after getting out of the hospital, 1959

ABOVE Louis appearing in traditional West African garb during his Pepsi-Cola sponsored tour of Ghana and Nigeria in 1960. From left to right, Trummy Young, Louis, Barney Bigard, and Mort Herbert

LEFT Ambassador Satch performs for the Great Sphinx of Giza in 1961.

Recording *The Real Ambassadors* with Dave Brubeck in 1961

Louis flanked by Jerry Herman and Dave Kapp on the day he recorded "Hello, Dolly!" in 1963. Herman's song combined with Kapp's production resulted in the biggest hit of Armstrong's lifetime.

Armstrong clowning around with three young girls while filming a Suzy Cute doll commercial in late 1964. Commercials such as this one led many younger fans to brand Armstrong as an out-of-date Uncle Tom.

ABOVE Offstage,
Louis didn't always
flash his trademark
smile. While the Suzy
Cute commercial was
airing in the United
States, Armstrong
was in Denmark in
1965, telling the press,
"They would beat
Jesus if he was black
and marched."

LEFT Taking bows
after cracking
the Iron Curtain
with a triumphant
performance in
Prague in March 1965

In the studio with producer Bob Thiele, recording "The Sunshine of Love" on August 16, 1967. The next song recorded that day would be "What a Wonderful World."

This Jack Bradley photo comes from a Central Park shoot for Armstrong's final album, *Louis "Country and Western" Armstrong*.

Armstrong spent much of his time off indexing his reel-to-reel tape collection and designing many of the empty boxes with collages. He shows off one such collage in this photo from circa 1969.

Louis and some children at his Corona, Queens, home. Today the home is a national historic landmark and a museum, visited each year by thousands of people from all over the world.

Rehearsing for his seventieth-birthday celebration at the Newport Jazz Festival, Louis holds court with guests: left to right, Tyree Glenn, Louis, unknown, Bobby Hackett, unknown, Jack Lesberg (with hand on bass, face partially hidden), Dizzy Gillespie, Jimmy Owens, and Oliver Jackson.

Armstrong was well enough to perform with the All Stars for two weeks in Las Vegas in early 1971. Here, he receives an award from Ella Fitzgerald and Duke Ellington, as Tyree Glenn looks on. It was Armstrong's next-to-last public engagement.

Louis and Lucille kissing in Armstrong's den after Louis's hospital stay in the spring of 1971

Probably the last photo ever taken of Louis Armstrong, just days before his passing on July 6, 1971

CHAPTER TWELVE

The Rigors of Touring at Home
and Abroad, 1957–1959

AS THE Little Rock controversy began to die down, Armstrong returned to the recording studio for what would turn out to be his final album for Norman Granz, a date with pianist Oscar Peterson's trio—the same rhythm section that had worked with him two months earlier on *Ella and Louis Again,* once more augmented by drummer Louie Bellson. While it seemed that Armstrong and Peterson, and the rest of the musicians, were comfortable with each other, many doubted the collaboration would be fruitful. "Despite the success of the pairing of vocalist Ella Fitzgerald and Armstrong (backed by Peterson), many of those who worshipped the trumpeter could not understand why this titan of early jazz, who was a central figure in the revival of small-band Dixieland, was making recordings with a leading exponent of what was then called modern jazz," John Chilton wrote. They feared that Peterson and the rest of the rhythm section's accompaniment would prove unsuitable for Armstrong's artistry. For their part, Peterson's growing army of fans saw the partnership as a retrograde step, which caused the brilliant young pianist to play with a veteran whose best work was in the past."[1]

Oscar Peterson had played with many a horn heavyweight by now—from Lester Young and Ben Webster to Stan Getz and Sonny Stitt. His meeting with Armstrong is somewhat neglected in writing about either artist, yet their recording was remarkable, and arguably the most underappreciated album of Armstrong's career, at least insofar as the jazz community is concerned. "All antipathy disappeared as soon as the fans heard the recording," Chilton wrote. "They realized it was a musical collaboration of the highest order, with Peterson's trio (plus Louis Bellson) providing the inspiration for Armstrong to make a recording that is among the most challenging that he created during the last two decades of his life." Armstrong was presented with twelve standards, nearly all of which he had never performed. As with the Armstrong-Fitzgerald albums, the emphasis is on the trumpeter's singing, and Armstrong shines on, among other tunes, "I'll Never Be the Same," "You Go to My Head," and "Sweet Lorraine." Though his trumpet work is not as majestic as it is on the Columbia and Decca recordings of the period, it is superior to his efforts on the Russell Garcia dates, especially on the up-tempo numbers "Just One of Those Things," "Let's Fall in Love," and "Moon Song." But the trumpet chorus on "Sweet Lorraine" is soulfulness itself, as if Armstrong were reflecting on his whole career in the light of recent controversies.[2]

Soon after recording with Peterson, Armstrong and the All Stars left the United States for a six-week tour of South America, including Argentina, Brazil, Chile, Uruguay, and Venezuela.[3] Before leaving, Joe Glaser decided to reward Armstrong with a little extra cash. Armstrong, who was generous to a fault and gave away thousands of dollars in handouts, knew what he wanted to do with it. Ernie Anderson remembered:

Just before the 1957 South American tour, Joe passed to Louis a bonus of $2,000 in twenty dollar bills. I came into the study to chat with Louis. He was sitting at his desk with a stack of white envelopes. On each envelope, he would scribble a name, even a nickname, with his green ink fountain pen. He didn't ever have a very legible hand but Doc Pugh could always read it. Louis must have had thirty envelopes so inscribed. Then he took out his stack of twenties. He would look at the name on an envelope, then he would insert one, two or, sometimes as many as five twenties and then he would seal the envelope. Finally the stack of twenties was completely gone. But he still had some envelopes with names on them left to fill. He picked up these unsealed envelopes and tore them up. "Just not enough money to go around," he exclaimed. Then suddenly Doc Pugh came rushing up the stairs. He had just run in from Harlem and his cab was waiting for him downstairs. Doc took all the sealed envelopes, dashed downstairs and got back into his cab and went back to Harlem where he distributed them. Of course Doc Pugh knew the address for every name on those envelopes; all people Louis thought needed a little cash. He had some so he was sending some along to them. There was no note in any of those envelopes, just the cash. Of course everybody who got one knew that green ink scrawl meant that it came from Louis.[4]

Armstrong's arrival in Buenos Aires was greeted with the usual chaos. "The famous trumpet player and his wife—here on a goodwill tour—had to be spirited away from the theater in a police car early today when screaming admirers swamped them and trampled over their automobile," the Associated Press reported. "Armstrong, who doesn't speak Spanish, drove around with the police for half an hour trying to make officers understand where he is staying. His tour manager said Armstrong was struck on the head, back and shoulders and is afraid he will be hit in the 'chops.' "[5] Armstrong humorously recounted the story in 1970. "They were so enthusiastic, when I'd go to the theater every night, they'd all come around, 'Let me touch your lips, touch your lips!' I'd say, 'Honey, I can't go for that!' Nobody knows the volume they're going to touch your lips in a crowd like that," he said. "So I wouldn't take that chance so I sent Mr. Joe Glaser, my manager, a wire. I said, 'Send me one of Yogi Berra's catcher's masks right away!' I put it on and when I got out of the car among all the people, I said, 'How do! How do!' " The sight of Armstrong in a catcher's mask was, needless to say, an unprecedented photo op; a spread appeared in the November 25 issue of *Life* magazine, even as *Life en Español* showed the trumpeter on its cover.

Armstrong now recalled "I Get Ideas" to the All Stars' live repertoire, Armstrong bellowing "Adios, muchachos" as he concluded his vocals, a nod to the Argentine tango on which the piece is based. Broadcasts from Buenos Aires find the All Stars in spectacular form, with Armstrong pushing himself even harder than usual on numbers like "Ain't Misbehavin'," "Tiger Rag," and "On the Sunny Side of the Street."

When Armstrong returned to the United States, his career was still suffering from the backlash against his Little Rock remarks. According to one newspaper item, "Louis Armstrong's engagement at the Copacabana has proven a great disappointment to all concerned. Apparently Satchmo, who rated Page One headlines when he rapped the President of the United States, isn't quite as effective as a supper club draw."[6] Columnist Jim Bishop used Armstrong's disappointing Copacabana showing as ammunition to fire at will:

> Armstrong, who has delighted millions of people with his jollity, his sandpapered throat, and his jazz, did le business poor. People did not want to see him. He is scheduled to star on an upcoming TV show. For one, I will not look . . . I was in Europe when this mess began. It was a big story here. It was bigger over there. Mr. Louis Armstrong's picture was plastered on the front pages in England, in France, in Italy, in Germany. He must have made a big hit in Russia because this was an American Negro telling the President off with scorn . . . When I returned from Europe, I was impressed with the enormity of damage Armstrong had done to the United States. So I checked with some leading musicians and inquired about Satchmo. They were unanimous in their opinions. They said that he is a good man, a fine musician, a good American. Most of them, including Eddie Condon, said that Armstrong is intelligent. That removes the prop of stupidity as an excuse. Then I checked the old newspaper files to see what Louis Armstrong had done for the people of his race in the past. I haven't found anything and now I rise to ask the musician himself: What have you done for your people, except hurt them?[7]

Bishop's column spread across the country like wildfire. Armstrong, as usual, didn't care. When asked about Bishop, he told Toronto writer Philip Sykes, "Man, so long as he don't ban the horn, I don't care a damn what he says." As to the charge that he had disappointed audiences at the Copacabana, Armstrong said, "I stayed there a month, playing two shows a night—and you don't do two shows if the business isn't there. AND I appeared on two TV shows columnists had suggested I would miss. That Mr. Bishop—he was in Europe when the row was on. He just wanted to climb on a bandwagon. He's a Johnny-come-lately. He didn't say nothing new. He just picked up the leavings of what other people had written . . . He spelt my name right. I'll sure give him credit for that. But he didn't say nothing, that hadn't been said before." Armstrong then stopped smiling and unburdened himself: "Mr. Bishop's been so busy being a white man, he don't know the life of a colored man."[8] Asked if he would like to revise his statement about his people not having a country to live in, Armstrong said, "I said the Negroes didn't have a country. But we're doing all right now. The colored man has no opportunities in Europe. He's better off in America. There are more rich Negroes in America than anywhere in the world . . . Man, I keep happy . . . I don't have no enemies. I want people to love each other all over the world."[9]

As much as Armstrong wanted the controversy to go away and concentrate on performing, he unwittingly generated more ill will. In early 1958, he managed to alienate the NAACP by not showing up at an NAACP rally in Detroit, as he had a musical engagement elsewhere. The NAACP's executive secretary, Arthur Johnson, chided: "It would further appear to us that Mr. Armstrong and his management should realize the performer's inescapable responsibility as both a citizen and a performer to the community."[10] Armstrong grew frustrated, citing the unfortunate double booking by his management, though he insisted a live performance would always trump a publicity appearance. The Glaser agency had promised Armstrong's appearance in Detroit even though it knew that he and the All Stars had a concert in Rochester, New York, at around the same time. Armstrong declared, "It's those people out there in the theater, the ones clappin' their hands together for our music, they're the important ones. If I gotta be honor guest here and honor guest there, and get citations and say howdy-do and be polite and all that stuff, then I got no time to go out there and perform for the people who paid to hear me." Yet he chastised the booking agency, rare for him in public: "All they gotta do in that New York office is sit there and count money, and I gotta drive all night from Rochester, New York, on Saturday night to make Detroit on Sunday, and if I gotta be guest of honor every place they say in New York I gotta be, than they gotta stop bookin' me to give performances, is what I told 'em in a telegram."[11]

By this point, the All Stars had a new rhythm section. Bassist Squire Gersh was the first to go, something that upset Armstrong, who enjoyed Gersh's rhythmic slapping style. As he related on a private tape at the end of 1957, "Squire Gersh . . . is leaving the band and we regret it terribly."[12] Gersh was replaced by Mort Herbert, a musician who had earned a B.A. from Rutgers University and a Bachelor of Law degree from New York

Law School. In a questionnaire for Leonard Feather's jazz encyclopedia, Herbert wrote that he wanted to concentrate on writing more arrangements and playing less bass, but his "ultimate ambition" was "a career in theatrical law." He had played in modernist settings, more so than the other All Stars, having performed with, among others, Don Elliott, Gene Krupa, Cozy Cole, the Sauter-Finegan Orchestra, Coleman Hawkins, Roy Eldridge, and Terry Gibbs, as well as being the leader on an album for Savoy. Herbert, however, had a solid beat and was a good soloist, especially on his many features, which included "I Cover the Waterfront," "These Foolish Things," and "I'm Beginning to See the Light." There was another personnel change when drummer Barrett Deems quit after four years on the road, though some have argued that he was forced to resign. According to trombonist Jim Beebe, "Deems had become a pariah with his prickly personality and had caused scenes throughout Europe. Deems told me that Glaser made it very difficult for him if he wanted to stay with the band. He was never honest about getting fired—for years he maintained that he quit."[13] Armstrong himself raved about Deems's playing when he first joined the band but later realized that his nervous temperament extended into his playing. In a 1956 discussion on drummers, Armstrong said, "With all respect to Deems, that's our biggest battle, wachin' that strict tempo. He's got that nervous streak so many drummers have."[14] Joe Glaser was more blunt about it. When bassist Jack Lesberg joined the group in 1956, Glaser's last instructions to him were, "By the way, your toughest job will be to hold that drummer down—he rushes like hell!"[15] In early 1958, Deems was still with the band, but Armstrong knew his time was up. Speaking privately, he said, "Deems, Barrett Deems, who also seems like the ax done hit him, but he's still with us. I don't know, I don't run Mr. Glaser's business. I just blow the horn."[16]

Deems's replacement was Danny Barcelona, who was suggested by Trummy Young. Barcelona had been Young's drummer in Hawaii, and Armstrong recalled his talent. Even though Deems had yet to leave the band, Barcelona arrived in New York at the beginning of 1958 and at first simply hung around, even attending, but not playing at, Armstrong's first recording session of 1958.

Armstrong and Sy Oliver reconnected and returned to Decca's studios to record *Louis and the Good Book,* another concept album, a collection of twelve religious-themed songs. Instead of strings, Armstrong was surrounded by a choir, the All Stars, and an organ—there was some righteous hand clapping now and then to add to the gospel flavor. Armstrong had recorded a powerful "Nobody Knows the Trouble I've Seen" a year earlier with a lush Russ Garcia arrangement for Verve, but remade it with Oliver with a bounce and a monologue. After the Little Rock and Jim Bishop contretemps, the irony of this selection was lost on no one.

Louis and the Good Book was Sy Oliver's favorite collaboration with Armstrong, "the most satisfactory thing that I ever did with Louis." He added, "While some of the things were swing, some of them weren't. 'Sometimes I Feel Like a Motherless Child' was ad-lib. It was very touching, and it was a performance completely unlike anything [anyone] ever heard Louis doing. That I enjoyed, I think, more than anything I ever did with him."[17] Two years later, Armstrong reprised "Sometimes I Feel Like a Motherless Child" on an episode of NBC's *Bell Telephone Hour*: "That's the first time I played 'Sometimes I Feel Like a Motherless Child' [since the recording] and even those cameramen and everybody was wiping their eyes . . . Well, that song's right in that feeling. I can see myself in that church sitting by my mother when I was a little old boy. You feel them things."[18] Still, reviews of *Louis and the Good Book* were far from heavenly. *DownBeat* gave it only two and a half stars, while condescendingly noting: "Although Armstrong remains astonishingly unchanged, tastes and manners have shifted since Louis first scored with spirituals in the 30s. There is today something vaguely offensive about Trummy Young, Hank D'Amico, and Barrett Deems, superimposed on the Sy Oliver choir and orchestra, echoing Louis' invocation to 'let my people go.' "[19] Nevertheless, the album was a strong seller and one of Louis's favorites.

After Deems's departure, Danny Barcelona began playing with the All Stars at a concert at Villanova University in February. Born on July 23, 1929, Barcelona was raised by Filipino parents in Hawaii. He began playing the drums around age eleven in a band on his father's sugar plantation. At age twelve, he performed professionally in a local dance band whose other musicians were already in their thirties, and by twenty-one he was a member of Trummy Young's band. When Young joined Armstrong in 1952, Barcelona took over its leadership, even taking the unit to Japan in 1954.

Now, without rehearsing once, Barcelona found himself inheriting Deems's and Cole's drum features, "Stompin' at the Savoy" and "Mop

Mop," the latter going back to Sid Catlett's days. Barcelona spent his first month with the band performing one-nighters in thirty different cities. "Geez, I couldn't believe it," Barcelona remembered. "Played thirty one-nighters in a row when I joined Louie, all through the States. Said, 'What am I doing here? I'm sleeping in the bus every night!'" Barcelona would remain with the All Stars for thirteen years. "I just adapted to it, you know," he said. "Get on that bandstand and give the best you got. Get all the rest you can, anyway, 'cause, you know with him, he's always moving, so you can't really mess around, you just have to keep yourself in good shape. Otherwise you're in trouble."[20]

Though Armstrong and the other members of the band might have been ebullient personalities who could drink and smoke a little weed when it suited them, it was not all one big party. "A lot of guys got the wrong idea," Barcelona said. "They think, it's Louie's band, every time we get through playing a concert or something we'd go around partying. I've got news for them! Man, when we get through playing, we're hungry, wanna get something to eat and get to bed because the next night, or the next day, it's traveling again."[21]

Still, Barcelona was witness to many moments of good humor during his tenure with the band. Early on, Armstrong gave him some Swiss Kriss to take without telling him what it was. Remembering the effects, Barcelona said, "Never again, man! Oh, that thing happened so fast, *boom!*" Thereafter whenever Armstrong offered it, Barcelona would reply, "I'm straight! I don't need it!" Those who saw the All Stars during Barcelona's years might remember Armstrong always introducing him as either "our little Filipino drummer" or "our little Hawaiian boy." Barcelona says this started when Armstrong overheard some Filipino fans in Boston comment that "Armstrong's got a Filipino drummer." One night at a gig in Portland, the governor of Hawaii was in attendance, compelling Armstrong to ask Barcelona, "What are you, Hawaiian or Filipino tonight?" "That's the way he was," Barcelona remembered. "Funny cat, man."[22]

The new configuration of the All Stars was greeted with yet more carping from critics. "Louis (Satchmo) Armstrong, who with the possible exception of Ed Sullivan has done more to revive vaudeville than any other man on this continent, held a full house in the palm of his hand for two and a half hours last night at Massey Hall," Patrick Scott wrote about an All Stars concert in Toronto. "There were two basic differences between this Armstrong concert and his previous performances during the past dozen years: Vocalist Velma Middleton did not do the splits (which was a bitter disappointment to me since I had hoped to see her break a leg), and Mr. Armstrong himself contributed a fat helping of first-rate jazz." Of Armstrong's playing, Scott wrote, "It was Mr. Armstrong . . . who furnished the most unexpected delights. He was in greater command of his trumpet than I have heard him, in the flesh, in about 13 years."[23]

Scott's assessment of Armstrong's playing is more than borne out by surviving broadcasts and concert recordings from this period—dramatic performances of, for example, "Muskrat Ramble" and "On the Sunny Side of the Street" on a *Timex All-Star Jazz Show* on NBC in April. A concert recording from North Bay, Ontario, in May finds Armstrong blowing the trumpet with breathtaking force, especially on a live-by-request performance of "Long Gone John" that dwarfs the version on *Louis Armstrong Plays W. C. Handy.* The Ontario recording is noteworthy for being perhaps the last documentation of arguably the greatest version of the All Stars Armstrong would ever lead.

On June 29, just days before the All Stars were set to make their annual appearances at Lewisohn Stadium and the Newport Jazz Festival, Edmond Hall left the band. Morris Duff reported that Hall did so "because he couldn't take it any more. After [quitting] he took a long vacation in California 'to get Louis Armstrong out of my system.' " Hall used the hackneyed critique of the band's repertory as an excuse to leave: "With Louis we played the same concert night after night without any variety," he told Duff. "It didn't matter if it was a dance, a night club or a concert hall. It was always the same. A guy's got to do something new once in a while to develop. We made records with the All-Stars but we wouldn't even play them. It was just the same concert night after night until I couldn't take it any more. This isn't jazz." Hall's gripe is, however, belied by the sheer variety of songs played by the All Stars during his tenure (the North Bay Ontario concert of May 1958, for instance, featured unusual fare).

Like most who left the All Stars, Hall was exhausted by the grind of touring: "I was tired of traveling around the world and back and forth through the U.S. I was with him exactly three years and Louis wouldn't take a vacation that whole time. That just got too much for me. He was afraid to stop playing for four or five nights for fear he'd go bad. He was afraid that his lip would give out. This was all mental, of course."[24]

Hall was replaced by Michael Hucko, known as "Peanuts." Eleven years earlier, Hucko had taken part in the historic Town Hall concert in New York City that helped bring about the birth of the All Stars, and had recorded with Armstrong at an RCA date soon afterward; in 1957, he had played in a band co-led by former All Stars sidemen Earl Hines and Jack Teagarden. Hucko's clarinet style owed a lot to Benny Goodman (he once played tenor saxophone in Goodman's band) and provided yet another new clarinet sound to the All Stars, somewhere between the liquid runs of Barney Bigard and the abandon of Edmond Hall. Yet in the wake of Hall's intensity, Hucko, whom Barcelona describes as being "on the quiet side," occasionally came off as a boring player who sometimes played by rote. The golden years of the band, with the front line of Armstrong, Young, and Hall, had ended.

At around this time, Armstrong's lips gave out again. His set at the inaugural Monterey Jazz Festival on October 3, 1958, was issued for the first time in 2007, and one hears Armstrong having a hard time with his chops. A master of pacing himself, Armstrong picked his spots and still hits the high notes, but on some songs, such as "Indiana," he was forced to forgo his solo. By the end of the night, he was playing on fumes during "When the Saints Go Marchin' In." That Armstrong was playing in pain is also evident from an October 8 Decca session. The session tapes capture multiple takes of four tunes recorded that day. The masters are edited to showcase Armstrong's best moments, but after listening to the entire session, one has to conclude that it was a difficult day for the trumpeter, marked by his grim determination to overcome his troubles.

A month later, Armstrong continued to struggle during another *Timex All-Star Jazz Show* on NBC, especially on a supercharged version of "South Rampart Street Parade" with an all-star edition of Bob Crosby's Bobcats. Armstrong was obviously in distress during the rideout choruses, barely able to hit high notes.

That same episode of the show featured Les Brown's band, with Wes Hensel on trumpet. According to Hensel's future student Boston trumpeter Phil Person, Armstrong went up to Hensel, his lips "half bleeding," and said, "Man, you gotta help me." According to Person, "Pops took Wes to his dressing room, where he had a towel laid out with needles and surgical tools. Wes said Louis felt he had to pick off the dead skin so it wouldn't 'clog up the mouthpiece.' Wes folded up the towel and threw it in the trash can. Pops said, 'Wait a minute, man! I spent [a lot of money] on that stuff!' Wes said Pops 'was the type of guy who needed to be told what he should do and he would usually listen.' Wes told him, 'Leave them alone. They'll heal right up.'" Armstrong listened, and a few months later he spotted Hensel and said, "Man, you was right. They healed right up. I got a high F like you wouldn't believe!" Hensel laughed and responded, "You always did."[25]

Two months later, on January 7, 1959, on the fourth Timex show, Armstrong seemed to have heeded Hensel's advice. As if to make up for his previous appearance, Armstrong pushed himself hard, blowing with fury on "Tiger Rag," "Ole Miss," and a closing, chaotic jam session on "Perdido." This show, however, is best known for Armstrong's historic appearance with Dizzy Gillespie. No one was prepared for what took place, years after the sniping between boppers and moldy figs had died down in the press. Gillespie was in the midst of a standard comic routine, singing "Umbrella Man" with his small group playing, when Armstrong suddenly joined him on stage. The two traded impromptu trumpet phrases for a couple of choruses. Gillespie was clearly the quicker man, but Armstrong's tone is so big, he sounds like he's playing another instrument altogether. It wasn't a cutting contest but rather a conversation highlighting why each was a maverick. Following the trumpet exchange, Gillespie, ever the showman, engaged Armstrong in a vocal duet. As Gillespie sings about his "parasol," he accidentally spits in Armstrong's face; Armstrong jokes, "Your parasol is juicy, boy," before once again extolling the efficacy of Swiss Kriss. Viewers could feel the love between the two performers, and this is one of the great moments in the history of jazz on television. It's also the only known footage or recording of Armstrong and Gillespie together.

While most of 1958 was spent on home ground, Armstrong left the United States soon after the Timex show for a world tour that would consume most of 1959. Many of the concerts were recorded, and they suggest that Armstrong was once again in top form, blowing with sometimes frightening power. He worked out on "Tiger Rag" again, playing it as if it were 1933, often taking three or four encores and hitting notes much higher than as a younger man. Armstrong now began to pace himself more, often letting the All Stars double up on their features; but even so, he didn't back down, often playing melodies an octave higher than normal, such as on Herbert's signature "Love Is Just Around the Corner" and Hucko's "The World Is Waiting for the Sunrise." Night after night Armstrong played with astonishing ferocity for someone his age.

Yet again European fans could not contain their joy at seeing Armstrong in the flesh. According to the *New York Times,* "A police riot squad used rubber truncheons and fire hoses to quell the enthusiasm of young Swiss who heard Louis Armstrong and his band in Zurich last night. The jive fans stormed the stage of Zurich's indoor sports stadium at the close of the Armstrong jam session demanding more music and seeking autographs. Mr. Armstrong and his musicians slipped out a back door under police protection. Disappointed fans then began throwing beer bottles and breaking up chairs. They battled with the police until fire hoses dispersed them. No one was reported injured and no arrests were made."[26]

It was on this European tour that Armstrong performed a bizarre one-night gig in the Netherlands village of Blokker, population 2,800. Twenty-five-year-old Ben Essing needed funds to build a clubhouse for his youth club, so he hit upon the idea of hiring Armstrong's band to play. Essing had fellow farmers from the town donate money to pay Armstrong, who was so touched by the project that he canceled two concerts elsewhere to play in Blokker. Ten thousand people showed up from all parts of Holland and Belgium for the concert, which was held at an auction hall where just a few hours before local farmers had been selling produce. The All Stars played for four hours before being asked to stop because it was getting late and the town did not have hotel accommodations for ten thousand. Armstrong said afterwards, "They didn't seem to know my music, but they were terribly grateful that I came. Man, I hope those kids get their clubhouse."[27]

In late March, the All Stars headed to the Middle East, with stops in Lebanon and Israel. According to a newspaper article from before the tour, "Glaser made it clear he would refuse any Near [sic] East dates if they stipulated that they would not accept Armstrong if he played Israel. Israel will definitely be reached, even if the whole Arab section has to be sanctified, sez Glaser."[28] Trummy Young remembered this part of the tour with great humor. Armstrong and the All Stars were booked to play Beirut by two brothers who were great smokers of hashish (Armstrong joined them). The brothers, together with some newspapermen, according to Young, asked Armstrong, "Say, how come you going playing for them damn Jews down in Israel?" Armstrong replied, "Let me tell you something. When I go down there, the first thing they going to tell me, how come you play for them damn Arabs over there?" He continued: "Let me tell you something, man. That horn, you see that horn? That horn ain't prejudiced. A note's a note in any language."[29] As Young recalled: "So, sure enough, when we got down there [to Israel], that's the first thing those guys told Louis; so Louis told them, he said, 'I told them that you guys are going to say the same damn thing. So ain't none of you no better than the other one. You's as bad as they are, man.' And so he told the press all that."

When the band played Egypt, Armstrong was asked if he supported Zionism. According to Young, he said, "What is that, Daddy?" "So they told him, said, 'You helped the Jews a lot.' He said, 'Yeah, I help them. I help anybody. I help you. You need help? I help anybody,' he said. So he told them. He said, 'Let me tell you something.' This is the way he talked. They're all about 24 newspaper reporters . . . He says, 'I'm going to tell you this. I got a trumpet, and I got a young wife, and I ain't got time to fool with none of the stuff you guys talking about,' and he walked off and left them all in the lobby, man."[30]

Some Egyptians must not have taken kindly to Armstrong's humor, for toward the end of the year there were rumors afloat in the newspapers that Armstrong was the leader of an Israeli spy network. According to the Cairo newspaper *Al-Ahram,* Lebanese security authorities had uncovered a spy ring reportedly working undercover with various artistic troupes. The report said: "Among the leading members of the gang was the famous American Negro musician Louis Armstrong, who had recently visited Beirut." Armstrong retorted, "It's all Greek to me. They claimed all that junk just because I played in Israel." He added, "I don't have to be a spy to earn my living. I make enough money blowing the horn and I have a very happy life doing it. Why don't you tell these people who are spreading all this stuff to come around. I'll tell them a few good traveling salesman jokes."[31]

Armstrong continued punishing his body throughout the trip, often playing multiple shows on certain days amid nonstop traveling. At one gig in Yugoslavia, the All Stars were supposed to go on at nine, but their plane was late, finally arriving at Zagreb Airport, ninety-five miles away from the concert, at ten p.m. Still wearing their traveling clothes, the weary All Stars headed on stage shortly before midnight. No one in the crowd of more than 3,500 had left. "Armstrong planned to play only a few numbers," newspapers reported. "But the crowd's enthusiasm was so high, he decided to go on. It was after 2 a.m. when the session ended. The musicians received a standing ovation from the happy fans."[32] Armstrong was appreciative: "You cats are like a living aspirin. You love music as much as ole Satchmovic."[33]

After wending their way through Italy in April, the All Stars played at Geneva's Victoria Hall, where the "Big Four" (the United States, France, England, and the Soviet Union) foreign ministers' conference was also taking place. "I don't know nothin' about politics," Armstrong said about the conference, "but if I could get them cats to sit still and listen, well then, daddy, maybe I can relax them a little. Get them cats to relax and daddy, they'll just relax this tension in the world."[34]

In early June in Germany, Armstrong was asked about the title of "goodwill ambassador." "I'm an American first of all," he said. "And I don't let my country down. And that's how it should be."[35] With his fifty-ninth birthday coming up, Armstrong looked to the future: "Nobody can stop that music that Satchmo plays . . . So, speaking for myself, I'll be blowing that trumpet a hundred years. With ease, the way I feel. Hallelujah."

Two weeks later, Louis Armstrong suffered a heart attack in Spoleto, Italy.

CHAPTER THIRTEEN

The Vicissitudes of Cardiac Arrest, 1959–1960

THE ALL STARS arrived in Spoleto on June 23 to play at composer Gian Carlo Menotti's Festival of Two Worlds, accompanied by impresario Ed Sullivan, who was intent on filming the festival for his television variety show. Upon briefly returning to New York after his most recent European tour, Armstrong flew to Rome, then proceeded on the two-and-a-quarter-hour drive to Spoleto, with Lucille, Sullivan, and Armstrong's personal physician, Dr. Alexander Schiff, in tow. Once there, Armstrong retired to his hotel room to rest, but began having difficulty breathing. Lucille called Menotti and Schiff, who found Armstrong on his knees in his room gasping for breath. Menotti phoned the hospital and had a tank of oxygen rushed over. A few hours later, Armstrong was rushed to a hospital. While there, he told Sullivan, "You've got to get me out of here, Ed. I've never missed a stage date in all my life." Told by Dr. Schiff he couldn't play Menotti's festival, Armstrong was inconsolable.[1]

On a 1970 episode of *The Mike Douglas Show,* Lucille Armstrong recalled the incident as the most important moment of her marriage. "We were in Italy, in Spoleto, it was a very small, picturesque town. One hospital. Nobody speaks English. And of course the diagnosis—we have our own doctor with us, Dr. Schiff, but Dr. Schiff is not allowed to practice [in Italy]. But he knows Louie's case history and he tells these doctors it's not a heart attack, it's pneumonia. And they keep saying, 'No, it's a heart attack.' They finally treated Louie for a heart attack for four days and the pneumonia is getting deeper. And Louie almost died."[2]

The first wave of newspaper reports called Armstrong's scare a heart attack, but the Associated Press reported on June 24, "The specialists said Armstrong's condition was not grave. His wife was at his beside."[3] The next day was filled with more good news, for Dr. Schiff had said Armstrong might be able to leave the hospital within a few days.[4] By now Armstrong was sitting up in bed, joking with reporters. Schiff told the Associated Press that Armstrong's heart was weakened by years of blowing the trumpet, but he had not suffered a heart attack.[5] Still, it appeared, Armstrong was being treated in accordance with a misdiagnosis; he soon took a turn for the worse. Alarmed, Countess Alicia Paolozzi, a friend of the Armstrongs, took control of the situation and sent for an English-speaking nurse and two heart specialists from Rome. In the wake of Armstrong's "heart disturbance," Lucille was called to his bedside at two a.m. The hospital said Armstrong had survived a "serious crisis" in the middle of the night but was now sleeping peacefully, though he still had a 102-degree fever. Italian heart specialist Corrado Tramontana was also at Armstrong's bedside, waiting for the other specialist to arrive.[6]

When details hit the United States, things looked grave. The *New York Post*'s front page headline was "Satchmo Goes Into a Coma; Rome Heart Doctors Called." The article inside, credited to the Associated Press, said, "Louis (Satchmo) Armstrong, who trumpeted his way to the top ranks of jazz, lay gravely ill in a coma here tonight. He was given oxygen and heart stimulants." Armstrong's condition was reported as "steadily worsening . . . The worsening in Armstrong's condition stunned members of his famous band. His rapid improvement earlier had given them hope he would be back with them within a few days. They were so cheered by this that last night, for the first time, they played on the program of the music festival. They said today, however, they would play no more while their leader is in the hospital."[7] Later in the day, Dr. Cataldo Cassano of Rome arrived to join Tramontana and Schiff. Hearing of the *Post*'s headline, Schiff made it clear that Armstrong "has not been in a coma at any time."[8]

The next day, Armstrong's condition stabilized, and he soon began to show signs of improvement. "Louie pulled out of it, he's got a very,

very strong constitution," Lucille said in 1970. "He pulled out of it and of course, this [particular] morning I'm taking this bath about six o'clock in the morning after Louie had gone into a sort of crisis when the fever breaks. And I hear Louie at six o'clock in the morning hollering, 'I want spaghetti! I want spaghetti for breakfast!' And I'm bathing and I said, 'This man's all right!' I couldn't get dressed quick enough to go in and look at him and he was just perfect."[9] Lucille propped him up on two pillows and asked him, "How do you feel, honey?" He answered, "I feel just dandy, just dandy." Armstrong's temperature was now only slightly above normal. Lucille, who kept an eighteen-hour vigil by his bedside, also made it clear that he was never in a coma.[10] Armstrong was then allowed to eat, after he had announced: "Bring it all, I'm hungry!" "He grinned, laughed and told his jokes from his hospital bed in this town in the central Italian hills," according to the Associated Press.[11]

Tramontana declared that Armstrong would still be able to play his trumpet, but he would have to take it easy for a while. So Glaser canceled Armstrong's upcoming gigs, including his appearance at what was to be a Fourth of July fifty-ninth birthday celebration at Lewisohn Stadium.[12] Upon leaving the hospital, Armstrong headed to Rome for some sightseeing, visiting St. Peter's Basilica "to thank the Good Lord for being so good to me."[13] A few days later, he wrote to Dizzy Gillespie, "There's one thing that you should always remember—you can't kill a nigger. Ha Ha Ha. Ole Sidney Bechet and Big Sid Catlett were trying to get me to come up there with them and hold that 1st chair down on the trumpet. Probably they would have had a little luck if they weren't so damn cheap. Huh—they only wanted to pay me union scale—shit."[14] On July 3, Armstrong arrived in New York. Apparently, he found time to jam with Jack Teagarden's band. "In Spoleto, if I wasn't in good shape, you know, don't no cat come out of the week with all the stuff the papers said and go right down there with Jack Teagarden, playing, when I come off the plane at two o'clock in the morning and went down and sit in that last hour with Jack," Armstrong would later say.[15]

The Lewisohn Stadium birthday concert was still on for the Fourth. Gene Krupa and Herbie Mann performed, before the All Stars took the stage with Wild Bill Davison filling in for Armstrong. At the conclusion of the concert, all hell broke loose. As the *New York Times* put it:

Then Satchmo showed up and, if there had been a roof, it would have been blown off . . . As he came on the stage, there was a moment of surprise, then a roaring, standing ovation from 8,000 persons present. Impromptu choruses of 'Happy Birthday' were clearly audible above the din, but Mr. Armstrong quieted them when he began to play. After a moment of suspense while he blew a few random notes, he went into his theme, "Sleepy Time Down South," adding a rousing vocal chorus for good measure. With the musicians behind him, he continued to delight the crowd with his playing and singing in "Back Home Again in Indiana" and "Gypsy."[16]

Armstrong played for about fifteen minutes and said after the show, "I didn't come here to prove I'm not sick. I came just to play."[17]

Armstrong would fully recover from his illness, and he would continue to downplay it for the rest of his life. He called it a mere "chest cold" he got from eating too much spaghetti late at night followed immediately by sleeping directly under an open window. And he wanted to make it clear that he had never been in a coma. "When I picked up our American paper where it said I was in a coma, I know they was wrong then, 'cause I'm from New Orleans, Louisiana, and all my life we was under the impression nothing but rich people went into comas! We went into a trance, maybe. But it all ended up nice."[18] Until the day he died, Armstrong, Lucille, Glaser, and everyone in his inner circle refused publicly to admit that Armstrong had had a heart attack in Spoleto. It wasn't until 1984 that Schiff, appearing in a British documentary on Armstrong, finally came clean. "All the time I said that Louie did not have a heart attack, Louie had a respiratory condition, pneumonia," Schiff said. "I brought this man up from Rome to agree with my diagnosis so that Louie's career would not be ended."[19] When Armstrong visited heart specialist Gary Zucker in 1968, Zucker performed a cardiogram that confirmed the heart attack, something Zucker spoke about after Armstrong's passing. As Schiff alluded, admitting a heart attack would have been bad for business. Club owners might have been skeptical about booking a frail, ailing artist.

By July 18, Armstrong was back with the All Stars, playing in front of six thousand people in Stony Brook, Long Island. "My main interest in driving out to Stony Brook was to hear just how much the ordeal had affected Louis, and to ask him personally how he had felt, and felt now, about his physical condition," Leonard Feather wrote. "The first question was soon answered, for Louis's pipes and chops obviously were completely unshaken. He played as much and as well as ever: his spirits were at their perennial ebullient level."[20] Of the two-hour show, Hugh Thomson said, "He is not only back to normal, which for him is highly exuberant, but seems to have gained gusto."[21] To Feather, Armstrong allowed: "I keep my body up good—I wasn't never in doubt about getting well. And I knew all along it wasn't my heart. What happened was, they worked me too hard—cut into the middle of my vacation, making me play a private performance for somebody's party. I needed a little rest, that's all."[22] Now that he was back on the road, the last thing Armstrong was about to get was a little rest. John Norris, in reviewing Armstrong's August set at the Toronto Jazz Festival for *Coda* magazine, was astounded by the amount of traveling Armstrong had to do in this period. "The ridiculous booking of the Armstrong band will have to be reviewed one day soon, for his agent surely cannot go on drawing blood from them for ever," Norris wrote. "The band travelled 500 miles from Columbus, Ohio, to make the festival. They left Columbus at 2 a.m. arriving in Toronto just before 6 p.m. the next evening. Their next engagement was in Milwaukee Sunday evening, when they were playing three 30-minute spots. This meant leaving straight after the show for another 600 miles of grueling travel by bus. This kind of thing was typical in the 1930s but is not what one would expect today." The scheduled bus trip proved to be a little too much; as Norris added, "Rather than face this sort of schedule and desirous of keeping fit, Louis, Velma and others in the band chose instead to fly at their own expense the following morning."[23] Though Armstrong was back to the grind remarkably soon after a heart attack, he wasn't acting any differently. When asked if he noticed any change, Danny Barcelona answered emphatically, "No! No, it was the same thing like he never left. It was a surprise, you know. I didn't think he'd come back that fast."[24] To all intents and purposes, Armstrong was still playing in peak form. He would go forward, traveling and performing as if nothing serious had happened.

From August 3 through August 5, Armstrong was in Chicago, back in the recording studio with Frank Assunto's Dukes of Dixieland, with whom he had shared a bill the previous summer. "They're home boys," Armstrong said of the Dukes. "Whenever we're playing in the same town, I go and sit in."[25] Much of the repertoire for the session was composed of

Dixieland warhorses, but Armstrong also included such All Stars set pieces as "Back o' Town Blues," "Someday You'll Be Sorry," and "My Bucket's Got a Hole in It." As their name suggested, the Dukes were very much an old-fashioned Dixieland band, but they swung, though not in the polished manner of the All Stars. While he acquits himself with power and brilliance on "Dippermouth Blues" and "Bill Bailey," Armstrong has some trouble executing the quick-fingered stop-time solo on "Cornet Chop Suey," which he had blazed through at the *Autobiography* sessions of 1957.

The recording with the Dukes was made for Audio Fidelity, a small label best known for releasing the first commercial stereophonic record in 1957. After his last recordings for Decca, Armstrong was now a free agent, open for business to the highest bidder, who would turn out to be the label's president, Sid Frey. After recording Armstrong with the Dukes, he lifted an idea for an album that George Avakian originally wanted to produce for Columbia in the mid-fifties: Armstrong and his All Stars performing the music of Armstrong's mentor Joe "King" Oliver. But unlike Avakian, who would have given much care and consideration to such a project, Frey did not want to pay extravagantly for rights to copyrighted Oliver material, so he ended up recording much public-domain material, including songs that had nothing to do with Oliver whatsoever, such as "My Old Kentucky Home" and "Frankie and Johnny." What is more, most of the All Stars were unfamiliar with Oliver's music. "A lot of the numbers, old King Oliver numbers, Billy Kyle and I didn't know," Trummy Young remembered. "We had never heard them before, so Pops had to play them over for us a couple of times, and show us where the breaks were. He taught me some of the phrases on one of those tunes, and made it a lot easier for me."[26] As a result, a certain stiffness creeps into the performances of "Snake Rag" and "Drop That Sack," among others, as the band sounds as if it is struggling to be a two-beat Dixie band.

Still, there are high points on the Oliver tribute: "I Ain't Got Nobody" features Armstrong's time-honored, but extremely difficult, playing of the melody an octave higher, nailing every note; his concluding cadenza on "St. James Infirmary" is unlike any other version in his career, ending on a piercing high concert E-flat; and, as in his youth, he figures out ways to transcend inferior material such as "My Old Kentucky Home" and "A Hot Time in the Old Town Tonight." Even John S. Wilson, implacable nemesis of the All Stars, agreed that *Satchmo Plays King Oliver* had its virtues.

In *DownBeat* he saw fit to give it three stars. "To say that this is the best recording to come from Armstrong's touring sextet in the last five years is fainter praise than the disc deserves," the review read. "The material gets the group away from the things it now does by rote, and Armstrong at least plays and sings with some semblance of creative fire."[27] As for the black media, Armstrong was applauded for changing "darkies" to "folks" in the lyrics of "My Old Kentucky Home." "Forget those old notions about Louis Armstrong being a 'handkerchief head,' " *Jet* magazine intoned. "He just had an impromptu session for a Dixieland album, which included 'My Old Kentucky Home.' When he came to the lyrics, 'It's summer and (you know who) is gay,' he sang: 'It's summer, and the folks they're all gay,' after first making certain he knew how the original words went. Salute!!"[28]

Armstrong and the All Stars, however, would not be saluted in New Orleans. Toward the end of the year, Jefferson Parish, part of metropolitan New Orleans, was dedicating the Louis Armstrong Playground. The parish wanted Armstrong to play at the dedication, but as he later wrote, "There's a state law that doesn't allow mixing of Negro and white musicians. They want me to leave the two white boys in my band home. But I say, 'That wouldn't be my band.' So I don't go."[29] Armstrong told a *New Orleans Times-Picayune* reporter that he would not return to his hometown until he was "received without racial distinction . . . I'm accepted all over the world, and when New Orleans accepts me, I will go home . . . I'm accepted in satellite nations behind the Iron Curtain, even before they see me . . . I feel bad about it, but will nonetheless stay that way."[30]

A New Orleans radio newscaster, retired school principal, and former friend of Armstrong's, O. C. W. Taylor, took umbrage at Armstrong's position. Taylor made insinuations regarding Armstrong's 1949 appearance as King of the Zulus in New Orleans: "So drunk was Louis at the time, and so rickety was the wagon, that both fell to pieces in the middle of the street, stopping the burlesque parade."[31] He added that Armstrong "was always contented to return a grinning, ape-like Sambo and help keep the Negro in his 'Uncle Tom' status. Maybe New Orleans does not accept him. New Orleans prefers to read about him, to remember him as a successful trumpet player . . . maybe New Orleans is rather tired of having him come down and lower the level of the Negro group." For his part, Armstrong simply dismissed Taylor's attack. He continued the boycott of his hometown into the next decade.

CHAPTER FOURTEEN

From the Dukes of Dixieland
to Dave Brubeck, 1960–1963

IN EARLY 1960, exhausted by the constant grind of touring, Peanuts Hucko left the band to pursue work as a studio musician. A rejuvenated Barney Bigard rejoined the All Stars; he no longer seemed tired and bored. Trummy Young, for one, was now impressed with his playing: "Barney Bigard sounds a whole lot better than when he was with the band before. He'll surprise you." Young also supposed the reason: "He's not drinking."[1] As Bigard tells it: "When I played my first job with Louis after being out of the band for so long I asked him, 'What are you going to open with, Pops?' ' "Back Home Again in Indiana," ' he said. Five years later it was still 'Indiana' . . . Trummy and Louis were as good as ever and it felt like old times to be back."[2]

Armstrong celebrated his sixtieth birthday while on tour in the summer of 1960, briefly accompanied by jazz writer Bill Coss and photographer Herb Snitzer, who were traveling with the band for a piece for *Metronome*. In the article Armstrong reminisced about one of his heroes: "You'd go back to his dressing room and Bill ["Bojangles"] Robinson would be crouched around the table, tears running down his face, in real agony, and the man would rap on the door and say, 'One minute,' and Bill would stand and wipe his face, and put his shoulders back, and grin, and dance on that stage. THAT's show business!" Here was Armstrong's philosophy of entertaining, and it accounts for why he continued to push himself so hard even as his health gradually declined throughout the 1960s.[3]

Behind the scenes, Armstrong continued having problems with Frenchy Tallerie. Armstrong had fired Tallerie after Tallerie frantically and presumptuously tried to cover up Armstrong's comments on the Little Rock crisis, but had allowed him back, most likely as a favor to Joe Glaser. Apparently, a few All Stars engagements were canceled and all the musicians in the group were reimbursed except for Armstrong. In a scathing letter sent to Joe Glaser on May 17, 1960, he didn't hold back. "Dear Mr. Glaser," he wrote. "Please don't ignore this letter like you didn't (ANSWER) concerning Frenchy giving every(one) their faire back and keeping mine and hasn't given (it) to me as yet. I just don't like to be *ignored*. I think that I am entitled a little bit somewhat as sort of being treated like a man instead [of] just a Goddam *Child* all the time. *That* we can forget. So please (don't) let me down (on) this issue."[4] How Tallerie still had a job at this point boggles the mind, but the letter is further proof that Armstrong was not afraid to stand up to Glaser when he felt he was being taken advantage of. Dan Morgenstern related that some time in the early 1960s, "I also overheard Louis on the phone with Joe, giving as good as he apparently was getting in the foulmouth department. No 'Mister Glaser' in evidence there, but it ended calmly. Armstrong was never afraid of Glaser's tough-guy demeanor."[5]

So it happened that Armstrong recorded two albums in 1960, neither with the All Stars. The first was another pairing with the Dukes of Dixieland, which took place at New York's Webster Hall. Many Armstrong insiders attended the sessions, including his publicist Ernie Anderson, his good friend Jack Bradley, guitarist Marty Grosz, Gene Krupa, and two very different trumpeters, Max Kaminsky and Dizzy Gillespie. Armstrong was his irrepressible self; on "South" he improvised an ode to red beans: "You eat a big plate and Swiss Kriss in the morning!" The repertoire this time around was comprised of songs not regularly performed by the All Stars, and Armstrong responded with scorching horn work on "Limehouse Blues," "Wolverine Blues," and an exceptional vocal and instrumental version of "Avalon." When he plays lead over Frank Assunto's second trumpet—as with his appearance with Gillespie—Armstrong sounds as if he were playing a heretofore unimagined instrument. Assunto was agog: "The old man is too much."[6] On two of the slower pieces,

"New Orleans" and "Just a Closer Walk with Thee," Armstrong was pre-ternaturally effective. In 2007, the band's helicon player, Rich Matteson, recalled Armstrong's playing the latter tune: "In that moment, he turned that place into a personal chapel. He looked up and he started talking to God . . . Nobody in the room but Louie and his God. It was absolutely frightening. And we got done with the first take, I'm standing there cry-ing. I turned and looked, the drummer's crying, the clarinet player's cry-ing, the trombones are crying, Lucille's crying, his own wife."

Armstrong called for a break when he noticed that even the engineer could not look him in the eye, having gotten too emotional. During the break, Matteson asked Armstrong how he could play like that in a stu-dio without a live audience. "Well, I always play for somebody I love," Armstrong responded. "That's all. You play for somebody you love all the time. I always play for Him because He gives me talent. I play for Lucille because she's my wife and I love her and if I make a mistake, she under-stands. They all want to listen, that's cool. And if they don't want to listen, it's still cool, because I was going to play for Him and her anyway."[7]

Armstrong's next recording partner would be an old friend he had been teaming up with for nearly twenty-five years: Bing Crosby. Though they had recorded singles and film soundtracks, this was to be their first full-length album together. But Armstrong was burdened by too overtly a Dixieland setting on this album, performing such songs as "Let's Sing Like a Dixieland Band," "Muskrat Ramble" and "At the Jazz Band Ball," the latter two chiefly jazz instrumentals now given corny lyrics for the occasion. Several numbers are marred by an intrusive choir, trashing the integrity of pieces like "Little Ol' Tune." All the same, there are some pleas-ant surprises, such as Armstrong's take on Horace Silver's "The Preacher," while "Rocky Mountain Moon," arguably the best track on the record, is stunningly beautiful from start to finish.

Billy May was hired for the date's arrangements, and Johnny Mercer for new lyrics. "That was a labor of love for John, because John loved Louis, and I know he's a good friend of Bing's," May remembered. He continued: "Louis was fun to work with. He enjoyed life, and he enjoyed recording. He enjoyed singing. He enjoyed playing. And he enjoyed talking to the musicians. And it was old home week . . . Almost all the musicians that I had in the band had worked with and were former—had something to do with him before. And Bing of course enjoyed being around musicians. It was really a fun gig."[8]

Armstrong continued touring into September before his first overseas trip since his near-death experience in Spoleto. On October 1, Pepsi-Cola International opened five bottling plants in West Africa to produce eight million cases of soda a year. A Pepsi spokesman said, "To help move these cases along to the nationals of Ghana and Nigeria, Pepsi-Cola is sending a jazz group headed by Louis Armstrong to entertain West Africans . . ."[9] One-half of the profits of Armstrong's stint in Southern Rhodesia in November were to go to Nyatsime College near Salisbury.[10]

Before heading for Africa, Armstrong spoke about the trip: "This is an important event, sure, but don't get me wrong—all dates are important. Whenever I play it's important to me; you still got to hit them notes."[11] The first stop was Accra, Ghana, where all fifty thousand seats in the city's sports stadium were sold in advance. Once there, Armstrong changed his tune; the African tour was no longer just another date, however important, but "the most important event in my life."[12] At the airport, he was met by three thousand Ghanians. Banners welcomed him throughout the city while musicians played and sang everywhere Armstrong looked. A Pepsi press release noted, "At times even Satchmo, who has been mobbed by admiring fans in every country he has visited, became anxious about his immediate future. One moment of truth came when a few over-jubilant Ghanians suddenly hoisted him to their shoulders and tossed him around like a medicine ball."[13]

The night of the first show, it rained so hard, the stage Armstrong was supposed to play on collapsed. It was propped up with cement blocks and wooden boxes and the show went on, but here was an ominous sign of things to come. "The magic of Louis (Satchmo) Armstrong's trumpet went a little sour in Lagos, Nigeria, last night," said a report after an October date. "It seems the Africans don't dig jazz while the American horn-blower doesn't dig calypso . . . Before the U.S. goodwill ambassador and his all-star combo had blown three numbers, the locals were swinging for the exits. Their beat was for home. The harder Satchmo blew the more fans he blew out the door. When he was finished only a handful of the 15,000 spectators remained."[14]

Offstage, Armstrong met with Sir Ahmadu Bello, the premier of

Northern Nigeria, a visit he remembered ten years later on *The Mike Douglas Show.* "The king, he couldn't take us over there, you know, so I stayed with all his men," Armstrong recounted. "He took Lucille and Velma Middleton, my vocalist, to meet all his harem. Boy, he must have had about a hundred wives. Yes sir, they must keep a muzzle on him or something with all those wives!" Pepsi's support of the tour would soon come to an end, proclaiming it "an enormous success."

The State Department, via the U.S. Information Agency, stepped into the breach and sponsored the next leg of the tour. Armstrong received a tumultuous reception from the Congolese, who called him "Okuka Lokole"—jungle wizard, the man who can charm beasts. He was entering the Belgian Congo at a volatile time: the country was in the midst of a civil war between followers of Prime Minister Patrice Lumumba and President Joseph Kasavubu, the latter's forces led by future dictator Mobutu Sese Seko. But in honor of Armstrong's visit, both sides stopped fighting and welcomed him grandly, bearing him on a red throne, which was reported in many newspapers and even in a movie newsreel. "The Congolese briefly forgot their differences to give Satchmo a triumphant welcome to Leopoldville," is how the Associated Press reported it in a story headlined, " 'Wizard' Satchmo Unites the Congo!" "They cheered and jived in the street as Satchmo drove past behind a truckload of native dancers . . . The army of Col. Joseph Mobutu and the police force loyal to ex-Premier Patrice Lumumba joined forces to provide a heavily armed cordon 'round Satchmo and his party from the moment they stepped off the Congo River ferry from Brazzaville. Satchmo shook his head sadly at the sight of all the rifles. But he cheered up when Congolese girls in colorful costumes turned up to pose for pictures with him and his wife, Lucille."[15] "We came off that ferry and then we got in the automobile and no more shooting," Armstrong recounted in 1970. "And then they paraded all through the city. And the day of the concert they put me in this chair—and you know, you've got to be somebody to ride in that chair. That's better than ol' rocking chair!" Asked if he was scared, Armstrong responded, "With my people? That's all they know. 'Ol' Satch-e-mo,' all through the jungles."[16] When he got to the stage, Armstrong announced, *"Merci beaucoup, beaucoup,"* to thunderous ovation.

At the evening's concert in front of 175,000 people at a Leopoldville soccer stadium, members of warring parties sat together, danced, and cheered the music. No sooner did Armstrong and the All Stars leave the Congo than fighting resumed. Such was the power of "Ambassador Satch." Back in the United States, Armstrong's trip to Africa was receiving praise as well. One editorial that appeared in many newspapers in mid-November stated: "Having been around the world numerous times, and as a representative of the State Department, this man with his trumpet is able to overcome barriers between peoples in a way beyond the capacity of polished diplomats."[17]

Armstrong must have been proud of the work he was doing now at age sixty. He was blowing the trumpet in particularly fine form. "If I'm in the gutter, I still got enough strength to blow in the ceiling," he said at this time. "I mean, you got to live with that horn. That's why I married four times. The chicks didn't live with the horn. They got too carried away, all but the last, and forget everything about the horn. I don't. I don't want a million dollars. See what I mean? No medals. I mean, I don't feel no different about the horn now than I did when I was playin' in the Tuxedo Band. That's my livin' and my life. I love them notes. That's why I try to make 'em right."[18] Feeling his oats, he couldn't resist a dig at the younger jazz trumpet players, something he hadn't done publicly in quite some time: "How many modern trumpet players could play my solos? You'd have to carry 'em out on stretchers."[19]

And even though at sixty he was an elder statesman, Armstrong was not about to stop playing any time soon. "I look at it this way, too," he said. "I get outa that bed every day, see? I make a good salary and my horn still sounds good. And I *feel* good. So I don't think nobody in the world [is] any richer than I am. Musicians don't retire. They stop when there's no more work. We never thought about that in New Orleans. Like we say there, 'That our *hustle*,' you know, a day's work. But anybody sit down with their money and look at the four walls, they don't live long; they die. There's nothin' I can say other than I've set *myself* up to be a happy man. *And*—I made it."[20]

Armstrong took a break from the African tour in early December to head to Paris, where he performed two new Duke Ellington numbers, "Battle Royal" and "Wild Man," in the film *Paris Blues*. In Paris, excepting two concerts on Christmas Eve and two on New Year's Eve, the All Stars waited for filming to conclude. Asked what they were up to, Billy Kyle responded with a smile: "Getting over that African tour."[21] "The rest of us, Trummy, myself, Barney, Mort Herbert, Billy Kyle, you know, we just played tourists," Danny Barcelona remembered. "Went all over Paris for five weeks. Not bad, huh? You got paid for it, you got a hotel paid for . . . while Louie was working!"[22]

Once the break was over, Armstrong and the All Stars returned for more dates in Africa. Tragedy would strike Velma Middleton, Armstrong's comic foil and female vocalist for nearly twenty years: she collapsed of a stroke while climbing steep stairs. Her health had been slipping and the intense African heat had not been salubrious. As her stroke occurred at the tail end of the tour, the band could not wait for her to get better. She was put in a Sierra Leone hospital, and *Jet* magazine reported she was partially paralyzed.[23]

A traumatized Armstrong wrote to Joe Glaser in the wake of Middleton's stroke. "She's got a stroke that's a Bitch," he wrote.

> Mr. Glaser, I ain't never in my whole life, seen anyone with a Stroke like Velma's. She has a stroke (all the way) down her whole right side. Even her (Eye) is paralyzed. Hump. Ain't that 'somphin'? What she needs now is to be taken from that small Hospital from Freetown, Africa and brought to America, USA, put into Hospital right away, where they may save her life. Because she is in a Bad Condition. Pray to the Lord that she won't have another Stroke before she get a chance to see (at least see) the good 'ol' American soils again. 'Gosh.' We're still 'Carrying on with our concerts, just like nothing happened. But it's hard to do.[24]

She never did recover, and died alone there on February 10, 1961, the site of her burial in question, and Louis and the band away on tour. "They didn't have the facilities to treat someone like that," wrote Bigard. "I'll never forgive Joe Glaser and Louis for that, because they said it would take too many people to lift her on the plane to France. I said to myself, 'This woman gave her all, and they just leave her here, like that, in some little African town.' "[25]

Armstrong and Lucille would have taken Bigard to task about Glaser's handling of the situation. In a private tape made with friends shortly after Middleton's passing, Louis and Lucille talked about the episode. All along the Armstrongs had wanted Middleton buried in America for her family's sake, and she eventually was. "But for Joe Glaser, she wouldn't be there," Lucille said caustically. "Joe Glaser pulled all—that's why it took ten days to get her here—all kinds of strings to get her over here. She would have been buried in Africa." For his part, Louis insisted: "If it don't be for Joe, her mother would never had had that body." Their only regret was that it took so long to transport Middleton's body to the United States. Because of the severity of her stroke, only half of her body could be embalmed; in the long waiting period, the body had deteriorated and was ravaged by maggots. "Couldn't open the casket," Armstrong lamented. "And if you had seen her, she wouldn't look like herself after being four days buried there." With solemnity, Armstrong made a bizarre comparison. "People don't stay the same after they die," he said. "Just like a pile of shit, you put it in the street, in the morning, when the sun hit it, anything li'ble to be coming out of there. That's what I'm talking about."[26]

Middleton had served Armstrong loyally for nineteen years and, in their timeless duets, had given pleasure to audiences around the world. In the final documentation of Middleton's contribution, an African concert recording from November 1960, she sang as she did night in and out, but in retrospect she is poignant. On "St. Louis Blues," she sang her own lyrics about Armstrong blowing "nice and high," ending with "I'm gonna love that man till the day that I die." On their final show stopper, "That's My Desire," Middelton's last lines are "Though you've found someone new, / I'll always love you, / That's my desire." Critics might have scoffed at her dancing and splits, but she was part of the family, the band, and things would never be the same without her. Armstrong knew Middleton was irreplaceable. "It ain't necessary to have another female singer," he told *Jet* magazine, "because there ain't no more Velmas."[27] Dan Morgenstern wrote, "This was a trouper's passing, and Velma was a trouper to the bone."[28]

After the heart scare in 1959 and Middleton's passing in 1961, Armstrong perhaps was finally forced to confront the punishing work schedule he continued to embrace. In the same letter to Glaser in which he lamented Middleton's stroke, he also introduced a novel idea, though he did so in a way to show he was serious. "You're my man," he began. "But, just one thing. You're skeptical of my abilities and myself 'knows' you are frightened of my assuredness." Having established this, Armstrong sprung his idea on Glaser: an extended run on Broadway. "Yeah man Dig this Shit," he wrote. "The title of our band concert only our Show A Night With 'Satchmo' And His All Stars. Do you hear me Mr. Glaser? It is about time Dammit. If I can please people, all over the world, why can't you rent a theatre with just a stage. Any kind of stage. With the right lights and right mikes. 'Shit.' We're in business."[29] Perhaps realizing he was being too forceful, Armstrong backed away a bit and heaped on some flattery. "I am just pulling your leg buddy. You keep me with the best and for that I love your dirty Drawers for it." But in his postscript, Armstrong couldn't resist one more plug for his idea: "P.S. Always remember the same people whom we play for all over the world comes to New York some time or other. And just them alone will buy tickets (You Dig?). Will be great. Wow."

Glaser obviously disregarded the idea, because Armstrong continued a string of one-nighters as soon as he returned home from overseas; the money was just too lucrative to turn down. It was around this time that columnist Jack O'Brian spent an afternoon at Glaser's Associated Booking office with both Louis and Lucille Armstrong. "We conversed an hour and suddenly Louis rasped: 'Show Jack the books,' " O'Brian later wrote. "Joe reacted as if mad. 'Why should I show him the books?' he demanded in mock anger. 'Because I want him to see them,' Louis said, simply. Joe went to a huge walk-in wall vault, reached high for a large leather case, upended it on his desk, and said, 'Start counting. There's $15,000 to $20,000 in every book—all insured by the government.' They were bankbooks. Joe ticked them off: more than a million dollars, maybe much more; we couldn't keep up with Joe's count."[30] Armstrong proudly asked Glaser to show O'Brian the books because he knew he was responsible for much of that money. He also knew that when the money was rolling in, he and Lucille could only benefit, as evidenced by a letter Glaser wrote to Armstrong in the summer of 1961 before sending Armstrong on another tour: "It will be a pleasure for me to give you some extra going away bucks."[31] For the time being, there was nowhere else for Armstrong to go than back on the road. But just the fact that Armstrong himself was envisioning staying put and doing his show on Broadway—a short distance from his home in Corona, Queens—demonstrates that perhaps the grind on the road was beginning to wear on his mind as well as his body.

Back in the United States, Armstrong's next step made consummate sense. Having played with Duke Ellington on the Timex show in 1959 and having performed his music in *Paris Blues*, Armstrong teamed up with

Ellington for a studio album. Bob Thiele, a producer at Roulette Records, had finally succeeded in getting the two jazz giants to record a program of Ellington tunes, Duke himself on piano. Over two days in April 1961, Armstrong, Ellington, and the All Stars met in RCA's New York City studios for seventeen songs. With time in short supply, arrangements were scant, nor was Ellington able to prepare anything new, as he had in previous meetings with Ella Fitzgerald and Coleman Hawkins. Still, the music that resulted was nearly flawless. It is joyous to hear Armstrong put his inimitable stamp on such standards as "Drop Me Off in Harlem," "It Don't Mean a Thing (If It Ain't Got That Swing)," and "Don't Get Around Much Anymore," and on ballads such as "Solitude," "I Got It Bad (and That Ain't Good)," and "Mood Indigo." He was battling a slight cold, and his voice sounds deeper than usual, his singing nonchalant and forceful even as his trumpet playing was that of a man half his age. The session's biggest surprises were two anomalies: a track Ellington made up on the spot, "The Beautiful American," an uptempo blues in a minor key, and "Azalea," written with Armstrong in mind years earlier—an intricate melody deftly handled by Armstrong's horn, the beauty of whose wily lyrics lies in such Ellington rhymes as "azalea" with "failure" (pronounced "fail-ya") and "assail ya." Armstrong charmingly breezed through the twists and turns of the song, Ellington brilliantly comping behind him. So it was that the two managed to create a classic.

The Armstrong-Ellington collaboration was a happy experience for all involved. "To see Louis at work under these circumstances was, for us, a rare privilege," said critic Stanley Dance, who was present at the sessions. "He never spared himself and he was so quick to grasp the whole conception of an interpretation . . . At the piano Duke was full of ideas and a great source of inspiration."[32] Barney Bigard, who had worked with Ellington for fourteen years, recalled, "Duke and I reminisced a while before we started, but the main thing was that Louis got along so great with Duke. I mean two prominent leaders on one date could have been rough, but we had no problems . . . The session came out real well."[33] For Bigard, though, this would be his final stand with the All Stars. One of its charter members, he would continue touring until July of 1961, when he again decided to leave, this time for good.

Bigard was replaced by another New Orleans clarinetist, Joe Darensbourg. Born in 1906, Darensbourg remembered hearing Armstrong play as a young man in the Crescent City. "That's one of the things that really made me want to be a musician, hearing a sound like that," he would later write. "What a man!"[34] In the 1920s, Darensbourg played with trumpeter Oscar "Papa" Celestin and pianist Jelly Roll Morton, among others; but he really didn't begin making his mark until the New Orleans jazz revival of the 1940s. Based on the West Coast, Darensbourg played for years with trombonist Kid Ory. In the mid-fifties he joined the band of Armstrong-inspired trumpeter Teddy Buckner before good fortune struck in 1957 when his Capitol recording of "Yellow Dog Blues" became a bona fide hit record. The novelty of the recording was that it featured Darensbourg playing in an old-fashioned, slap-tongue style that somehow appealed to the public.

The clarinetist joined Armstrong during a rare night off in Buffalo and made his debut on July 17, in Bala, Ontario. "One of the first things Louis said to me was, 'Well, Joe, now you with the All Stars, so *you* a star. Let's see you shine.' "[35] It didn't take long before Darensbourg began featuring himself on "Yellow Dog Blues." "When you got ready to play, Louis would say, 'This is your solo, play whatever you want, long as you want, short as you want, just do it.' Those were his very words. He never told anybody how to play. He wasn't one of them bandleaders that would tell you this or that . . . We always had a lot of fun and, certainly, I never worked for a better guy or a better bandleader."[36]

Darensbourg signed a one-year contract but wound up staying three years. In that time, he got along beautifully with Armstrong, but he also saw the sterner side of the trumpeter at times. "I was about a minute late getting on the stand, for some reason—I had to go to the men's room," Darensbourg told drummer and writer Barry Martyn. "And when I got up there, he says, 'Look, that's one thing I won't tolerate. You men be on this stand. Listen, homeboy, we hit. We *hit*.' And another time, Billy Kyle was taking a solo, and me and Trummy started talking. Boy, Louis got mad . . . He said, 'When a man is taking a solo, anything you do to distract him . . . That's his spot, and you don't do nothin' to distract him, because you wouldn't want him to do it on your solo.' He says, 'I don't do it.' And then he says, 'You guys just be quiet, that's all.' "[37]

Darensbourg also witnessed an altercation between Armstrong and one of the band's other new faces, bassist Irv Manning. Mort Herbert had left the group in early June to practice law full-time, which he continued to do until his untimely death at the age of fifty-seven in 1983. Manning had performed with many jazz greats, including Eddie Condon and Benny Goodman, before joining the All Stars. After Darensbourg joined a month later, Armstrong called a rare rehearsal in Boston to go over features and background parts. Manning wanted to do a comedic skit on "The Rain in Spain" for his feature, "but nobody liked it and finally Louis got fed up and he says, 'I don't know, Irv, I don't think it will fit.' Irv says, 'The only reason I was doing it was to get *you* a laugh.' When he said that, Louis got mad as hell. He said, 'I been playing music before you was born. I don't need you to get a laugh for me.' " Manning called Armstrong a "sonofabitch" and Armstrong told him to quit on the spot; Manning quickly apologized.[38] He was safe for the time being, but the incident would prove a harbinger of what was to come.

Darensbourg was full of anecdotes that shed light on Armstrong's offstage persona. "He spent a lot of money on people, orphanages, things that you never seen in the papers," Darensbourg wrote. "Like when we went down to Tennessee, where they had the only all-colored medical school. Louis and Joe [Glaser] had donated thousands of dollars to help them build a new wing for heart research and we went down to play for them. I felt it was a beautiful thing to play for something like this and I enjoyed meeting some very prominent doctors. Louis never turned anybody down. I seen him give away cash money to all sorts of people that was having a hard time."[39] Darensbourg was careful to explain that Armstrong's charity was consistent with his unique working relationship with Joe Glaser. "A lot of people used to say Louis was gonna wind up broke because of his generosity," he said. "Louis told me himself that him and Joe didn't have any kind of written contract. People would say that nobody knew how Joe was splitting the money, but Louis wasn't as dumb as they thought. Once every six months him and Joe would have a meeting so he knew what was happening, or Lucille did. Anyway, when he died he'd wound up a millionaire and Lucille had all the money she needed."[40]

Darensbourg also noted the pleasure Armstrong took in simple things. "Louis was crazy about [Cracker Jack] popcorn, so every time I'd pass a place I'd pick up about half a dozen boxes for him . . . As soon as he opened that box he'd look for the prize. One time it was a little trumpet, made a whistling sound when he blew it, so he says, 'I hope it's a Selmer.' He played it all the time on the bus. He was just like a little kid that had found a diamond ring."[41]

Darensbourg spent much free time with an ebullient Armstrong, usually sampling Darensbourg's Creole cooking, but he also witnessed the trumpeter more subdued when he was alone. "For all his popularity, Louis could be sitting in his dressing room and he looked like the saddest guy in the world. That always amazed me. He'd be sitting with his horn in his hand, just looking at it, turning it over, looking at the bell, picking it up and blowing a little, that's all."[42]

Velma Middleton had been well-nigh impossible to replace, and for several months Armstrong had not bothered even to try.[43] Now, in addition to Darensbourg and Manning, Armstrong added a new vocalist, Jewel Brown, a twenty-three-year-old Houston native, to the band, but how she became one of the All Stars was instructive. After working with Earl Grant in Los Angeles, she had settled into the Chalet Club in Dallas, working for the infamous Jack Ruby. There Tony Papa, a representative of Joe Glaser's ABC booking agency, had heard her. After Middleton's death, Glaser had his people across the country search for a singer, even though, as Brown remembers, "they weren't very sure that Louie would even want another singer because of the tie between he and Velma, and he was quite hurt at losing her."

On Papa's recommendation, Glaser flew down to Texas and caught one of Brown's shows without letting her know he was in the audience. "I did not know that he had done that until later on," she recalls. Impressed, Glaser flew immediately back to New York, where he began brainstorming a way to get her into the band. When the All Stars were next in Texas, Glaser had Brown audition by working with the band for two weeks. Brown remembers that altogether some five hundred singers all over the country were after the job, but after hearing many of them and letting some sit in, the band was given final say. "I believe they asked the boys in the band what did they think about me," Brown says. "And they said, 'Well, that little girl down there in Texas got it going on!'" Brown officially joined the band in June of 1961.[44]

Of meeting Armstrong, Brown recalls, "He seemed delighted in me. I mean, I didn't know what to think or say. I've never been afraid of anybody. I just went in, all whole hog, you know." When asked what Armstrong was like offstage, Brown replied, "The same as he was onstage. He was just the same, personable kind of guy. He was the same personable fellow offstage as what people saw onstage, and I guess that was his success. He was always personable, like he was sitting in somebody's lap, singing to them, performing. And Pops was just friendly to all people, whether he understood their language or whatever. It seemed like they understood his gestures whether they understood English or not. And I believe that was his success."

The new faces in the band did not stem the negative criticism showered on the All Stars, especially after an October 12 performance at Massey Hall in Toronto. "Mr. Armstrong still calls his band the All-Stars, but any resemblance between professional jazz musicians and the collection of mediocrity Mr. Armstrong dragged behind him all night, last night, is strictly wishful thinking," Patrick Scott wrote in a devastating review in the *Globe and Mail.* According to Brown, Armstrong was never bothered by what critics wrote about him. "Critics are not the people that buy the tickets," she says. "So what they say is really insignificant. As a matter of fact, [Armstrong] gave me a lesson on that. He told me, he said, 'If you ever see a [review] that is not what you would desire, don't let it bother you.' He said, 'That's one person's opinion. He didn't buy a ticket.' He said, 'You just always get out there and do the best you can do.' And that's what I always did."[45]

Still, it is hard to imagine that Armstrong was not offended by Scott's reference to his band as "Louis Armstrong and his All-Nonentities." Scott trashed every one of the All Stars that night, continuing a trend that had started after the early version of the band that included Jack Teagarden, Earl Hines, and Sid Catlett broke up. But most of succeeding musicians in the group—Trummy Young, Edmond Hall, Billy Kyle, Joe Darensbourg, Peanuts Hucko, and Mort Herbert—while not possessed of the same star power, were team players with impressive résumés and were well respected by their peers.

As Armstrong rightly wondered in 1956: "There's a lot people . . . say that I play with musicians sometimes that's not up to my standard. Well, how do they know what my standard is? I mean, we was just taught there weren't but two kinds of music. Jack Teagarden always said that, 'There's only two kinds of music, good and bad.' And that's why you hear those hands when we finish playing our tunes, 'cause we try to play them right.

But I don't listen to fanatics that try to tell me how to blow my horn. And I guess that's why I've been playing forty-something years, you know?"[46]

Joe Glaser was usually responsible for finding new All Stars, but as Dan Morgenstern told me, "People who say that . . . it was Joe Glaser's call who came into the band and all that, that's pretty much bullshit, because Louie naturally had final approval of anybody who came in."[47] In the case of a musician like drummer Kenny John—the opposite of a team player, and with a drinking problem—once Armstrong had had it with him, he was out. Russ Phillips did his best trying to fill Teagarden's shoes, but Armstrong wanted someone different and asked Trummy Young to join the band as his replacement. While Glaser may have found the musicians, if Armstrong had a problem with them, they were gone.

In addition to musicianship, character was key for Armstrong, as is evidenced by the long tenures of Danny Barcelona and Mort Herbert. Cozy Cole remembered that it was important that nobody in the All Stars ever started arguments. "That's the way Louie would hire you," he said. "Of course your character first and he'd have to like your playing, but Louie with that personality that he had, he didn't want anybody to be in there that's going to be a drag. He wants everybody in there to get along."[48] Barcelona provided tremendous swing to the band, but he wasn't a great soloist like Sid Catlett, sometimes rushing the tempo during his breaks. When the trumpeter Wes Hensel asked Armstrong why he used Barcelona, Armstrong responded matter-of-factly, "Oh, he's a nice fella."[49] As Armstrong's friend Jack Bradley said, Barcelona "just did his job. He wasn't the world's greatest drummer but he always showed up on time and did what he was supposed to. And I think Louie would prefer someone like that than some so-called star that didn't show up all the time and you couldn't depend on."[50]

In September, the All Stars settled in New York to make one of the most challenging records of Armstrong's career. Pianist-composer Dave Brubeck and his wife, Iola, had collaborated on a musical project titled *The Real Ambassadors,* which was informed by social protest suggesting that jazz musicians would make better politicians than those then in charge. It touched on many issues of the day, especially race, and the Brubecks had conceived of the project with Armstrong in mind after his incendiary Little Rock comments. "I think that's what we really tried to overcome when we wrote *The Real Ambassadors*," Iola Brubeck remembered, "because before we got into this project we didn't really know Louis that well, but we sensed in him a depth and an unstated feeling we thought we could tap into without being patronizing, and I think that's why he took to it."[51]

While they intended eventually to stage a play, the Brubecks wanted to record the score first. Singer Carmen McRae and the vocalese group Lambert, Hendricks and Ross agreed to participate, but Armstrong proved difficult to get hold of, as Dave Brubeck related. "Louis's road manager wouldn't give me access when I wanted to discuss the project with him in Chicago, so I found out the number of Louis's hotel room, sat in the lobby until room service came and hollered, 'Hi, Louis' when the door opened . . . Louis invited me in, ordered me a steak and thought the idea was interesting. I gave him copies of the tunes to listen to on the road; and at the session, he was the first one in the studio and last guy to leave."[52]

Brubeck's demo tapes of the material are at the Louis Armstrong House Museum in Queens. Listening to them today, one hears a very polite Brubeck explaining the nature of the project and what Armstrong means to it. It is possible, that Brubeck gave Armstrong the demo tapes of the songs in the summer of 1961 before an All Stars' four-day tour of Germany, for Brubeck is heard saying, "I've just talked to Joe Glaser and he's told me how difficult it will be for you to record any of these things before going to Europe. But I'm hoping you can figure out the backgrounds with my group playing and me singing the songs like you asked me to do."

To his meeting in Chicago, Brubeck had brought along the lyrics to a song called "Lonesome." Without knowing the melody, Armstrong gave an impassioned reading that greatly affected Brubeck. "Now I told my wife about the way you read the song 'Lonesome' in Chicago," Brubeck says in the tape. "You didn't sing it, you just read it, and it was such a moving job that I thought maybe you would be able to read this on tape and send that back to us because this wouldn't involve you singing or trying to match your voice with the backgrounds that I've sent you by my combo." Brubeck went on to tell Armstrong about Iola's regard for him: "She's always considered you the greatest ambassador we've ever had." Iola herself then tells the trumpeter: "I saw you tonight on [the television program]

You Asked for It and I was very, very impressed with your performance on the show. It thrilled me particularly because I heard you deliver some lines in a way that I knew it was possible for you to do some of the scenes in the show I had written for you. Now, I had the feeling all along that you could do them, but I had never heard you do anything like that before, and when I saw you tonight and saw the sincerity with which [you spoke] some various lines, it impressed me terrifically." The rest of the tape features Brubeck and his trio playing the show's originals with Brubeck singing the melodies ("I'm ashamed of the horrible way in which I sing," he tells Armstrong at one point).[53]

Armstrong practiced the Brubecks' material whenever he had the rare luxury of free time. "Louis told everybody that we had written him an opera," Brubeck remembered. The only problem was finding someone who wanted to record it. "All of the producers I took it to, thought it was great, but they'd give me all these excuses . . . You weren't supposed to have a message. I forget the word they used, but it meant you weren't entertaining. We couldn't lecture the American public on the subject of race."[54]

Eventually, Brubeck's own label, Columbia, agreed to take on the project, which was completed over the course of three sessions in September 1961. The first song recorded was "They Say I Look Like God," a mournful piece that pitted Armstrong's blues-infused singing against Gregorian-chant-like lines delivered by Lambert, Hendricks and Ross. The Brubecks intended the song as satire, with Armstrong wondering if God could be black. "If both are made in the image of thee," he sings, "Could thou perchance a zebra be?" Expecting Armstrong to deliver the line with his usual jocularity, they were shocked and moved by Armstrong's chilling seriousness. Armstrong had tears in his eyes when he got to the song's final line, "When God tells man he's really free"; he repeated "really free" with haunting sincerity. "Goose pimple, I got goose pimple on this one," Louis said after recording it.[55] For me, this is arguably the most emotionally wrenching recording of Armstrong's career—a performance that dispels any notion of Armstrong as merely a clown in his later years.

Not every song on *The Real Ambassadors* is quite so serious; some, such as the romping "King for a Day," are full of good humor. The first session ended with the title tune, "The Real Ambassadors," on which Armstrong sang autobiographical lyrics:

I'll explain, and make it plain, I represent the human race
And don't pretend no more.

The next day, Armstrong was joined by Carmen McRae for heavenly vocalizing by both singers. "I Didn't Know Until You Told Me" is mainly McRae, but Armstrong harmonizes with her sublimely at the end. Next up was a vocal version of Brubeck's well-known instrumental "The Duke," retitled "You Swing Baby." The performance was left off the original album, but it contains some stunning trumpet, with Armstrong interpreting the tricky melody made famous by Miles Davis after his own fashion. "One Moment Worth Years" features an absolutely gorgeous melody, Armstrong and McRae demonstrating deep chemistry, in one of the most charming performances of Armstrong's later years.

The highlight of the day, however, was "Summer Song," a heartbreaking ballad that would become the album's most lasting track. "On his poignant performance of 'Summer Song,' you can hear the elder Armstrong accepting the inevitability of death and looking ahead towards his final peace, even as he casts a parting glance at all of his remarkable achievements," writes Chip Stern in the liner notes to the CD reissue.[56] Dan Morgenstern was present at the recording session and vividly remembered that "Summer Song" was accomplished in one take, before which Brubeck at the piano had played the song for Armstrong as he mastered the lyrics. In the documentary *The Wonderful World of Louis Armstrong*, Morgenstern said, "Brubeck was totally overwhelmed. As a matter of fact, tears came to his eyes when he heard Louis do this thing, and the record of it is marvelous." Jack Bradley, who was also present, described the session as a "a love fest, especially between Dave Brubeck and Louie. Dave would run up and hug and kiss Louie after every take. It was a wonderful session, and it went well, considering they didn't have time to rehearse."[57]

The lack of rehearsal led to Armstrong having trouble with some of the Brubecks' tricky lyrics. One song, "Since Love Had Its Way," required fifteen takes to get the lyrics right. After take one of "King for a Day," Armstrong remarked, "That was a real tongue twister." Brubeck asked, "Pops, what do you want to do next?" A game Armstrong replied, "I don't care, you call 'em." Brubeck said, "I was thinking of your lip." Armstrong answered, "It ain't the lip, it's the lyrics. You don't have to worry 'bout my chops." After another tricky lyric on "Nomad," Bradley remarked to Armstrong, "You'll get your tongue worn out with those lyrics." Armstrong replied, "More than that, I'll get my brains worn out."

But in the end, the hard work was worth it. At the time of the sessions, Brubeck exclaimed, "This is a miracle that it came off. I didn't think it would come off, without even any rehearsal." On the final night of the sessions, Bradley watched as every musician left until the only ones left in the empty studio were a satisfied Brubeck and Armstrong. "Boy, oh boy, what a night we've had," Brubeck said. "We've done everything on schedule. God, boy, we had such a ball."[58]

While in Germany the following year, Armstrong was interviewed on television by Joachim-Ernst Behrendt. "The latest thing I've done is with Brubeck," he told Behrendt. "It turned out nice. Yeah, I told a guy, 'I just made a record with Brubeck.' 'Brubeck!?' I said, 'Yeah! I'll play with anybody, man, you kidding?' That's my hustle. Good, too!" (Nor was Armstrong kidding about playing with anybody. Only two weeks after the Brubeck session, he had reunited with trombonist Kid Ory at Disneyland.)

Having recorded the tracks for *The Real Ambassadors,* the Brubecks set about staging the play, but could not get it off the ground. But by the time Armstrong was interviewed by Behrendt, things seemed more promising. "We're going to do a concert with everybody that was in this session, right from the stage," Armstrong said. "It even might be on TV. . . And we're going to have the ranks and everything, same as opera, you know what I mean. It's going to be all right. We're doing it at the Monterey Jazz Festival."[59]

On September 23, 1962, at the Monterey Jazz Festival, *The Real Ambassadors* had its first and only performance, complete with costumes and scenery. The performance opened with a speech read by a narrator that showed no doubt that this work was written with Armstrong in mind:

Our story concerns a jazz musician not unlike the musicians you have seen on this stage the past three days. The personal history of our hero reads like the story of jazz—up from the shores of Lake Pontchartrain to Chicago and beyond—from New York to San Francisco, London to Tokyo and points in between. The music which poured from his horn became his identity—his passport to the world—the key to locked doors. Through his horn he had spoken to millions of the world's people. Through it he had opened doors to presidents and kings. He had lifted up his horn, as our hero would say, and just played to folks on an even soul-to-soul basis. He had no political message, no slogan, no plan to sell or save the world. Yet he, and other traveling musicians like him, had inadvertently served a national purpose, which officials recognized and eventually sanctioned with a program called cultural exchange.[60]

Brubeck remembered a funny story about the Monterey performance. "At dress rehearsal, I said to Louis, 'You're the real ambassador, will you wear this top hat and carry the attaché case? The audience will immediately identify you as the real ambassador,' and he said, 'Dave, I'm not wearin' a top hat and I'm not carrying that case.' It came time to open and it was time for the concert to begin, Louis to make his entrance, and he came in, there's the top hat, the attaché case and he struts right by me and he says, 'Pops, am I hammin' it up enough to suit you now?' " There was no hamming when Armstrong reprised "They Say I Look Like God." Before an audience, Brubeck still expected the lyrics to get a laugh, but once again Armstrong remained completely serious. "There wasn't a smile in the audience, Louis had tears," Brubeck remembers. "He took those lines that we thought would get laughs right to his heart and everybody in that audience felt what he felt."[61]

The Real Ambassadors was a triumph for Armstrong, but because of Joe Glaser no film of the live performance survives. "Well, the reviews were fantastic," Brubeck said. "[Ralph] Gleason and [Leonard] Feather—to give you an example of two people who weren't too kind to me—they flipped over it. They had tears in their eyes after the concert, and said they felt it was the greatest thing ever done at Monterey. But Glaser wouldn't allow me to have the TV crew turn the cameras on—and they were standing right there."[62] Glaser's insistence on not filming *The Real Ambassadors* has deprived jazz fans of the chance of witnessing one of the most important evenings in the careers of both Armstrong and Brubeck, but the studio recordings are still in print and grow in stature with each passing year. Armstrong remained proud of the project, telling Feather, "It was five years ahead of its time and the big shots that buy shows for Broadway were afraid of it . . . I had to learn all that music, and I'd never done nothing at this kind before. Brubeck is great!"[63] And Brubeck wrote: "When *The Real Ambassadors* was performed . . . the most critical jazz audience in the world rose as one body to give Louis Armstrong and the cast a standing ovation. It was an electrifying moment."[64]

Between the studio recording of *The Real Ambassadors* in September 1961 and the Monterey performance in September 1962, Armstrong continued business as usual, touring both at home and abroad. Yet as much as he had traveled the globe, Armstrong regretted not being able to play at two destinations. "Two places," he told Leonard Feather. "Russia and New Orleans. I haven't been home to New Orleans since 1956, and I've turned down any number of offers, because I won't go until I can take *all* my men."[65] "Sad, isn't it?" he said. "I've been all over the world with my band. In Wiesbaden, Germany, Lucille and I slept in the same bed the Kaiser and Hitler slept in. I've played for the kings of England, Sweden, Belgium, Holland; I've been invited to banquets with the president or prime minister of the countries I've visited. Yet I can't take my own band to my own town."[66] Armstrong also publicly hinted at a never previously discussed longing: time off. "I'll tell you, though, if I took any time off now, I'd want to take a whole year. I'd like to go to all the places I've worked and just listen. Let me hear the cats and catch the bands—let me be a civilian for a change! And there's so many things I want to do with my tape library. I've got all kinds of history in there, and things we did after the sessions, and it all needs to be edited. I'd like to get me a secretary and put all that stuff in order. I don't mean I'd retire. During the year off I'd warm up every day for fifteen minutes to keep my chops up to par."

Before the interview came to a close, Armstrong told Feather, "You know, I'm serious about taking a year off. Of course, we have to plan it way ahead. We're in San Francisco in January, then Sun Valley, then another tour of England and the Continent . . ."[67] Except for his private idea about performing on Broadway in 1961, never before had Armstrong talked this way publicly, badly wanting a vacation but not having it within him to stop performing. Armstrong knew he was aging, something that was occasionally beginning to show in his live performances. A *Coda* magazine review of an Armstrong show in 1962 related what must have been a rough night for the trumpeter at the Brant Inn on July 18th." The review read, "The evening was not one of the happiest ones for Louis looked very tired and drawn even before the dance started. Then midway through the evening he slipped and fell awkwardly. Although he finished the show without fuss he asked to see a doctor afterwards and complained that it hurt when he blew. X-rays revealed nothing. However much we love to see and hear Louis year after year, the grueling pace and miserable travelling conditions would tax the strength of a man half Louis's age."[68]

Joe Darensbourg recalled that Armstrong nearly got his wish at one point during his three years with the band. Armstrong, feeling a bit tired, was told by his personal doctor, Alexander Schiff, to take a break. "They told us that Louis was taking off for an eight-week Caribbean cruise with Lucille and that we was having a paid vacation," Darensbourg said. "They paid us for the eight weeks, post-dated all the checks. Man, I started singing, I was so happy. Nobody in the band could believe it. A vacation with pay! I came on home and relaxed for about three weeks, just thinking about five more solid weeks, enjoying my swimming pool."

As it turned out, things were too good to be true for Darensbourg and the rest of the band. "I didn't take any jobs, just took my horn out and blew for fun, when here comes a call from the office saying to get ready to come back to New York 'cause Louis was itching to go back to work . . . He wasn't having any fun on that cruise. We kept the money, although it wouldn't have mattered about the money. Louis just loved playing that horn, he never really wanted to lay off. The guys once told me that Louis had the feeling that, if he ever had a long lay off, he was afraid he wouldn't be able to come back."[69] Jewel Brown says, "He worked so hard that we would beg for days off. And he loved working, he loved working." Brown first visited Europe on two tours of the continent in 1962. She was thrilled by the experience: "Every single solitary place, everywhere, there was never not a packed house. Never, ever. It was amazing. Either they did good advertisements or there's a lot of people during that time that plain old loved Louis Armstrong. And he gave them a show."[70]

One member of the band who didn't make the European trips was bassist Irv Manning. In Feather's piece, Manning was full of compliments about his time with the All Stars: "My mouth still drops open at the fantastic conception that Louis has. And it's a wonderful group to work in—all the guys are just like a family."[71] But Manning had a short temper that would often get the best of him, and he was thrown out of the band after an altercation with everyone's nemesis, Frenchy Tallerie. "This Frenchy was a miserable guy, evil, and nobody in the band liked him," Darensbourg wrote. "Why Joe kept him as the road manager I don't know." Apparently, Tallerie borrowed a dollar from Manning and refused to pay him back. "Eventually one thing led to another, Irv got mad and he pushed Frenchy on to a stanchion or something," according to Darensbourg. "The floor had just been mopped and Frenchy slipped. Somebody told Louis that they had got into a fight and Frenchy was down on the floor."[72] Jewel Brown remembered Armstrong yelling, " '[Manning's] fired! Get rid of him!' . . . And Pops didn't want to know why or anything, that was it. That was it." When she was asked whether Frenchy could be overbearing, Brown replied: "Yes, he was, yes he was, and nine times out of ten, Frenchy deserved it. But you're supposed to have discipline as adults, and that was not the [answer], punching him out like that."[73]

Manning was replaced by Billy Cronk, a veteran of such groups as Bob Crosby's Bobcats and the Dorsey Brothers Orchestra, who went to Europe with the All Stars. There was something curious about Armstrong's European appearances in 1962, which are documented on film and audio tape: the set lists are repetitive. While no two set lists are identical, the pool of songs had dwindled. Almost every concert on this European tour relied on performances of Armstrong's most popular tunes, among them "A Kiss to Build a Dream On," "Mack the Knife," and "Blueberry Hill"; New Orleans favorites like "My Bucket's Got a Hole in It," "Tin Roof Blues," and "Tiger Rag"; and the *High Society* numbers "Now You Has Jazz" and "High Society Calypso." Armstrong was clearly intent on chiefly performing songs that accounted for his contemporaneous celebrity. His gambit was greeted by the rapturous delight of packed crowds everywhere, but back at the office Joe Glaser was worried about the criticisms of Armstrong always playing the same songs. "Joe Glaser wanted [the tunes] changed, but all of them was afraid to tell Louis," Darensbourg wrote. "I'd go up to the office and Joe would say, 'Why don't you guys play some different tunes? Do you want to talk to Louis about it?' " But Darensbourg wouldn't do it, and neither would anyone else, including Frenchy. What Louis did on stage was a subject that everyone knew was off limits. Armstrong's previous manager, Johnny Collins, once made the mistake of trying to get Armstrong to change his program back in the early 1930s. Armstrong remembered his reaction in 1953: "I said, 'Listen, cocksucker! You might be my manager and you might be the biggest shit and book me in the biggest places in the world but when I get out on that fucking stage with that horn and get in trouble, you can't save me. So we'll play THIS, THAT and . . .' "[74] Surely, Glaser must have had similar experiences with Armstrong, so he wasn't about to broach the subject again. But as Darensbourg admitted, "People used to criticize Louis for sticking to these songs, but he knew if we didn't play them the audience would holler and demand them."[75] Recordings from the 1962 European tour do capture Armstrong occasionally playing unexpected tunes like "I Get Ideas" and "Jazz Me Blues," but with less frequency. For the most part, he still played magnificently, but on other occasions he struggled a bit with his velocity. At one Paris concert, he even had difficulty with his "Indiana" solo. His sound was still huge, and he still had years of great trumpet playing left in him, but the first small signs of a decline were evident.

After returning from Europe in May, the All Stars had downtime of only one day before departing for South America. And so it went on for the rest of the year, the touring sometimes bordering on absurdity. As Darensbourg recalled: "Had some pretty crazy distances to travel . . . I know one time we flew from New York to Copenhagen for a few days just to play at the Tivoli Gardens for their anniversary, but the biggest jump we ever made was from Tokyo, Japan, to Houston, Texas, for some big oil tycoon's daughter's party at the Shamrock Hotel in Murchison."[76] Danny Barcelona vividly remembered a typical day of traveling with the All Stars. "So we got up early and, okay, Frenchy, the road manager, and Doc Schiff, everybody, baggage count at six, leave at seven . . . and then Louie gets down at eight! So we get on that bus and then stop on the way for lunch and then you're in that city, and sometimes you don't have the time to check in [at] the hotel, it was straight to the concert hall or whatever . . . Really, that's part of it. And I mean it's a whole bunch of them all at once, not just one or two at a time, you know. Yeah, we could do about thirty one-nighters straight in a row, or forty . . . One time we were finishing in Toronto, left at one o'clock in the midnight, you know, after midnight and got in the bus and went straight to the Waldorf-Astoria. We didn't even have breakfast! I mean, we had breakfast when we stopped, but went straight to the gig! And now that's rough. I mean, you know, geez, no shower, no nothing . . . I guess you get used to it, you know."[77] To Brown, the All Stars were "family" and Armstrong never once acted as if he were better than any of them. "Pops was right there with us," she recalled. "He was never without us and we was never without him. He was constantly right there. We did everything together."

By this point in his career, Armstrong had a pretty set routine, something witnessed countless times in the 1960s by his friend Jack Bradley. "He had a philosophy I believe probably from the old days of show biz . . . that the show is the ultimate thing and everything he did during the day was for the show and whatever appointments or whether he ate or whether he practiced, it was all geared to that," Bradley said. "If showtime was at 8:00 say, he'd always be one of the first ones there . . . He'd be there at least an hour ahead of time and he had his whole ritual he'd go through with in his dressing room. On the counter, he'd line up his medicines and salves and creams and his handkerchiefs and his piles of samples of Swiss Kriss to give out and his 8x10 photos and everything had its place. And he'd do the same thing no matter where he went. He'd know when to go on and he'd very often be the first one in the wings before the rest of the band. And that's what he's here for and that's what he wanted, to be straight."[78]

Armstrong's postshow routine was also set in stone. "So once the show was over, he'd very often announce, 'Folks, thank you everybody and good night and Pops will be in the dressing room if you want any autographs,' " Bradley continued. "And then he'd sit at his—always, somehow, a little table would appear, not like a card table size, usually smaller. He'd always make sure there'd be one. He'd sit behind it. He'd line the people up. He'd have pictures, a sample pack of Swiss Kriss and with everyone, he wouldn't just go, 'Here.' He'd go, 'Hi,' he'd greet them with a big smile and sincerity and say, 'What's your name?' The people would be nervous as hell most times and he'd try to get them to relax. 'What's your name?' Sometimes if he didn't know how to spell it, he'd ask them and they'd tell him. Not that they expected their name on the picture, but he felt that was more personal and he strongly felt that without these people, he couldn't exist, he wouldn't exist and he owes them this and he didn't mind doing it at all. And very often, it went for so long, the rest of his band would be back in the hotel in bed and Louie would still be doing that. So it shows you what kind of person he was. And he didn't do it as a chore. He did it as part of his being. These were his fans. They were important to him."[79]

Armstrong, ever on tour, was making so much money for Glaser and himself that the trumpeter felt no need to make new records. The year

1963 in Armstrong's life was more or less lost in a haze of travel, so much so that few broadcasts and articles about him survive.

The band was still selling out every performance, but by year's end it was clear that as busy as he had been, Armstrong had lived through the quietest period of his life. He had not recorded an album solely with the All Stars since 1959's *Satchmo Plays King Oliver.* His albums in the 1960s so far were collaborations with Bing Crosby, the Dukes of Dixieland, Dave Brubeck, and Duke Ellington. He had stopped recording the pop songs Decca had forced on him in the 1950s. He had not been in a film since *Paris Blues* in 1961. And he had not set foot in a recording studio for more than two years, since September 1961. Nonetheless, when he did again, Armstrong would find himself atop the music world at the unlikely age of sixty-three.

CHAPTER FIFTEEN

Hello, Dolly! 1964

WHEN LOUIS ARMSTRONG and the All Stars entered a New York City recording studio on December 3, 1963, it was a quick detour in yet another stretch of grueling one-nighters. As in the old days, the purpose of the session was to take an unpromising show tune and turn it into gold, here as a favor to Jack Lee, a friend of Joe Glaser's. The song was from a musical that hadn't even opened yet. Armstrong was hired to record the show's title tune, "Hello, Dolly!," for added publicity. Glaser claimed that five companies turned him down before he got approval from Kapp Records, a small label run by Dave Kapp, brother of Jack Kapp, the man who had founded Decca Records and who'd overseen so many of Armstrong's recordings in the 1930s and early 1940s. It was to be a quick session, just a momentary pause in between more stretches of one-nighters. "There was no two or three days' rehearsing," Danny Barcelona remembered. "That's how we did 'Dolly.' You know, we happened to be in town—'Okay, be at the studio at so and so.' We do two numbers, we're out of town."[1]

Some stories about the recording of "Hello, Dolly!" have made it sound like Armstrong went into the studio blind, not knowing what he was about to record. However, in Armstrong's reel-to-reel tape collection is one that consists of nothing but demo versions of two songs from Jerry Herman's score, "Hello, Dolly!" and "Penny in My Pocket," as well as

Bobby Darin's recording of "A Lot of Livin' to Do."[2] Throughout the tape, Armstrong's voice can be heard faintly in the background as he sat there, listening to each song multiple times to get the feel of it. By the time he arrived at the studio, "Penny in My Pocket" had been cut from the show, leaving Armstrong with only two songs to perform.

"A Lot of Livin' to Do" was up first. The song was from the score of *Bye, Bye Birdie,* a Broadway musical from 1960 that had been turned into a popular movie released earlier in 1963. The tune seemed to fit Armstrong like a glove, featuring a hip vocal and ending on a swinging trumpet solo capped by a final, fat high note. Everyone in the studio was pleased, including Jack Bradley, who felt that the song could turn into a hit if it were properly promoted.

Next up was "Hello, Dolly!" Billy Kyle had sketched a simple arrangement of it off of a lead sheet. The All Stars sailed through the tune, but no one was impressed, least of all Armstrong. Though Armstrong might have familiarized himself with a demo version of the song before heading to the studio, he was clearly dismayed at having to record such a trifle. Arvell Shaw, who had rejoined the band on bass in 1963, remembered Armstrong asking, " 'You mean to tell me you called me out here to do this?' He hated it, you know?"[3] Some tinkering would have to be done to make the record salvageable. Dave Kapp's son Mickey was running the show, and he offered up some changes, which were added to Armstrong's copy of the "Hello, Dolly!" lead sheet, now housed at the Louis Armstrong House Museum.[4] For the vocal reprise at the end of the record, Louis scratched out the lyrics "Take her wrap" and wrote in "Golly gee." Another line, "Find her an empty lap" was also replaced in Armstrong's hand with "Have a lil faith in me." But there was one more change to the lyrics marked on Armstrong's lead sheet, and it wasn't in the trumpeter's handwriting. For the titular lyrics, "Hello, Dolly. Well hello, Dolly," someone else—probably Mickey Kapp—scratched out the second "Hello" and wrote, "it's Louie." It was only a suggestion, but, as Kapp later recalled, Armstrong's reply was, "It's not Louie, it's *Louis!*"[5] With the recording light on, Armstrong sang a take in his own fashion: "Hello, Dolly, this is Louis, Dolly." The accented "s" on the last syllable of his name left no doubt as to where Armstrong stood in the "Louis" versus "Louie" debate on how to properly pronounce his first name.

After listening to the playback, Darensbourg recalled, Armstrong said, "I don't like that. Can't something just be done with this record to kind of pep it up a little or do something?"[6] Trummy Young suggested a banjo player he knew who lived nearby, Tony Gottuso. Gottuso showed up and, after a few attempts, nailed the introduction that would serve as the record's opening wake-up call. Armstrong and the All Stars left the studio to head to a concert, but session producer Mickey Kapp still wasn't finished. After dubbing in Gottuso's banjo introduction, he added discreet strings to the record. When Kapp sent a copy of it to Glaser, Glaser exclaimed to his associate Cork O'Keefe, "Listen to that, Cork, it's a fucking hit!"[7]

The Broadway musical *Hello, Dolly!* opened on January 16, 1964, and Armstrong's single was released soon thereafter. By then the All Stars were returning from another trip abroad, ringing out the old year, 1963, in San Juan, Puerto Rico, and heralding the new in Bermuda. After co-hosting *The Mike Douglas Show* for a week, Armstrong and the All Stars headed for the American Midwest. On a bus every day in the middle of nowhere, the band was unaware of what was happening: meant only as the flip side of "A Lot of Livin' to Do," "Hello, Dolly!" had stirred a huge sensation. Soon, inexplicably, the All Stars started hearing audiences chant "Hello, Dolly! Hello, Dolly!" at live performances. Nobody in the band immediately recalled the tune they had recorded nearly two months before. " 'Hello, Dolly!'? What's 'Hello, Dolly!'?" asked Barcelona. "I never heard of it."[8] Joe Darensbourg also was baffled. " 'Hello, Dolly!'?" he remembered thinking. "I had forgot about the tune completely."[9] Finally, when the audience request was repeated evening after evening, Armstrong turned to Arvell Shaw and wondered, "What the hell is 'Hello, Dolly!'?" Shaw replied, "Well you remember that date we did a few months ago in New York? One of the tunes was called 'Hello, Dolly!'; it's from a Broadway show.' "[10] Armstrong asked, "Any of you guys remember this damn tune?" Nobody did, and as with "Mack the Knife" in 1955, the band boy had lost the sheet music, so Armstrong had a record flown to where they were. The band reacquainted itself with the song and performed it live for the first time later that night. "He had to take about eight curtain calls, so he knew right then he had a hit," Darensbourg remembered. "They wouldn't let him off the stage."[11] "The first time we put it in the concert, pandemonium broke out," according to Shaw.[12] "Oh my God, people, I don't know, they knew it," says Danny Barcelona, "We hit the first note—

Billy hit the first note on the piano—and they're already clapping, they knew what it was."[13]

"Hello, Dolly!" hit the *Cash Box* Top 100 singles chart on February 22, ranked sixty-eighth. One week later it jumped to number thirty-five and the week after to twenty-two. By March 14, it had climbed to number fifteen, before landing in the top ten at number eight on March 21. During the initial rise of "Hello, Dolly!," Armstrong spent time in a New York hospital as he had trouble with his left foot. Armstrong had trouble with varicose veins and was diagnosed with phlebitis, which would plague him for the rest of his life (but it also gave him a funny line, as he quoted his doctor telling him, "Man, you've got very-close veins!"). However, it was in the hospital where Armstrong really got to experience the impact "Dolly" was having, especially regarding the seemingly simple change suggested by Mickey Kapp. Armstrong said

> The nurse that came in when I had phlebitis in the hospital say, "I bought 'Hello, Dolly!' just because you said 'Hello, Dolly, this is *Louisss.*'" She went and bought the record just from [that]. She ain't heard the rest of it![14]

Two nights after getting out of the hospital, Armstrong was the mystery guest on the CBS game show *What's My Line?* Signing in simply as "Satchmo," Armstrong turned in one of the most entertaining segments in the history of the popular, long-running show, the trumpeter doing his best to disguise his famous sandpaper voice before the blindfolded panel. When his identity was revealed, regular panelist Arlene Francis asked him to sing "Hello, Dolly!" As the audience cheered wildly, Armstrong delivered an entire chorus a capella, swinging, mugging, and waving his handkerchief. It was his first performance of the song on television.

It was clear that Armstrong had made peace with his initial reservations about "Hello, Dolly!"; he now owned it. "It was his big number from then on and he started liking it, singing it, kept improvising on it and he'd even do a little dancing to it," Darensbourg wrote. "A lot of people thought 'A Lot of Living' was a better number than 'Hello, Dolly!' Matter of fact, I did, too."[15] But the question of which was better was now irrelevant: Armstrong was riding the wave of the biggest hit of his career. With "Hello, Dolly!" creeping up the charts, producer Mickey Kapp called the All Stars to a Las Vegas studio to record a follow-up album to the hit single. To re-create the sound of "Hello, Dolly!" the All Stars were augmented by Glen Thompson's banjo. As the formula would have it, Kapp saddled Armstrong with more show and film tunes; some worked (a gorgeous "Moon River"), others didn't (a hokey "You Are Woman, I Am Man"). However, the former outnumber the latter. Armstrong beams on "I Still Get Jealous" and "Be My Life's Companion," on which he gives a shout-out to wife Lucille. Armstrong also took the opportunity to wax definitive versions of some songs he'd popularized, such as "Blueberry Hill" and "A Kiss to Build a Dream On." While the original versions of these songs are still more famous, Armstrong's performances on this date are enhanced by maturity. To me, the revisions transcend the originals. Too, Armstrong's trumpet playing was in exceptional form throughout the sessions, as evidenced by a propulsive extended solo on "Jeepers Creepers."

Sadly, the album lacks a sound that had been integral to the All Stars for more than a decade: Trummy Young's trombone. After eleven years with the band, Young had left on New Year's Day. Young's wife had gotten more than a little tired with his continual absence from home, and was pressuring him to settle down and help raise their young daughter. The situation became even more tense when Young's wife fell ill. "So finally when I found my wife was sick, I left the band, and Joe Glaser got so mad with me, he hardly spoke to me, you know, about that, because he wanted to give me more money," Young said. "I said, 'No, I got to go home. My wife is sick.' And so it's a good thing I did because I found out my wife had cancer, and we caught it, you know, just in time."[16] Young moved back to Hawaii, where he would remain until his death in 1984, returning to the United States only now and then for an occasional jazz party or festival. "Trummy and Louie had a very special relationship," according to Dan Morgenstern. "They got along beautifully. They were the closest friends, I think, throughout the All Stars, more than Jack [Teagarden] and Louie . . . There was a special thing between them . . . Trummy just, you know, he understood who Louie was . . . They were really close. And when Trummy left, that left a big hole in the group, and it was a blow to Louie, you know."[17] "I think out of all the people I played with, Louis did more for me," Young reflected in 1973. "He inspired me when I listened to him. He was truly a great artist. The nights that Louis was on, you would never hear anything like that again. I used to forget to come in on my part sometimes. Just listening he would make you cry when he played pretty things. I'm sure I'm not alone in feeling like this. A lot of other musicians feel this same way. If there's any such thing as a giant in this field, he was it."[18]

A double blow was dealt Armstrong when Jack Teagarden died on January 15, 1964, at fifty-eight. The official cause of death was pneumonia, but he had been a heavy drinker for many years, which all but certainly had contributed to his premature death. Teagarden had planned to rejoin the All Stars as Young's replacement. "What a character!" Armstrong said of Teagarden during a radio interview the following year. "And he was getting ready to come back to the band when he died. Yeah, he was getting ready to come back. He got all tired of all that rat race, you know, hustle and bustle."[19] In his later years Teagarden had always maintained a hectic schedule, largely attributable to the great success he had enjoyed as a member of the All Stars. The constant traveling and the gargantuan appetite for booze had finally taken their toll. Armstrong would always be quick to cite Teagarden when asked to name his favorite musicians. When one listens to one of their duets, such as "Rockin' Chair," the extraordinary bond between two jazz legends is immediately apparent.

To fill the trombone chair, Armstrong delved into the past and hired Russell "Big Chief" Moore, a member of the trumpeter's big band from 1945 until its demise in 1947. An imposingly large man, Moore was one of the few full-blooded Native Americans in jazz, a member of the Pima tribe. His punchy style of playing was congruent with the styles of other New Orleans musicians such as Red Allen and Sidney Bechet, and he got along with Armstrong well. "Louis, he's so congenial and so great and he taught me a lot of stuff, things about performance and projection," Moore said. "It was beautiful just to be with him. Louie and I never had a cross word. He's the same on the bandstand and he's the same off the bandstand, too, and all the guys in the band respected him as a leader and as a musician and on top of all, a human being. He treated everybody the same way . . . We could tell that he's one of the greatest."[20] According to Moore, "At a later time I heard that they were after Vic Dickenson, too. But Joe Glaser said, 'No, no, no, I don't want Vic Dickenson, he got no personality. Get me Chief. Get me Chief.' So Arvell decided he would call me and get in touch with me."[21] After a spell of negotiation with Glaser, Moore joined the band in Bermuda, before "Hello, Dolly!" took off, and immediately made an impact on his fellow All Stars. When asked about Moore, Jewel Brown simply started laughing happily and said: "He was one big old fun guy . . . Big Chief was a great big ol' guy, boy, I tell you. I used to tell him, 'Boy, you need to work some of that off doing your war dance!' Boy, I tell you, he was something else. He was a big old bundle of fun."[22]

For his part, Moore was ecstatic about joining the band: the All Stars of this period were "a beautiful group"; the *Hello, Dolly!* album sessions in Las Vegas were "beautiful, beautiful."[23] He admitted that the album went off without a hitch because the band had already been playing many of the songs night after night. "I venture to say that on all my engagements with Louie, with the small band, we played this so often, you know," he remembered. "Each one knows what to do and sometimes I have night-mares of the same thing all over and over and over, but what we did over and over and over, I never regretted it. I never regretted the nightmares because it was beautiful working with Louis, that we were doing what we did on the albums, we did it all the time, because that's the way people like us. That's the way the people liked Louie. Believe me, it was wonderful to work with Louie again."[24]

Even as the *Hello, Dolly!* album was being readied for release, Arm-strong appeared on the ABC variety show *The Hollywood Palace* to per-form both "A Lot of Livin' to Do" and "Hello, Dolly!" By now both songs had become staples of the All Stars' repertoire, but "Dolly" was getting four or five encores each night. On the charts, it continued gathering momentum, hitting number two in *Billboard* and *Cash Box* by the end of April. At the time, it seemed impossible that it would reach the number one position: the Beatles had ruled it since their arrival in the United States in February. Their "I Want to Hold Your Hand" had been the number-one song in America for seven weeks; it was supplanted by "She Loves You" for two; and "Can't Buy Me Love" was next to ascend to number one. Armstrong himself admitted to being a fan of the Beatles. In a 1965 interview, he said, "I buy the Beatles. Everything they put out, I got 'em in my house and I put 'em on tape. They're very good—they swing. They're good boys. Yeah, and they made a wonderful reputation, which they deserve. Because they put everything in it. And I thought it was awful nice. They upset the world!"[25] As much as the charts were now ruled by the lads from Liverpool, at the height of Beatlemania a beloved

New Orleans jazz trumpet player, more than sixty years old, would shock the music world with a corny Broadway show tune.

On May 9, "Hello, Dolly!" hit number one on the *Billboard* Hot 100 singles chart. The next week, it hit *Cash Box*'s number one. The *New York Post* estimated that the song was being played ten thousand times a day in North America. Everywhere one went, "Hello, Dolly!" could be heard in the background. But why? Why not any other recording Armstrong had made over the years? Gary Giddins is eloquent in his explanation of the record's success:

> The trite song, which has had virtually no life beyond Armstrong and the show itself, was an unswinging set piece on Broadway, pompous and logy. Armstrong had transformed dross into gold once again, and even got to play a full chorus of trumpet. The banjo was an ingenious touch . . . The eight-bar banjo intro, oddly electric and percussive, worked like an alarm clock to introduce a performance unlike anything else on the Top Forty . . . Louis's rhythm section and the backing by Trummy Young and Joe Darensbourg were right on the money, and his trumpet solo and burnished vocal were ringingly, inimitably Armstrongian. The whole performance was casually flawless.[26]

After May 16, "Hello, Dolly!" gradually began its descent down the charts—the Beatles were not to be denied. Still, according to New York's WABC, "Hello, Dolly!" was the best-selling record of 1964. It was cause for celebration for both jazz and Armstrong fans, among them Frank Sinatra, who stepped into a recording studio on June 10, 1964, to cut his own version, backed by the Count Basie Orchestra and featuring an arrangement by Quincy Jones with new lyrics paying tribute to the trumpeter's newfound success. "You're back on top, Louie," Sinatra sang. "Never stop, Louie / You're still singing, you're still swinging, you're still going strong." Sinatra's sentiment was shared by a perennial Armstrong detractor, John S. Wilson of the *New York Times,* in a piece called "Still the Champ": "There was undoubtedly a good deal of unexpected satisfaction among those beyond the age of Beatlemania when the Beatles' reign of several months at the top of the list of best-selling popular disks was ended recently not by a younger and louder group of Superbeatles but by

63-year-old Louis Armstrong singing and playing 'Hello, Dolly!,' a tune so obviously melodious that you hum it on the way into the theater."[27]

The "Hello, Dolly!" goodwill spread even to Patrick Scott, who had been withering about the All Stars in 1961. Scott's July review of a Toronto gig was positive through and through: "Louis Armstrong, aged 64, demonstrated again last night at O'Keefe Centre that, in addition to being one of the world's great comedians, vaudevillians and all-around showmen, he can still be the most heart-stirring performer in the history of jazz." Of his trumpet playing, Scott wrote, "We have had many formidable trumpeters in our midst this season, but Armstrong's one solo on 'Struttin' with Some Barbecue' made them seem like children."[28]

To some critics, of course, "Hello, Dolly!" hardly counted as jazz. Reviewing the same performance as Scott, Barrie Hale wrote, "It's many, many years too late to lament the passing of the Hot Five and the Hot Seven, but what is often said should be said again. Those groups were jazz. The All Stars are Pop. But as a Pop group, the All Stars provide solid package." All the same, in spite of his nostalgia, Hale was sufficiently observant to note that Armstrong was now drawing more fans than ever: "The pattern hasn't changed in years and years, and regardless of the changes in the Showbiz winds, Louis continues to keep picking up new generations of audiences."[29] While he might be amassing new and a greater number of fans, Armstrong had not exactly been in a rut before "Hello, Dolly!" was released. When asked if she noticed a difference in Armstrong's audiences before and after "Dolly," Jewel Brown said, "They were always the same. I mean, we always had a full house before that and we always had a full house after that."[30]

Joe Glaser reveled in the success of "Hello, Dolly!" At the height of its popularity, money was pouring in, and Glaser was coy when asked how much Armstrong had earned: "Hell, Pops hasn't made less than a half-million bucks in any given year during the past 20 years . . . It's between us and Uncle Sam how much he actually takes in, but I can tell you this, for tax reasons we won't let it go over a million a year."[31] Armstrong was not one to keep tabs, as long as he had enough money to lavish on pretty much anyone who needed it. "We don't tell many people this but it's no lie," Glaser said. "Pops actually gives away—I mean *gives* away—$500 to $1,000 every damn week. I don't mean every month. I mean every damn week. We just hand it to him in a brown envelope and he chuckles and says, 'O.K., this is some more of Old Pops's pissing away money.' He honestly gets his biggest thrill just giving away dough. He just gives it away—no strings attached. We don't kick about it. Hell, any man who's worked as long and hard as he has ought to get some pleasure out of life." Armstrong put it this way: "Well, I don't keep up with it too much, but I greases a few palms here and there. What good is all the dough doing me and Lucille just laying around accumulating?"[32]

Even as he mostly kept his fiercest opinions on race to himself, Armstrong was also guarded about dispensing cash. As to why he had not started a philanthropic foundation, Armstrong explained: "Me or Joe Glaser go out here and start setting up foundations and funds and all that kind of stuff and some cat gets the idea I'm trying to be Henry Ford or one of the Rockefeller brothers or somebody. Then he'll want me to lay a whole pile of dough on his pet project. Then here comes the newspapers wanting to know why you did this or why you didn't do that. You get yourself caught in a trick bag trying to play the big shot. I figure you lay a little here and a little there and everybody's happy. That's how I get my satisfaction. And let me tell you something, Pops. A man's satisfaction is better than all the dough in the world."[33]

It is very conceivable that Joe Glaser was taking advantage of Louis financially, but as has been demonstrated elsewhere in this narrative, Armstrong always knew the score and would stand up for himself when he really felt cheated. But this son of New Orleans, who grew up dirt poor in one of the roughest neighborhoods in that city, wasn't about to start counting dollars and cents any time soon. He was just glad to be comfortable. "What's money anyhow?" Armstrong asked soon after the release of "Hello, Dolly!" "You make it and you might eat a little better than the next cat. You might be able to buy a little better booze than some wino on the corner. But you get sick just like the next cat, and when you die you're just as graveyard dead as he is. So what's the difference between me and some cat that's making it at the Salvation Army Lodge? All I got was a little better roll of the dice." Lucille Armstrong was definitely more materialistic, something her husband was quick to point out. "Now you take my wife, Lucille. She's got everything she thinks she wants. She buys all them clothes from Paris and Rome and places. But them minks she wraps her fine self up in don't keep her no warmer than some old lady wrapped up in gunny sacks and dirty rags."[34]

Armstrong never had to worry about money anymore, thanks to Joe Glaser, which probably made it easier for him to overlook some of Glaser's character flaws. Though Glaser loved Armstrong and made millions off the talents of black entertainers, he still proved to be a man of contradictions when it came to issues of race. Shortly before the recording of "Hello, Dolly!" a black trumpeter named June Clark fell gravely ill. Clark had retired from playing years earlier, but he remained a longtime part of Armstrong's entourage. When Jack Bradley told Glaser that Clark was sick, Glaser grew upset and demanded they go visit Clark in the hospital immediately. On the way to the hospital, Bradley shared some gossip from the jazz world. Glaser asked, "Who told you that?" When Bradley responded that the information was given to him by a black musician, Glaser callously said, "Don't ever believe anything *they* tell you."[35] Bradley was offended by Glaser's comment but didn't say anything. Minutes later, they arrived at the hospital and Glaser was sweet as could be to the ailing Clark, staying for hours and making sure Clark had everything he needed.

Glaser was one man that nobody could ever quite figure out. After the success of "Hello, Dolly!" writer Jimmy Breslin attempted to do just that in his piece "A Normal Day with Joe Glaser." In it, he asked Armstrong about Glaser. "What can I tell you? Askin' me about Joe is like askin' a chile 'bout its daddy," Armstrong said. "That's what he is. He's my daddy. He's been my daddy for 40 years and we ain't never gonna die, not one of us, so he goin' be my daddy for 40 more years." Breslin asked, "Did he make a lot of money for you, Louis?" Breslin then reported: "The laugh started down in his stomach, then it went through his body and he began to shake. It came out of him in a deep chuckle. 'Next year, we gonna start on a new program,' Louis said. 'We gonna burn it in bonfires.' "[36]

More popular than ever before, the All Stars suffered yet another departure by one of its members in the summer of 1964: not in good health, Joe Darensbourg left. Darensbourg told Glaser to secure a replacement for him before a high-profile appearance at the 1964 World's Fair, but it wasn't easy. With no immediate prospect, Glaser threatened Darensbourg: if he didn't play the World's Fair gig, Glaser would not pay for his transportation home. Darensbourg insisted that he was prepared to incur the cost, though "I can go to the Musicians' Union and they'll make you pay for it." Glaser backed down. "Joe knew it and he says, 'Well, I'm just kidding. You know I'm gonna send you back home. We love you.' All that shit."[37]

Before leaving, Darensbourg had noticed a difference in Armstrong's trumpet playing. "When I joined the band Louis was going strong, still playing well. It seemed to me after I had been there a couple of years his lip would get sore. He had quite a problem there," he wrote. "The wonder of it was that his lip lasted that long." While the pure tone of Armstrong's trumpet playing was still there, as were its power and range, Armstrong was rapidly losing velocity. That his lip was giving him trouble at the apex of his popularity was no doubt disconcerting, but he could still provide many a spine-tingling moment night after night. Darensbourg distilled his impression of his former boss: "The man had so much strength and so much talent that the Lord himself must have picked him out. Yes, the Lord picked out Louis."[38]

Darensbourg ended up playing the World's Fair concert on June 30, but at a concert the very next night he was replaced by Eddie Shu, a talented multi-instrumentalist who had once studied violin, guitar, and harmonica. Later, he would focus on reed and brass instruments, chiefly alto and tenor saxophone. After serving in the army, Shu had played in the bands of Tadd Dameron, George Shearing, Buddy Rich, Lionel Hampton, Charlie Barnet, and Chubby Jackson before joining the Gene Krupa trio. Shu was an interesting choice in that he had very little experience playing New Orleans–style jazz and was unfamiliar with much of the All Stars' repertoire. (According to Darensbourg, Shu got the job only because his father was a friend of Glaser's.)

Still, Shu managed to define a role for himself. He brought a Benny Goodman–inspired conception to his clarinet playing that was unlike the more traditional New Orleans–based style of such Crescent City clarinetists as Darensbourg himself, Edmond Hall, and Barney Bigard. However unfamiliar with the repertoire he may have been, Shu's contributions to the band were not inconsiderable. As one of Armstrong's subsequent clarinetists, Joe Muranyi, would say: "Eddie Shu was a very good clarinet player—especially considering he was a saxophone player. He had a nice tone, nice and clean. And I don't think his heart was really in that kind of music, but he did it pretty well. You won't hear me putting him down, so you gotta take it as it comes and live in the present."[39]

But audiences were not paying money to see Eddie Shu; they were coming for the maestro, Armstrong. Hugh Mulligan, who spent time traveling with the All Stars in the summer of 1964, summed up his experiences for the Associated Press; his story appeared, in various forms, in several newspapers during August. The All Stars were performing grueling one-nighters and Mulligan noticed Armstrong "slumping wearily" in the bus. When he approached the trumpeter, Armstrong was rueful: "What else am I going to do? A man's got to do what he knows and loves."[40] Mulligan also caught Armstrong's performance at a baseball stadium in West Virginia where the All Stars had to use the visiting team's locker room to get ready for the show. "Any place to hang my trumpet, just so long as the folks still want to hear it," Armstrong remarked.[41] Armstrong seemed vaguely concerned with his own mortality. He talked about the jazz funerals that he played growing up in New Orleans: "It's corny, I know, but that's the way I want to go, with a band out to the cemetery and back. I told my wife Lucille to give the boys all the whisky they want, let them get snookered with ol' Satch, just so long as they blow me on home."[42]

On September 3, the All Stars entered Mercury's New York City office to begin yet a new relationship with another label, with some recording sessions overseen by Quincy Jones. Armstrong recorded singles for Mercury until 1966, a series of erratic performances that tried too hard to fit the mold and achieve the success of "Hello, Dolly!" (banjo or guitar was added to insipid material). Not all the songs were failures; another number from *Hello, Dolly!*, "So Long Dearie," showcased a powerfully infectious Armstrong vocal, the band swinging mightily from the start. The record became a minor hit for Armstrong, though it also was notable for the conspicuous absence of any trumpet playing. This didn't bother Joe Glaser one bit. "Not a note on the trumpet," Glaser told Jimmy Breslin. "He don't blow a note on the trumpet. I said in 1939, when everybody said his lip was shot and he couldn't play anymore and I wouldn't let him hit 100 high C's in a night, that one day Louis Armstrong wouldn't even have to play the trumpet. Here it is. Sold 500,000 copies already." Breslin then provided this memorable snapshot of Glaser enjoying his prized client's work: "Joe's fingers started to snap and he began to jiggle. Then he started to turkey trot around a leather chair, fingers snapping, feet shuffling, his voice, perhaps the worst voice in all of America, mumbling along with the song."[43]

Armstrong's Mercury sessions capture him in various states of physical fatigue, his chops in compromised condition. At times he was stunning, as on 1964's "Pretty Little Missy" and 1965's "Short but Sweet," one of his finest records of the sixties. At others he sounded exhausted, as on a lackluster version of "When the Saints Go Marching In" from 1966. So it is that the Mercury sessions, suffering by comparison with the Columbia and Decca sides of the fifties, are mostly forgotten today.

After almost an entire year of performing in the United States, the All Stars, in November, went to New Zealand, Australia, India, and Japan on a month-long tour. International reaction to "Hello, Dolly!" was as wildly enthusiastic as in the United States: unbeknownst to Armstrong and the All Stars, the song had also become an international sensation. Danny Barcelona, accounting for its popularity, was agog: "And I don't mean in the United States. I'm talking India, Korea, wherever, you know. I guess that record really hit, because doing it all through these different countries . . . as soon as they heard the first four bars, they're already clapping, stomping. Yeah. Amazing, huh? First time I ever had seen something or heard something like that."[44]

Having conquered the East, Louis Armstrong might have been on top of the world as the year ended, but he still wasn't through playing the role of jazz's greatest ambassador. After years of speculation, he and the All Stars were about to breach the Iron Curtain.

CHAPTER SIXTEEN

From the Iron Curtain to the
Crescent City, 1965–1966

AFTER YEARS OF speculation and rumors, Louis Armstrong stood poised to pierce the Iron Curtain in early 1965. Though the All Stars never visited the Soviet Union, as had been assumed they would, they toured Prague, East Berlin, Bucharest, Belgrade, and Sofia from mid-March to the beginning of April, with a new trombonist, Tyree Glenn, who had joined the band in late February.

Russell "Big Chief" Moore had served the All Stars well for more than a year, but as Dan Morgenstern puts it, "Big Chief didn't last long because Big Chief was Big Chief. Big Chief was huge. Big Chief was what we nowadays call obese. And he simply decided that being on the road at that pace wasn't going to be good for him. He was absolutely right."[1] Moore remembered the last relentless trip from Japan to San Francisco to Iceland to the Virgin Islands as the one that did him in. He gave notice, and Glenn met up with the band in Memphis. "I told Tyree Glenn that I can't take it," Moore remembered, "I want to be home with my wife and my family. He said, 'Yeah, I'll take over, Chief.' "[2] Moore reconnected with his former employer Lester Lanin, with whom he remained well into the 1970s. Moore died in 1983 at the age of seventy; according to Morgenstern, "He was a good, good trombone player. Boy, I liked Big Chief."[3]

In Tyree Glenn, the All Stars had a musician with impeccable credentials; he had had long stints with the orchestras of Cab Calloway and Duke Ellington. Glenn could also double on vibraphone, and after a while he began taking vibes features with the All Stars. Glenn's tenure got off to a rocky start, however, during his first rehearsal with the band. When Billy Kyle tried to teach him the same backgrounds that Moore had played, Glenn became peeved and said, "I'm not Chief, I'm Tyree Glenn. I'll play my own background."[4] Armstrong, as always, must have seen something in the newcomer that others didn't, because soon he made him his comic foil. While performing in Honolulu, Armstrong called up old friend Trummy Young and had him teach Glenn some of their old routines. Within a year or so, Glenn proved to be an adept partner, turning in fun versions of "Rockin' Chair" and joining Armstrong in his revival of the routine with Velma Middleton on "That's My Desire." On trombone, Glenn wasn't as brash as Young, but he had a fluent way of swinging and was a master of the plunger mute. Hardly the greatest trombonist in the history of the All Stars, Glenn was nonetheless crucial to the group in Armstrong's twilight years.

The All Stars arrived in Prague on March 12 and were greeted by Prime Minister Alexander Dubcek. "*That's* how big Louis was then," Arvell Shaw recalled. According to Shaw, "The first night was reserved for the VIP's, the diplomatic corps and everything. They had all the VIP's, the diplomats from China, from Africa, from all over Europe, Eastern Europe and Russia. Everyone was there. They had three rows in front for the American Embassy staff and the American Ambassador." But those three rows were empty; when Armstrong asked why nobody from the American embassy was there, the tour's promoter replied that he didn't know.

The All Stars received a massive ovation at the conclusion of their program. The next day, their success was celebrated in newspapers around the world. "The next night," Shaw continued, "we walked out on the stage to play, the theatre was packed, and right in front the place was filled by the Americans with flags waving, calling 'That's our boy, Louis.' Louis said, 'Those jive turkeys, they thought I was going to bomb out, and they wouldn't come to support me.' But we laughed it out—it was a diplomatic thing."[5]

Some of Armstrong's Prague performances at Lucerna Hall were recorded, and they more than show that Armstrong was ready for the challenge of this trip. He dusted off demanding pieces such as "Royal

Garden Blues" and "Struttin' with Some Barbecue," compensating for his diminishing speed with brute strength. In Prague an old song found its way back into Armstrong's live repertoire: "Black and Blue." Three versions survive from March 1965; all are moving experiences, but none more so than the one captured on video (March 22) in East Germany, the next stop on the tour.

The All Stars arrived at Berlin's Schönefeld Airport on March 19 to greetings from a jazz band, Jazz Optimisten Berlin, in the form of a rendition of "When It's Sleepy Time Down South." He had never performed in East Berlin before and not a single Armstrong recording was available for purchase in East Germany. None of this mattered: he was an icon, an institution, arguably the most recognizable entertainer on the planet. However, the East Berlin press was eager to see Armstrong for entirely nonmusical reasons: they wanted him to comment on the Berlin Wall and, more important, they hoped for him to comment on some explosive remarks he had made before leaving for Prague. In February, the Student Nonviolent Coordinating Committee had unsuccessfully tried to institute a voter-registration program in Selma, Alabama. Under the aegis of Martin Luther King Jr. and the Southern Christian Leadership Conference, numerous marches were held in Selma, with more than 250 demonstrators arrested. On March 7, six hundred people left Selma to march fifty-four miles to Montgomery, the capital of Alabama. Early on, police had attacked the demonstrators, brutally beating many; at least sixteen had to be hospitalized. The horrifying images were broadcast on television for the world to see.

Louis Armstrong watched in a hotel in Denmark. When asked for his reaction, Armstrong said he "got sick." As to why he'd never taken part in such a march, Armstrong allowed: "Maybe I'm not in the front line, but I support them with my donations. But maybe that's not enough now. My life is music. They would beat me on the mouth if I marched and without my mouth I would not be able to blow my horn." A newspaper reporter asked Armstrong whether, given his stature and celebrity, he could imagine being so attacked. "They would even beat Jesus if he was black and marched," Armstrong cooly responded.[6] He wondered: "How is it possible that human beings can still treat each other that way? Hitler is dead a long time—or is he?"[7]

Armstrong's words made headlines around the world, as had his

remarks regarding the Little Rock incident of 1957. But this time there
was a difference: possibly as a result of prodding by Joe Glaser, Armstrong
began to recant. On March 19, when he arrived in East Berlin, there was
a press conference with local reporters eager for Armstrong to criticize
the United States, which at the time did not recognize East Berlin. Armstrong was the first American entertainer to play there, and before he even
blew a note, he was mired in controversy. "I've got no grievances," he said
when asked about how he had been treated in the American South. "I love
everyone. All through the South, some of my greatest friends are white
people." Even more, Armstrong went out of his way to say: "I have been
treated fine in the South. In the South, we stay in the best hotels and get
courteous treatment. We play to mixed audiences there and some of my
best audiences are in the South . . . both whites and blacks are my fans
and I am not going to abuse either one."[8] Armstrong refused to comment
publicly on the Berlin Wall. "I ain't worried about the Wall, I'm worried
about the audience I'm going to play to tomorrow night," he told the press.
"I don't know nothing about no Wall. See, when you get in the concert
hall, forget about everything and concentrate on Satchmo." When the line
of questioning didn't cease, Armstrong turned frank: "I can't [say] what
I want to say, but if you accept it, I'll say it: forget about all that other
bullshit."[9] With those words, a deadly serious Armstrong stopped talking,
lit a cigarette, and pointed at himself. Such testiness would have made
headlines in the United States, but it didn't make an impression in East
Berlin. The Communist reporters were "visibly disappointed," according to one account, but Armstrong was savvy enough not to add fuel to
the fire of his Denmark quotes. As a black man from the United States
performing in a Communist country, Armstrong was in a conundrum.
When all was said and done, he just wanted to play his music; he felt better communicating with his horn than with mere words.

On the evening of March 22, 1965, Armstrong and the All Stars performed at the Friedrichstadt Palast, a program that was broadcast on
both German television and radio. After opening with standards "Sleepy
Time" and "Indiana," Armstrong called for something special. "Thank
you very much, folks. Here's one of our recordings, a beautiful number
called 'Black and Blue.' Yessir." A murmur went through the audience; the
choice of "Black and Blue" was a loud clarion call.

Originally from the 1929 Broadway show *Hot Chocolates,* "(What Did I

Do to Be So) Black and Blue" was a dark-skinned woman's lament about losing out to lighter-skinned women when trying to get a man. In July 1929, Armstrong, a cast member, had daringly recorded it for Okeh, stripping it of its womanly associations while turning it into essentially a powerful protest song. After Armstrong formed the All Stars in 1947, "Black and Blue" had become a mainstay. By the mid-fifties, Armstrong had recorded a definitive version for Columbia and had performed it in Ghana, moving Kwame Nkrumah to tears. But, inexplicably, Armstrong had stopped performing the tune, perhaps because he found it too confrontational, too controversial in the wake of Little Rock. From May 1956 until March 1965, only two versions of "Black and Blue" survive from countless broadcasts and concerts recorded, and in both instances Armstrong announced the song as a request. But the events in Selma had so infuriated him, and his East Berlin press conference could have been construed as so compromising, that on March 22, Armstrong chose to break his silence on certain matters with his music.

No sooner did he call the number than pianist Kyle began playing a solemn introduction. When the rhythm section kicked in, it was clear that they were playing "Black and Blue" at a tempo slower than that of any previous version. Back in the 1950s, "Black and Blue" had a hint of a bounce to it, and when Armstrong sang it, he couldn't quite repress a smile. In East Berlin, the bounce was gone. Armstrong stoically played a full chorus of melody, pacing himself dramatically with sympathetic support from Glenn's trombone and Shu's clarinet. Armstrong stuck closely to the melody, holding the last note of each phrase and shaking it slightly for emphasis.

At the end of the chorus, Armstrong slowly made his way to the microphone. He stared at the floor and unburdened himself of a nearly inaudible sigh. As he reached the microphone, he gave his face a quick wipe with his handkerchief and proceeded to sing Razaf's lyrics.

He sang the first eight bars hinting a smile, unable to mask his delight in the beautiful number, but there was none of the mugging and eyerolling routinely lambasted by younger black musicians in America. During the second eight bars, Armstrong's smile began to fade, as he manipulated his handkerchief as a prop to dramatize the hurt contained in the lyrics. By the time he got to the bridge, his smile had disappeared. He now assumed the air of a preacher, pointing a finger skyward as if to say, "Listen up to my sermon." In perhaps the most disturbing stanza of the piece, Razaf's original lyrics ran, "I'm white inside / But that don't help my case," and that's how Armstrong had sung it from 1929 through 1956. But by the time of his "by request" versions in 1959, Armstrong had made an important change to the lyrics, a change he retained in East Berlin. "I'm *right*," he now sang, a telling alteration indeed. As Armstrong made his way across the bridge, he instinctively tried to smile but, engaged as he was in serious business, fought it off and finished out the bridge with a dramatic scat break delivered with a pained frown. He sang the last stanza as if to clarify what he had been unable to express to reporters only a few days earlier: "My only sin," he intoned, "is in my skin."

His smile reappeared at the end of the vocal; he was awash in the audience's adulation. He took two steps backward and put the horn back to his lips. He wasn't done preaching yet. He blew a reflective quote of a song he loved, "I Cover the Waterfront," before quickly ascending into the upper register in a scorching manner. Refusing to peak too fast, he withdrew to his lower register for some somber, blues-infused phrases, his eyes closed, his horn pointing to the floor. He pulled the horn from his lips for a second, put it back, flickered his valves for good measure, leaned back and resumed playing. As the band began throbbing beneath him, Armstrong's playing grew more intense. He closed out the bridge with a shattering tremolo, tension building as the rhythm section turned up the heat with a series of triplet accents.

The tension exploded when he began his final eight bars with a three-note phrase leading to a screaming high concert B—not the highest note he had ever hit, but arguably the angriest, the most passionate single note he would ever play. Back in America, avant-garde jazz was in its "New Thing" phase, younger musicians frequently unleashing their anger at racism by way of music full of instrumental screams and shrieks. The high B Armstrong played on "Black and Blue" rivaled their ferocity. As he hit the note, he was leaning back, his trumpet pointed to the heavens, his eyes rolling back into his head, his eyebrows furrowed—here was dangerous intensity personified. Arvell Shaw let out an emotional yell, urging Armstrong on as cameras caught drummer Danny Barcelona, laying down an unyielding backbeat, slack-jawed, agog at his boss's impassioned outpouring.

Armstrong still wasn't done. He continued to play in almost operatic

fashion, nailing another high B along the way. He concluded with a signature chromatically ascending phrase, ending on a sky-high C, shaking
it for all it was worth. The audience was beside itself, ecstatically shouting
its approval. Armstrong beamed and started shouting back, mostly gib-
berish, at once as appreciation of their response and acknowledgment that
he had just created something special. When he took what he thought
would be his final bow that night, he was besieged by continuous applause
for more than two minutes. He encored with "Hello, Dolly!" but still the
East Berlin fans wouldn't let him leave. He came out for bow after bow,
finally appearing in his bathrobe. Louis Armstrong had breached the Iron
Curtain, and "Black and Blue" was as powerful a musical statement about
race as he would ever make.

Mindful of appealing to his East German audience, Armstrong eventually found time to visit the Berlin Wall. "This is where the truly musical
mixed with that which was outside of the realm of music," wrote Karlheinz Drechsel, a German jazz musician and journalist who had spent
almost the entire tour with the All Stars.

> There—in the shadow of the "Wall"—one could see not only Louis
> Armstrong the world famous jazz musician but an ambassador, a sym-
> bol of humanitarianism, of people living together in a life of liberty.
> Armstrong had perhaps never been so conscious of this as he was dur-
> ing that tour. His deep distress when he saw the inhumane reality of
> the "Wall" for the first time with his own eyes at the Brandenburg Gate
> made a very great impression on me, and his thoughtful words during
> the drive in the tour bus, "That's even more terrible than Jim Crow!
> What cruel hardship and pain for millions of people! I will do my best
> to give my very best to make them happy. Yes, that's what I'll do."[10]

On the bus ride from Magdeburg to the Erfurt freeway, Drechsel witnessed a remarkable scene. "During a brief rest in a poor village pub whose
'menu' comprised nothing but sausage with or without bread the musicians suddenly found themselves surrounded by lively school kids," he
wrote. "The news 'Louis Armstrong is sitting in the Konsum' had spread
like wildfire, followed by a turbulent autograph hunt using scraps of paper,
beer mats, playing cards, copy books and the like. Louis Armstrong was

literally surrounded, but his joy was obvious and, with careful lettering and the typical Satchmo smile, he let every kid have his 'Louis "Satchmo" Armstrong.' It was a wonderful, heart-warming scene."

But Frenchy Tallerie busted up the scene, shouting, "Cut the crap immediately!" and telling the band members to "move your asses to the bus." "Dead silence ensued," Drechsel continued, "and then Louis Armstrong, with an aggressive outburst that was not his style anyway and especially unusual against a white man, said to the road manager, 'We're not in the States here. And even there you won't be able to boss us around much longer! Get out: slavery is over once and for all. Listen here, the joy and happiness of these kids here are a thousand times more important to me than your orders. We won't leave here before I've signed the last autograph!' And that's what happened."[11] Coincidentally or not, this would turn out to be Tallerie's last tour with Armstrong, ending a rocky relationship that went back to 1942.

Armstrong wasn't going to allow Tallerie's antics to mar such a historic occasion. "Six years before his death, Louis Armstrong had once again reached a really impressive artistic zenith," Drechsel wrote of the historic tour. "And the jazz audience in East Germany (where until then there had not been one officially issued Armstrong record) celebrated the 'King of Jazz' with an enthusiasm that had never been known before. No concert ended without standing ovations that went on for several minutes."[12]

Armstrong was only back in the United States for a matter of days when he became the recipient of a major award. On April 13, Armstrong won a Grammy award for "Best Vocal Performance, Male" for the song "Hello, Dolly!" beating out Andy Williams, Dean Martin, João Gilberto, and Tony Bennett for the honor. Armstrong might not have known it at the time, but Joe Glaser campaigned pretty hard for this to happen. In late December 1964, Glaser received a phone call from George T. Simon, the esteemed jazz writer and president of the National Academy of Recording Arts and Sciences, asking if Armstrong would be available to give out an award during the ceremony. Glaser didn't think Armstrong should solely be handing out awards, he insisted that he should be on the receiving end of one. Apparently, Glaser used some pretty strong language, because minutes after the fractious phone call ended, Glaser composed a letter to Simon, apologizing for his emotional outburst, but continuing to hammer his point home.

> I repeat and add to what I said, that it is a shameful situation when you see obscure artists, and Johnny-Come-Latelies [sic] who have gotten lucky with one record and who have not served the Public or the Industry as long as a man called Louis Armstrong, receive an award and Louis Armstrong's latest record "Dolly" sold over two million, and one Million so far of the albums, should be asked to present an award to these questionable "hits."

Glaser was particularly miffed that N.A.R.A.S. presented Bobby Darin with an award for his record of "Mack the Knife" during an episode of *The Ed Sullivan Show,* but never bestowed such an honor on Armstrong. Glaser could not control his feelings, which eventually spilled out in a remarkable run-on sentence:

> I appreciate the fact your organization has great merit, and I have the greatest respect and admiration for the people you mention who have made awards and presentations, but the important thing is *who* receives an award, not who gives it out, therefore when you asked that Louis Armstrong, who has one of the greatest hits on earth, to give an award, I had no alternative but to express myself as I did, even admitting it may be a secret who is going to get an award and who is not—from all indications it doesn't appear as if a man of Louis Armstrong's caliber, ability, and prestige is going to get anything, only lend his great showmanship to *giving,* and I for one would not want Louis Armstrong's feelings to be hurt even though he is a Champion and one of the "greats" of the world.[13]

Glaser's passionate appeal may or may not have had any effect on the voters, but the end result was another major award for Armstrong. Though it must have been nice to conquer the Iron Curtain and receive a Grammy all within a matter of weeks, this period served as something of a farewell to Armstrong at the peak of his powers. As it turned out, Armstrong's fierce trumpeting during the tour had not been without pain.

Within a week of his return to the United States, Armstrong underwent dental surgery, which required a long recuperative hiatus. With a mouth full of intricate bridgework, Armstrong's trumpet playing would never again be the same.

While Armstrong recovered, the All Stars managed a rare vacation, six weeks off, from April 12 to May 24. It was then that Arvell Shaw left the band yet again to freelance, and was replaced by the very talented George James Catlett, better known as Buddy. Catlett was a product of the Seattle jazz scene, having jammed while still a teenager with Ray Charles and Quincy Jones, among others. Before joining Armstrong, Catlett amassed experience playing with the small groups of Eddie "Lockjaw" Davis and Coleman Hawkins and with the Count Basie and Quincy Jones big bands. For Catlett, becoming an All Star was a dream come true, for he had always admired Armstrong profoundly. "I had seen him perform when he'd come to Seattle and I had his records," Catlett said. "My first musical experience was my father had bought me a Czechoslovakian cornet and I had learned to play Louie's 'Back o' Town Blues' without knowing my scales or anything. So I could kind of feel where Louie was coming from." Catlett never grew tired of listening to what Armstrong could do night after night with many of the tunes he himself had practiced. "Watching him style himself was something, like he would play 'Hello, Dolly!' or something like that until it was coming out of your ears and he would still come up with, every once in a while, a new note or an approach to his phrasing on tunes like that," he said. "It was really something to experience listening to that."[14]

Having recovered from his dental work, Armstrong led the All Stars back on the road for another grueling tour of Europe: London, Paris, Copenhagen, and Budapest, where they played to an outdoor crowd exceeding one hundred thousand. Upon their return to the States in mid-June, there was yet another change in personnel: Eddie Shu was replaced by Buster Bailey. Born in 1902, Bailey was a technically advanced clarinet player who had studied with Franz Schoepp of the Chicago Symphony, who would later be Benny Goodman's teacher as well. Bailey had first met Armstrong when they played in King Oliver's Creole Jazz Band in 1923 and 1924 and then with Fletcher Henderson in 1924 and 1925. Bailey's consummate virtuosity provoked some to complain that he didn't swing. But after the bored Barney Bigard, the bland Joe Darensbourg, and the sometimes blasé Peanuts Hucko, Bailey was a godsend, one of the best clarinetists Armstrong ever played with; he turned "Memphis Blues," W. C. Handy's ode to Bailey's hometown, into a memorable feature.

Bailey's first night with the band was July 4, which Armstrong celebrated as his birthday every year. To honor the day in 1965, Armstrong performed three shows for twenty thousand fans at Atlantic City's Steel Pier. The crowd was chiefly young people there to hear the man who had turned "Hello, Dolly!" into a hit. Armstrong didn't mind; he was inspired by their enthusiasm: "Man, them kids are something else. Who say they don't know good music from bad?"[15]

While the All Stars were on the road, the July 15 issue of *DownBeat* hit newsstands, featuring a "Salute to Satch" cover story together with tributes to the trumpeter, and a long interview with the magazine's New York editor, Dan Morgenstern. "It's wonderful—but nobody lasts forever," Armstrong said of his fame before summing up his career. "After 52 years of playing, I had a wonderful experience for a man who came up from New Orleans selling newspapers and who just wanted to blow the horn . . . The people put me in my seat, and I'll never let them down. And there's no problem: they love music, and I love music too." Regarding his critics, Armstrong was sanguine: "If you perform, you're going to have your up and downs, but what is said about you, good or bad, is forgotten tomorrow. The public is ready for tomorrow's news. That's how fast our America is . . . it's wonderful to be around and to see so many things happening with the youngsters. And you're right in there with them. Today. That's happiness—that's nice. I don't regret anything. I still enjoy life and music."[16]

Critic Patrick Scott begged to differ. Reviewing a lackluster Toronto concert of July, Scott was struck by Armstrong's seeming exhaustion; four days later, he dwelled on it some more in an article titled "An Ominous Streak Shows Up in Satchmo." "I think it is a genuinely humble awareness of this universal affection that keeps this man going—and that eventually will kill him," Scott wrote. "Even iron men grow rusty, and the first ominous streaks are beginning to show on Armstrong. The characteristic ebullience and effervescence were not in conspicuously large supply at O'Keefe Centre. He smiled his trademark smile (and rolled his eyes and shook his jowls and brandished his handkerchiefs) when the occasion demanded, but he spent much more of his time—right there on the stage, in front of all those people!—slump-shouldered against the piano, staring somberly at his shoes, or off into space. For the first time in all the times and places I have seen him he seemed to be uninterested, almost to the point of obvious boredom, in what was going on around him." Scott concluded: "I would like him to stop being a musical zombie, and start to enjoy life—and his own work—again, and to hell with goodwill ambassadorships and 'Mack The Knife' and Tyree Glenn."[17]

In Toronto, Scott had wanted to spend a day with Armstrong. Both Joe Glaser and Armstrong himself had agreed, but plans were scuttled when the above review appeared. Scott was cut off by Armstrong's new road manager, Ira Mangel, who replaced Frenchy Tallerie after the Iron Curtain tour, for his unflattering piece. But Armstrong followed through, telling an irate Mangel to allow Scott and him privacy. Scott was then allowed to spend an entire evening in Armstrong's company, from his late-afternoon wake-up through his entire preshow ritual of Swiss Kriss, vitamins, dinner, and warming up. Scott was with him throughout the show and watched him sit at a small table and sign autographs long after the final notes sounded. Scott's resulting piece, "The Offstage Satchmo," was a fascinating glimpse of Louis's daily routine and featured numerous quotes from the trumpeter himself.

However, Scott left some things out of the profile, as he related elsewhere in the very same issue. "He also talked so freely and frankly that some things he told me will remain unpublished until he dies," Scott wrote. "Others—such as the fact that he knows he is in a rut and intends to get out of it as soon as he can—gave me a rather eerie sensation, since I knew (but he didn't) that I had just written a piece, already going to press, in which I had said that Armstrong was in a rut, and that he seemed determined to die in it. What he told me confirmed the first point—he even used the phrase 'prisoner of this grind I'm in'—and proved me completely wrong on the second—which was the happiest discovery that I was wrong, I had ever made."[18]

In fact, in the profile Scott quoted Armstrong as saying, "Gotta keep myself in shape for that grind. And not just for the grind, either. I wanna be in shape when I put down that horn. I'm 65 years old now, Daddy, and I sure as hell don't figure to be playing that horn when I'm 70. That's when I wanna be relaxin' and enjoyin' life, and I plan to be in shape to do that, too."[19] Not long after, Louis told Associated Press writer James Bacon, "Man, there just ain't no days off. Just looking at that itinerary makes me tired." Armstrong was about to embark on forty-two straight one-nighters in September without any sustained time off until January 1966. "I got 12 weeks off next January and I may just dig this retirement jazz for size."[20] There was now a buzz building, with numerous blurbs appearing in print throughout the country hinting that Armstrong was considering retiring. Scott even tracked down Armstrong's second wife, Lillian Hardin, a driving force behind Armstrong's career in the 1920s, who said, "But I'll tell you one thing—and I hope it doesn't sound like sour grapes, because it isn't. If Louis and I had stayed together he'd've retired long ago. The first time he hit a bad note, that would have been it. Sure, he's the greatest jazz musician that ever lived—but he's the stubbornest, too. He should have quit long ago, and he'd be a happier man today."[21]

Armstrong realized he had to intercede on all of this retirement talk. While in Eugene, Oregon, for a gig, he tried to clarify matters. "I told a reporter I thought it's time to start taking things a little easier. You know, goof for three or four months, then lay off for three or four, but man, I'm not retiring." In the wake of this statement, Scott went to press in October with what Armstrong and he had discussed in private: "His two greatest fears, Armstrong told me last July, were: a) that when it came right down to it he would be 'scared stiff' to tell his manager, Joe Glaser, that he wanted out; and b) that Glaser would die before he did—and 'then what a hell of a mess I'd be in,' " Scott recounted. He added, "He knows he is not playing as well as he used to (which is why he is not playing as much), and he knows he is not going to improve with age. But this is not his chief concern." Scott used Armstrong's own words to describe his "chief concern." "I don't feel I have to prove anything now," Armstrong said:

> And I've been so tired for so long that I couldn't if I had to. All I want to do is get the hell out of this grind while I still have my health, so Lucille and I can enjoy what's left of our lives as civilians. I don't want to be Satchmo any more. I can't go where I want to go or do what I want to do. I don't resent the acclaim—it's been wonderful all these years—but we just haven't had a life of our own. So mark my words: about a year and a half from now, old Satchmo is gonna disappear—me and Lucille will go underground for about six months—and when we come up again it's gonna be as Mr. and Mrs. Armstrong, civilians, period.[22]

Armstrong also told Scott his postretirement plans: "I'd like to give trumpet lessons to little kids," he said. "I think maybe I could still show 'em a thing or two. But once I lay down that horn I'll never pick it up in public again." All the same, Armstrong was sure to insist: "But all this is just me talking to you, for now. Make all the notes you like, but please keep them in your pocket till I give you the signal. If Glaser ever knew what I was thinking—well, I just don't know how I'm gonna get up the nerve to tell him. I guess maybe I'll let Lucille do it for me." Scott believed that Armstrong's statement in Oregon was tantamount to his giving him "the signal." This was his rationale for publishing their July conversation: "Armstrong has decided that he never will get up the nerve, and that he can't, when the chips are down, let Lucille do it for him. Which means that the greatest performer that jazz has known will go on—and on and on—being a sad, scared Satchmo."[23]

Scott's article is singular in the body of literature about Armstrong published during his lifetime. Armstrong's remarks contradict others he made privately and publicly at the time. Two weeks before Armstrong's conversation with Scott in July, he was quoted as saying, "You don't quit when you're still strong and enjoy your work," and "I love music just as much as when I first started to play."[24] It is conceivable that Scott caught Armstrong in the dumps in July. Armstrong's trumpet playing was not the same after his dental surgery, and this must have depressed him greatly. He began cutting out some solos, while on others he changed some of his set patterns because he could no longer aim for the stratosphere. But as Lil Hardin had alluded, Armstrong's stubbornness was legendary. He admitted as much in a letter to Lucille on September 24, 1965, when he related how a reporter from *Life* magazine had inquired about his dental work. "He really did Blush when I showed him my new Dental work with so many teeth missing—and this Big Ass removal Bridge I have in my mouth. He wondered his Ass off how 'n' the hell Can you play with all that Bridge work into your mouth. I told him, there ain't But one *Game Sommitch* in music and that's Louis Armstrong."[25]

As game as he might have been, after over fifty years of being able to do whatever he desired on his horn, Armstrong now found his chops deserting him at the height of his popularity. His fans still adored him, of course, as he related in a letter to Lucille from September 31, 1965, just days before Scott published Armstrong's words, writing, "I am fine, doing Great. My public still loves me all the way."[26] But though the adulation was nice, Armstrong's personal standard remained high, and the fact that he couldn't get around the trumpet like he used to must have been crushing. There was probably nothing that scared him more, and it was in a depressed moment that he discussed quitting the business with Scott.

Oddly enough, for all the weightiness, Scott's piece about Armstrong does not seem to have been picked up by any other news outlet or jazz magazine at the time. There is no record of anyone commenting on it.

Perhaps the article was ignored because the prospect of Armstrong's retirement was inconceivable to all who knew him. When Jewel Brown was asked whether Glaser worked Armstrong unconscionably, she replied: "That's what Louie wanted. And Louie wanted to die onstage like Big Sid Catlett."[27] Buddy Catlett agreed: "One of the things he used to talk about was he was going to die onstage." As for Glaser pushing Armstrong too hard, Catlett said, "He wanted to be there. What else was he going to do? You can't just go and pick the jobs you want. I don't care if you're Louie or whoever you are. If you want to play, you got to do that in order to keep some chops up. He couldn't play two months from now if he hadn't played at all."[28]

Armstrong's friend trumpeter Ruby Braff remembered a phase late in Louis's life when the trumpeter became interested in situation comedies on television. "He was screaming about the situation comedies—he says, 'Jesus Christ, I could make up twenty-five situation comedies with me, then go out on the road, put them all in the can.' He said, 'I don't know,' 'cause he mentioned Redd Foxx, he said, 'he's not as funny as the shit I know.' He says, 'We could have some characters,' he says, 'people would go insane. But nobody wants me to do anything but play.' He wanted to do all kinds of shit." When asked if Armstrong ever made his desires known, Braff said, "Yeah, he spoke up about it, but the thing is, there was so much quick money in his concerts every night and he was booked so far ahead—five, six, ten years ahead, man—that it was hard to separate anything already. It was very complicated. And part of it was his fault, because he insisted on never having a night off, which nobody knows about. He told Joe Glaser, 'You ever give me a night off, go find yourself a new boy.' Everyone thought that Joe was a guy that kept pushing him to work. Joe was trying to get him to stop working for four or five weeks at a time so he could figure out other things to do to make more money off of him. But Pops always kept the pressure on him. You know why? Every night was a party for him. For him to have four weeks of no parties was like 'What are you doing me, a big favor?' "[29]

Whether the sentiments he expressed to Scott were heartfelt or not, Armstrong refused to relent: even as he was always on tour, he had not played in New Orleans, his hometown, in ten long years because of Jim Crow laws preventing integrated bands from performing publicly. Now when these laws had been repealed, Armstrong made a triumphal return to his native city to perform an afternoon concert on October 31 at the Loyola Field House, a benefit for the New Orleans Jazz Museum. Armstrong was greeted by a crowd of hundreds at the New Orleans International Airport (renamed the Louis Armstrong New Orleans International Airport in 2001). While being whisked around town in a motorcade, Armstrong reminisced a bit about his youth. "These are my old stomping grounds," he said. "Everybody was blowin' good stuff here when I was a kid." Armstrong also reconnected with Peter Davis, the man responsible for teaching the troubled youngster how to play cornet while he was at the Colored Waif's Home for Boys as a teen. Armstrong told the eighty-seven-year-old Davis, "You sure taught us the rudimentals."[30]

As 1965 drew to a close, Armstrong found himself in front of movie cameras again. He had a role meatier than he was accustomed to in *A Man Called Adam,* a film directed by Leo Penn and starring Sammy Davis Jr. as the title character, fictional jazz trumpeter-singer Adam Johnson, a bitter and angry man so unsympathetic that Howard Thompson concluded his review of the film by writing, "But it's hard to appreciate a paranoid hero who is his own worst enemy, with more collected misery than even he can shake a trumpet at."[31] The film, however, gave Armstrong a rare opportunity for serious dramatic acting.

Although he appeared in over thirty films, Hollywood rarely utilized Armstrong's acting abilities. "See, no one in America, unfortunately, knows what an actor he was," Ruby Braff recalled. "They never found out he was one of the greatest actors that ever lived. Laurence Olivier acknowledged him. He said, 'Him and Chaplin are two of the best actors I've ever seen.' And that comes from a person who is not an idiot. I mean a man who could, in a studio, when the light goes on, a two-and-a-half-minute record, can make up a 'Laughin' Louie' thing or anything and do a whole drama in three seconds, impromptu, do anything—they don't have actors like that. He told me he was very frustrated about it."[32]

In the film, Armstrong plays a thinly veiled version of himself, Willie "Sweet Daddy" Ferguson, an aging trumpeter whom Davis's character treats poorly, regarding him as old-fashioned and out of date. Late in the film, Ferguson is seen sitting alone at a party, a poignant moment not unlike what Armstrong's co-star Ossie Davis had witnessed on the set:

> One day at lunch, everybody'd gone out. The set was quiet. As I came back to the set I looked up and there was Louis Armstrong sitting in a chair, the handkerchief tied around his head, looking up with the saddest expression I've ever seen on a man's face. I looked and I was startled and then I started to back away because it seemed such a private moment, but he heard me backing away and he broke out of it right away, "Hey, Pops, looks like these cats are going to starve old Louis to death, hey, man, wow . . . " And everything you know, I went into it with him but I never forgot that look and it changed my concept of Louis Armstrong. Because I, too, as a boy had objected [to] a lot of what Louis was doing. I figured all them teeth and that handkerchief—we called it 'ooftah,' by which we meant you do that to please the white folk. You know, you make them happy and all that stuff, make us look like fools. But it was only then I began to understand something about Louis. He could put on that show, he could do that whole thing, because in that horn of his he had the power to kill. That horn could kill a man. So there was where the truth of Louis Armstrong resided. Whatever he was, the moment he put the trumpet to his lips, a new truth emerged, a new man emerged, a new power emerged and I looked on Louis for what he truly was, after that. You know, he became an angelic presence to me after that moment.[33]

In his private moments, the wear and tear of decades of one-nighters was beginning to take its toll on the aging trumpeter. The punishing life on the road was instanced by the tragic death of All Stars pianist Billy Kyle on February 23, 1966. Kyle collapsed on February 16 after a gig at the Stambaugh Auditorium in Youngstown, Ohio. Kyle had a history of heavy drinking that had led to past battles with ulcers and ailments that would force him off the bandstand for weeks at a time, but by 1966 he was on the wagon. However, it was the middle of winter, and the All Stars were making another grueling tour, traveling from gig to gig in an unheated bus. By the time they reached Ohio, Kyle was already ailing. Catlett remembered this Ohio performance and Kyle's condition well: "Number one, they had to help him up the stairs—there were some stairs to get up to the stage. And he was out of breath and couldn't hardly make it. But he played everything he knew. It was just magnificent playing. That's the way I heard it."[34] Jewel Brown knew something was wrong when the usually punctual Kyle did not come out of his room the following morning.

Dr. Alexander Schiff, who still traveled with the band, suspected misfortune. He called security to open Kyle's room, and when they did, according to Brown, "it looked like they had slaughtered a hog. His liver had erupted. Blood was all over the place, from what I understand. I never shall forget, he lived for like a week or so and I understand they had blown balloons up in him in order to try to stop the bleeding or something there. And the night we were in—I forget what city we were in—we had to leave, and that's when they got Marty Napoleon to take his place. And of course, Louie sent Marty Napoleon out, like, in a hurry, in a jiffy. And we never missed a gig or anything."[35]

Even as the band continued performing, Kyle remained in hospital for a week. A preternatural chill overcame one performance, and it remained forever vivid to Brown. She recalls, "Pops started playing, out of the clear blue sky, Pops started blowing 'Just a Closer Walk with Thee.' And when we came off the bandstand, Dr. Schiff walked up to Pops and told him, he said, 'I just got a call. Billy just passed.' So it's like Pops felt it."[36] The official cause, according to the *New York Times* obituary, was "complications resulting from hemorrhaging ulcers."[37] Though Kyle was only fifty-three, thirteen years of nonstop traveling had aged him greatly, much as it had Velma Middleton, the only other All Star who died on the road.

Of the pianist, Brown said, "Billy Kyle enhanced that band and enhanced everything that Louie was doing. He was great. He was just absolutely great . . . He did so many pretty things on piano that pulled so much out of me that I didn't even know I had . . . When he had a chance, it was pretty. Just absolutely pretty."[38] To Danny Barcelona, Kyle was "a sweetheart, a gentleman all the time."[39] His elegant, Earl Hines–inspired playing was a perfect fit in the small group, and his simple but effective arrangements greatly enriched the All Stars' book. Was Kyle's fate a har-

binger for the sixty-five-year-old Armstrong? Armstrong seemed uncon-
cerned, for he and the All Stars spent February and March wending their
way through Michigan, Illinois, Pittsburgh, and Los Angeles.

It was around this time that Armstrong sat down for an extensive
and expansive interview with Richard Meryman. Meryman edited
Armstrong's responses into an autobiographical first-person account of
Armstrong's life. Titled "An Authentic American Genius," the piece was
the cover story of the April 11 issue of *Life* magazine. It allowed Armstrong
to offer candid viewpoints on a variety of subjects, including his relationship with Joe Glaser. On that subject, Armstrong unburdened himself of
complex feelings: "I've always known my manager Joe Glaser is the only
cat that dug Louis Armstrong—like a baby or a little dog always knows
the one who ain't slapping him on the rear all the time. So I go all out
to do everything I possibly can to keep him satisfied."[40] Glaser was given
his own sidebar in the piece, in which he said of Armstrong, "I guess to
me he's like a son," before likening him to "a brother. He's like a younger
brother with me." Glaser also admitted, "I build my whole business, my
whole career on my success with Louis Armstrong." He took credit for
turning Armstrong into more of an entertainer: "An entertainer, singer,
and musician can make ten times as much money as an ordinary trumpet
player. So I used to say, 'Louis, forget all the goddamn critics, the musicians. Play for the public. Sing and play and smile."[41] But Armstrong had
never been "an ordinary trumpet player."

Armstrong himself discussed his role as entertainer: "See, I think when
I commenced to put a little showmanship in with the music, people
appreciated me better . . . long time there we just played one number after
another—just another blasting band—and pretty soon you got everybody's backs. I was blowing my brains out, standing on my head trying
to please the other musicians. And the first thing those cats ask, 'Was you
high? Sho' was blowing, man. Was you high?' Here you trying to show
your art-tis-try and this son-of-a-bitch come up with a bust right off the
reel and drag you. And I come to realize the audience, the ordinary public,
thought I was a maniac or something, running amuck. I forgot them and
it didn't do me no good." And so it was that Armstrong always put his
audience first. "So I found out, the main thing is to live for that audience.
What you're there for is to please the people—I mean, the best way you
can. Those few moments belong to them."[42]

But most conspicuously, some of the tiredness and regret that perme-ated Patrick Scott's 1965 profile were present in the *Life* profile. Armstrong dwelled on growing up in New Orleans, but he also spoke philosophically about his later years. "I'm always wondering if it would have been best in my life if I'd just stayed like I was in New Orleans, having a ball . . . I never did want to be no big star. Some people say, 'Shoot, he wants to be a big deal, an individual,' and even from your own musicians you won't get that same warmth. And all those beggars with their phony poor this, poor that, always got their hand out every time they catch you. What do they do when I ain't around?" Armstrong addressed his relentless touring: "And this life I got, few can do it, making those gigs sometimes seven days a week—feel like I spent nine thousand hours on buses, planes, getting there just in time to play with cold chops, come off too tired to lift an eyelash—nothing but ringing and twisting and jumping and bumping."[43] Yet Armstrong was quick to point out that he wasn't complaining. "Don't get me wrong . . . I ain't lazy, I'm grateful. I've had some great ovations in my time, had beautiful moments. But seems like I was more content, more relaxed growing up in New Orleans—just being around, playing with the old timers."[44]

Meryman's profile was long to begin with, but he published an extended version of it five years later in which he conveyed Armstrong's state of mind during this period with quotes on even more serious subjects. Speaking of old timers, Armstrong also discussed his favorite subject, his New Orleans mentor Joe "King" Oliver. Armstrong always spoke of Oliver in happy, reverential terms, but now, as his health and playing ability began to fade, Armstrong began to focus on Oliver's tragic ending. "See, I don't never forget what happened to Joe Oliver," he told Meryman. "By the time he got to New York, they had to tell him he ain't got nothing to offer. He'd aged up, lost that certain something—the reflexes around the lips . . . Didn't have an agent to look after him. Nobody never did stick with him."[45] Armstrong was particularly disgusted by how young musicians treated Oliver, taking advantage of him, laughing at him, even taking his food. "Pulled him down like a barrel of crabs," he vented. "They should have glorified the man, 'cause he represented so much." Clearly, Armstrong saw a parallel in how he was being received by young musicians. But most cryptically, he hinted at his own death: "But if I do play till I faint and fall out with a heart attack—wouldn't get no credit for that," he told Meryman. "Nooo. They going to say what a darn fool he was. What's the use of ripping and running and batting my brains out and killing myself. And pretty soon it's going to be, 'Ladies and gentlemen, this is it.' "[46]

Between the Patrick Scott article and the *Life* cover story, a fair amount of bitterness and a whiff of mortality had crept into Armstrong's words, something that was not lost on those close to him. When the *Life* magazine story was published, Jack Bradley wrote to a friend, "We agree with you when you say that you felt Pops's *Life* mag. article had bits of bitterness in it. Unfortunately, for the past year or more Pops has developed this attitude and undoubtedly for very good reasons—we know he has been having painful and bad trouble with teeth and chops—and Glaser still cracks that whip—not allowing Louis time to get dental work done properly—with Louis still doing one-nighters although, thank God, not as many as he has done all his life. Still not time for him to mend body and soul."[47]

Armstrong finally got some respite from touring during the unusually relaxed summer of 1966; he and the All Stars remained in New York from July through September. The band was appearing in a revue called *Mardi Gras* at the Jones Beach Marine Theater. Forty years later, Danny Barcelona was still mystified by so long a stretch without one-nighters. "Yeah, we were there through, would you believe, sitting down for three months?" he remembered. "The whole summer, man—Jesus! Actually unbelievable, you know?"[48]

Armstrong was happy to be a part of the show because it featured Guy Lombardo's orchestra. The revue, produced by Lombardo with choreography by June Taylor, had a second act depicting New Orleans in 1905. Armstrong and the All Stars played for thirty minutes each night, after which there was a grand finale uniting the All Stars and Lombardo's orchestra. Of the experience, Armstrong said, "Nice working for Guy Lombardo. I always said he was best."[49]

During the *Mardi Gras* run, Armstrong found success with two more Broadway show tunes. First up was "Mame," his final recording for Mercury, which aped the "Dolly" formula to a tee. Jerry Herman, who had written "Dolly," had a new musical opening on Broadway in May, *Mame*. Once again, to help publicize it, Armstrong agreed to record the theme song, which would soon appear at number sixty on the *Cash Box* singles chart. Like "Dolly" it's catchy—banjo and all—but Armstrong's trumpet is absent. "Mame" quickly lost steam and progressed no further up the chart, but it was a big enough success to become part of the All Stars' stage repertoire.

A few months later, Armstrong was back in the recording studio of Columbia Records, which had released many an Armstrong classic in the 1950s. It was ironic that Armstrong returned to the label in 1966, because this would have been the tenth and final year of the ten-year contract George Avakian tried to get Armstrong to sign in 1956. Who knows how history would have changed if Armstrong had stayed with one label—a label that took so much care and consideration over his music—for all those years? Even though Avakian was no longer there, Columbia still treated Armstrong with more respect than Mercury, allowing him to record a complete instrumental in King Oliver's "Canal Street Blues." It was an odd choice in the middle of all of Armstrong's attempts to land another pop hit, but it made for one of Armstrong's finest latter-day recordings. With his superhuman chops finally showing a bit of mortality, Armstrong was forced to more or less invoke the ghost of Oliver, his mentor, playing straight lead for five ensemble choruses. Armstrong doesn't play any real high notes, but he obviously had Oliver in mind as he fell back on every lesson the King taught him while he was growing up in New Orleans; a very soulful record. That same day, Armstrong also recorded a terrific Broadway show tune, John Kander and Fred Ebb's "Cabaret," which fit like a glove. Armstrong knew he had a winner, and just two weeks later, he debuted it on *The Ed Sullivan Show,* the same night the Rolling Stones performed their famous version of "Let's Spend the Night Together." Here, Armstrong's trumpet is extremely weak, with such a delayed entrance, one can see him mentally preparing himself before uttering the first, fragile statement. He recovers and again comes up with something pretty, but it's clear that at this point in his career, Armstrong's singing had officially overtaken his powers as a trumpet player. Fortunately, his singing is wonderful as he puts "Cabaret" over like a pro, muttering to Sullivan as he approaches him, "Show business!"

Armstrong offered a lot of "show business" in his television appearances of the period. His popularity was at such a high level that he had begun doing TV commercials for products such as Schaefer beer and Suzy Cute dolls. (On the latter, Armstrong sang and danced with a group of young girls, uttering such lines as "You can bend her legs, bend her arms, and bathe her too!") He appeared with Bing Crosby on a September episode of *The Hollywood Palace* and sang the corny lyrics of "Muskrat Ramble" and "Let's Sing Like a Dixieland Band" with Crosby, as well as performing "Cheesecake," a bizarre novelty number he made for Mercury. Armstrong's personality was just as vivacious as ever, but with his trumpet prowess lessening and his new material being of inferior quality, his television appearances were becoming more and more cartoonish. Thus, if you were a young, impressionable person watching Armstrong sing "Cheesecake" or dance with little girls on a Suzy Cute commercial, it was easy to think of him as being more of a funny old out-of-date entertainer than a jazz pioneer. Nevertheless, if these fans went to see Armstrong perform live, they might have been surprised at how much great music he still created night after night. He now had more hits than ever before, and no show would be complete without "Hello, Dolly!" "Mack the Knife," "Blueberry Hill," "Mame," and "Cabaret." But he also still had that trumpet, and though he couldn't quite execute anything he wanted to as he had just a few years earlier, his sound was still unlike anything else in jazz, and he continued to push himself on numbers like "The Faithful Hussar" and "A Kiss to Build a Dream On." Jazz historian Ed Berger caught Armstrong live around this time and remembered, "I saw him in person for the first and only time in 1966, when he appeared in Lambertville, NJ with the All Stars for a one-nighter. I was 17, and had recently heard Dizzy, Miles, Jonah Jones and the Ellington orchestra in person. Armstrong gave his usual show which included a lot of novelties and features for the sidemen. But when he played, it was a revelation. Even at that stage, it sounded as if he were playing a different instrument, so commanding was his presence and the depth of his sound."[50]

sel, Armstrong mused: "Well—God Bless All of them. We never know when our time will come to go. As for myself—I have had a pretty nice life. So—I am ready to go any time the 'Man up above' (The Lord) will call me. 'Yessir.' "[2]

Four days later, Armstrong was dealt another blow when his clarinetist, Buster Bailey, died of a heart attack. The band had just returned from a stint in Las Vegas and was enjoying a rare two-week vacation when Bailey suddenly died in his New York home at age sixty-four. "Buster Bailey, when he finally got the call, was very happy and he fit beautifully, both personally and musically," Dan Morgenstern recalls. "But he was not up to it anymore. He had not worked at that pace, I think, since he left Fletcher Henderson or John Kirby and even then. So he was a victim of that. I mean, he just couldn't do it."[3]

Five days after Bailey's passing, Red Allen, a New Orleans trumpet master who had performed for years in Armstrong's big band, passed away at age sixty. "The same time we went to Buster's funeral, Red Allen died," Buddy Catlett remembers. "That was like a double mourning. We were going to the church and got the news that Red Allen passed on." Asked if Armstrong took these deaths hard, Catlett says, "I think he was more or less used to death in the musical circle he traveled in. And that's the only way I can look at it because I never heard him talking about it at all."[4]

Armstrong quickly replaced Bailey on clarinet with Johnny Mince—a CBS studio musician and veteran of bands led by, among others, Tommy Dorsey and Bob Crosby—and was soon on the road again. But a few weeks later, Armstrong contracted bronchopneumonia. The iron man of yore might have shrugged it off, but now Armstrong played it safe, cancelling all bookings from late April to mid-June. (Though this didn't stop him from luring Tyree Glenn into an impromptu rehearsal of "That's My Desire" during one of the trombonist's visits!)[5] The respite was salubrious, and Armstrong returned to performing a reenergized man. On June 22, he appeared on *The Tonight Show,* his trumpet playing stronger than it had been in quite some time, surpassing any of his 1966 studio recordings. On "Hello, Dolly!" he soloed well, in complete command, and he even took a spot on "Mame," a song that usually featured no trumpet playing. Clearly, for now at least, Armstrong was ready to blow and eager to show it.

When Armstrong had been recuperating, clarinetist Mince returned to being a studio musician, perhaps daunted by the wearying prospect of the

constant touring that may have contributed to Bailey's and Kyle's premature deaths. While the All Stars clarinet position had been commanded by
many prestigious musicians, Armstrong's new man was relatively unher-
alded: thirty-six-year-old Joe Muranyi. Born of Hungarian descent in
1928, Muranyi studied with pianist Lennie Tristano for three years and
had performed with such great trumpeters as Max Kaminsky, Jimmy
McPartland, and Yank Lawson. A tall, skinny white man with a mustache
and glasses, Muranyi looked more like an accountant than a jazz musician. In fact, he remembered Armstrong once introducing him by saying,
"How about a hand for Joe Muranyi. Come on, Joe. He's going to play
a clarinet solo for you—although he does look like a college professor!"[6]

Muranyi was playing with the Village Stompers, another group booked
by Glaser, when he got the call to join Armstrong. Glaser told him, "You're
on, if Louie approves." "So the first rehearsal, I was more than a little nervous," Muranyi remembers. "I mean, how the fuck can I play with Louis
Armstrong? But then he recognized me, he had heard me play. I don't
know if he knew my name, it was one of those things. But the rehearsal
went well."[7] Muranyi joined the band and quickly got along well with
its other members, especially with Armstrong: "I was the only one in the
band that knew all the records and the history and stuff."

On one of Muranyi's first nights as an All Star, Armstrong asked him,
"How the fuck do you pronounce your name?" Muranyi responded:
" 'Muranyi, like [blues singer] Ma Rainey.' Oh, he loved that! He broke up
laughing, he never forgot it. A lot of cats in the business call me 'Hey, Ma
Rainey!' " Muranyi felt that Armstrong admired his comportment offstage as much as his clarinet playing. "The thing was, I wasn't a fall-down
drunk or anything and I had a couple of young kids and I'm a college
graduate . . . I think it meant something to him that I had the wife and
the two kids and I wasn't coming from the—I don't know what kind of
milieu, a drug-addict milieu or whatever."[8] Armstrong was loath to tolerate offstage carousing if it interfered with music making onstage.

According to Muranyi, Armstrong "did not like cats being drunk or
carrying on in the band. [Others say] 'Oh, he smokes pot.' But [perform-
ing] was very serious to him. Take care of business. And the line I heard
him yelling at (I think) Buddy or somebody that was drunk and he says,
'Don't fuck with my hustle.' Which is great. But in a way, the thing is, he
thought what he did *was* a hustle. It was just an expression, but it was like

street smart. He certainly was street smart." About Armstrong's persona, Muranyi says, "He could be, you know—he had good sides, bad sides, he wasn't always an angel, but . . . He was the greatest star I've encountered because he really was a star but he didn't act like one. He was very real. There wasn't a phony bone in his body. And he liked people. And he liked poor people. And he liked crippled people and fat ladies. He loved the humanity aspect. And he was just wonderful, I can't tell you."[9]

Armstrong was obviously feeling good at the time of Muranyi's arrival, as evidenced by seven songs from a concert at Ravinia Park in Highland Park, Illinois, on June 30, 1967. Armstrong's second wife, Lil Hardin, was in the audience, as might have been a few other associates from his early Chicago days, and the trumpeter responded by blowing with tremendous force, especially on "St. James Infirmary." Soon after, journalist Larry King managed to spend an evening with Armstrong. His account of the night appeared in *Harper's* and is one of the finest portraits of Armstrong to ever appear in a magazine.

King spent one night interviewing Louis, drinking and smoking and singing "That's My Desire" together with the maestro. The most captivating aspect of King's piece concerned race, including a quote from Civil Rights activist Julius Hobson on Armstrong. "He's a good, happy black boy. He hasn't played to a black audience in ten years. I'm glad I saw him though, but I wouldn't come here if I had to pay. He's an interesting example of the black man's psychology but if he had took this band—two whites, three Negroes, a Filipino—down on U Street it would start a riot." King added, "Clearly Armstrong, who remembers that not long ago everyone cheered him for having an integrated band, is genuinely puzzled by such comments."

Armstrong insisted to King that he had been a racial pioneer:

When I was coming along, a black man had hell. On the road he couldn't find no decent place to eat, sleep, or use the toilet—service-station cats see a bus of colored bandsmen drive up and they would sprint to lock their restroom doors. White places wouldn't let you in and the black places all run-down and funky because there wasn't any money behind 'em. We Negro entertainers back then tried to stay in private homes—where at least we wouldn't have to fight bedbugs for sleep and cockroaches for breakfast. Why, do you know I played ninety-nine *million* hotels I couldn't stay at? And if I had friends blowing at some all-white nightclub or hotel I couldn't get in to see 'em—or them to see me. One time in Dallas, Texas, some ofay stops me as I enter this hotel where I'm blowing the show—me in a goddamn *tuxedo,* now!—and tells me I got to come round to the back door. As time went on and I made a reputation I had it put in my contracts that I wouldn't *play* no place I couldn't *stay.* I was the first Negro in the business to crack them big white hotels—Oh, yeah! I pioneered, Pops! Nobody much remembers that these days.[10]

And Armstrong addressed the issue of a black man needing the support of a white man to succeed. "If you didn't have a white captain to back you in the old days—to put his hand on your shoulder—you was just a damn sad nigger . . . If a Negro had the proper white man to reach the law and say, 'What the hell you mean locking MY nigger?' then—quite naturally—the law would walk him free. Get in that jail *without* your white boss, and yonder comes the chain gang! Oh, danger was dancing all around you back then." Naturally, Joe Glaser was brought up, of whom Armstrong said, "Ya know, Pops, my manager, Joe Glaser—Papa Joe, bless his ole heart he's *my* man, we been together since we was pups, why to hear us talk on the phone you'd think we was a couple of fairies: I say, 'I love you, Pops,' and he say, 'I love *you,* Pops.' "[11] But when it came to issues of race, Armstrong added, "Sometimes Joe Glaser says I'm nuts. Says it wasn't as bad as I recall it. But then Papa Joe didn't have to go through it. He was white. Not that I think white people is any naturally meaner than colored. Naw, the white man's just had the upper hand so long—and can't many people handle being top cat."[12]

Armstrong had resumed playing for less than a month when his busy schedule began taking a toll on his chops. He was in erratic form on a broadcast from Atlantic City, and matters didn't improve much when he headed overseas. During a concert in Copenhagen, Armstrong forgot the melody to "Tenderly" and started playing a disturbing passage of wrong notes.

On the next two nights, Armstrong performed at the Festival d'Antibes at Juan-les-Pins, France, where he was filmed by Jean-Christophe Averty.

Armstrong was visibly annoyed onstage because the television crew kept getting between him and the audience, which responded by booing. Shots of him in the wings during features by Tyree Glenn and Jewel Brown show him looking weary and solemn. Though he still played strong solos on "Hello, Dolly!" and "Cabaret," among other tunes, and led the ensembles with his usual charge, he no longer played the more demanding solos on instrumentals like "Indiana" and "Muskrat Ramble."

Muranyi remembered the poignancy of how the band would know that Armstrong wouldn't be soloing on those songs. "What happened was when he physically wasn't up to it, Ira Mangel would come to the band and say, 'The trumpet solo is out. No trumpet solo.' 'Cause Pops would tell him and then he'd tell us. So it was not in." But as Muranyi was quick to point out, Armstrong compensated in other ways. "It varied but he never, it was never a question of he couldn't do the show or anything. He did his things and he just sometimes worked less. But I tell you something, with him, the audience got their money's worth. If he chose not to do it [play trumpet], he would go out of his way for his audience. He loved his audience. And it wasn't ego so much as he took it seriously. I mean, he loved his audience."[13]

According to Tyree Glenn, Joe Glaser didn't want to see his prized client struggling onstage and offered a suggestion. "Mr. Glaser, he says, 'Let Tyree do the playing, you do the singing. You don't have to work that hard.' But man, you know he's going to get out there and play, play his trumpet, you know. He never let up on nothing. When he'd hit that night, he'd be feeling bad, but you'd never know that he was sick. When he hit that stage, that was something else. He never let down one bit, man."[14]

Three weeks after the Juan-les-Pins concert, Armstrong again entered a recording studio. The session was organized for ABC-Paramount by Bob Thiele, who'd been responsible for the studio pairing of Armstrong and Duke Ellington in 1961. "Some years later, in the mid-1960s during the deepening national traumas of the Kennedy assassination, Vietnam, racial strife, and turmoil everywhere, my co-writer George David Weiss and I had an idea to write a 'different' song specifically for Louis Armstrong that would be called 'What a Wonderful World,'" Thiele would later recount. "We wanted this immortal musician and performer to say, as only he could, the world really *is* great: full of the love and sharing people make possible for themselves and each other every day."[15] Aware that Armstrong's recent records had fallen into the rut of trying to mimic "Hello, Dolly!" Thiele, for "What a Wonderful World," decided to surround Armstrong with a full orchestra and choir.

Joe Glaser approved the song, but according to Muranyi, Armstrong's first reaction to it was "What is this shit?" But Muranyi said that Armstrong began to warm to it, perhaps because he related it not so much to the social upheavals of the 1960s as to his own life.[16] "There's so much in 'Wonderful World' that brings me back to my neighborhood where I live in Corona, New York," Armstrong said in 1968.

> Lucille and I, ever since we're married, we've been right there in that block. And everybody keeps their little homes up like we do and it's just like one big family. I saw three generations come up on that block. And they're all with their children, grandchildren, they come back to see Uncle Satchmo and Aunt Lucille. That's why I can say, "I hear babies cry / I watch them grow / they'll learn much more / than I'll never know." And I can look at all them kids's faces. And I got pictures of them when they was five, six and seven years old. So when they hand me this "Wonderful World," I didn't look no further, that was it. And the music with it. So you can see, from the expression, them people dug it. It *is* a wonderful world.[17]

Thiele wrote, "In fact, Louis agreed to record it for minimum union scale (approximately $250 at the time) because he liked both the song and this new concept for him, and was mindful of the expense required for the extra string musicians to achieve the desired effect we envisioned."[18] The first song recorded on that August date was another Thiele composition, "The Sunshine of Love." From the opening notes of the arrangement by Tommy Goodman, it's clear that Thiele succeeded in creating a recorded sound for Armstrong that was different from his other output of the period. This may not have been all to the good. The opening seconds of "The Sunshine of Love" are painfully saccharine: a slurping sax section, weepy strings, a harpsichord, and a stiff two-beat rhythm invite a listener to dismiss the tune. But Armstrong starts singing and all is forgiven. He manages to get the band to swing as he embarks on one of his patented lyric transformations. Goodman smartly keeps the strings playing the melody the entire time, allowing the listener to marvel at the rhythmic liberties Armstrong takes with it. Hopelessly commercial and corny though it might be, "The Sunshine of Love" still ranks as a choice Armstrong vocal.

With one tune in the can, it was now time to record Thiele's new opus, "What a Wonderful World." Goodman's arrangement is ultra-sentimental—more weeping strings, guitar arpeggios, and, later, even an angelic choir. Yet Armstrong managed to infuse the triteness of it all—the melody bears more than a passing resemblance to "Twinkle, Twinkle, Little Star"—with so much emotion as to have created one of his best-known songs. What is singular about his performance is that he stuck to the melody almost entirely throughout, something he rarely did. He occasionally plays with the rhythm, but for the most part he sings it as written—and beautifully, as the song seems to speak to his philosophy of life. Here there is also no trumpet playing and no scatting, though Armstrong's inimitable "Oh yeah" is a definitively fitting conclusion. "What a Wonderful World" hardly changed the musical landscape like "West End Blues," but, even though it's been ubiquitous in recent years, there's no denying that it is a magical recording.

Larry Newton, the president of ABC-Paramount Records, however, demurred. Newton thought Thiele was crazy to record a ballad instead of an uptempo number like "Dolly" and didn't hesitate to tell him so throughout the session. "As the recording progressed, he became increasingly incensed and disruptive as his agitation about this 'radical' concept intensified," Thiele wrote. "Finally, he declared he wanted to cancel the date and fire the musicians and me as well."[19] Thiele told Newton to leave the control room, as he was verging on becoming the first person "who ever threw Louis Armstrong out of a recording studio." Still angry, Newton had to be physically restrained from re-entering the studio. "Miraculously, with all the sinister drama and ominous distractions, the recording of one of the most optimistic songs ever written was completed," Thiele wrote. When Glaser heard of Newton's behavior, he offered to buy "What a Wonderful World" outright. Newton refused. But the drama of "What a Wonderful World" was far from over.[20]

Armstrong's hectic pace in the summer of 1967 caught up with him in September. For the second time in five months, he was stricken with pneumonia. Forced to cancel a string of gigs in Reno, Nevada, Armstrong was hospitalized for a few days, which was reported in many newspapers at the time.[21] Back home, he discussed his recent illness in a letter to clarinetist Slim Evans. "My manager Joe Glaser was so happy that I was OK all he said—take it easy on your two weeks' off. After all . . . we ain't '39' anymore. Speaking of age of course. So I agreed."[22]

On September 28, Armstrong was released from the hospital, spending a short time recovering at his Queens home. A few days later, he was back on the road, appearing on *The Tonight Show,* where he debuted "What a Wonderful World." Armstrong twice returned to the studio in October and November to record seven numbers for an album for Brunswick. Though it included a couple of songs from the Broadway songbook that had provided him with some of his recent hits, most of the album's selections come from films. Instead of backing him again with a Motown-inspired orchestra and letting the All Stars be the All Stars, Brunswick saddled Armstrong with an orchestra conducted by Dick Jacobs.

Joe Muranyi minced no words vis-à-vis Jacobs: "Schmuck. Schmuck . . . Mr. Square . . . I'm not saying he was a bad guy or anything. He was just a commercial arranger."[23] The "orchestra" was composed of the All Stars, an organ, a choir, a banjo, a guitar, the drums of Grady Tate, and the intruding bounce of Everett Barksdale's electric bass. Early in 1968, Armstrong and Jacobs collaborated on three more songs in a similar vein. The resulting album, *I Will Wait for You,* cannot be described as one of Armstrong's finer moments. On the entire ten-song album, he blows a total of forty bars of trumpet; even his singing is upstaged by Jacobs's cloying choir and corny arrangements. "The Happy Time" must vie for the dubious distinction of being the worst recording Armstrong ever made, marred as it is by the egregiously weak material, syrupy chorus, and stiff arrangement. But Armstrong's dramatic vocals on "You'll Never Walk Alone" must be reckoned with. He had been performing the tune as an instrumental for years, but with the Vietnam War raging he began singing the lyrics more and more in live performances and television appearances, always dedicating the song to the soldiers and the mothers of the soldiers fighting in Vietnam.[24] "I Will Wait for You" is also undoubtedly a highlight of Armstrong's twilight years for its stirring opening trumpet cadenza and righteous vocals.

Dick Jacobs may not have been the man for the job, but he and Armstrong weren't through collaborating after the Brunswick album of movie and show songs. Their next project would be more successful, but arguably the most unusual in Armstrong's career thus far: four songs with vocals sung by Armstrong *in Italian*—recorded in New York City for the Discografica Italiana label and slated for release in Italy. An Italian instructor from the Berlitz School was on hand to teach Armstrong to sing the lyrics phonetically. During the recording sessions, the instructor stood next to Armstrong and whispered the correct pronunciation of each phrase seconds before Armstrong had to sing it. The scene cracked Danny Barcelona up almost forty years later. "Yeah, well, he had this guy right next to him showing him," Barcelona said, breaking into laughter, "showing him how to pronounce his words and stuff like that, you know. It was funny—this guy right on Louie's ear, you know. Then you got that Italian words coming out, stuff like that."[25] On the recording itself, the instructor's voice can now and then faintly be heard; he had apparently sometimes been whispering a little too closely to the microphone!

But the Italian coach aside, this was far from an easy session for Armstrong. Muranyi remembered Armstrong's frustration over the arrangements making for a tense situation: "And I start to laughing and—the only time he did anything like this—he turns to me and says, 'You don't like your job?' Isn't that a riot? Oh, man, I fell out laughing—not there, to his face. 'You don't like your job?' He was so pissed, you know, that he had to do all this work and they didn't have it together enough so that the music fit the words."[26]

These recordings are virtually unknown today but are worth tracking down, especially "Dimmi, Dimmi, Dimmi," with its passionate, upper-register trumpet solo, and "Mi Va di Cantare," a song that inspired one of the last great spontaneous trumpet solos of Armstrong's career. There are also live versions of the latter, performed at the San Remo Song Festival in Italy on February 2 and 3, 1968, where Armstrong played with a combo led by clarinetist Henghel Gualdi (pianist Marty Napoleon accompanied Armstrong on the trip). During the February 2 performance, Armstrong's "Mi Va di Cantare" followed the record itself right down to the twelve-bar trumpet solo and "Stormy Weather" quote, though his horn work was a little hesitant. The following night Armstrong began the song the same way, but once he started playing his trumpet, he improvised an entirely different solo, still a bit shaky at first, but after the "Stormy Weather" quote, he improvised new variations on the melody, his blowing becoming stronger and stronger, right into an unplanned second chorus full of fierce runs, leading to a heroic ending: six high A's in succession before a glide up to a high concert C. Here is one of Armstrong's last great hurrahs. His lip was no longer in peak shape, but his pride was altogether another matter. Here is the last great extended solo of his recorded career.

Armstrong continued to prove his mettle throughout 1968. He recorded yet another curious concept album: *Disney Songs the Satchmo Way*. The most important jazz musician of all time found himself singing such ditties as "Bibbidi-Bobbidi-Boo" and "Heigh-Ho" amidst a studio orchestra and mixed choir—not a promising venture, an apparently desperate attempt at commercialism after the fashion of the Brunswick fiascos of the period. The results, however, disabuse all low expectations. *Disney Songs the Satchmo Way* is one of Armstrong's finest albums of the 1960s. The record was produced by Tutti Camarata, who had been responsible for Armstrong's tremendous 1953 Decca date with the Commanders. Camarata, "another wonderful cat" in Joe Muranyi's parlance, intelligently picked ten songs that suited Armstrong perfectly and handed arranging duties to Maxwell Davis, who kept things fun yet interesting, with no trace of the awkwardness of Dick Jacobs. To be sure, there is a little schlock on "Heigh-Ho" and "Whistle While You Work," but Armstrong's infectious enthusiasm is convincingly winning. His trumpet playing, too, is in surprisingly good form for so late a date; his harmonic note choices and dexterity are deft. He's at his most rhythmically free on this album; everything coheres on the nearly seven-minute "Chim Chim Cher-ee," which features two completely different sixteen-bar trumpet solos, each—haunting and even modern—performed over a descending minor vamp.

Yet "Chim Chim Cher-ee" isn't the album's highlight; the towering "When You Wish Upon a Star" is. This beautiful song inspired Armstrong to give one of his most heartfelt performances ever. Davis's arrangement is gorgeous and the choir sounds heavenly, though it's placed far enough in the background so as not to distract from Armstrong's primer in jazz singing. When he sings "Mama, when you wish upon a star," you don't know whether to laugh or cry. Seconds later, when he starts to play the trumpet, the results are profoundly moving—it's time to cry. Armstrong opens with simple quarter-notes as the band slowly begins to swing along with him. His first eight bars are low-key, mellow, before he ascends to a concluding eight. It's an astonishing solo for its sheer passion and emotion, a wise solo, the sound of an old man summing up a lifetime in brief.

Muranyi fondly remembers listening to the playback of "When You Wish Upon a Star" with Armstrong and Camarata. "Here comes Louis with a white handkerchief and he's standing there . . . Camarata's standing there, too. And he said, 'You'll be glad to hear it.' I think I grabbed his hand or grabbed him around and said, 'Pops, I think it's wonderful. That's the one.' I don't know that he said, 'You think so?' but that look he gave me, a very soulful look, 'cause he liked it, too. A wonderful moment. Every time I hear that, I think of that."[27]

Armstrong was clearly affected by his performance. In a letter to Camarata that was reprinted on the back of the original LP's cover, he wrote, "I listened to the record that you gave me of the tune 'When You Wish Upon a Star.' It knocked me out—but way out, Tutti!!! . . . You could still put 'Wish Upon a Star' with the rest of the tunes in the album, which I am very fond of and very happy I did, but this goldarned 'Wish Upon a Star' is so beautiful—and more than that, man—I listen to the tune three or four times at night." It was another magical moment in a lifetime full of them.

When Armstrong resumed touring with the All Stars, prominently featuring "What a Wonderful World," John S. Wilson wrote the song off as "a dreary bit of sentimental claptrap."[28] There was good reason for Armstrong to plug "What a Wonderful World" in May 1968: the previous month, it had become a number one hit in England, selling more than six hundred thousand copies. Strangely, the record had done almost no business in the United States, largely because of the still-simmering animosity between the song's composer-producer, Bob Thiele, and ABC-Paramount president Larry Newton. Newton, still upset with Thiele for recording the number, sabotaged its marketing by not at all promoting the record in the United States. Armstrong did his best on its behalf, singing "What a Wonderful World" in live shows and on television, but according to Thiele, months after its release the record hadn't cracked a thousand copies in America. Newton was blind to the success of the recording not only in England, where it became a smash, remaining number one for thirteen weeks, but also in other European countries as well as in South Africa.

As Newton and Thiele persisted in their tug-of-war, Armstrong headed to England in June for a three-week tour to take advantage of the "What a Wonderful World" mania. British journalists Max Jones and John Chilton, co-authors of the biography *Louis,* spent much time with Armstrong on this trip. As they relate it, the tour began with that rarity of rarities: a two-week stint in one place, the Batley Variety Club in West Yorkshire. Jones and Chilton recalled Armstrong's patience with his fans as he happily signed autographs for, and answered questions from, each and every one of them. They also report that a travel-weary Armstrong grew impatient with "a persistent and somewhat racist-sounding drunk" who asked Armstrong, "Do you know who I am?" Armstrong snapped, "All you white folks look alike to me, Pops."[29]

On July 2, Armstrong and the All Stars filmed two concerts for the BBC. In the footage, it's striking how physically small Armstrong had become; he had slimmed down tremendously since the Juan-les-Pins concerts of July 1967. As to the cause, Joe Muranyi says: "I think he had a lifelong fixation with dieting and stuff. People thought he was ill, said, 'Gee, he's got cancer.' He dieted; no, he wanted to lose the weight."

Swiss Kriss was still central to Armstrong's regimen, so much so that he now started handing out postcards with a picture of himself on a toilet, with the inscription: "Swiss Krissly—Leave It All Behind You!" Muranyi describes one episode on an airplane when Armstrong was proselytizing with his postcards and samples: "Everybody's left the plane and . . . he walks down the aisle and [Bob] Sherman, the valet, had handed out the postcard pictures to the crew and stuff, and he gets [to the cockpit] and they're all laughing and he shakes hands . . . There's a cute little blond hostess, you know, she's got one of them Swiss Kriss packets, a cute little blond thing—she says, 'What is this? What is this?' He said, 'It'll make you shit!' "[30] Addressing the issue of his weight to British writer Steve Voce, Armstrong tried to clarify matters: "Speaking about my weight, there's a lot of people think 'Oh Louis Armstrong, my God, he must have some kind of disease, or something,' but they ain't thinking that if a person eats sensible and eats on time and the right food . . . I lost a hundred pounds with a diet sheet that I saw in *Harper's Bazaar*—I didn't pay but 25 cents for it."[31]

In the BBC performances Armstrong is seen making a strong go of it. He still didn't play his old, fiery solos on "Indiana" and "Ole Miss," but both tunes featured strong lead playing and humorous new quotes: "Sidewalks of New York" on the former, "Bye and Bye" on the latter. On

"A Kiss to Build a Dream On," he pushed himself to play higher than usual on what was by now a set solo. On "You'll Never Walk Alone" and "What a Wonderful World," his vocals are singularly passionate, even melancholy. As was his wont, he dedicated "Alone" to the mothers of Vietnam soldiers, managing to look at once somber and warm and inviting. A review of a Canadian gig in May 1968 accurately captures this quality of Armstrong's: "If he doesn't happen to be playing the sort of impeccable, trailblazing trumpet he was 40 years ago (and who does these days?) he offers something in its place—a warmth and humanness that is all too sadly lacking in many younger musicians today," Peter Harris wrote.[32]

Back home, the contretemps between Bob Thiele and Larry Newton took an unexpected turn. The European market was demanding an album assembled around "What a Wonderful World." Newton relented, but only if Armstrong would record the rest of the album for $500. Joe Glaser wanted a $25,000 advance. Thiele became their go-between and recalled their spirited exchanges. Glaser: "I heard what went on. You tell that fat bastard to go fuck himself and give us twenty-five thousand dollars for eight more sides." Newton: "Tell him to go fuck himself and why do we give a shit about those European companies? Screw 'em all." Back and forth it went until pressure from abroad finally persuaded Newton to green-light the rest of the album and agree to Glaser's demand. Seven additional songs would be recorded once Armstrong returned to the United States.

As always, Armstrong never had the luxury of complete availability during a recording session; Thiele had to squeeze the date in while the All Stars were playing in Las Vegas. The producer booked two sessions, one featuring just Armstrong's group and another featuring the All Stars and a small string section. Armstrong played trumpet on a few numbers, sounding tired for the most part, but he still conveyed wisdom on such tunes as "Dream a Little Dream of Me" and "There Must Be a Way." But his singing rarely sounded better than on the session with strings. He performed another song written by Thiele and Weiss, "Hello Brother," which assuredly would have sounded laughably corny and dated if sung by any other vocalist of the period. Yet Armstrong is quite moving in this ode to the working man.

Ironically, Armstrong also sang a tune called "The Home Fire" at that final session. He sounds wistful, as if brooding on his home in Corona, Queens, and all the people, young and old, in the neighborhood whose lives he had touched since moving there with Lucille in 1943. Armstrong was about to spend more than a year at home, away from the stage. The indestructible Satchmo had finally broken down.

CHAPTER EIGHTEEN

Winter of His Discontent, 1968–1970

IN SEPTEMBER 1968, Armstrong's regular doctor, Alexander Schiff, thought it might be time for Armstrong to see a specialist, so he sent him to see Gary Zucker of Beth Israel Hospital in New York. Armstrong's legs were swollen and he had great difficulty breathing when he arrived at Zucker's office. When told that it looked like heart failure, Armstrong "practically ran out of my office," according to Zucker. For two weeks, Armstrong disappeared with the rumor circulating that he was living it up in Harlem, partying with fans from the old days, and refusing to believe anything was wrong. "It was a kind of last exfoliation and it nearly killed him," James Lincoln Collier wrote. "By the end of perhaps two weeks his whole body was swollen with fluid, to the point that he had trouble walking and could not get his shoes on his swollen feet."[1] Armstrong, finally realizing he was no longer made of iron, returned to Zucker, who deduced that Armstrong's weakened heart had put too much strain on his kidneys, allowing fluid to build up in his body, causing the swelling. A heavy dose of diuretics reduced the swelling, but Armstrong would be forced to stop performing until he fully recovered.

When the news reached *DownBeat* magazine in October, it put the blame on Armstrong's weight loss. "Louis Armstrong was hospitalized in

New York City Sept. 17 for what was initially described by a spokesman as 'an examination and tests,'" the article read. "Subsequently, *Down-Beat* learned that the 68-year-old trumpeter was apparently suffering from exhaustion due to excessive loss of weight. After a week in an intensive care unit at Beth Israel Hospital, Armstrong was reportedly making an excellent recovery . . . It was expected that the trumpeter would rest at least until early November. A number of scheduled appearances, including a major one in Vienna, Austria, have been cancelled at presstime."[2] For the time, the rest seemed to do Armstrong some good, as he related in a letter to some friends in December: "I'll soon be back on the mound wailing away again, as usual. I really enjoyed the rest at home for a change. Been so busy through the years—I did not realize how nice it is to sorta lay around home and cool it awhile. I didn't realize how tired I was."[3]

But Armstrong wasn't out of the woods, yet. As 1969 began, Armstrong's health continued to deteriorate. In February, he went back to Beth Israel with more heart problems. Zucker didn't want to take any chances and kept Armstrong at Beth Israel until April. Zucker began talking to Armstrong about retirement, a subject Armstrong wouldn't even begin to think about. "He made it abundantly clear that the only thing that was important to him was to continue to make music," Zucker said. "If he couldn't make music then he was through, and life wasn't worth anything."[4] Though Louis had occasionally seemed weary and beaten in interviews in the late 1960s, he knew that this was the only life for him, once telling an interviewer, "If I ever quit—or even think about it—I'm dead. That's the way to start to die, by stopping. I just keep on going. For me, it's the only way."[5]

As much as it probably hurt to see his prize client in such bad shape, Joe Glaser knew the end was near. He told his friend Cork O'Keefe that he planned on visiting Armstrong in the hospital to tell him it was time to finally slow down a bit or even retire. But before he could do so, Glaser suffered a debilitating stroke in the spring and also wound up in Beth Israel, where he immediately fell into a coma. Lucille Armstrong thought it would be best to keep this information from Louis, as she knew it would upset him and possibly harm his recovery; but the plan failed when Dizzy Gillespie and Tyree Glenn came to the hospital to visit both men. Upon visiting Louis, they said, "We came by to give blood for Joe Glaser." A surprised Armstrong asked, "Blood for Joe Glaser for what?" "Why man," they said, "Joe Glaser's sick as a dog right around the corner in the hospital here."[6]

"Well, the worst thing they could have told Louie was that," Lucille Armstrong remembered. "And when the doctor came Louie chewed the doctor out. By the time I got to the hospital he had enough left in him to chew me out." Armstrong, too weak to walk, demanded to be taken to Glaser's intensive care unit in a wheelchair. "I went down to see him and he didn't know me," a shaken Louis told Lucille. Glaser passed away on June 4, never having emerged from his coma. A month later, Armstrong wrote to blues pianist Little Brother Montgomery, "Man, I was a sick ass. Yes, my manager + my God Joe Glaser was sick at the same time. And it was a toss up between us—who would cut out first. Man it broke my heart that it was him. I love that man which the world already knows. I prayed, as sick as I was that he would make it. God Bless his Soul. He was the greatest for me + all the spades that he handled."[7]

Naturally, Glaser's will became the object of much scrutiny. For thirty-four years, his partnership with Armstrong existed on the sole basis of a handshake. There were no documents to officially show every dollar Glaser made off Armstrong. Armstrong was always happy as long as he had enough money to do whatever he needed, and Glaser saw to that. But critics of Glaser couldn't help feeling that he spent the better part of those decades ripping off his star client. "But, in some mysterious way, Joe's will made Louis a rich man," according to Ernie Anderson. "This seemed to be the work of Oscar Cohen, who was now President of Associated Booking Corp. and twenty per cent owner of the agency, operating under pressure from Lucille."[8] Armstrong received all of Glaser's shares in his music publishing firm, International Music. According to Collier, "Glaser had also set aside money in savings accounts and trust funds, all of which was turned over to the Armstrongs after his death."[9] Of course, being a booking agency to the end, ABC split Armstrong's total sum in two—"That was fair enough," according to Lucille, since Armstrong and Glaser were "essentially partners"—and took an extra 15 percent commission. But even with this, Armstrong did well: he "told Bobby Hackett, who was very close to him, that it amounted to 'a bit more than two million dollars,'" Anderson related. "It was not all in cash, one item was a piece of prime real estate on Rodeo Drive in Beverly Hills."[10]

It's impossible to know exactly how much Glaser made off of Armstrong and how much of that Armstrong received. But it's certain that for all of its faults—and there were many—the relationship worked, and from the time their partnership started until the end of Glaser's life, Armstrong had everything he wanted. Louis himself summed it up on a later appearance on *The Dick Cavett Show,* saying, "Everybody loved Joe Glaser. Everybody . . . And to me, he was Jesus."[11] When Joe Glaser died in 1969, part of Louis Armstrong died with him.

The combination of Glaser's death and the inability to perform sent Armstrong into a tailspin. While recuperating in the hospital before Glaser passed, Armstrong fought off depression by telling his doctors and nurses stories about the old days, especially about growing up in New Orleans. On March 31, Armstrong decided to write some of these memories down in a document titled "Louis Armstrong + the Jewish Family in New Orleans, La., the Year of 1907." Under the title, Armstrong wrote, "Written by Louis Armstrong—Ill in his bed at the Beth Israel Hospital." When Glaser passed away two months later, Armstrong picked up the manuscript and added a dedication to his deceased manager:

I dedicate this book
to my manager and pal
Mr. Joe Glaser
The best Friend
That I've ever had
May the Lord Bless Him
Watch over him always

His boy+disciple who *loved* him *dearly.*

Louis
    Satchmo
        Armstrong[12]

The memoir was apparently inspired by Dr. Zucker's humming of "Russian Lullaby," a song Armstrong was taught to sing by the Karnofsky family while a boy in New Orleans. The Karnofskys had taken Armstrong in, given him a job delivering coal, taught him to sing "from the heart," and even helped him buy his first cornet. Armstrong went on to write about how he would always love Jewish people because of how people like the Karnofskys and even Joe Glaser treated him throughout his life.

Fueled by depression, Armstrong used this document, which he referred to as a "book," to air out some grievances, especially when it came to issues of race. After he had been such a popular attraction to black audiences for years and years, by 1968 Armstrong's audience had become almost entirely white. Writing twenty years later, Gerald Early explained why the black audience abandoned Louis in his later years:

> It was because of his adamant refusal to change, his strenuous insistence that he should continue to perform as if social and cultural history in America had stopped in 1930 that he went from being praised as a black cultural hero to being denounced as an Uncle Tom. He had not changed, but the world and especially black America clearly had . . . In a way, his black audience was right for throwing him over because he was an Uncle Tom. He did say, after all, that he needed to be "some white man's nigger," that is, taken under the protective, paternalistic wing of a white man who would "look out for him."

Early did end his essay by acceding, "Yet if Armstrong ever felt outrage or despair over this abandonment because he thought that black folk had misunderstood him and judged him unfairly, he would have been right, too."[13]

Armstrong was outraged and in despair and let all of his hurt out with the mighty power of his pen. While discussing his admiration for the Jewish people, Armstrong wrote that he believed blacks had it better than Jews, "But we didn't do anything about it. We were lazy and *still* are. We never did try to get together, and to show the younger Negroes such as myself to try and even to show that he has ambitions, and with just a little encouragement—I could have really done something worthwhile. But Instead, we did nothing but let the young *up* starts know that they were young and simple, and *that* was *that*. *Never* a warm word of doing anything important came to their minds."[14] Armstrong's words only grew more cutting as he continued. "Negroes *never* did stick together and they *never* will. They hold too much *malice—Jealousy* deep down in their heart for the *few* Negroes who *tries*. But the odds were (are) *against* them."

Armstrong was justifiably proud of where he came from and what he made of himself, all because of hard work and common sense. Yet the knocks from the black community had obviously hurt him no end. "*Those* days were like some of these *Modern* days—*one* Negro who has *no* ambitions, or any intention of doing the *right* things, will bring sufferings to a *whole* Flock of *Negroes* that is at least trying to live like *Human* Beings," he continued.

> Because they know within themselves that they're doing the wrong things, but expects *everybody* just because he is a *Negro* to give up everything he has *struggled* for in life such as a *decent* family—a *living,* a *plain* life—the *respect.* This Trifling *Negro* expects him to *give* up everything just because of his *Ignorant, Lazy Moves. Personally* I think that it is *not fair.* And the *Negro* who *can't see* these *foolish* moves from some *over Educated fools' moves*—then *right* away he is called a *White* Folks *Nigger.* Believe it—the White Folks did *everything that's decent* for *me.* I wish that I can *boast* these *same* words for *Niggers.* I think that I have always done *great* things about *uplifting* my *race* (the Negroes, *of course*) but *wasn't appreciated.*[15]

Armstrong's document wasn't made public for another thirty years, at a time when he was still unappreciated by many for his role as a racial pioneer. Though undoubtedly motivated by depression and ill health, Armstrong's unflinchingly raw 1969 document features a hurt and betrayal that are very real. And as Early concluded, he was right, after all, to feel that way.

Even though he was back home and feeling a little better (his weight was up to 155 pounds, having hit a low of 124 pounds the previous November[16]), Armstrong's depression occasionally made its way into published interviews. "I never did want to be no big star," he told a *New York Times* reporter. "It's been hard goddam work, man. Feel like I spent 20,000 years on the planes and railroads, like I blowed my chops off. Sure, Pops, I like the ovation, but when I'm low, beat down, wonder if maybe I hadn't of been better off staying home in New Orleans."[17]

Around this time, Louis and Lucille received visitors from France, Louis Panassié, the son of Hugues, and his wife. The Panassiés visited the Armstrongs for a casual dinner and, naturally, Armstrong let his tape recorder roll. The results more than sufficiently conveyed the state of Armstrong's being. He's unusually low-key throughout the visit, often letting Lucille take charge in discussing Armstrong's various ailments. Armstrong did talk about seeing a proctologist and was pleased with the results. "See, it was in my favor, taking that laxative every night to keep my system cleaned out, because I went to that examination, you know, where they turn you upside down and they put that long iron pipe in your booty, your behind, you know, and you could hear me hollering for five hundred kilometers," he told the Panassiés. "When [the doctor] finished, he said, 'Thank God, you have no disease and no cancer or anything.' So don't let nobody tell you I had disease, because between that and Swiss Kriss and that piece of iron down there, that told everything, kept all the disease. So this kidney trouble and heart problems come from other things, like over-work, no rest, probably had one nip too much." Looking back at his life, he solemnly intoned these unthinkable words: "Now all I got to do is scan my life back and see what I was doing wrong. Like I didn't get enough rest. I was always afraid I was going to miss something."[18] After dinner, Armstrong put on some music. He didn't reach back to the Hot Fives and Sevens. Instead, he played a recording he had made during a BBC television show with the All Stars the previous summer before he grew ill. For the rest of the tape, Armstrong barely spoke, obviously depressed and sorely missing the world of show business.

Armstrong spent the rest of 1969 recovering at home in Corona. Friends frequently came by to visit and he delighted in entertaining the local children. Reporters caught up with him in July for his sixty-ninth birthday celebration. He used to celebrate his birthdays with big public performances at places such as the Newport Jazz Festival or Lewisohn Stadium, but now he spent it with Lucille, some friends, and some of the neighborhood children. "The kids and some of the cats (Satch's jazz colleagues) are always poppin' by, but mostly I'm taking it nice and easy 'till September," Armstrong said, adding, "I've never had a rest like this in my life."[19] By October, Armstrong still wasn't ready to perform again, but he was spotted on national television during game five of the World Series, cheering on the New York Mets with Lucille. Twelve days after watching the Miracle Mets clinch the World Series in Queens, Armstrong made his first small steps back to performing. John Barry, the composer behind the music of all the James Bond films, personally visited Armstrong in New York to present him with an opportunity to sing a brand-new song to be featured in the next Bond film, *On Her Majesty's Secret Service*. Armstrong was honored that Barry had selected him to perform the song, "We Have All the Time in the World." However, the younger fans of the film might have been puzzled by the choice, as Barry admitted. " 'All the Time in the World' is my own personal favorite," he said. "I think that might have had a lot to do with the experience we had in New York with Louie Armstrong and that afternoon we recorded it. It wasn't the popular choice at the time, because we always used, you know, the Tom Joneses, the Nancy Sinatras. And I said, 'Look, it's about a man singing about the September of his years.' And I thought Louie Armstrong singing 'We Have All the Time in the World,' it just rung true and [producer Albert "Cubby" Broccoli] loved the idea, there were no arguments. But to work with this guy in the studio, he was the sweetest, humblest guy."[20]

Armstrong had not set foot in a recording studio for over a year. The song's lyricist, Hal David, could sense that Armstrong was still recovering, but he remained impressed by his innate professionalism. "He was a sick man at the time," David said. "After he did his first take, he came over to me and, you know, 'Did I do it good? Don't be afraid to tell me, I want to do it good.' " In the end, Armstrong was more than just good. Always known for his gravelly singing, the year off seemed to wear down his voice more than ever, as it now sounded, in the words of Gary Giddins, "burned to a husk." But if anything, the extra rawness and fragility of his health made him connect even deeper with the song's emotions. Armstrong was truly in his September years, just thankful to be alive, and the joy and love in his voice is contagious throughout the performance. Armstrong loved the song and was happy to have had the opportunity to record it. "He came across and he thanked me for asking him to sing the song in the movie, which—I mean, I was in such awe of the gentleman that the fact that he took it upon himself to sing the song for us, we were so honored that he should come across and very gently say, 'Thank you,' " Barry remembered. "It was a testament to the gentleman, the kind of gracious gentleman that he was."[21]

The song had little impact upon the film's release, probably because the audience expected and wanted to hear a younger star performer. How-

ever, almost twenty-five years later, it was used on a Guinness beer commercial in the United Kingdom and soon vaulted to the top of London's
music charts. Since then, it's become one of Armstrong's best-known
later recordings, and, along with "What a Wonderful World," a favorite
at weddings. Yet nobody ever mentions that another song was recorded
at the same session: an updated version of Armstrong and Billy Kyle's
old 1955 composition "Pretty Little Missy." Torrie Zito wrote a beautiful
string-laden arrangement of the tune and cut its regular tempo in half,
adding an effective organ and underpinning it all with a gentle, loping
shuffle. Armstrong responded with one of the happiest vocals of his entire
career. But more unexpected are the sixteen bars of trumpet he plays.
Armstrong hadn't performed live in a year, but that trumpet was his life,
and he still managed to practice a little every night. On "Pretty Little
Missy," he sounds slightly rusty on a couple of high notes, but otherwise
he sounds stronger than he did on some of the records he made in 1966
and 1967. He even concludes with the patented sign-off phrase he used to
end so many of his records, both vocally and on the trumpet. He didn't
know it at the time, but it was the final trumpet solo he would ever take
inside of a recording studio.

Armstrong must have felt revitalized by the return to recording. In
December, he told *Esquire* magazine, "There's no such thing as on the
way out. As long as you are still doing something interesting and good.
You are in business as long as you are breathing."[22] A short time later,
Armstrong was back on the big screen once again. His short cameo scene
in the movie *Hello, Dolly!*, which was filmed in 1968, was finally released
on December 16, 1969. Audiences would cheer when Armstrong's beaming face appeared to sing a chorus of the title tune with Barbra Streisand.
As the lyrics of Armstrong's biggest hit said, it was so nice to have him
back where he belonged. Just two days later, *On Her Majesty's Secret Service* was released, featuring Armstrong's voice singing "We Have All the
Time in the World." Just like that, after sixteen months of recovery, Louis
Armstrong was in the public's mind again. He knew he was too weak to
go back to performing with the All Stars, but he still had a need to entertain, to be in front of the public. Louis Armstrong was about to make his
comeback.

.   .   .

On January 13, 1970, Armstrong began the New Year by appearing on Dick Cavett's late night talk show. Armstrong, probably eager to show the world that he hadn't slowed down, actually brought along his trumpet, performing two original compositions, "Someday You'll Be Sorry" and "Pretty Little Missy." Unfortunately, his chops weren't ready for the comeback, especially on the former, which featured a new arrangement that had him taking two full choruses up front, a shorter solo in the middle, and even a closing coda. In 1960, it would have been a piece of cake, but it was entirely too much for the Armstrong of 1970, who sounded almost like a beginner in his reading of the melody, his tone thinner and his pitch sounding a little sour and nowhere near as golden as it once did. As he soldiered on, his playing began boasting equal amounts of good ideas and faltering execution. And in his final coda, apparently out of gas, he had to pull the trumpet off his lips and instead sang the final note. It was a painful struggle for the man who was once the greatest trumpet player in the jazz world. Armstrong's doctors soon told him that he would have to cut out the trumpet playing entirely, and after his shaky performance on national television he probably agreed that that would be the best idea. For the time being, he would go back to practicing after dinner.

But he could still sing and he could still talk, which made him a worthwhile guest on many television talk shows. He spent the first part of the year cracking up audiences and singing songs on *The David Frost Show, The Tonight Show,* and *The Mike Douglas Show.* He usually told stories about growing up in New Orleans or about Swiss Kriss. He was especially lively on the Frost show in February, discussing his upbringing in New Orleans with tales of prostitutes and the frequent gunfights he witnessed. Frost asked him, "Is that a good atmosphere for a musician?" Armstrong, without missing a beat, answered, "Well, I thought it was lovely," breaking up the audience. Before he was done, Armstrong talked about stealing as a child, getting into trouble with the police, and eventually getting thrown into the Colored Waif's Homes. He ended the show lit only by a spotlight and, backed only by Billy Taylor's piano, sang a stunningly poignant version of "What a Wonderful World"; he had come a long way from that rough beginning in New Orleans. Before singing it, Armstrong said about the lyrics, "They mean so much." Few people could really know the meaning of the phrase "wonderful world" as much as Louis Armstrong.

Though many black listeners and hardcore jazz fans had abandoned him, Armstrong's overall popularity had never diminished. But the serious illnesses of 1968 and 1969 made him appear more mortal than ever. Also, everyone knew that in July, Armstrong would be celebrating his seventieth birthday (though truthfully, he'd be turning sixty-nine in August). Because of these circumstances, he began getting more respect than ever before. Armstrong co-hosted Douglas's show for an entire week while every other guest, including young artists such as Tom Paxton and the Four Tops, talked about what an honor it was to be on the same program as such a legend. Douglas talked about going to a Tom Jones tribute at the Friars Club in April when Armstrong received a tremendous standing ovation. Fellow guest Sammy Davis Jr., who once criticized Armstrong over his Little Rock comments in 1957, now took great pains to convey to the audience just how important Armstrong was to the world.

But Armstrong didn't show up just to receive love. He sang during every show, material ranging from "Zip-A-Dee-Doo-Dah" from his recent Disney album all the way back to "I Surrender Dear," which he first recorded in 1931. He put so much into his vocals that the trumpet wasn't even really missed, even on songs he used to love blowing on, such as "St. Louis Blues," proof that he could continue to have a thriving career without his horn. Armstrong even got to interact with all the other guests, swapping show-business stories with Cesar Romero, singing "The Whiffenpoof Song" with Shari Lewis and Lamb Chop, and talking about the music business with Artie Shaw, who delighted in telling a story about Armstrong: "Erroll Garner—and I found out it was true—Erroll Garner was listening to Louie when Louie played at Basin Street East, a club in New York at that time," Shaw related. "And Erroll was going out past the dressing rooms, he saw Louie in the dressing room with the door open. He stuck his head in, he said, 'Hey, Pops, how's everything?' And Louie said, 'White folks still in the lead.' " Armstrong literally doubled over with laughter remembering his line. Armstrong's wit showed no signs of slowing down throughout the week. When Shari Lewis remarked that she didn't know how Armstrong came up with his scat-singing improvisations, he replied, "You get hungry, you'll do it!" Later in the week, Pearl Bailey called the show for an on-air phone conversation with Armstrong. When she asked if President Lyndon Johnson was the one who named Armstrong a goodwill ambassador, Armstrong replied, "Eisenhower, Johnson—one of them boys there," sending the audience into hysterics.

On the final day of the week, Douglas asked Armstrong to name the five most admired people in his life. In addition to the expected choices of Lucille, King Oliver, Joe Glaser, and his mother, Armstrong now added Dr. Gary Zucker to the list. "And there's my doctor, Dr. Gary Zucker, that's the man that really brought me back to breathe again, because I was in bad shape when he took hold of me and brought me down to intensive care," Armstrong said. "Very serious, you know. When you go down there, you're getting ready to say bye-bye to the world, you know that. And this man brought me on in there and after he finished, he took me out of intensive care and put me on the floor where all the VIPs was. My room was among them. And when I was so sick, they'd come to see me, and when I got a little better, he had me to go around and visit them and we had a nice time. Then finally, he called Lucille, my wife, who took me home, and for the two years I stayed out, she's the one that nursed me very beautifully, you know, took good care of me. I still visit Dr. Zucker once a week." Armstrong was now singing on television again, but his horn was still on his mind. "I asked Dr. Zucker, I says, 'What about the horn?' So he reminded me of the Lord when Gabriel was getting ready to make some riffs on that horn—the Lord said, 'No, Gabe, not yet, hold it! I'll tell you when!'"

In May 1970, Armstrong began working on a new project, his first studio album in over two years. The album became known as *Louis Armstrong and His Friends* and was produced by Bob Thiele. Though Joe Glaser had died, his successor, Oscar Cohen, had very much the same mentality as his former boss: get Louis Armstrong a hit record. Thus, when planning Satchmo's seventieth-birthday album, Cohen turned to Thiele, who was now running the Flying Dutchman label, which featured records from an eclectic mix of musicians ranging from Johnny Hodges and Oliver Nelson to Gato Barbieri and Gil Scott-Heron. Thiele enlisted Nelson to arrange and conduct the Armstrong sessions. Nelson was originally a modern-jazz saxophonist, but he soon became better known as a composer and arranger. By the late sixties, he was doing a lot of film and television work, and that "commercial" sound began to creep into his jazz writing, something that can be heard especially on the dated arrangements he turned in for Thelonious Monk's *Monk's Blues* album (1968) on Columbia. Still, he loved Armstrong and was quoted in the July 1970 issue of *DownBeat* as saying, "We couldn't have had what we now know as American music without him. He created a style and he opened up this whole thing."

Nelson definitely had that commercial sound down and the combination of his orchestrations and Thiele's talents as a producer looked as if they could give Armstrong one last hit. Unfortunately, that's where *Louis Armstrong and His Friends* failed. Of the album's ten performances, only five are home runs: two beautiful standards, "Mood Indigo" and "My One and Only Love,"; an autobiographical take on "When the Saints Go Marchin' In" titled "Boy from New Orleans"; a soulful remake of "What a Wonderful World"; and a moving version of the civil-rights anthem "We Shall Overcome." But Armstrong could only do so much with the rest of the material, which included inferior songs such as "His Father Wore Long Hair" and "This Black Cat Has Nine Lives," the latter ending with the rumbling Armstrong voice letting out a gravelly "Meow!": not one of his finest moments.

The sessions were, by all accounts, a joyous celebration. A birthday cake was served before the recording went down in the studio, and over 250 guests came in to pay their respects to Pops. Rock journalist Al Aronowitz was in attendance and painted a good picture of the atmosphere of that first day of recording. "As the party dwindled, many remained as an audience for the session, and there were rows of folding chairs," he wrote. "Tony Bennett was sitting in one. Leon Thomas and Bobby Hackett and Eddie Condon also stayed. Ornette Coleman sat dangling his feet over the edge of the stage, sucking up a whistle every time he thought sick, old Pops hit a home run or made a shoestring catch. Miles [Davis] told me that it was as if the songs, the arrangements and the register of the orchestra had been designed to make it easy for Satchmo . . . But Satchmo fooled everybody by doing some unexpected fancy footwork."[23] Aronowitz also remembered Miles Davis remarking, "He don' sound like a dyin' man," after hearing Armstrong sing. True, his voice is raspier than ever before on this recording, but his heart shines through, though apparently Miles was so concerned, he went up to Armstrong between takes and whispered, "Isn't the orchestra too low for you?" Armstrong responded that he didn't care about that and, after conversing for a while, shouted, "Always glad to see you, Miles!" as Davis walked back. When Davis was ready to leave, he told Aronowitz, "They take advantage of his age. When you're that old, they really drain you to make you sound as if you're in heaven. It don't matter. He's got so much soul, he makes it sound good anyway."

Armstrong's soul really shines through on "We Shall Overcome," which remains one of his most heartfelt recordings, benefited by a choir made up of many of the guests who dropped in to pay tribute to the aging performer. The idea to record the civil-rights anthem was Thiele's, though he admitted he was skeptical about whether Louis would want to do it. "But when I mentioned it," Thiele said, "Louis' eyes lit up. He reached up and pulled down a tape of the Martin Luther King funeral that he'd made. We played it and he said he loved the way the choir sang the piece during the service. We talked a lot about King and religion. Louis said that when he was sick in the hospital, he knew he was near death and he talked to God. Louis is very sincere about this. He sincerely believes a lot of trouble in the world today is because people don't take the trouble to talk to God. I think Louis is quietly religious. He told me he hopes the Lord does help the poor black man. Then he added—'Not the poor lazy black man though.' " [24]

Armstrong was all business when it came time to actually record the tune with his star-studded choir. "Pops quieted everybody down and said, 'Now I want all you people out there to sing like you never sang before. This is a beautiful song and it's our song,' " wrote Ralph J. Gleason. "And they sang it with him. A guest at the party told me it was the most moving experience of his life. 'Louis gave that song, which even if it is the hymn of the Sixties' integration movement, is still a tattered and threadbare song, almost a cliche, the kind of vocal sound you would expect from the celestial chorus.' " [25] Eyewitnesses claimed he had tears in his eyes by the end of the performance. To think about Armstrong singing those lyrics and all the obstacles he overcame to achieve what he did—poor childhood, racism, becoming the scorn of younger black musicians and writers—he overcame it all to become the greatest, most important jazz musician of them all.

By July 1, Armstrong was just days away from celebrating his seventieth birthday and he became a constant presence in the press. All the depression surrounding his illness was gone, as were any regrets he had about his hard life as an entertainer. "I think I had a beautiful life," he said, before imparting his philosophy. "I didn't wish for anything I couldn't get, and I got pretty near everything I wanted because I worked for it. I don't keep nothing that I can't use right now, so everything I have I'm still enjoying it." While he remained upbeat and cheerful, he also knew he wasn't going to last forever. Cryptically, he began discussing his funeral, still dreaming of a New Orleans send-off. "They going to enjoy blowing over me, ain't they? Cats will be coming from California and everywhere else just to play . . . If anybody plays a bad note, Lucille'll slap 'em right in the face. She'll take care of that for me. I don't want no part of it. Once I cut out forget it." Armstrong even discussed the afterlife, saying, "When I go to the Gate, I'll play a duet with Gabriel. Yeah, we'll play 'Sleepy Time Down South' and 'Hello, Dolly!' Then he can blow a couple that he's been playing up there all the time. He wants to be remembered for his music, just like I do."[26]

But before Armstrong could get that far, he had some celebrating to do. On July 3, he flew out to Los Angeles for a tribute concert arranged by promoter Floyd Levin at the Shrine Auditorium. Hoagy Carmichael was the emcee and Armstrong got to enjoy the entire show from a rocking chair onstage—an appropriate choice, as Carmichael wrote and sang on Armstrong's original 1929 recording of "Rockin' Chair." The two reprised it as a duet and Armstrong even got to close the show by singing three numbers.[27] As he later wrote Levin, "That was my happiest birthday!"

One week later, George Wein devoted an entire evening of the Newport Jazz Festival to Armstrong's honor. Wein brought the Preservation Hall Jazz Band, the Eureka Brass Band, and the New Orleans Classic Rag-time Band to the festival from New Orleans, hired gospel legend Mahalia Jackson, and even scored five famed jazz trumpeters to pay tribute to Armstrong, including Dizzy Gillespie. Proving that any hard feelings were officially in the past, Gillespie opened his tribute by saying, "Louis Armstrong's station in the history of jazz, all I have to say, is unimpeachable. If it weren't for him, there wouldn't be any of us. So I want to take this moment to thank Louis Armstrong for my livelihood." Jackson summed up the feelings of everyone present when she said, "If you don't love him, then I don't think you know how to love." Wein filmed the entire day's events, including the rehearsal, which captured an incredibly shrunken Armstrong greeting his fellow musicians. The only snag in the rehearsal came when Wein told Armstrong he wanted him to appear on stage unannounced in the middle of "Pennies from Heaven." Armstrong wouldn't hear of it. "No, 'Sleepy Time' should be first," he told Wein. "That's my theme song!" After some more discussion, Armstrong emphatically said, "They expect 'Sleepy Time,'" meaning his audience. Bobby Hackett agreed and told Wein, "Yeah, if that's the way he feels." Tyree Glenn was also on hand to stand up for his old boss, and finally Wein relented. The lyrics and theme of the song had made some younger audience members, black and white, uncomfortable for decades, especially after the uproar that surrounded his 1951 Decca recording. But it was his theme song, and no other song meant more to him, and that evening at Newport, Armstrong opened with "Sleepy Time." "When he dressed up for that evening—he had on a nice brown suit, as I remember—and there was a glow in his face, a glow in his eyes, there was a glow in his skin," Wein recalled. "And he just sang so beautifully and he projected, it was like, 'Hey, I'm here again. I'm still here, I'm still Louie Armstrong and I'm still going to give you a great evening of music and entertainment.'"[28]

Armstrong continued making the rounds on television throughout the summer of 1970 and even found time to record another album in August, *Louis "Country and Western" Armstrong,* for the Avco Embassy label. Armstrong had backed legendary country music pioneer Jimmie Rodgers on a 1930 record and he had recorded covers of "Your Cheatin' Heart" and "Cold, Cold Heart" for Decca in the 1950s, so it wasn't exactly unfamiliar territory. Armstrong seemed to enjoy himself, imparting tunes like "Miller's Cave" and "Almost Persuaded" with great amounts of humor. Some songs, such as the Youngbloods' "Get Together," aren't exactly a natural fit, but overall the album has some very nice moments, though it is almost forgotten today, having never been issued in the CD or MP3 eras. It would turn out to be Armstrong's final album.

Armstrong still occupied most of his time in his Corona den, transferring music to his reel-to-reel player, listening to and annotating the tapes, and even decorating the tape boxes with artistic collages. "Been off two years and haven't been bored yet," he wrote to Max Jones in 1970. "When I get through sending out photographs, [illegible] tapes that I receive from fans. And I got reels up there that I am trying to listen to because there was tape of me forty years ago." But Armstrong's retirement was about to come to an end, and he couldn't be more excited. "I am rehearsing, blowing the trumpet and getting ready to open at the International Hotel [in

CHAPTER NINETEEN

Good Evening, Everybody, 1970–1971

WITH TWO WEEKS of performances booked at the International Hotel in Las Vegas in September, Armstrong felt rejuvenated toward the end of the summer of 1970. He was even able to admit that perhaps the two-year layoff from steady work had done him some good. "For 54 years I went through that one-nighter routine, and I didn't know what my home looked like," he said at the start of the International Hotel engagement. "I don't want to get too active and overdo it. I'm not ready for that big funeral yet. Frankly, I've never had a rest like these two years in my life. I'm getting regular meals, sleeping regular hours and taking it easy—just like the doctors suggested. There were times I went back to work after I'd been sick when I had no business going back to work. It's ruined a lot of cats. Suddenly I realized what a fool I was when I could have been home in bed."[1]

This was an important event for Armstrong. Besides having a steady gig again and getting the green light to play the trumpet, Armstrong would finally be reunited with the All Stars, who hadn't been asked to appear at the Los Angeles or Newport tributes, much to the chagrin of Joe Muranyi. "That would bother me very much," Muranyi said. " 'Cause Pops felt more comfortable with his band. That Newport one there, too, that, I was furious about that. He was rehearsing 'Hello, Dolly!'—you know, come on, have his band already! . . . The guy's old and it's the end of his career and he's made a hundred million dollars, God knows what he's made to the office, fly his band out there. Come on. That bothered me very much. I felt left out. And I just felt that my interests [were] Pops's interests. He could hire somebody better than me, but at least I know Pops's shit."[2]

Aside from the birthday tributes, Armstrong hadn't performed a full show in public in two years, leading to a bit of rare tension in the dressing room. "Lucille, with a warm embrace, kissed her man on the cheek and left to take a seat in the overcrowded dining room [of the International]," Eddie Adams wrote. "Ira [Mangel] left the room to take a position outside the dressing-room door. Only Pops and I were left. He sat on a chair facing a mirror tinged with lights, wearing his tuxedo trousers, a white shirt, and a bib around his neck. He picked up his horn, played a couple of notes, gently laid the shiny instrument on his lap, and stared at it as though he was either spellbound or reminiscing. He looked frightened." At that point, a voice yelled, "Five minutes!" That was all Armstrong needed to hear to loosen up. "Wearing a bright smile, holding his horn in one hand, Pops came bursting out of the dressing room door, stopped abruptly, stretched out both arms, chuckled devilishly: 'My debut.' "[3] At the end of the evening, the ecstatic crowd gave him a long standing ovation.

After opening night, Armstrong told the *National Enquirer*, "I just took it nice and easy out there. I proved to those doctors and I proved to myself that I can still blow that horn in public. Let me tell you something. I lived two years just waiting for that opening night. I knew the doctors had to be wrong. Twice them hospital cats had me under intensive care. And when you get in that ward, you can kiss the world good-bye. But Ol' Satch ain't ready to go upstairs yet. I'm gonna live for another 100 years."[4] Leonard Feather attended Armstrong and Bailey's show at the International Hotel and raved. "It was not just Louis himself we applauded as he ambled onstage to the opening stanza of 'Sleepy Time Down South'; it was the fact that he was once again able to play his horn, for the first time after two years of illness," he wrote. "Satchmo and his combo (most of his 1968 men were back with him) cruised through their traditional show, with the usual 'Indiana' for openers, followed by 'Someday,' 'Tiger Rag,' and 'The Saints,' among others. His horn had lost none of its incandescence. His sound might have been stronger, but we told ourselves that time would take care of that. Each note was perfectly on target and Armstrong-pure."[5]

Bailey, who would later call the engagement "two of the most beautiful weeks of my life," said after one of the shows, "There was an awful lot of love in the house tonight."

Though the Vegas shows were a giant love fest, one incident demonstrated that Armstrong's almost fatherlike defense of his All Stars was still very much intact. Bailey would open backed by an orchestra led by her husband, Louie Bellson, a tremendous jazz drummer, who had backed Louis on his 1957 Verve sessions with Ella Fitzgerald and Oscar Peterson. Armstrong was determined to protect Danny Barcelona, a fine drummer in his own right but out of Bellson's league when it came to dynamic showpieces. "I mean, Louie Bellson, one of the world's great drummers, he's got his two bass drums and everything, and he does his feature," Dan Morgenstern related. "Louie's immediate reaction is that . . . Danny Barcelona is going to have to follow that, not immediately, but he's following it. So he knows Pearl—he takes her aside and says, 'Look, Pearl, you know, I would really be happy if you didn't do this. Louie's great and everything's wonderful but you're showing up my guy, you know, and your show is not a jazz show, I mean, you got your thing, and . . .' Well, she wouldn't do it."[6] According to Muranyi, Armstrong "went ballistic. He got very pissed off." At the end of the show, which closed with Armstrong and Bailey singing some duets, Muranyi recalled, "Louie took his mike and threw it up in the air. It must have gone fifteen feet and down into the piano, *boom boom boom!*—you know, like 'fuck it!' "[7] Morgenstern continued, "On the next night, when Bellson starts his solo, Louie walks out from the wings with his horn and starts to play over him, you know—and of course completely, you know, steals the show, which is what he intends to do. So after that, Bellson's act was cut from Pearl Bailey's show."[8]

With a two-week engagement behind him, a confident Armstrong appeared on an episode of ABC's *Johnny Cash Show* in October. There to promote his new *Country and Western* album, he looked resplendent in a blue suit with a comically oversized cowboy hat and sang a medley of "Crystal Chandeliers" and "Ramblin' Rose." After the performance, Cash surprisingly invited Armstrong to re-create his famous 1930 duet with Jimmie Rodgers on "Blue Yodel Number 9." Armstrong pulled out his trumpet and instantly transformed into the young Louis Armstrong of 1924, the master of the obbligato whose horn work was a hallmark on so many seminal blues recordings of the 1920s. Armstrong hadn't really played obbligatos since Velma Middleton's days in the band; but on Cash's set he showed that he hadn't lost any of his inventiveness or his sound, which was just as warm as ever. Armstrong didn't go for many high notes, but he didn't have to. He unleashed an incredible stream of ideas throughout the nearly four-minute performance. Anyone who was unaware of Armstrong's health troubles wouldn't have known he was ailing. Sure, he looked skinnier than usual, but he played and even scatted with the command of a man who wasn't ready to give in just yet.

Though Armstrong's trumpet playing sounds wonderful on the Cash program, it soon became clear that he no longer had the endurance to play for extended periods of time. At the end of October, he flew to London to perform a charity concert for the National Playing Fields Association. It would be a one-night-only performance, documented by a camera crew shadowing Armstrong for the day. Armstrong's friend trumpeter Humphrey Lyttelton was on hand and remembered that "Louis Armstrong's final appearance in Britain, witnessed in all its detail by his friends here, assumed the elements of Greek tragedy." Lyttelton was taken aback by Armstrong's appearance. He may have been skinny during the 1968 trip, but now he clearly had trouble walking. "To me, he seemed for the first time an old man. The always jaunty, stiff-limbered walk had a frail jerkiness about it and in repose his face wore a crumpled, defeated look," Lyttelton continued. "When he arrived in London, this frailty was marked—it seemed as if the head of a fifty-year-old was perched on the body of a man of ninety." Armstrong had a packed, nonstop day, including television appearances, receptions, and even rehearsals. The finished documentary, *Boy from New Orleans,* features small snippets of Armstrong playing trumpet during rehearsal, and though he sounds fairly strong, it was clearly quite taxing. "Now the trumpet notes really were laboured and the effort needed to produce them obviously painful," Lyttelton wrote. "It is hard to imagine any other artist of international repute in his old age being subjected—or perhaps in Armstrong's case we should still say subjecting himself—to the routine of that day."[9]

At the concert, the camera caught his time-honored warmup routine in the dressing room—a beautiful segment—but by the time he got onstage, Armstrong was out of gas. As he tripped down a step and almost fell before his opening vocal, "When It's Sleepy Time Down South," his fragility was on display for all to see. "His show-business reflexes came to the rescue and he covered up with a crack to the effect of 'You want to watch that step!' But he was clearly shaken," said Lyttelton. Footage of Armstrong playing "Hello, Dolly!" is truly a tragic moment. "When he started to play the trumpet, it must have been apparent to him before anyone else that the renowned chops had no strength left in them," Lyttelton wrote. "And the man . . . whose majesty on the instrument had never been challenged by any other trumpet player, surrendered to a ruthless and irresistible opponent and played the trumpet with his back to the audience."[10] The image of Armstrong fumbling to produce a note, turning around, and surrendering the lead to Tyree Glenn is perhaps the saddest of Armstrong's career. Fortunately, it lasted less than a minute. The rest of the concert was a smash, thanks to Armstrong's singing and stage presence as he traded jokes with host David Frost and delivered heartfelt vocals on pieces like "What a Wonderful World." Back in the United States, Armstrong proudly discussed the performance on various talk shows, especially delighting in a story about receiving a gift from Prince Philip, the Duke of Edinburgh. Naturally, Armstrong immediately responded by giving the duke a packet of Swiss Kriss and enthusiastically explaining its purpose!

Following a slow November, Armstrong brought the All Stars back to Las Vegas for another two-week engagement. There was little fanfare this time around as things seemed to go smoothly onstage. But offstage, something was wrong: Armstrong began experiencing shortness of breath. Dr. Schiff was already with Armstrong, but he knew he had to write Dr. Zucker. Probably fearful that Zucker would make him stop playing, Armstrong broke the ice in his letter of December 30 by opening with a dirty joke and assuring him "Everything's going real well here. Everybody loves us." He then continued, "I thought it best to wait an write you after Dr. Schiff consult you concerning the shortening of my Breath. And Since he talked to you—and with your Instructions I feel much better already. Thanks Daddy."[11] Zucker couldn't have been pleased at Armstrong's shortness of breath but with his assurance that he was okay, Zucker allowed him to play a few engagements spread out over January and February. On January 23, 1971, he and Tyree Glenn appeared with some local Washington, D.C., musicians for a concert at the National Press Club. Armstrong opened with "Sleepy Time Down South" and played a wonderful, fresh solo on "Hello, Dolly!," even managing to insert a quote from the old

New Orleans standard "I Thought I Heard Buddy Bolden Say." Feeling confident again, he appeared on *The David Frost Show* later that month, singing "Blueberry Hill" with Bing Crosby and playing "Sleepy Time" and "That's My Desire" on the trumpet again. Although he complained his "chops are dry," the broadcast sounded very good. On February 21, Armstrong wrote to clarinetist Slim Evans, "Your boy Satchmo is getting pretty sassy these days. Blowing his black ass off. I knew I could, all the time. My fans and friends, quite naturally they'd be a little uneasy about things, but as for me, they're my chops. I wear them 24 hours a day, and I keep them in good trim."[12] On *The Dick Cavett Show* the very next night, as if to prove a point, Armstrong daringly called "Ole Miss," a demanding instrumental that was a highlight of Armstrong's shows in the fifties and sixties. The choice did not come without its consequences, as Armstrong had trouble maintaining the fast tempo during his solo. However, he sounded very strong throughout the ensemble and ended the tune on a perfectly paced high-note climb. Cavett's announcer, Jack Barry, then backstage with Lucille, reported that she had said, "You know, Louie's been quite sick. I'm so happy to see him back there. All he was worried about, would he ever blow that horn again."[13]

By the time of the Cavett appearance, Armstrong's next engagement was already booked and advertised in the *New Yorker*. Beginning on March 2, Armstrong and the All Stars, augmented in some numbers by a big band, would perform for two weeks at the Empire Room of the Waldorf-Astoria. After Vegas in December and his performance on television, he felt confident about the gig. The night before he opened, a vivacious Armstrong appeared on *The Tonight Show*. He told stories, sang "Blueberry Hill," and even played one of his best trumpet solos of this period on "Pretty Little Missy." Excited at the Waldorf appearance, Armstrong told Johnny Carson, "We was over there rehearsing today, me and the boys, my band and the band that's over [there], we had a nice time. I have some big stuff they play behind me, too, you know, when we all get grandioso, you know!"[14] He was ready to entertain, singing and playing well. However, the Waldorf-Astoria gig is generally known to be one of the saddest stories of Louis Armstrong's life. When talking about it on Ken Burns's documentary *Jazz*, Arvell Shaw broke down crying and couldn't continue. According to Joe Muranyi, "Well, Louis was wobbly, but it wasn't [that sad]."

The truth seems to lie in the middle. A short amount of footage survives from the Empire Room and, though skinny, Armstrong looks perfectly fine, singing beautifully and holding his horn proudly. Armstrong's old critical nemesis John S. Wilson reviewed a show for the *New York Times* and didn't notice anything wrong. "His appearance at the Waldorf is his first engagement in New York since his illness," Wilson wrote. "Yet, despite the physical impact that this must have had on a man in his late 60's, he seems little changed from the Louis Armstrong who was constantly touring the world during the decade before." Wilson mentioned that Armstrong played "Indiana," "Some Day You'll Be Sorry," "Hello, Dolly!," "What a Wonderful World," "That's My Desire," "Blueberry Hill," "Mack the Knife," and "Boy from New Orleans," in addition to giving the All Stars their regular features. "Looking slim and trim in a light-blue suit, Mr. Armstrong sings with the deliberate, toothy emphasis that is his trademark and blows his trumpet sparingly but with enough emphasis to let it be known that he is back at the old stand."[15]

However, it is clear that a two-week engagement was more than he could handle, and some time in the middle Armstrong began to decline rapidly. Knowing about Armstrong's shortness of breath in Las Vegas in December, Dr. Zucker had predicted this and told Armstrong so before the Waldorf performances even began. During a visit to Zucker's office, Armstrong was barely able to breathe. Zucker told him, "Louie, you could drop dead while you're performing," to which Armstrong responded, "Doc, that's all right, I don't care." According to Zucker, "He did a very interesting thing. He got into this transported state. Sitting there on the examining table he said, 'Doc, you don't understand. . . . My whole life, my whole soul, my whole spirit is to blooow that hooorn.' And he sat there for a moment sort of removed and went through the motions of blowing that horn. 'I've got bookings arranged and the people are waiting for me. I got to do it, Doc, I got to do it.' "[16]

Armstrong's longtime physician Alexander Schiff agreed that the engagement should have been canceled. "Even at the end, when his last date was at the Waldorf-Astoria here in New York City, we wanted to cancel that contract," Schiff said. "But he said, 'Oh, you can't do that to me. This is the first big engagement I have in New York City at the best hotel, and I'm gonna finish that contract.' He was very, very sick at that time, and he had lost so much weight that people didn't even recognize him."[17]

Writing about the performances a few months later, Richard Meryman inferred Armstrong probably saw it as too important a gig to cancel. "He had to be helped on and off the stage," Meryman recounted. "To Louis, no doubt, that date—his first at the Waldorf—was a kind of pinnacle, a very specific measurement of the distance from squalid James Alley. For that—and for him—I am much more happy than sad."[18]

As the Waldorf run continued, Armstrong's trumpet playing suffered. "His playing the trumpet was—I wouldn't say 'shameful,' but it wasn't Louie," Schiff said. "It was a different person playing that trumpet."[19] Muranyi, too, remembered Armstrong's chops deserting him on a recorded version of "Indiana." "He plays 'Indiana' and he's got no chops at all, he's physically in terrible shape," he says about the tape. "And the old man, I cried when I heard it a couple of times and I couldn't play it anymore. He plays 'Indiana' with all the mistakes and he tries to make something happen with the mistakes. And it's, you know, he wouldn't give up."[20]

Armstrong was so determined to keep playing that he focused all of his offstage time on resting. On March 8, six days into the run, gossip columnist Earl Wilson reported, "Louis Armstrong, 71 on July 4, blew his famous horn when he opened at the Waldorf Empire Room though it took so much strength that he went to bed in between shows. His wife said he had been in bed much of the month resting so he could blow the trumpet while performing with his All-Stars."[21] Phoebe Jacobs, a friend of Armstrong's and today vice president of the Louis Armstrong Educational Foundation, remembered that during those rest periods, Armstrong had to use oxygen to ease his breathing.[22] From the beginning Dr. Zucker had insisted Armstrong stay at the Waldorf for the entire two weeks and only leave his room to take the elevator to the Empire Room. Though Armstrong never left the hotel, the performances began to take a toll. "Once, coming downstairs to do our show with Ira [Mangel], the road manager, Pops threw up in the elevator," Muranyi recalled. "I saw Ira wiping off Louis's patent-leather shoes and Ira making a comment on the happening." Nothing would stop Armstrong, as he lived to perform. If he couldn't entertain, he couldn't be happy. His health already had kept him from doing what he loved for almost two years, and it had depressed him tremendously. Now back onstage, he was determined to stay there, even if it killed him.

Armstrong had been suffering from varicose veins (which he called "very-close veins") since at least 1964. It turned into phlebitis, which Armstrong had to endure for the rest of the decade.[23] Throughout his 1970 television appearances, Armstrong showcased a stiff, troubling gait but still seemed to get around without much difficulty. However, at the Waldorf, Armstrong's leg problems were so severe he had to be helped on and off stage. Arvell Shaw, who had played intermittently with Armstrong since the mid-forties, knew the trumpeter's larger-than-life stage presence and was struck by the now fragile Armstrong. Shaw recalled the impact Armstrong's performance had on the band augmenting the All Stars. "They had a big, sixteen-piece show band there, you know. And they had all these hardened New York musicians. We used to call them 'the thugs,' that's how hard—all jazz musicians and good musicians. The guys that you'd think nothing could faze them. And I'd look back, especially every night [when] we would end the show with . . . 'What a Wonderful World,' and he did it with such emotion, these guys would be like this, tears running down. So that was one of the worst two weeks."[24] Armstrong did play "What a Wonderful World" each evening, but he closed every night with "Boy from New Orleans," the autobiographical take on "When the Saints Go Marchin' In" that he first recorded for *Louis Armstrong and His Friends* in May 1970. At a strutting medium tempo, Armstrong told his life's story, from growing up a youth in New Orleans to being named a "jazz ambassador" and appearing in films with "Bing and Princess Grace." It was an upbeat song, but as the band slowed the tempo to dirgelike status Armstrong always recited:

> *Now all through the years*
> *Folks, I've had a ball.*
> *Oh, thank you, Lord*
> *And I want to thank you all.*
> *You were very kind,*
> *To old Satchmo*
> *Just a boy from New Orleans.*

Those were the final words spoken by Louis Armstrong onstage, thanking the fans for making his life a "ball," a very fitting epitaph. Armstrong was practically killing himself onstage at the Waldorf, but he knew that without them, he'd probably still be struggling in New Orleans. Photographer Eddie Adams attended Armstrong's final performance and recalled, "That night, Pops ended his performance with a song about his life, 'The Little Boy from New Orleans.' I think he was trying to tell us something."[25] Road manager Ira Mangel was tremendously affected by Armstrong's final performance. "He had tears in his eyes as he walked off the stage during his last night at the Waldorf," he said. "In all my years with him, I have never seen him cry before. He played his horn like he never played before and even told his audience stories about his trips to Africa."[26] Adams had attended Armstrong's triumphant comeback performance in Las Vegas the previous September and was horrified by his condition at the Waldorf. "I waited offstage for Pops. He wasn't the same Satchmo I had seen in September. Now he was frail, seemed to be wasting away. He moved slowly, haltingly. Six months had made a very old man of Pops."

Armstrong knew he was a sick man at the end of the Waldorf-Astoria run, but he didn't think it would be his last gig. "In fact, just before he left, right after the gig, Pops said, you know, 'Hey, kid, see you in Miami, Florida, in June,' or something like that," Danny Barcelona recalled. "That's what I can remember. I guess they had something booked, you know, during the summer."[27] Joe Muranyi told a similar story. "That night, it's the last set of the last night, I'm seated with Louis Armstrong and Tyree's taking the solo, or somebody . . . and he says, 'Josephus,' he says, 'I want you to know,' he said. 'When we're through here, I'm checking into a hospital, Beth Israel. I've got some things that have to be done for me but I don't want you to worry. I'm all right. I'm going in on my own. There's not going to be an emergency. Don't worry. We're going to go around the world one more time.' "[28]

Adams later wrote about the offstage moments after Armstrong's final performance at the Waldorf. "After a standing ovation, Pops, Ira, and I started for his suite, but through the lobby of the hotel a crowd of well-wishers and autograph seekers surrounded Pops. He obliged. A New York columnist latched onto Ira. The crowd disappeared. Pops disappeared. At the far end of the lobby the light was reflected from his horn. It made me look up. I saw Pops walking away alone. He seemed in a daze, swaying as he walked. I thought he was going to collapse before he got to his room. His doctor answered the door."[29] Back in Dr. Zucker's care, Armstrong knew he was sick, he just didn't know the extent. The Waldorf engagement ended on March 13 and two days later, on the 15th, Armstrong suffered a heart attack and was rushed to Beth Israel. The attack was induced by kidney trouble that resulted in uremic poisoning, affecting the heart in the process. Armstrong's liver and gall-bladder were also barely functioning. Now more than ever, Louis Armstrong was staring death in the face. Though he was in critical condition, the moment Armstrong's pain eased, he would sing and entertain the hospital staff. On March 29, Armstrong took a turn for the worse, suffering another heart attack. This time, his heart stopped beating completely. "For thirty seconds he was clinically dead," Lucille said.[30] Zucker had to insert a tracheotomic tube to save Armstrong's life. He was later placed on a respirator but once again fought for his life, and in mid-April he moved from intensive care to a private room. "His breathing is comfortable and his heartbeat is regular," Zucker told the press. "He is eating very well and is out of bed in a chair several times a day. His spirits are much brighter now."[31] Armstrong even joked about the tracheotomy, confessing, "I was afraid that would take away my dulcet tones, but it didn't affect me at all."

Truthfully, Armstrong was miserable. He was especially upset about the tracheotomy. "At first I was furious at Lucille for giving permission for this operation," he said when he got out. "I thought, now it's finished with talking and blowing the horn. But, thank heavens, I was wrong." Lucille sat at his bedside for sixteen hours a day for over eight weeks; on some days, he didn't recognize her. But she believed in his will to survive. "Not for one second did I really believe Louis could possibly die," she said. "This was it," Louis said. "That helped me. I couldn't disappoint her." On May 8, feeling slightly better, Armstrong called his wife at 2:30 in the morning and shouted, "Get me out of this damned hospital! I can't look any longer at the nurses in their uniforms. Get me out of here—or I'll quit on my own." Lucille responded that there was nothing she could do at that time of night. Finally, after repeated phone calls from Louis, Lucille called Dr. Zucker, who agreed that sending Louis back home could be "good therapy for Louis."[32]

Back in Corona, Lucille had her hands full. Armstrong still couldn't get around, falling down on his second day at home and bruising his knee. Because Louis couldn't walk, Lucille had to carry him out of the bed every four hours to change the sheets, in addition to washing, shaving, and feeding him. The ever-stubborn Louis was even reluctant to take his medicine, so she had to stay on him for that, as well. It took Louis ten days before he could get out of bed alone. Lucille had an electric lift installed to help Louis get up and down the stairs. This, too, did not please him. "Louis was mad at me when I first told him [about the stair lift]," Lucille said. " 'I am not a cripple yet,' he yelled. 'I am not an old man and not paralyzed. Beside this, I am convinced, you have demolished half the house to get this stupid chair installed.' He wanted me to remove the chair immediately, but of course I didn't." Finally, on May 23, two weeks after his return home, Louis came downstairs for dinner on his own. "He was feeling amazingly well and we enjoyed a lovely, entertaining evening with some close friends," Lucille said.[33]

Foreseeing another long stay at home, Louis and Lucille turned their efforts to improving their residence. "When we bought this house twenty-nine years ago, we figured it would be a temporary home while looking for something better," Lucille said. "But we stopped looking for something else. We really got to love this area."[34] The first thing they did was purchase the empty lot next door. The Armstrongs wasted no time in installing a lavish Japanese-inspired garden area. "I'm going to landscape this lot with trees, bushes, and flowers and maybe even a small croquet court," Armstrong told the press in late May. "Then, I'm just going to sit out there and enjoy my garden and maybe even blow my horn a little. I'll let my wife Lucille do the gardening. She has a green thumb." The same *New York Daily News* article about this expansion of the Armstrong property ended with these words: "He said he hopes to be recovered enough by Fall to resume concerts but added that he would never play one-nighters again."[35] Next, the Armstrongs covered their house with a brick façade. "Not wishing to be perceived as 'putting on airs,' " director of the Louis Armstrong House Museum Michael Cogswell explains, "Louis offered to cover the house of his next-door neighbors, Adele and Selma Heraldo, with brick as well. The Heraldos declined, but did allow the brick masons to extend the brick face along the retaining wall in front of their house."[36] The gesture typified how Armstrong felt about his Corona neighborhood. Armstrong's generous spirit continued, and in June 1971 he donated a thousand dollars to the Milne Boys' Home in New Orleans "for the purchase and maintenance of musical instruments." Milne was the new name for the Colored Waif's Home, where Armstrong first learned to blow his horn in 1913. He knew, even at the end of his life, that he wanted to help struggling kids from his hometown become musicians.[37] This desire to give back also led him to become the first jazz musician to lend his name to a foundation when the Louis Armstrong Educational Foundation was founded in 1970. The Foundation's purpose, according to Lucille in June 1971, was to "Help where help is necessary, regardless of the political views of those who need help."

Armstrong's next task was to alert friends that he was doing okay. On May 30, he wrote to Slim Evans, "This was a tough one this time (in the Hospital). Hmmm. The Cats (people) Everywhere out East were Betting money that I wouldn't make it this time. 4 weeks I was in Intensive Care, Sick as a Bitch. But Doctor Zucker—Lucille and the Lord and Mee (Tee-Hee) we had something going. Ol Swiss Kriss was in there with us. Yas Lord—Ol Satch is back on the mound again." Armstrong told Evans that he had even begun playing the trumpet again. "My Doctor a ('Hip Rascal') gave me permission to Blow a little lightly every day before My Dinner. Sorta slip on it and getting a strong lip and building up an Embusure or Amberschure. [Embouchure] Hmm. You know? I am trying to say good strong crumb crushers (Lips)."[38]

By late June, Armstrong began to feel better. He was now walking with a cane—when he chose to. "He is supposed to walk with the help of a walking stick," Lucille told a German reporter, "but now that he feels strong again he often forgets it. After walking a while, he naturally gets a little weak. Then he calls and I know. Now he is standing up clutching at the furniture, because he can't go on. And only because he was too stubborn to use his walking stick." Armstrong knew that the reports about his illness were dire and he didn't care for such speculation. "I never was interested in the life of Caruso or the death of Mario Lanza," he said. "But today it is different. Everybody wants to know how I am going to die. And I am going to be at least ninety years old. And they think I want to prove something by playing the trumpet as soon as possible and give at least four concerts a year. I don't want to prove anything. I just like to blow my horn. And I enjoy hearing myself play."[39]

In order to prove he was on the road to recovery, Armstrong invited the press to visit him in Corona. *Rolling Stone* magazine sent photographer Annie Leibowitz on her first travel assignment for the magazine. "Leibowitz hoped to do unposed photo reportage on Armstrong and was disappointed to find that the show business veteran had his own ideas about picture taking," Marc H. Miller wrote. "Without any encouragement from Leibowitz, he went through his complete repertoire of poses: taking out his handkerchief, pretending to blow his trumpet, and giving her his famous smile. After a few hours, Leibowitz left, feeling that the session was largely a failure. It was only later that she saw the true poignancy of the photos, which were among the last taken of Armstrong." Leibowitz recalled, "You know something is not 100 percent right. You admire the professionalism. You admire that the show must go on. You admire that even in this sort of tired and exhausted state, he's going to give you his best. Those are all very fascinating and admirable moments."[40]

On June 23, Armstrong sat down in his den and composed an open letter to the most important people in his life, his fans:

> This is Louis Satchmo Armstrong speaking from his home in Corona. I've Just gotten out of the Beth Israel N.Y. Hospital. I've had a million things that happened to me, including the operation for TRECHEOT-OMY. And I'm coming along just fine and I'm getting my strength back even in my legs. I thought that it is real thrilling to send a message to my fans and friends from all over the world. Which I'd like to thank all of them from every nook and corner of the world for their lovely get well cards and prayers. Which did wonders for me. I also want to thank my personal Doctor Gary Zucker—His staff of Doctors, Mrs. Lucille Armstrong, Dr. Alexander Schiff, our company Doctor, Ira Mangel, our road manager for many years for many years [sic], and still is. That is, if I ever get back to work again. I am looking forward to it. I feel that I owe them, my public and fans, my service again. Which they are eagerly waiting for.[41]

Later that day, Armstrong held court in his home for various reporters and photographers. "I'm one old cat that you just can't kill . . . and I'm definitely going back to work as soon as my legs get a little stronger," he assured them. "Work, that's my life—oh yeah! But I wouldn't want to go out on the stage with a walking cane. Soon as my pins get back in shape, ole Satch will be back."[42] Lucille was on hand to speak of Armstrong's yearning to get back on stage. "Just the other day he asked me 'what's my next job?' He's doing so well and he looks so great," she said. "And he plays his horn every day . . . sounds great, just great." To prove it, Louis pulled out his trumpet and began playing "When It's Sleepy Time Down South," backed by his friend Tyree Glenn, who had dropped by for a visit. As a United Press International reporter summed it up, "Taking a chorus, eyes closed, ever-present white handkerchief clutched in his left hand, Satchmo ran off a series of clear, clean notes, whose mellowness and phrasing proclaimed that he has lost none of his touch. Then he laid down his horn, wiped his chops with the handkerchief, pointed to a photograph of himself and mused: 'See that cat? You can't kill him, man. That cat ain't ever gonna die. We just gonna keep on going, just going. Yeeeaaah man!' "[43]

According to one report, Armstrong played three more short songs with Glenn and ended the mini-set with one of his own compositions, "If We Never Meet Again."[44] Armstrong found time to read his "open letter" to his fans, and according to the *New York Times,* he ended his visit with the press by asking them to deliver a message to the fans: "Tell 'em I love 'em, that's all."[45]

In his alone time, Armstrong pursued his hobbies, including writing, listening to his tapes, and designing collages for the boxes. He had begun to recatalog his massive reel-to-reel collection while recuperating at home in 1970. For more than a year, Armstrong spent much of his free time transferring recent and older recordings to numbered tapes. He frequently dubbed his own music, revisiting his 1920s work on occasion, but spending most of his time on later albums such as *Louis Armstrong Plays W. C. Handy, Ambassador Satch, Louis and the Good Book, Louis and the Angels, The Real Ambassadors,* and *Satchmo: A Musical Autobiography,* sometimes making multiple copies of the same albums. He transferred joke-telling sessions with now-deceased friends such as Velma Middleton and Doc Pugh. He continued copying other people's records, not only expected musicians such as King Oliver and Jelly Roll Morton but also more modern jazzmen such as Dizzy Gillespie and Clifford Brown, proof that his old stance against bop had, for the most part, dissipated. Classical music and opera remained a favorite, but he also made room for new music by Neil Diamond and the Plastic Ono Band. Once done making a reel, he would write down the tape's contents and stick the paper inside the tape box. In his final year, he had begun transferring the contents of his tapes into a catalog. He prenumbered the first 233 pages, leaving room for 155 reels, but would only manage to fill it up to reel 123.

The exteriors of the tape boxes were saved for his special collages, which often had nothing to do with the contents of the tapes. He would take photos from throughout his career, cut them up and arrange them in the most creative fashions. Now each photo turned into a memory. Before he got sick, he viewed them with Associated Press reporter Mary Campbell. "Here's Velma Middleton," he said, looking at one. "She killed them when she sang. I'll never find another one like her." He picked up another one and remarked, "Edmond Hall, probably playing 'Dardanella.' "[46] Armstrong's entire life was contained in these boxes, on the inside and the out. As June turned into July, Louis was still busy decorating boxes with at least five different newspaper headlines and magazine articles from May or June of that year. Two of his final collages consisted of headlines from the June 24 issue of the *Orange County Register* ("Satchmo Talking . . . 'Tell all the cats the Choirmaster up there in Heaven will have to wait for old Louis.' ") and the June 25 *Miami Herald* ("Satchmo Bouncing Back, Eager to Work Again").

On July 4, Armstrong celebrated his seventy-first birthday in his backyard garden area, welcoming friends and listening to a radio marathon of his music. The next day, he was ready for yet another comeback. He called Dr. Schiff and told him that he wanted to get the All Stars together for a rehearsal. "We'll get the boys together, rehearse and go back to work," Armstrong told Schiff.[47] Preparations were underway for Armstrong to perform again, starting in California. Louis Armstrong, happy with the knowledge that he could one day perform with his All Stars again, went to bed. He would never wake up.

Louis Armstrong died in his sleep at 5:30 a.m. on July 6, 1971. Lucille Armstrong noticed her husband stopped breathing and immediately summoned Drs. Schiff and Zucker, who pronounced Armstrong dead of "kidney failure, attributable to heart failure."[48] Though he had just celebrated his seventy-first birthday, Armstrong was in fact sixty-nine years old at the time of his death, four weeks shy of actually turning seventy. It doesn't seem like a particularly old age until one considers how much Armstrong packed into it. The one-nighters, the powerful trumpet playing, the cigarettes, the marijuana, the endless laxatives . . . in some ways, it is a miracle Armstrong lasted that long. Perhaps he would have lasted longer if he hadn't worked himself so hard but it was the only life he knew.

Armstrong's death was front-page news around the world. The papers were filled with tributes from the likes of Bing Crosby, Eddie Condon, Dizzy Gillespie, Earl Hines, and Duke Ellington. Gillespie penned a column for the *New York Times* and wrote, "Never before in the history of black music had one individual so completely dominated an art form as the Master, Daniel Louis Armstrong." Proof the bop-war days were over, Gillespie, who once called Armstrong a "plantation character," wrote, "Louis is not dead, for his music is and will remain in the hearts and minds of countless millions of the world's people, and in the playing of hundreds of thousands of musicians who have come under his influence."[49] Ellington, who once bitterly made insinuations about Armstrong being an Uncle Tom, was quoted as saying, "If anyone was Mr. Jazz, it was Louis Armstrong. He was the epitome of jazz and always will be . . . He is what I call an American standard, an American original."[50] Miles Davis, an unabashed fan who also vehemently criticized what he perceived as Armstrong's Uncle Tom ways, said, "You can't play anything on that horn that Louis hasn't played."[51] Lucille Armstrong filled multiple scrapbooks with personal condolences from celebrities and friends. Crosby wrote to her, "The too infrequent times I spent in his company were joyous experiences and I know of no man for whom I had more admiration and respect. He was a true genius, but more."[52]

The NAACP obituary, written by Executive Director Roy Wilkins, praised Armstrong: "Unlike many of the Negro youngsters of today, Armstrong was not always feeling sorry for himself, bemoaning the fact that he was black, while looking around for someone whom he could flim-flam for assistance," echoing sentiments Armstrong had expressed in his private 1969 manuscript on race. Wilkins concluded:

> Louis Armstrong is one answer to those who maintain that excellence is not necessary, that all a black person has to be is black. In his time this man was simply the best trumpeter alive. Through his own sheer talent he won the place that jazz occupies today in American music. No faking. With today's crime news, it may not seem that devotion to excellence pays off. The slick operators seem to have it, all the way from lunch money muscled from schoolboys to dubious deals in the board rooms of great corporations. But Louis Armstrong, growling out his gravelling singing, fluttering one of his snow white handkerchiefs and blowing ecstasy into the air with his trumpet, pipes piercingly, "Taint so, Honey, taint so."[53]

Armstrong's body was laid out for three days at the New York National Guard Armory for the more than twenty-five thousand fans who went to say good-bye. When Lucille organized Armstrong's funeral as a sober New York affair, she was criticized for not planning the joyous New Orleans–styled celebration Armstrong himself explained as his ideal send-off. *Jet* magazine ran the headline "Satchmo's Funeral 'White and Dead' in New York, but 'Black, Alive and Swinging' in New Orleans." The article read, "For a man who contributed so much to the world of music, Armstrong's last laying-out moments on this earth were bereft of any of the strains that brought comfort and joy to millions around the world, although his widow, Mrs. Lucille Armstrong, insisted that this was the way 'Pops' wanted it . . . The so-called attempt at 'dignity' was stifling to any sense of real feeling or emotion."[54] Ella Fitzgerald, in attendance, did not sing despite her storied collaborations with Armstrong. Instead, Peggy Lee sang a quiet "Lord's Prayer" while Al Hibbler sang mournful versions of "Nobody Knows the Trouble I've Seen" and "When the Saints Go Marching In." Thousands of people lined up outside Corona's Congregational Church, but only five hundred were admitted, including Gillespie, Earl Hines, David Frost, and Ornette Coleman. Joe Muranyi recalled, "You had to have tickets to get into the church. And they were stamped 'Associated Booking Corp.' And I had to laugh and I said, 'Jesus, even his funeral was booked by Joe Glaser!' "[55]

Muranyi was dismayed by the lack of music at the funeral: "I took my horn and I didn't know, I figured maybe we should play, but we didn't." "If Joe Glaser had been alive Louis would have had a grand send-off," Dan Morgenstern declared. "But Lucille wanted to be respectable and had ties to the community—she was under some pressure to have it there."[56] According to *Jet,* "Not a trumpet sounded, nor a funeral note, for the man who started his career playing at funerals and who said on his 70th birthday last year, 'They going to enjoy blowing over me, ain't they? Cats will be coming from California and everywhere else just to play.' Cats came from everywhere, but apparently they were not allowed to play at the funeral . . . Many New Orleans musicians traveled to New York on their own to be at the funeral and to play, if they were allowed. But no permission came."[57] Those musicians would have been better off staying in New Orleans, where fifteen thousand people crowded City Hall for the official tribute to the city's most famous son. Multiple brass bands performed, but the music did not last long. However, trumpeter Teddy Riley closed the ceremony by performing "Taps" on the battered cornet

Armstrong first learned to play on while at the Colored Waif's Home in 1913: a beautiful touch the New York affair sadly lacked.

Louis Armstrong was officially gone. Soon after his heart stopped beating, the now standard story of Armstrong's later years began to develop. In his eulogy, John S. Wilson stated: "Because he made these essential contributions to the development of jazz in the 1920's when jazz . . . was largely an underground music, most of Mr. Armstrong's career was, in a sense, an anticlimax."[58] Barely a month after Armstrong's death, Craig McGregor began sowing the seeds for the theory that Louis's life was a "tragedy" and a "despairing story." "What we may not know or don't always remember is that in many ways Armstrong is a tragic figure, and his tragedy is part of a larger one in which we all share," he wrote in the *New York Times*. Regarding Armstrong's ability "to adapt his art to the demands of the time," McGregor argued: "Armstrong survived by compromise, and it was a compromise which destroyed his art. It should never have been necessary, and unless we learn from his fate how commercialism can corrode even a creative genius like Armstrong, jazz will continue to be created by a unique minority who are willing to sacrifice their lives for their art."[59]

This line of thinking continued throughout the 1970s and into the 1980s. For example, James Lincoln Collier said, "I cannot think of another American artist who so failed his own talent," and Gunther Schuller referred to Armstrong's "need to scratch out a living as a good-natured buffoon." Gerald Early, a young black essayist and critic, protested: "Armstrong, at the time of his death in July 1971 was not only quite wealthy but was probably the most famous American entertainer in the history of the American performing arts. But it is not Armstrong the entertainer, Armstrong the performer, Armstrong the darkie minstrel, who needs to be remembered." In the late 1980s Early described why Armstrong's later career turned off so much of his black audience:

> The pain that one feels when Armstrong's television performances of the middle and late sixties are recalled is so overwhelming as to constitute an enormously bitter grief, a grief made all the keener because it balances so perfectly one's sense of shame, rage, and despair . . . One shudders to think that perhaps two generations of black Americans remember Louis Armstrong, perhaps one of the most remarkable geniuses America ever produced, not only as a silly Uncle Tom but

as a pathetically vulnerable, *weak* old man. During the sixties, a time when black people most vehemently did not wish to appear weak, Armstrong seemed positively dwarfed by the patronizing white talk-show hosts on whose programs he performed, and he seemed to revel in that chilling, embarrassing spotlight. To this current generation of young black adults, Armstrong's greatness, if he ever had any, occurred in such a remote, antediluvian time as to bear almost no relation to modern American music or modern American culture.[60]

The tide began to turn in the 1980s with Dan Morgenstern's liner notes to various Armstrong releases, including Columbia's *Chicago Concert* set. Gary Giddins, the first to gain access to Armstrong's manuscripts and tape recordings, published *Satchmo* in 1988. The book, a loving appreciation of Armstrong, defended the trumpeter's entertaining ways and provided new insight into his writings. Armstrong's personal archive did not become available to the public until 1994, when the Louis Armstrong Archives opened at Queens College. It is a haven for researchers and fans alike.

Probably of little coincidence, perceptions about Armstrong began to change when Armstrong's private views about life and music became public. In the 1990s, younger black jazz musicians such as Jon Faddis, Wynton Marsalis, and Nicholas Payton began to preach about the wonders of Armstrong's entire career, including his later years. And 1994 also marked the year of the traveling Smithsonian exhibit about his life, the release of *Portrait of the Artist as a Young Man,* and Jazz at Lincoln Center's weeklong "Armstrong Continuum," the first time a cultural institution devoted significant time to celebrating Armstrong's life and art. But the critically lauded boxed set redirected the focus to Louis's 1920s recordings as a jazz maverick, thereby allowing critics to praise his early work at the expense of the later. "Hello, Dali, goodbye 'Hello, Dolly!'" wrote David Hadju in *Entertainment Weekly.*

The Armstrong juggernaut continued over the ensuing years. Armstrong was featured on a postage stamp in 1995; numerous biographies and books about the trumpeter were published; an annual "Satchmo Summer-Fest" was founded in 2001, drawing thousands of people to New Orleans to celebrate the city's most famous son. Ken Burns's *Jazz* documentary made Armstrong its "star," even devoting time to the All Stars, the Little Rock comments, and other episodes from Armstrong's final decades. Armstrong's historic Corona home opened as the Louis Armstrong House Museum in 2003. As I write this, Forest Whitaker is planning a big-screen biopic on Armstrong's life.

And yet, and yet. As chronicled in the first chapter, Armstrong's later years continue to be shrouded in myths. People still hurl the "Uncle Tom" epithet. Hardened jazz fans focus on the Hot Fives and Sevens and ignore the All Stars. There are nonjazz fans who only know Armstrong though "What a Wonderful World" and other coffeehouse pop songs that showcase yet another side of his genius, a more "neutered" one. My hope is that in reading this book people from all musical backgrounds will finally begin to understand that the later years of Louis Armstrong's life were epic. His music was masterful and he consistently challenged himself in studio recordings and live performances. It was then that Armstrong experienced his greatest popularity, touring the world and touching the lives of fans everywhere. Offstage, though he delighted in laxatives, marijuana, and women, he also showcased an indomitable spirit of generosity, treating friends and fans, royalty and strangers, all like gold. With regard to race relations, Armstrong's private conversations and public actions proved he was nobody's Uncle Tom.

Although Armstrong was overwhelmingly popular throughout his career and died a national icon, his detractors have always had the loudest voices, which is why the negative view of his later years remains the standard after all these years. Armstrong's composition "Someday You'll Be Sorry," which he sang from the earliest All Stars gigs in 1947 until his last performance at the Waldorf-Astoria, perfectly epitomizes Louis's misunderstood final period: "Someday you'll be sorry / The way you treated me was wrong."

Miles Davis may have criticized Armstrong's entertaining style, but he couldn't deny how Armstrong transcended his stage persona, saying in 1970: "To me, the great style and interpretation that Louis gave to us musically came from the heart, but his personality was developed by white people wanting black people to entertain by smiling and jumping around. After they do it they call you a Tom, but Louis fooled all of them and became an ambassador of good will."[61] Few names better capture Armstrong's mission in life. He addressed the title "Ambassador of Goodwill" in 1957:

I say my public, they ain't thinkin' about politics when they call me Ambassador. They thinkin' about that horn and them notes and that music and them riffs. Oh, yes, that what they thinkin'. They prob'ly want to rest up on Satchmo, you know, when they call me Ambassador Satch. Which *is* nice, you know. 'Specially when the chicks, they say, "Hellew there, Ambassador Satch." And the cats, "How you doin' there, ol' Ambassador Satchie-matchie!" Long as I'm playin', I don't want 'em to feel nothin' else. I'm not lookin' to be on no high pedestal. They get their soul lifted because they got the same soul I have the minute I hit a note. There's three generations Satchmo has witnessed—the ol' cats, their children and their children's children, and they still all walk up and say, "Ol' Satch, how *do* you do!" I love my audience and they love me and we just have one good time whenever I get up on the stage—it's such a lovely pleasure.[62]

Acknowledgments

It can be argued that I began writing this book the minute I saw Louis Armstrong in *The Glenn Miller Story* when I was a fifteen-year-old kid in 1995. Days later, my mother took me to the local library, where I checked out a cassette compilation of Armstrong's 1950s Columbia recordings entitled *16 Most Requested Songs*. By track 14 ("St. Louis Blues"), my life was changed, and right there, one could say, I planted the seed of writing a book on this music that moved me so.

Hundreds of people helped me over the fifteen-year journey from that October day to the publication of this book. I wish I had the time to thank each person individually, but that would require a volume in itself. First, I would like to thank my parents, who never stopped encouraging me from the moment I was born. They always supported my wide-ranging interests, even as it led them to spend much of my childhood in bookstores, video stores, and record shops. When I got into Armstrong, they, too, got into Armstrong, and often rewarded me by buying me CDs and allowing his music to form a large part of our family vacation soundtracks. They never stopped in their support for a single second, which truly meant the world to me. When I finally got the book deal and my dream job at the Louis Armstrong House Museum in Queens, there was nobody in the world happier than they. I will never truly be able to thank them enough for their tireless encouragement, but I will never tire of trying.

I also had the guidance of some very influential teachers, namely Nick Cucurese, Michael Aiello, Barbara Smith, and Karen Bosley, who acted like a second mother to me during my time on the newspaper at Ocean County College, teaching me more about writing during those Tuesday production nights than I ever learned anywhere else.

In 2003, I was accepted into Rutgers's master's program in jazz history and research. My thesis formed the basis for this very book. I am grateful to the friends I made during that time, namely Ryan Maloney, Flip Peters, Corey Goldberg, Shannon McCarty, Todd Weeks, and the other two-thirds of "the Power Trio": John Wriggle and Michael Heller. I benefited from the teachings of Henry Martin, John Howland, and especially my mentor, Lewis Porter. Lewis became one of the most important people in my life, encouraging me to develop my thesis into a book at every turn. My gratitude to him is endless.

While at Rutgers, I spent much of my time conducting Armstrong-related research at the Institute of Jazz Studies. Thanks to the entire staff, especially Tad Hershorn, Ed Berger, and Vincent Pelote, for all their help. Dan Morgenstern, director of the IJS, had been my Armstrong writing idol since I was a high-school student absorbing his liner notes. I was thrilled to meet him, honored to become his friend, and am grateful for his input on this book. No one has ever written better about Louis Armstrong, and no one ever will.

Ed Berger booked my first "Research Roundtable" discussion at the IJS in February 2006. It was a life-changing event that helped me realize I needed to expand my research into a book. This led me to the Louis Armstrong House Museum in Corona, Queens, where I came to know director Michael Cogswell, a terrific guy and a patron saint of Pops. I marvel at the heroic way he turned Armstrong's home into a museum and at the way he has organized and run the Armstrong Archives, where I spent the majority of my time listening to Armstrong's private tapes. I would like to thank Michael, Deslyn Dyer, Baltsar Beckeld, and Lesley Zlabinger for all their help when I was merely a researcher. My current position as project archivist for the House Museum, which allows me to work with such great people, is a dream come true. Anyone remotely interested in Louis Armstrong should visit the museum for an experience that will never be forgotten. When the Visitors Center opens across the street from the house in 2013, it will be a banner day for Armstrong fanatics and music lovers around the world.

My thanks also go to the Louis Armstrong Educational Foundation, and particularly to Phoebe Jacobs and Oscar Cohen, for continuing to do so much in the name of Louis. Phoebe has been an enthusiastic supporter of mine, even taking the time to attend some of my Armstrong film presentations, and I'm grateful for all of her help.

I must also thank the All Stars themselves, whose music always inspired me and who have been criminally neglected by previous writers. I tracked down five members of the illustrious group, each a gigantic help in making those years of one-nighters come to life. My never-ending thanks to Joe Muranyi, Marty Napoleon, Jewel Brown, Buddy Catlett, and the late Danny Barcelona.

I couldn't tell the story of Armstrong's later years without consulting two of the trumpeter's closest friends, Jack Bradley and George Avakian. Both men not only were tremendously helpful from a research standpoint, but also took the time to look over my manuscript when the clock was ticking. And, more importantly, they've both become friends of mine, and for that I'm eternally grateful.

Without a book deal and with too many thoughts about Armstrong on my brain, I started a blog, "The Wonderful World of Louis Armstrong." I was almost immediately Satch-urated with e-mails from Armstrong fans around the world. I would like to thank each and every person who has ever visited the blog and dropped me a line. I've become quite close with some of my readers and must thank Dave Whitney, Phil Person, Al Basile, Bernard Flegar, Uwe Zanisch, David Sager, Augustin Perez, Michael Johnston, Al Pomerantz, and Fernando Ortiz de Urbina for their cherished correspondence. Special thanks to Michael Steinman for all of his support and encouragement (and rye bread).

And special thanks goes to the peerless Armstrong discographer Jos Willems, who, without being asked, generously filled my mailbox with dozens of incredibly rare Armstrong CDs and DVDs, allowing me to listen to and see things I previously had only dreamed about. I am fortunate to have Jos as a great friend. Special thanks also to the group I dubbed "the Swedish Hot Four": Håkan Forsberg, Peter Winberg, Sven-Olof Lindman, and, especially, the late Gösta Hägglöf. I had always admired

Gösta's work regarding Armstrong, but I never expected to strike up such a fruitful association with him. We traded e-mails for over a year, and he became a mentor of sorts. His stories, pictures, wisdom, and encouragement always provided a great deal of inspiration. The fact that he did not live long enough to see this book published is heartbreaking.

I would like to thank Jon Pult and Marci Schramm of French Quarter Festivals for taking a chance and inviting me to give three presentations at the Satchmo SummerFest in 2008. It was an unforgettable experience, and I'll always have them to thank for it. I've made many great friends at the SummerFest over the past three years, namely Yoshio Toyama, Gary Giddins, Robert O'Meally, Michael Gourrier, Randy Sandke, and David Ostwald. David, especially, has become a close friend, providing hours of rare tapes for my use. I treasure his friendship.

I would like to thank two very important people without whom there would not have been a book: Tony Outhwaite of JCA/Midpoint, my agent and chum, who always remained positive, even when I would call him in a panic; and Erroll McDonald, my fantastic editor at Pantheon, who believed in the importance of my work. The first time I met Tony, he struck up a discussion on Billy Kyle. The first time I met Erroll, he brought up Armstrong's neglected RCA Victor recordings of the early 1930s. I knew, in both cases, I was in the right hands. They have coaxed me off numerous ledges and helped turn a monstrous thesis into the book you are currently holding. Credit for that also goes to production editor Kevin Bourke and copyeditor Patrick Dillon, who both did heroic jobs in catching not just typos and formatting issues (of which there were thousands) but also any inconsistencies that cropped up. I'm sure few writers have ever been as excited to read through a copyedited manuscript as much as I. Thanks to Alissa Kleinman in permissions and Josie Kals in publicity for all their help and enthusiasm. And big thanks to Erroll's assistant Lily Evans for all of her help, too, especially when it came to preventing various nervous breakdowns!

Thanks to Chris Albertson for sharing his treasure trove of correspondence between Columbia Records and Joe Glaser in the 1950s. Thanks to Loren Schoenberg for giving me a chance to preach the gospel of Pops at the National Jazz Museum in Harlem and to Terry Teachout for all of his guidance through each stage of the writing process. I'd like to thank Ingo Ruppert, Guy Thalman, Donna Fields, and Len Pogost for helping me acquire rare video footage. And thanks to Swiss photographer Milan Schijatschky for permission to use his beautiful, never-before-published photos. (And thanks to Ronnie Hughart for helping me locate Milan . . . what a story!)

As a piano player in New Jersey, I've led my own small combos for over a decade. I would like to thank some of the many musicians I've been fortunate to play with, including Dennis Valencia, Dan Liotti, Jon Kahnt, Dave Williamson, Mark Ipri, Jake Suskevich, Brendan Castner, Angelo Basilone, and the late Shane Gooding. I must thank Mike Wellen and Tom McGovern, as well as the entire OCC crew, for all their help, support, and laughter over the years.

I'm fortunate to come from a very large Italian family, all of whom I love dearly and thank for all of their interest and love. I must make special mention of my brother, Jeff, with whom I'm insanely close, and my brother-in-law, Mike Adams; we've all shared thousands of laughs. And thanks to my sister, Michele, and her two children, Tyler and Connor, both of whom learned early on that their birthdays would often be celebrated by watching live performances of Louis Armstrong's music at Birdland.

Finally, and most importantly, the biggest thanks go to the two ladies of my life: my wife, Margaret, and my baby daughter, Ella. In Margaret, I truly married the woman of my dreams. Writing this book was absolutely no fun for her, but she always supported me when I would disappear to write for hours and hours. She was with me for the thesis, for the blog, for the book, for the lectures, for the rejections, for the celebrations. She's my best friend in the world, and I love her more than words can describe. And finally, to baby Ella, whose smile goes through me like a high C. She will get to know her uncle Satchmo very well over the course of her life. She was identifying photos of "Louie" at age one and can even identify his trumpet sound! I'm blessed and thankful to have their love.

Notes

The majority of my research was done using the clippings files at the Institute of Jazz Studies at the John Cotton Dana Library, Rutgers University, a treasure trove of newspaper and magazine articles arranged chronologically. However, because they were not full periodicals, some clippings were missing information such as article title, date, periodical title, page number, and even author. I've tried to piece together as much information as possible in these source notes, but often resort to an "IJS" to denote an item from the Institute's files.

Material found in the IJS's Jazz Oral History Project of the National Endowment for the Arts, has been indicated by a "JOHP."

EPIGRAPH

1 Louis Armstrong, Voice of America interview, July 1956. Courtesy of David Ostwald.

INTRODUCTION

1 Scrapbook 1987.8.2, Louis Armstrong House Museum.
2 Scrapbook 1987.8.83, Louis Armstrong House Museum.
3 *Louis Armstrong Talks About Louis Armstrong* (Mark 56 Records, 1975).
4 Tape 1987.3.345, Louis Armstrong House Museum.
5 Louis Armstrong, Voice of America interview, July 1956. Courtesy of David Ostwald.
6 Larry King, "Everybody's Louie," *Harper's,* November 1967, 68.
7 Dan Morgenstern, interview with the author, 19 April 2004.
8 Joshua Berrett, *The Louis Armstrong Companion* (New York: Schirmer Books, 1999), xiv.
9 Gilbert Millstein, "The Most Un-Average Cat," liner notes to *Satchmo: A Musical Autobiography* (Decca DXM-155, 1957).
10 Humphrey Lyttelton, *It Just Occurred to Me . . .: The Reminiscences & Thoughts of Chairman Humph* (London: Robson Books, 2006), 39.
11 Joe Evans and Christopher Antonio Brooks, *Follow Your Heart* (Illinois: University of Illinois Press, 2008), 66.
12 Laurence Bergreen, *Louis Armstrong: An Extravagant Life* (New York: Broadway Books, 1997), 439.
13 Richard Meryman, "Louis Armstrong: An Authentic American Genius," *Life,* 11 April 1966, 116.
14 Tape 1987.3.218, Louis Armstrong House Museum.

15 Charles Sanders, "Louis Armstrong: The Reluctant Millionaire," *Ebony*, November 1964, 143-144.

16 Louis Armstrong, as told to David Duchs, "Daddy, How the Country Has Changed!," *Ebony*, May 1961, 81-90.

17 Stuart Nicholson, *Reminiscing in Tempo* (Boston: Northern University Press, 1999), 329.

18 Armstrong, "Daddy," 85.

19 King, "Everybody's Louie," 66.

20 Tape 1987.3.715, Louis Armstrong House Museum.

21 Sanders, "Louis Armstrong," 143.

22 Wilfred Lowe, "The Jazz Jester?," *Jazz Journal*, September 1954, 7.

23 Whitney Balliett, "Jazz Records: The Three Louis," *New Yorker*, 28 September 1957.

24 Armstrong, Voice of America interview.

25 John Norris, "Trummy Young: An Interview," *Coda*, August 1973, 9.

26 *Louis Armstrong: The Portrait Collection*, DVD (Hip-O B0010365-09, 2008).

27 Richard Meryman, *Louis Armstrong: A Self-Portrait* (New York: Eakins Press, 1971), 55.

28 Ibid., 42-43.

29 Armstrong once told an interviewer, "Listen, I've got everybody's records. I buy everybody from Stravinsky to 'Gizzard'! Thelonious Monk, everybody, yeah. Because I think you should hear everybody. I mean, it makes you appreciate your work, too, and you check up on yourself." Tape 2003.197.10, Louis Armstrong House Museum.

30 Tape 1987.3.424, Louis Armstrong House Museum.

31 1960s handwritten notes, Jack Bradley Collection, 2008.3.397, Louis Armstrong House Museum.

CHAPTER ONE

1 Billy Rowe, "Armstrong Breaks All Records at Paramount," *Pittsburgh Courier*, 24 April 1937, 19.

2 "Louis Armstrong Sets Tour; Waxes 'I Wonder,' " *Pittsburgh Courier*, 17 March 1945, 20.

3 Barry Ulanov, "Louis and Jazz," *Metronome*, June 1945, 33–34.

4 Leonard Feather, " 'Jazz and Swing?—No Difference!'—Says Armstrong," *Melody Maker*, 28 July 1945.

5 "Louis Armstrong on 'Re Bop,' " in Lewis Porter, *Jazz: A Century of Change* (New York: Schirmer Books, 1997), 182.

6 "Reverend Satchelmouth," *Time*, 29 April 1946.

7 Armstrong wasn't playing anything close to New Orleans jazz with his big band, but he was no stranger to small groups in the mid-1940s. He took part in the two famous *Esquire* magazine all-star concerts in 1944 and 1945, sharing the stage with the likes of Roy Eldridge, Sidney Bechet, Jack Teagarden, Coleman Hawkins, Art Tatum, and others. On December 7, 1944, Armstrong unexpectedly showed up at a midnight V-Disc session to blow the lights out on two numbers, "Jack Armstrong Blues" and "I'm Confessin'," fronting a band filled with jazz greats and future associates, including Teagarden, Bobby Hackett, and Cozy Cole. And on January 10, 1946, Armstrong contributed a solo laced with modern touches on an all-star studio recording titled "Snafu." All these small-group appearances found Armstrong in superb form, relaxed

and improvising more than he did with the big band. He still sounded great with the orchestra, but arguably played with more fire and inspiration in the small-group settings.

8   Louis Armstrong, letter to Leonard Feather, 5 December 1946, 1987.9.10, Louis Armstrong House Museum.

9   "Louis, Long-Distance," *Music Business,* March 1947, 33. Armstrong's horn was stolen a day before the concert, but fortunately, cornetist and Armstrong worshipper Bobby Hackett was in attendance. "I knew my horn would be closest to his, and the easiest for him to play," Hackett said. Hackett made it back to Carnegie in time with a horn of his own for Armstrong to perform with. Armstrong still had his mouthpiece, Hackett noticed. "He always carries it in his pocket," Hackett said. "Smart."

10 Ibid.

11 Ernie Anderson, "Louis Armstrong & Joe Glaser, Part 1: The Early Years," in *Storyville* 160, 1 December 1994, 132.

12 "Vote to Indict Joe Glaser in Liquor Robbery," *Chicago Tribune,* 9 April 1935, 5.

13 Anderson, "Joe Glaser & Louis Armstrong, Part 1," 129.

14 *Louis' Lost Tapes,* BBC4 broadcast, 22 January 2005. Courtesy of Håkan Forsberg.

15 Jack Bradley, "A Symposium on Louis Armstrong," *Saturday Review,* 4 July 1970. Quotes taken from the cassette containing the entire original, unedited interview, Jack Bradley Collection, 2005.1.2184, Louis Armstrong House Museum.

16 Tape 1987.3.493, Louis Armstrong House Museum.

17 Richard Meryman, *Louis Armstrong: A Self-Portrait* (New York: Eakins Press, 1971), 27-28. In the same interview with Meryman, Armstrong recounted Glaser's reaction to this story: "You're nuts."

18 Tape 1987.3.493, Louis Armstrong House Museum.

19 Anderson, "Louis Armstrong & Joe Glaser, Part 1," 129.

20 Louis Armstrong, "The Goffin Notebooks," in *Louis Armstrong in His Own Words,* ed. Thomas Brothers (Oxford: Oxford University Press, 1999), 160.

21 For a time, Armstrong's old New Orleans rival Sidney Bechet was also scheduled to be on the bill. The two had not seen each other since a debacle at the 1945 *Esquire* concert in New Orleans, when the rivalry between both men led to some sloppy, tension-filled playing. When the night of the Town Hall concert came, Bechet was absent. Later, he would claim to have fallen ill while on the subway en route to Town Hall. However, trumpeter Max Kaminsky could swear he saw Bechet playing later that night at Jimmy Ryan's nightclub. "I don't know if he was taken ill on the subway," said Bob Wilber, Bechet's student at the time. "If he was, he soon recovered. I think the feeling against Louis got too strong for him to go and play at the concert." John Chilton, *Sidney Bechet: The Wizard of Jazz* (New York: Da Capo, 1987), 195.

22 Peter Tanner, "Louis Is Still Tops," *Melody Maker,* 7 June 1947.

23 Max Jones and John Chilton, *Louis: The Louis Armstrong Story, 1900–1971* (Boston: Little, Brown and Company, 1971), 172.

24 "Interview with Louis Armstrong: 'They Cross Iron Curtain to Hear American Jazz,' " *U.S. News & World Report,* 2 December 1955, 60. Ernie Anderson felt Armstrong's lyrics to "Someday You'll Be Sorry" revolved around his third wife, Alpha. "Anyone who

has any doubts of Louis's use of his subconscious need only listen to his song, perhaps his favorite composition, 'Someday You'll Be Sorry,' " Anderson wrote. "He was crazy about Alpha, his third wife. She shocked him to the quick by running off with the white drummer, Cliff Leeman." Anderson concluded, "If you listen to the lyric you can see that it is addressed directly to Alpha." Anderson, "Louis Armstrong & Joe Glaser, Part 1," 135.

25 Dan Morgenstern, "Pops in Perspective," *Jazz Journal,* May 1962, 3.

26 "Louis Center of New Commotion," *DownBeat,* 2 July 1947.

27 Ron Welburn, interview with Russell "Big Chief" Moore, 1980, JOHP.

28 "Louis Armstrong and Jack Teagarden at Apollo Theatre," *New York Amsterdam News,* 5 July 1947, 10.

29 Louis Armstrong, *Satchmo: My Life in New Orleans* (New York: Da Capo, 1986), 188.

30 Barney Bigard and Barry Martyn, *With Louis and the Duke: The Autobiography of a Jazz Clarinetist* (New York: Oxford University Press, 1986), 113.

31 Dick Cary, unpublished interview with Floyd Levin, 8 July 1991. Transcribed by Richard Miller. Courtesy of Håkan Forsberg.

32 Burt Korall, *Drummin' Men* (New York: Schirmer Books, 1990), 180.

33 Cary, interview with Floyd Levin.

34 Patricia Willard, interview with Barney Bigard, 1976, JOHP.

35 Ernie Anderson, "Louis Armstrong & Joe Glaser, Part 2: The All Stars," in *Storyville* 161, 1 March 1995, 167.

36 "Satchmo Comes Back," *Time,* 1 September 1947.

37 John Lucas, "Louis, Born with Jazz, Still Its King—and Success on Coast Today Is Proof," *DownBeat,* 27 August 1947, 14-15.

38 "Satchmo Comes Back."

39 Ibid.

40 Gene Norman, quoted in *DownBeat* advertisement, 22 October 1947, 7.

41 Floyd Levin, *Classic Jazz: A Personal View of the Music and the Musicians* (Berkeley: University of California Press, 2000), 149.

42 Joshua Berrett, *The Louis Armstrong Companion* (New York: Schirmer Books, 1999), 165-166.

43 *The Wonderful World of Louis Armstrong,* directed by Peter Davis and Terry Henebery (KAY Video Jazz, 1981). Courtesy of Håkan Forsberg.

44 Dan Morgenstern, liner notes to *The California Concerts* (Decca GRD-4-613, 1992), 11-12.

45 Berrett, *Armstrong Companion,* 175.

46 George Hoefer, "Louis Armstrong Concert," 10 November 1947, IJS.

47 Ibid.

48 Berrett, *Armstrong Companion,* 166.

49 "Program by Armstrong," *New York Times,* 17 November 1947, 26.

50 John Norris, "Trummy Young: An Interview," *Coda,* August 1973, 8.

51 Anderson, "Joe Glaser & Louis Armstrong, Part 1," 134.

52 Dan Morgenstern, interview with the author, 19 April 2004.

53 Joe Muranyi, interview with the author, 26 October 2006.

54 Tape 1987.3.115, Louis Armstrong House Museum.

CHAPTER TWO

1   "Louis Armstrong Sought for French Jazz Festival," 6 December 1947, 16, IJS.

2   *DownBeat* originally reported that Hines was supposed to join the band for Billy Berg's debut, but that must have been unofficial speculation.

3   Stanley Dance, *The World of Earl Hines* (New York: Charles Scribner's Sons, 1977), 103.

4   Henry F. Whinston, "Soon I'll Be Leaving Louis—to Record with My Own Band," *Melody Maker,* 6 October 1951.

5   Dick Cary, unpublished interview with Floyd Levin, 8 July 1991, transcribed by Richard Miller. Courtesy of Håkan Forsberg.

6   Barney Bigard and Barry Martyn, *With Louis and the Duke: The Autobiography of a Jazz Clarinetist* (New York: Oxford University Press, 1986), 116.

7   Jack Bradley, interview with the author, 13 October 2007.

8   Dan Morgenstern, interview with the author, 19 April 2004.

9   "Satchmo a Happy Man; No Headaches for Him As He Approaches 50," *Capitol News,* April 1950, 7.

10 Morgenstern interview.

11 Cary, interview with Floyd Levin.

12 Ibid.

13 Humphrey Lyttelton, *Last Chorus: An Autobiographical Medley* (London: JR Books, 2008), 169.

14 Max Jones, "Louis As Good As Ever," *Melody Maker,* undated, IJS.

15 Hugh Rees, "Let's Take Stock of Armstrong," IJS.

16 Carl L. Biemiller, "Armstrong and His Hot-Noters Point a Trend," *Holiday,* October 1948, 16.

17 "Interview with Louis Armstrong: 'They Cross Iron Curtain to Hear American Jazz,' " *U.S. News & World Report,* 2 December 1955, 57.

18 Dizzy Gillespie and Al Fraser, *To Be, or not . . . to Bop* (New York: Doubleday, 1979), 296.

19 George T. Simon, "Bebop's the Easy Way Out, Claims Louis," *Metronome,* March 1948.

20 Ibid.

21 Ernest Borneman, "Bop Will Kill Business Unless It Kills Itself First: Louis Armstrong," *DownBeat,* 7 April 1949.

22 "Louis Armstrong Takes Lead in Popularity Poll for Small Bands," *Chicago Defender,* 29 May 1948, 8.

23 Biemiller, "Armstrong and His Hot-Noters," 16.

24 Ibid., 14.

CHAPTER THREE

1   Tape 1987.3.571, Louis Armstrong House Museum.

2   Humphrey Lyttelton, *Satchmo: The Story of Louis Armstrong,* 10-part BBC radio series broadcast in 1971. Tapes courtesy of David Ostwald.

3   Thomas Brothers, *Louis Armstrong's New Orleans* (New York: W. W. Norton & Company, 2006), 81.

4 "Louis the First," *Time,* 21 February 1949, 52.

5 Brothers, *Louis Armstrong's New Orleans,* 81.

6 Leonard Feather, "Satchmo—The Three Lives of Louis Armstrong," *Esquire,* March 1955, 81.

7 Audio of this version of "Shoe Shine Boy" can be heard on my "Wonderful World of Louis Armstrong" blog from 3 September 2009, http://dippermouth.blogspot .com/2009/09/shoe-shine-boy.html.

8 WDSU radio broadcast, 27 February 1949; courtesy of Jos Willems. Before the big parade, Armstrong and the All Stars played a dance in New Iberia, 135 miles away from New Orleans and the hometown of the hero of the moldy figs, Bunk Johnson. Though ailing, Johnson managed to attend the dance as an honored guest, and when asked to sit in on a few numbers, he ended up playing for hours. He would pass away on July 7 of that year. Armstrong said of the night: "They should have let him play two or three numbers on a program, and let it go at that. But everybody wanted to hear Bunk, and the promoters wanted to make that money. An old man can't blow a horn like that. It makes a man go all to pieces inside. That's what killed Bunk." Johnson always claimed he taught Armstrong how to play the trumpet, but it wasn't until he died that Armstrong told the truth: "Bunk didn't teach me shit." Tape 1987.3.218, Louis Armstrong House Museum.

9 Laurence Bergreen, *Louis Armstrong: An Extravagant Life* (New York: Broadway Books, 1997), 445.

10 Nick Gagliano, "King Louis' Triumph Tempered," *DownBeat,* 8 April 1949, 18.

11 One of the handful was Armstrong's first wife, Daisy Parker. Her tumultuous marriage to Armstrong when he was a teenager in New Orleans had ended almost thirty years before, but that didn't stop her from coming to Armstrong's performance claiming she was the real "Mrs. Armstrong." (She passed away in Gretna, Louisiana, the following year, at the age of forty-five.)

12 "Solo," *Playback,* March 1949, 2.

13 "Louis 'Satchmo' Armstrong Praised and Cussed: Bouquets and Brickbats for Mardi Gras in N.O.," *Courier Louisiana Bureau,* IJS.

14 Lyttelton, *Satchmo.*

15 Michael Cogswell, *Louis Armstrong: The Offstage Story of Satchmo* (Portland: Collectors Press, 2003), 158.

16 Burt Korall, *Drummin' Men* (New York: Schirmer Books, 1990), 203.

17 Sinclair Traill and Gerald Lascelles, *Just Jazz* (London: Peter Davies, 1957), 7.

18 Tape 1987.3.248 Louis Armstrong House Museum.

19 Bill Kirchner, interview with Cozy Cole, 1980, JOHP.

20 Stanley Dance, *The World of Earl Hines* (New York: Charles Scribner's Sons, 1977), 104.

21 *The Wonderful World of Louis Armstrong,* directed by Peter Davis and Terry Henebery (KAY Video Jazz, 1981). Courtesy of Håkan Forsberg.

22 "Armstrong Puts the 'Bee' on Bebop," IJS.

23 Robert L. Lyon, "Swing Finds a Defender in Jazzman Louis Armstrong," *Eve Leader* (Corning, NY), 27 July 1949.

24 Leonard Feather, "Lombardo Grooves Louis!," *Metronome,* September 1949.

25 Leonard Feather, "Pops Pops Top on Sloppy Bop," *Metronome,* October 1949.

26 Ibid.

27 Ibid.

28 "Louis Armstrong Set for Broadway's Bop," *Chicago Defender,* 27 August 1949, 26.

29 Hal Webman, "Armstrong's Nostalgia Envelops Bop City; Others Share Honors," 27 August 1949, IJS.

30 George T. Simon, "Armstrong Commercialism and Music," *Metronome,* October 1949.

31 Ibid.

32 Dan Morgenstern, liner notes to *The Complete Decca Studio Recordings of Louis Armstrong and the All Stars* (Mosaic MD6-146, 1993), 4.

33 Joe Benjamin, "Roses for Louis," *DownBeat,* 9 July 1970.

34 Bruce Jenkins, *Goodbye: In Search of Gordon Jenkins* (Berkeley, California: Frog, Ltd., 2005), 58.

35 Ibid., 56.

36 Steven Lasker, liner notes to *Billie Holiday, The Complete Decca Recordings* (Decca GRD2-601, 1991), 30.

37 "Satchmo Hottest Package to Hit Europe in Years; Does Italo Film Stint," *Variety,* 1 November 1949.

38 Ernie Anderson, "Louis Armstrong & Joe Glaser, Part 2: The All Stars," in *Storyville* 161, 1 March 1995, 168.

39 "Welcome," *Time,* 7 November 1949.

40 Louis Armstrong, "Europe—with Kicks: Jazz's Ambassador Extraordinary Tells How He Blew Hot in Nine Different Languages," *Holiday,* June 1950, 7-8.

41 *The Wonderful World of Louis Armstrong.*

42 Armstrong, "Europe—with Kicks," 12.

43 Anderson, "Joe Glaser & Louis Armstrong, Part 2," 170.

44 All Stars bassist Arvell Shaw used to tell a detailed version of this story, but in actuality, he was not present at this meeting with the Pope, only Louis and Lucille and Ernie Anderson. Also, there's no concrete proof that Armstrong ever uttered this sentence. Anderson was a publicist and might have seen the opportunity for a great story. Armstrong, too, liked a good line and might have continued to use it because it was a guaranteed laugh. This quote comes from Louis's own mouth, uttered at the 1958 Newport Jazz Festival in the film *Jazz on a Summer's Day.*

45 Anderson, "Joe Glaser & Louis Armstrong, Part 2," 170.

46 Dance, *World of Earl Hines,* 104.

47 Ibid.

48 Armstrong, "Europe—with Kicks," 20.

49 "Welcome."

CHAPTER FOUR

1 John Davis and Gray Clarke, "Collector's Angle on Armstrong," IJS.

2 Frenchy Sartell, "Louis Armstrong—Crooner! How Commercial Can One Get?," *Musical Express,* 19 October 1951.

3 *The Mike Douglas Show,* 25 May 1970. On Douglas's show, Armstrong demonstrated how the Karnofskys taught him how to sing "Russian Lullaby," saying, "They're the ones who told me, 'You should sing more,' " and adding, " 'Cause on my side—on the other side of the tracks—they didn't want to hear that." He then sang a real lowdown

blues, the music then popular in the black part of town. Even back then, Armstrong was already facing opposition in the black communities from people who wanted to hear jazz and gutbucket blues all night instead of something pretty like "Russian Lullaby."

4 Louis Armstrong, "Louis Armstrong + the Jewish Family in New Orleans, La., the Year of 1907," in *Louis Armstrong in His Own Words,* ed. Thomas Brothers (Oxford: Oxford University Press, 1999), 8.

5 Richard Meryman, *Louis Armstrong: A Self-Portrait* (New York: Eakins Press, 1971), 24.

6 Ibid. 43-44.

7 International Jazz Club broadcast, September 1952. On cassette, Armstrong Transcriptions, Jack Bradley Collection, 2005.1.2158, Louis Armstrong House Museum.

8 George Avakian, liner notes to *Louis Armstrong: An American Icon* (Hip-O HIPD3-40138, 1998), 15.

9 Louis Armstrong, Voice of America interview, July 1956. Courtesy of David Ostwald.

10 " 'Satchmo' Record Sets New Sales Record," *Jet,* 31 January 1952, 63.

11 Tape 1987.3.520, Louis Armstrong House Museum.

12 Armstrong always talked about King Oliver playing it back in the red-light district, and it had been a favorite of New Orleans revival bands such as Bunk Johnson's and Kid Ory's in the 1940s. However, the song didn't really become well known until country-music legend Hank Williams had a hit with it in 1949. Thus, it only made sense for Armstrong to cover a song he had known since he was a teenager. Unlike Williams's jaunty version, Armstrong performs it very slowly, the way most New Orleans bands played it, building to quite a passionate, blues-infused ending. The song became a staple in Armstrong's live shows, though through the years its tempo would double.

13 Gary Giddins, *Satchmo* (New York: Doubleday, 1988), 168. To clear up any confusion: Armstrong always referred to "Indiana," or whatever other song followed "When It's Sleepy Time Down South," as his "opener." Technically, "Sleepy Time" opened every show, but it was regarded as a theme song and not the actual "opener."

14 Humphrey Lyttelton, *Satchmo: The Story of Louis Armstrong,* 10-part BBC radio series broadcast in 1971. Tapes courtesy of David Ostwald.

15 John Chilton, *Let the Good Times Roll: The Story of Louis Jordan and His Music* (Ann Arbor: University of Michigan Press, 1997), 218.

16 Jack Bradley, interview with the author, 13 October 2007.

17 Don Freeman, "We'll Get Along Without Hines' Ego, Says Armstrong," *DownBeat,* 22 February 1952, 3.

18 Tape 1987.3.218, Louis Armstrong House Museum.

19 A few months after the filming, while doing a radio interview in Hawaii, Armstrong cleaned up this tale and made it sound much nicer: "Every time I go to warm up between scenes, somebody holler, 'Quiet, please!' I said, 'Listen, man, you can have this movie, I'm going back on my one-nighters.' " Tape 1987.3.199, Louis Armstrong House Museum.

20 Tape 1987.3.218, Louis Armstrong House Museum.

21 James L. Hicks, "Louis Armstrong Makes New D . . . Y Recording," *Baltimore Afro-American,* 8 January 1952, 12.

22 Ibid.

23 Tape 1987.3.199, Louis Armstrong House Museum.

24 Barney Bigard and Barry Martyn, *With Louis and the Duke: The Autobiography of a Jazz*

Clarinetist (New York: Oxford University Press, 1986), 123-124. Bigard remembers this scene happening during a film with Bing Crosby. Armstrong never performed "Sleepy Time" in a Crosby film, and Bigard never made a movie with Crosby, either. It's probably a case of a faulty memory, as everything else he says about the incident relates to the Decca recording.

25 Private tape made with George Avakian, 24 October 1953. Courtesy of David Ostwald.

26 Ernie Anderson, "Louis Armstrong & Joe Glaser, Part 1: The Early Years," in *Storyville* 160, 1 December 1994, 130.

27 *Louis Armstrong: The Portrait Collection,* DVD (Hip-O B0010365-09, 2008).

28 Frankfurt interview, 1952, Jack Bradley Collection, 2005.1.2267, Louis Armstrong House Museum.

CHAPTER FIVE

1 Don Freeman, "We'll Get Along Without Hines' Ego, Says Armstrong," *DownBeat,* 22 February 1952, 3.

2 Ibid.

3 Hugh Barr, "Satchmo Serious About His Music," *Erie Times,* 22 December 1958.

4 Russ Phillips Jr., e-mail to the author, 29 December 2007.

5 Tape 1987.3.115, Louis Armstrong House Museum.

6 Tape 1987.3.6, Louis Armstrong House Museum.

7 Tape 1987.3.160, Louis Armstrong House Museum.

8 Tape 1987.3.115, Louis Armstrong House Museum. One month into his tenure with the band, however, Jones was involved in a tragic event in Canada. On August 5, 1951, the All Stars were playing the Standish Hall Nightclub and Hotel in Hull, Quebec, right across the river from Ottawa. At ten o'clock in the morning, a fire broke out in the basement. Velma Middleton was one of the first who noticed. Panicking, she woke up Armstrong and the rest of the band. They all made it out safely with their instruments, except for Jones, who jumped from the roof and badly injured his back. However, he didn't have it anywhere near as bad as Ralph Gomez, a drummer from New York, who perished in the blaze. Gomez was only twenty-two. The entire front of the Standish Hall was destroyed, and the All Stars were lucky to make it out alive. Tape 1987.3.49, Louis Armstrong House Museum.

9 Stanley Dance, *The World of Earl Hines* (New York: Charles Scribner's Sons, 1977), 105.

10 Freeman, "We'll Get Along," 3.

11 Dance, *World of Earl Hines,* 105.

12 Jos Willems, *All of Me: The Complete Discography of Louis Armstrong* (Lanham, Maryland: Scarecrow Press, 2006), 437.

13 Freeman, "We'll Get Along," 3.

14 Tape 1987.3.115, Louis Armstrong House Museum.

15 Marty Napoleon, interview with the author, 27 August 2007.

16 *Louis' Lost Tapes,* BBC4 broadcast, 22 January 2005. Courtesy of Håkan Forsberg.

17 Ibid.

18 Ernie Anderson, "Louis Armstrong, A Personal Memoir," *Storyville* 148, 1 December 1991, 132-133.

19 Armstrong must have been proud of this moment, as he copied the audio of it on

multiple reel-to-reel tapes in his private collection. He even repeated the moment later that year when he was honored on a live radio broadcast from Boston's Storyville club in December, telling the same joke and mentioning how he had told it in New Orleans. That version can be heard on Tape 2003.197.9, Louis Armstrong House Museum.

20 Napoleon interview.

21 Bruce Jenkins, *Goodbye: In Search of Gordon Jenkins* (Berkeley, California: Frog, Ltd., 2005), 60.

22 Barney Bigard and Barry Martyn, *With Louis and the Duke: The Autobiography of a Jazz Clarinetist* (New York: Oxford University Press, 1986), 122. Napoleon remembers Bigard's leaving having to do more with money than with rest. "[Bigard] didn't want to go to Europe because he asked Joe Glaser for some more money and Glaser wouldn't come up with it so he said, 'Well, I'm not going.' "

23 Napoleon interview.

24 Louis Armstrong, letter to Jeann Failows, December 1948. Jack Bradley Collection, 2008.1.34, Louis Armstrong House Museum.

25 Patricia Willard, interview with Trummy Young, 1976, JOHP.

26 Ibid.

27 Dan Morgenstern, liner notes to *The California Concerts* (Decca GRD-4-613, 1992), 16.

28 Dan Morgenstern, liner notes to *The Complete Decca Studio Recordings of Louis Armstrong and the All Stars* (Mosaic MD6-146, 1993), 8.

29 "Satchmo Toots Horn for LP's As Best Hypo," *Variety,* 8 October 1952.

30 Gösta Hägglöf, liner notes to *Louis Armstrong in Scandinavia, Vol. 2* (Storyville 101 8349, 2005), 3.

31 For more proof that the All Stars changed it up more than they were given credit for, the band played the same piece on an Italian broadcast less than a month later, this time with a quicker tempo, clocking in at only three minutes and forty-six seconds!

32 "Wild Crowds, Broken Records Greet Armstrong Abroad Again," *DownBeat,* 19 November 1952.

33 Art Buchwald, " 'Satchmo' Abroad," *New York Herald Tribune,* 1 December 1952.

34 Ibid.

CHAPTER SIX

1 Barney Bigard and Barry Martyn, *With Louis and the Duke: The Autobiography of a Jazz Clarinetist* (New York: Oxford University Press, 1986), 122.

2 Marty Napoleon, interview with the author, 27 August 2007.

3 John McDonough, interview with Norman Granz, Geneva, Switzerland, 1 February 1999, transcribed by Tad Hershorn. Courtesy of Tad Hershorn.

4 Ibid.

5 Tape 1987.3.571, Louis Armstrong House Museum.

6 John Hammond with Irving Townsend, *John Hammond on Record* (New York: Penguin Books, 1981), 315.

7 Ross Firestone, *Swing, Swing, Swing: The Life & Times of Benny Goodman* (New York: W. W. Norton and Company, 1993), 378.

8 Bigard, *With Louis and the Duke,* 111.

9   Marc Myers, "Interview: Al Stewart (Part 2)," 29 September 2009, http://www.jazz-wax.com/2009/09/interview-al-stewart-part-2.html.

10   McDonough, interview with Norman Granz.

11   Patricia Willard, interview with Trummy Young, 1976, JOHP.

12   McDonough, interview with Norman Granz.

13   Firestone, *Swing, Swing, Swing,* 378.

14   Gary Giddins, *Satchmo* (New York: Doubleday, 1988), 198.

15   Howard Taubman, "Atom Bomb on Carnegie Hall? No, Man! Goodman and Satchmo Armstrong's All Stars Beat It Out," *New York Times,* 18 April 1953.

16   Ibid.

17   Hammond, *John Hammond on Record,* 316.

18   Max Jones, *Talking Jazz* (New York: W. W. Norton, 1988), 119-120.

19   McDonough, interview with Norman Granz.

20   Jones, *Talking Jazz,* 120.

21   McDonough, interview with Norman Granz.

22   Tape 1987.3.233, Louis Armstrong House Museum.

23   Jones, *Talking Jazz,* 120.

24   Michel Boujut, *Louis Armstrong* (New York: Rizzoli International Publications, 1998), 52.

25   Napoleon interview.

26   *The Wonderful World of Louis Armstrong,* directed by Peter Davis and Terry Henebery (KAY Video Jazz, 1981). Courtesy of Håkan Forsberg.

27   Tape 1987.3.424, Louis Armstrong House Museum.

28   *Louis' Lost Tapes,* BBC4 broadcast, 22 January 2005. Courtesy of Håkan Forsberg.

29   Louis Armstrong, radio interview on BBC's *Be My Guest,* London, 2 July 1968. Courtesy of Jos Willems.

30   Tape 1987.3.571, Louis Armstrong House Museum.

31   Armstrong seemed proud to have Hinton in the band, too. On a broadcast from the Blue Note in Chicago in July, Hinton takes a typically fun solo on "Royal Garden Blues," quoting "Mona Lisa" and generally breaking up Armstrong, who, after encouraging him to "lay it on 'em, Hinton," proudly announces to the crowd, "That's Milt Hinton playing the bass! He just left Joe Bushkin!"

32   Tape 1987.3.19, Louis Armstrong House Museum.

33   Milt Hinton and David G. Berger, *Bass Line: The Stories and Photographs of Milt Hinton* (Philadelphia: Temple University Press, 1988), 206.

34   Bigard, *With Louis and the Duke,* 123.

35   Tape 1987.3.241, Louis Armstrong House Museum.

36   Bigard, *With Louis and the Duke,* 121.

37   "Pops' Japan Tour a Smash," *DownBeat,* 27 January 1954.

38   "Interview with Louis Armstrong: 'They Cross Iron Curtain to Hear American Jazz,' " *U.S. News & World Report,* 2 December 1955, 55.

39   George E. Pitts, "After Twelve," *Pittsburgh Courier,* 3 December 1955.

CHAPTER SEVEN

1   "Louis Armstrong's Wife Seized in Hawaii for Dope," *Jet,* 14 January 1954, 57.

2   "People," *Time,* 11 January 1954.

3   "Satchmo's Wife Held on Narcotics Charge," *Hartford Courant*, 1 January 1954, 2.

4   Audio letter from Louis Armstrong to Joe Glaser, 16 January 1954, Tape 2003.197.23, Louis Armstrong House Museum.

5   Milt Hinton and David G. Berger, *Bass Line: The Stories and Photographs of Milt Hinton* (Philadelphia: Temple University Press, 1988), 209.

6   Audio letter from Louis Armstrong to Joe Glaser, 16 January 1954.

7   Richard Gima, "4,000 Turn Out for March of Dimes Show at Auditorium," *Honolulu Star-Bulletin*, 5 January 1954.

8   "Lucille Armstrong Is Fined $200 on Marihuana Charges," *Honolulu Star-Bulletin*, 6 January 1954.

9   Audio letter from Louis Armstrong to Joe Glaser, 16 January 1954.

10   According to Milt Hinton, Armstrong's engagement at the Brown Derby was canceled at some point, though this wasn't reported in local Honolulu newspapers. "We were cancelled," Hinton wrote. "In fact, when we went to the theater to get our instruments we found them piled up out on the street and it took us hours to put things back in order." Hinton and Berger, *Bass Line*, 209.

11   "Local Union Would Bar Satchmo from Island Engagements," *Honolulu Star-Bulletin*, 11 January 1954.

12   Audio letter from Louis Armstrong to Joe Glaser, 16 January 1954.

13   "Local Union Would Bar Satchmo."

14   Audio letter from Louis Armstrong to Joe Glaser, 16 January 1954.

15   Jack Bradley, transcription of an unpublished interview with Richard Shaw, Jack Bradley Collection, 2005.1.2186, Louis Armstrong House Museum.

16   Hinton and Berger, *Bass Line*, 206.

17   Tape 1987.3.17, Louis Armstrong House Museum.

18   Milt Gabler, liner notes to *Louis Armstrong: An American Icon* (Hip-O HIPD3-40138, 1998), 9.

19   Ibid.

20   Louis Armstrong, letter from the Oriental Theater in Chicago dated 6 June 1950, *DownBeat*, 14 July 1950.

21   Bruce Jenkins, *Goodbye: In Search of Gordon Jenkins* (Berkeley, California: Frog, Ltd., 2005), 59.

22   Ibid., 60.

23   A concert at the University of North Carolina in Chapel Hill on May 8, recorded by a member of the audience, shows the All Stars of this period to greatest advantage, especially on a stunningly accomplished version of "Lazy River" and a riotous version of "When the Saints Go Marching In" that lasts for more than ten minutes. On "Saints," Armstrong commands numerous encores, doubles the tempo, plays the melody an octave higher, improvises with preternatural brio, holds high concert G's as if it were 1931. Just an afternoon gig (he'd play again later that night), but here was confirmation that when sufficiently inspired, Armstrong could still push himself to the limits of musical genius. This material can be heard on a commercially released two-CD set on the Avid label, *Louis Armstrong & the All-Stars at the University of North Carolina* (AMSC 870).

24   Tape 1987.3.17, Louis Armstrong House Museum.

25   Dan Morgenstern, interview with the author, 19 April 2004.

26 Bigard, *With Louis and the Duke,* 123.

27 Tape 1987.3.341, Louis Armstrong House Museum.

28 Dan Morgenstern, liner notes to *The Complete Decca Studio Recordings of Louis Armstrong and the All Stars* (Mosaic MD6-146, 1993), 11.

29 Armstrong, "It's Tough to Top a Million," *Our World,* August 1954.

CHAPTER EIGHT

1 George Avakian, liner notes to *Louis Armstrong Plays W. C. Handy* (Columbia/Legacy CK 64925, 1997), 13–14.

2 George Avakian, interview with the author, 22 February 2007.

3 Ibid.

4 Ibid.

5 Avakian, liner notes to *Louis Armstrong Plays W. C. Handy,* 19.

6 George Avakian, conversation with the author, 4 August 2008.

7 Tape 1987.3.341, Louis Armstrong House Museum.

8 Avakian, liner notes to *Louis Armstrong Plays W. C. Handy,* 15.

9 Tape 1987.3.520, Louis Armstrong House Museum.

10 Tape 1987.3.341, Louis Armstrong House Museum.

11 Ibid.

12 John Norris, "Trummy Young: An Interview," *Coda,* August 1973, 10.

13 Nat Hentoff, "Review of *Louis Armstrong Plays W. C. Handy,*" *DownBeat,* 1 December 1954.

14 Leonard Feather, "The Three Lives of Louis Armstrong," *Esquire,* March 1955, 83.

15 Leonard Feather, "Satch Mellows a Little on Bop, but Only a Bit," *DownBeat,* 11 August 1954.

16 Leonard Feather, "Louis Still Lauds Guy, Digs Turk but Not Bird," *DownBeat,* 25 August 1954.

17 Feather, "Satch Mellows a Little."

18 Murray Kempton, "The Kicks," *New York Post,* 20 August 1954.

19 Wilfred Lowe, "The Jazz Jester?," *Jazz Journal,* September 1954, 7.

20 Ibid.

21 Dan Morgenstern, "Introduction to *Satchmo: My Life in New Orleans,*" in *Living with Jazz,* ed. Sheldon Meyer (New York: Pantheon Books, 2004), 52.

22 Whitney Balliett, "Good King Louis," *Saturday Review,* 27 November 1954.

23 *The Wonderful World of Louis Armstrong,* directed by Peter Davis and Terry Henebery (KAY Video Jazz, 1981). Courtesy of Håkan Forsberg.

24 Jack Bradley, interview with the author, 13 October 2007.

25 Avakian interview.

26 Ibid.

27 George Avakian, letter to Joe Glaser, 17 May 1955. Courtesy of Chris Albertson.

28 Dan Morgenstern, interview with the author, 19 April 2004.

29 Barney Bigard and Barry Martyn, *With Louis and the Duke: The Autobiography of a Jazz Clarinetist* (New York: Oxford University Press, 1986), 124.

30 Dan Morgenstern, liner notes to *The Complete Decca Studio Recordings of Louis Armstrong and the All Stars* (Mosaic MD6-146, 1993), 12.

31 Louis Armstrong, letter to Joe Glaser, 8 September 1955, 2008.1.44, Louis Armstrong House Museum.

CHAPTER NINE

1   Joe Glaser, letter to George Avakian, 19 May 1955. Courtesy of Chris Albertson.
2   George Avakian, letter to Joe Glaser, 19 September 1955. Courtesy of Chris Albertson.
3   George Avakian, liner notes to *Louis Armstrong: 16 Most Requested Songs* (Columbia/ Legacy CK 57900, 1994), 5.
4   George Avakian, interview with the author, 22 February 2007.
5   Ibid.
6   Felix Belaire Jr., "United States Has Secret Sonic Weapon—Jazz," *New York Times,* 16 November 1955.
7   Gösta Hägglöf, liner notes to *Louis Armstrong in Scandinavia, Vol. 3* (Storyville 101 8350, 2005), 3.
8   "The 'Riot' Over Armstrong in Europe," *Record Mirror,* 14 January 1956.
9   "Interview with Louis Armstrong: 'They Cross Iron Curtain to Hear American Jazz,' " *U.S. News & World Report,* 2 December 1955, 59.
10 "The Trumpet Madness," *Newsweek,* 19 December 1955.
11 "Interview with Louis Armstrong: 'They Cross,' " 59.
12 Ibid., 58.
13 Ibid., 62.
14 "The Trumpet Madness."
15 Tape 1987.3.14, Louis Armstrong House Museum.
16 George Avakian, interoffice memo to Goddard Lieberson, 29 December 1955. Courtesy of Chris Albertson.
17 Avakian, liner notes to *Louis Armstrong: 16 Most Requested Songs,* 5.
18 O.K., "Jazz and Swing," *Gramophone,* May 1956, 82.
19 *The Wonderful World of Louis Armstrong,* directed by Peter Davis and Terry Henebery (KAY Video Jazz, 1981). Courtesy of Håkan Forsberg.
20 Humphrey Lyttelton, *Satchmo: The Story of Louis Armstrong,* 10-part BBC radio series broadcast in 1971. Tapes courtesy of David Ostwald.
21 Ibid.
22 Tape 1987.3.28, Louis Armstrong House Museum.
23 Arvell Shaw, interview for *Jazz: A Film by Ken Burns,* www.pbs.org/jazz/about/pdfs/ ShawA.pdf.
24 Tape 1987.3.14, Louis Armstrong House Museum.
25 "56 Jazz Reviews," in *DownBeat,* undated, IJS.
26 Sinclair Traill and Gerald Lascelles, *Just Jazz* (London: Peter Davies, 1957), 4–5.
27 Louis Armstrong, Voice of America interview, July 1956. Courtesy of David Ostwald.
28 Joe Glaser, letter to George Avakian, 16 March 1956. Courtesy of Chris Albertson.
29 George Avakian, interoffice memo to Goddard Lieberson and J. B. Conkling, 19 March 1956. Courtesy of Chris Albertson.
30 Financially, Armstrong was doing well, having earned a total of $22,089.74 from the label as of January 31, 1956. C. J. McClinch Jr., interoffice memo to George Avakian, 28 February 1956. Courtesy of Chris Albertson.

31 George Avakian, interoffice memo to Goddard Lieberson and J. B. Conking, 20 March 1956. Courtesy of Chris Albertson.

32 Joe Glaser, letter to George Avakian, 22 March 1956. Courtesy of Chris Albertson.

33 George Avakian, interoffice memo to Goddard Lieberson and J. B. Conkling, 27 March 1956. Courtesy of Chris Albertson.

34 Joe Glaser, letter to George Avakian, 28 March 1956. Courtesy of Chris Albertson.

35 George Avakian, interoffice memo to J. B. Conkling and Goddard Lieberson, 2 April 1956. Courtesy of Chris Albertson.

36 George Avakian, interoffice memo to Goddard Lieberson, 20 April 1956. Courtesy of Chris Albertson.

37 Joe Glaser, letter to George Avakian, 25 April 1956. Courtesy of Chris Albertson.

38 Eddy Gilmore, untitled Associated Press story, 3 May 1956, IJS.

39 Kenneth Allsop, "Genius is rationed," *Evening Standard,* 5 May 1956.

40 Eddy Gilmore, "Happy Ambassador for U.S. That's Our Satchmo Abroad," *Hartford Courant,* 27 May 1956, 16E.

41 Ibid.

42 Eddy Gilmore, "Princess Meg Digs That Ol' Satchmo Big," *New York Daily News,* 10 May 1956.

43 "Armstrong's Jazz 'Sends' a Princess," *New York Times,* 10 May 1956. The Duke of Kent also attended a show at Empress Hall, but only one unknown reporter noted the following: "At one point in his concert the unpredictable Satchmo announced with a mischievous grin, 'We'll drape this one on the Duke of Kent, one of our fans here tonight. Here it is—"Ain't Misbehavin'." ' " Seeing how that quote didn't spread, it's possible that it was made up to ride the coattails of all the other Princess Margaret stories.

44 Humphrey Lyttelton, "Satchmo Post-Mortems," *Musical Express,* 1 June 1956.

45 Robert Raymond, *Black Star in the Wind* (London: Macgibbon & Kee, 1960), 221.

46 Ibid., 223.

47 "Armstrong's 'Axe' Gasses Ghanese Fans," *Pittsburgh Courier,* 2 June 1956.

48 Raymond, *Black Star,* 225.

49 "Satchmo Gets Big Greeting on Gold Coast," *New York Daily News,* 24 May 1956.

50 "Just Very," *Time,* 4 June 1956.

51 George Padmore, "A Holiday Honored 'Satchmo' Armstrong," *Crisis,* June/July 1956.

52 Raymond, *Black Star,* 228.

53 Ibid., 230.

54 Ibid., 230–231.

55 Ibid. 231–232.

56 Ibid., 235.

57 "Good Will with Horns," *Newsweek,* 4 June 1956.

58 Raymond, *Black Star,* 239.

59 Ibid., 240.

60 "Good Will with Horns."

61 Raymond, *Black Star,* 240.

62 When Murrow included this scene in his eventual documentary, *Satchmo the Great,* it featured Armstrong's voice dedicating "Black and Blue" "to the Prime Minister." For over fifty years, that has been a central part of the story. However, Armstrong's private reel-to-reel tape collection contains the audio of almost an hour of this concert, now

housed at the Louis Armstrong House Museum. According to the tape, Armstrong did play "Black and Blue," but he didn't dedicate it to Nkrumah. Instead, he dedicated the next number, "Stompin' at the Savoy," a drum feature for Barrett Deems, perhaps knowing how important drums were to Africa. In the finished film (and resulting soundtrack album), Armstrong's words have been edited to make it appear that he dedicated "Black and Blue" to Nkrumah. However, Raymond recalled that the CBS camera crew set up their equipment to film only one number, which was "Black and Blue." Thus, the footage of Nkrumah listening, smiling, and appearing to wipe away a tear is all from "Black and Blue," but the introduction is fake. Tape 1987.3.284, Louis Armstrong House Museum.

63 Raymond, *Black Star,* 242.
64 Ibid., 243.
65 Ibid., 246.
66 "Just Very."

CHAPTER TEN

1   " '50 Years of Jazz' to Medinah," *Chicago American,* 23 May 1956.
2   "Helen Hayes Concert Narrator," *Chicago News,* 17 May 1956.
3   Joe Glaser, letter to George Avakian, 26 May 1956. Courtesy of Chris Albertson.
4   Nat Hentoff, liner notes to *Satchmo the Great* (Columbia/Legacy: CK 62170, 2000), 12.
5   George Avakian, interoffice memo to Walter Dean, 17 July 1956. Courtesy of Chris Albertson.
6   Louis Armstrong, telegram to Joe Glaser, 6 August 1955, 1997-34, Louis Armstrong House Museum.
7   Ernie Anderson, "Louis Armstrong & Joe Glaser, Part 2: The All Stars," *Storyville* 161, 1 March 1995, 174.
8   Louis Armstrong, "Letter to Joe Glaser," in *Louis Armstrong in His Own Words,* ed. Thomas Brothers (Oxford: Oxford University Press, 1999), 157–163.
9   John S. Wilson, "Music: Jazz Is Tested at Stadium," *New York Times,* 16 July 1956.
10   Harold Lovette, "Louis Armstrong: Is He an Immature Jazz Fan?," *Metronome,* August 1956.
11   Ibid.
12   "Satchmo Plays, Negroes Barred in Indianapolis," *St. Louis Argus,* 6 July 1956, 9.
13   "Armstrong Indignant Over Race Ban Story—Says He Loves Race," *Pittsburgh Courier,* 28 July 1956, 15.
14   Jonathan Mark Souther, *New Orleans on Parade: Tourism and Transformation of the Crescent City* (Louisiana: Louisiana State University Press, 2006), 77–78.
15   Eddy Gilmore, "Happy Ambassador for U.S. That's Our Satchmo Abroad," *Hartford Courant,* 27 May 1956, 16E.
16   "Jazz Grew Up 'On the Wagon,' " *San Francisco News,* 25 September 1958.
17   Louis Armstrong, Voice of America interview, July 1956. Tapes courtesy of David Ostwald.
18   Ingrid Monson, *Freedom Sounds: Civil Rights Call Out to Jazz and Africa* (New York: Oxford University Press, 2007), 59–60.
19   Tape 1987.3.14, Louis Armstrong House Museum.

20   William Ruhlmann, liner notes to *The Complete Verve Recordings of Ella Fitzgerald and Louis Armstrong* (Verve 354 537 2842, 1997), 8.

21   Ibid., 9-10.

22   *DownBeat* review clipping.

23   "Lose Weight the Satchmo Way." Multiple versions of Armstrong's diet chart can be found at the Louis Armstrong House Museum, Jack Bradley Collection, 2008.3.462.

24   Art Chenoweth, "Satchmo 'Grabs Sleep' for Session Tonight," *Oregon Journal,* 2 October 1956.

25   William Kennedy, "Music Don't Know No Age," *GQ,* August 1992, 146.

26   "Satchmo Returns for Hungary Relief," *Melody Maker,* 24 November 24, 1956.

27   Humphrey Lyttelton, *Satchmo: The Story of Louis Armstrong,* 10-part BBC radio series broadcast in 1971. Tapes courtesy of David Ostwald.

28   "Satchmo Doesn't Dig the Maestro on Those British Bom-Bom Beats," United Press story, *New York World Telegram and Sun,* 18 December 1956, IJS.

29   "Satch Given Big Ovation by Britons," 19 December 1956, IJS.

30   Robert Musel, "Satchmo Buries Liszt As London Cats Roar," United Press story, 19 December 1956, IJS.

31   Ibid.

32   "Satch Given Big Ovation by Britons."

33   Max Jones, "Storm at Armstrong Relief Fund Concert," *Melody Maker,* 22 December 1956.

34   Musel, "Satchmo Buries Liszt."

35   Jones, "Storm at Armstrong Relief Fund Concert."

36   Dan Morgenstern, liner notes to *The Complete Decca Studio Recordings of Louis Armstrong and the All Stars* (Mosaic MD6-146, 1993), 5.

37   Ibid.

38   Morgenstern, liner notes to *The Complete Decca Studio Recordings,* 12.

39   Ibid., 13.

40   Whitney Balliett, "The Three Louis," *New Yorker,* 28 September 1957.

41   Randy Sandke, conversation with the author, 16 February 2006.

42   Dave Whitney, "*Satchmo: A Musical Autobiography* (1957)," *Pete Kelly's Blog,* 7 March 2009. http://petekellysblog.blogspot.com/2009/03/satchmo-musical-autobiography-1957.html

43   *Satchmo,* directed by Gary Giddins with Kendrick Simmons, 1989.

CHAPTER ELEVEN

1   "Takes More'n Tenn. Bomb to Stop Satchmo," *New York Post,* 20 February 1957.

2   "Dynamite Blast Fails to Move Those Cats," Associated Press report from Knoxville, Tennessee, 20 February 1957.

3   David Halberstam, "A Day with Satchmo," *Reporter,* 2 May 1957.

4   Ibid.

5   Ibid.

6   Interestingly, Armstrong changed his mind on rock not too long after Halberstam's article appeared, saying, "Nothin' wrong with rock n' roll. The cats have fun with it. It's nothing new. I been doin' it for years." Sidney Fields, "Satch Hits a Note and the

Angels Sing," *New York Mirror,* 7 May 1957. And in 1960, he said, "Well, I got all kinds of music, Beethoven, Bach, and a whole lot of that rock and roll will make you feel so good. Those lyrics and the chords and those tunes, that music will be here for a long time. Because it's the essence of jazz and everything comes from jazz." Tape 1987.3.5, Louis Armstrong House Museum.

7 Ibid.

8 Gary Giddins, *Satchmo* (New York: Doubleday, 1988), 160.

9 Dan Morgenstern, liner notes to *The Great Chicago Concert 1956 Complete* (Columbia/Legacy C2K 65119, 1997), 14.

10 Ibid., 15.

11 Laurence Bergreen, *Louis Armstrong: An Extravagant Life* (New York: Broadway Books, 1997), 470.

12 Tape 1987.3.158, Louis Armstrong House Museum.

13 Morgenstern, liner notes to *The Great Chicago Concert,* 15–16.

14 Murray Kempton, "Birthday Party," *New York Post,* July 1957, IJS.

15 Ibid.

16 Giddins, *Satchmo,* 160.

17 Morgenstern, liner notes to *The Great Chicago Concert,* 16.

18 Marc Myers, "JazzWax: Interview: Russ Garcia (Part 2)," 18 September 2008, http://www.jazzwax.com/2008/09/interview-rus-1.html.

19 William Ruhlmann, liner notes to *The Complete Verve Recordings of Ella Fitzgerald and Louis Armstrong* (Verve 354 537 2842, 1997), 6–7.

20 Dan Morgenstern, liner notes to *Let's Do It* (Verve 314 529 017-2, 1995), 8.

21 William Ruhlmann, "Interview with Norman Granz About Louis Armstrong/Ella Fitzgerald Recordings," unpublished, mid-1996. Courtesy of Tad Hershorn.

22 Patrick Scott, "Louis and Ella Do *Porgy and Bess,*" *Toronto Globe and Mail,* 13 June 1959.

23 Max Jones, "Louis Looks In," *Melody Maker,* 15 October 1960.

24 Humphrey Lyttelton, *Satchmo: The Story of Louis Armstrong,* 10-part BBC radio series broadcast in 1971. Tapes courtesy of David Ostwald.

25 Ruhlmann, "Interview with Norman Granz."

26 Ibid.

27 Ernie Anderson, "Joe Glaser & Louis Armstrong, Part 2: The All Stars," *Storyville* 161, 1 March 1995, 176–178.

28 Louis Armstrong, telegram to Joe Glaser, 25 August 1957, reproduced in *Jazz,* a catalog of jazz-related items being auctioned by Guernsey's, New York City, in 2005.

29 "Louis Armstrong, Barring Soviet Tour, Denounces Eisenhower and Gov. Faubus," Associated Press report, *New York Times,* 19 September 1957.

30 David Margolick, "The Day Louis Armstrong Made Noise," *New York Times,* 23 September 2007.

31 " 'Satchmo' Cancels Tour: 'My People' Mistreated," Associated Press report, *New York Herald,* 19 September 1957.

32 Ibid.

33 " 'Satchmo' Tells Off Ike, U.S.!," *Pittsburgh Courier,* 28 September 1957, 33.

34 Ibid.

35 Geoffrey C. Ward and Ken Burns, *Jazz: A History of America's Music* (New York: Knopf, 2001), 396.

36   Sam Lacy, "Theatrical Whirl," *Baltimore Afro-American,* 24 September 1957, 14.

37   "Satch's Sour Note," *Redlands Facts,* 23 September 1957.

38   Unidentified newspaper clipping, 25 September 1957, IJS.

39   "Aim Dixie Boycott at Satch, Others," *Daily Defender,* 23 September 1957, 3.

40   Robert M. Ratcliffe, "Behind the Headlines," *Pittsburgh Courier,* 19 October 1957, A4. Upon reading about the boycott, Norman Granz angrily wrote to a Mississippi radio station, "I am interested in this, not only because I feel Armstrong, as a citizen of this country, has as much right to his opinion as anyone else, but also because he happens to be an important artist on my label. I think it is unfair that he, Lena Horne and Eartha Kitt should bear the brunt of WBKH's prejudice and so I suggest that WBKH ban my entire label from their so-called radio station."

41   "Armstrong Lauds Eisenhower for Little Rock Action," *New York Times,* 26 September 1957.

42   U.S. Attorney General Herbert Brownell Jr. ("Brownwell" was an Armstrong mistake.)

43   Thomas Brothers, ed., *Louis Armstrong in His Own Words* (Oxford: Oxford University Press, 1999), 194.

44   "Eisenhower 'Has a Soul,' Satchmo Says," *Hartford Courant,* 10 October 1957, 2.

45   Robert Williams, "Satchmo's No Spokesman, Says Sammy Davis Jr.," *New York Post,* 4 October 1957. When the *Post* asked Joe Glaser about Davis's remarks, Glaser told them, "[Armstrong] doesn't want to talk about Sammy Davis Jr. If Sammy Davis Jr. wants to talk about Louis Armstrong and get some publicity, let him. But Louis is not interested into getting into argument with HIM. Who cares about Sammy Davis Jr.?"

46   Louis Armstrong, as told to David Duchs, "Daddy, How the Country Has Changed!," *Ebony,* May 1961, 81–90.

47   Tape 1987.3.715, Louis Armstrong House Museum.

48   Tape 1987.3.493, Louis Armstrong House Museum.

49   Krin Gabbard, "Actor and Musician: Louis Armstrong and His Films," in *The Louis Armstrong Companion,* ed. Joshua Berrett (New York: Schirmer Books, 1999), 210.

50   Ward and Burns, *Jazz,* 397.

51   Tape 1987.3.493, Louis Armstrong House Museum.

52   Alexander T. Goodale, "Answer to Satchmo," *Spartanburg Herald-Journal,* 22 September 1957, 14.

53   Irving Lieberman, "No Color Line at Satchmo's Ark. U. Date," *New York Post,* 14 October 1957.

54   "Arkansas U. Cancels Satchmo; His Manager Says 'Who Cares?'," *New York Post,* 16 October 1957.

55   Tape 1987.3.493, Louis Armstrong House Museum.

56   Louis Armstrong, "Louis Armstrong + the Jewish Family in New Orleans, La., the Year of 1907," in Brothers (ed.), *Louis Armstrong in His Own Words,* 9.

CHAPTER TWELVE

1   John Chilton, liner notes to *Louis Armstrong Meets Oscar Peterson* (Verve 314 539 0600-2, 1997), 3.

2   Once, when I was listening to this solo with him, jazz historian Lewis Porter commented, "He out-Mileses Miles!"

3   "Armstrong and Band to Tour South America," *Hartford Courant,* 28 October 1957, 8.

4   Ernie Anderson, "Louis Armstrong, A Personal Memoir," *Storyville* 148, 1 December 1991, 136.

5   "Louis Armstrong Asks Yogi's Mask to Protect 'Chops,' " *Lewiston Daily Sun,* 2 November 1957, 11.

6   Dorothy Kilgallen, "The Voice of Broadway," *Kentucky New Era,* 17 December 1957, 13.

7   Jim Bishop, "Jim Bishop, Reporter, Tells the Story of: Satchmo—The Telegram," *Toronto Telegram,* 30 December 1957.

8   Philip Sykes, "Satchmo in City Shrugs Off Critic," *Toronto Telegram,* 23 January 1958.

9   Ibid.

10   "They Get 'Blues' Waiting in Vain for Old Satchmo," *Hartford Courant,* 25 February 1958, 12A.

11   "Satchmo Toots 'Sour Notes' in Blast at NAACP," *Pittsburgh Courier,* 8 March 1958.

12   Tape 1987.3.158, Louis Armstrong House Museum.

13   David Bradbury, *Armstrong* (London: Haus Publishing, 2003), 108.

14   Sinclair Traill and Gerald Lascelles, *Just Jazz* (London: Peter Davies, 1957), 8–9.

15   Jack Lesberg, *Jazz Journal,* July 1970, 24.

16   Tape 1987.3.159, Louis Armstrong House Museum.

17   Humphrey Lyttelton, *Satchmo: The Story of Louis Armstrong,* 10-part BBC radio series broadcast in 1971. Tapes courtesy of David Ostwald.

18   Tape 1987.3.5, Louis Armstrong House Museum.

19   *DownBeat,* undated review, IJS.

20   Danny Barcelona, interview with the author, 7 January 2005.

21   Ibid.

22   Danny Barcelona, interview with the author, 9 January 2005.

23   Patrick Scott, "Satchmo Shows He Can Still Pack the House," *Toronto Globe and Mail,* 25 February 1958.

24   Morris Duff, "Quits Satchmo As Armstrong Music Bored," *Toronto Daily Star,* 4 October 1958.

25   Phil Person, e-mail to the author, 5 November 2008.

26   "Riot at Jam Session," *New York Times,* 25 March 1959.

27   "How to Do the Impossible," *DownBeat,* 25 June 1959.

28   "Satchmo Skips Only Tibet in '59 World Tour," 26 August 1958, IJS.

29   Patricia Willard, interview with Trummy Young, 1976, JOHP.

30   Ibid.

31   "The Egyptians Insist Louis Armstrong's a Spy," *New York Post,* 13 November 1959.

32   "Yugoslavs Sit Hours to Applaud Jazz," United Press International report, *Toronto Daily Star,* 2 April 1959.

33   " 'Satchmovic' Biggest Hit in Yugoslavia," *Pittsburgh Courier,* 24 April 1959.

34   Eddy Gilmore, " 'Satchmo' Offers Music to Relax Big 4 'Cats,' " Associated Press report, *Elmira Advertiser,* 14 May 1959.

35   " 'Satchmo' Shrugs Off Tag of Good Will Ambassador," United Press International story, *Baton Rouge Advocate,* 4 June 1959.

CHAPTER THIRTEEN

1 Ed Sullivan, "Little Old New York: Americans in Italy," *New York Daily News,* 26 June 1959. Menotti explained that opera singer Eileen Farrell would sing in place of Armstrong, fronting the All Stars. "An opera singer can't do it," Armstrong complained. However, Trummy Young responded, "Yes she can. We ran through it just an hour ago and she's terrific. That girl's just wasting her talents with the longhairs." Sullivan reported that Billy Kyle, Danny Barcelona, Mort Herbert, and Peanuts Hucko all told Armstrong to relax and take it easy. Farrell did the show and even won some laughs by picking up a trumpet and pretending she was about to play it.

2 *The Mike Douglas Show,* 26 May 1970.

3 "Satchmo Felled by Pneumonia at Italian Fete," Associated Press story, 24 June 1959, IJS.

4 "Louis Armstrong Improved," Associated Press story, 25 June 1959, IJS.

5 "Armstrong Very Ill: But Physicians Differ on the Exact Details of Sickness," Associated Press story, 25 June 1959, IJS.

6 " 'Satchmo' Has Relapse; Wife at Bedside," 25 June 1959, IJS.

7 "Satchmo Goes Into a Coma; Rome Heart Doctors Called," Associated Press story, *New York Post,* 25 June 1959.

8 Reynolds Packard, "Satchmo Takes Turn for Worse; Fever Up," 25 June 1959, IJS.

9 *The Mike Douglas Show,* 26 May 1970.

10 "Satchmo Gains, Fever Down," United Press International story, 26 June 1959, IJS.

11 "Hungry Satchmo Greedily Plays His Horn of Plenty," Associated Press story, *New York Daily News,* 28 June 1959, IJS.

12 "Armstrong Is Better," United Press International story, 26 June 1959, IJS.

13 "Satchmo Fine, Now in Rome," United Press International story, 29 June 1959, IJS.

14 Louis Armstrong, letter to Dizzy and Lorraine Gillespie, 1 July 1959, 1987.9.11, Louis Armstrong House Museum.

15 Tape 1987.3.5, Louis Armstrong House Museum.

16 Eric Salzman, "Armstrong Pulls a Jazz Surprise," *New York Times,* 5 July 1959.

17 Ibid.

18 Tape 1987.3.5, Louis Armstrong House Museum.

19 *Laughin' Louis: A Film Portrait of Louis Armstrong,* 1984 documentary.

20 Leonard Feather, "The Three Armstrongs," *Melody Maker,* 22 August 1959.

21 Hugh Thomson, "Satchmo Armstrong Hale, Hardy as Ever," *Toronto Daily Star,* 20 July 1959.

22 Feather, "The Three Armstrongs."

23 John Norris, "Second Chorus," *Coda,* August 1959, 21.

24 Danny Barcelona, interview with the author, 7 January 2005.

25 Mike Baillie, liner notes to *Louis Armstrong and the Dukes of Dixieland, Vol. 1* (Blue Moon BMCD 3071, 1997), 3.

26 Stanley Dance, *The World of Earl Hines* (New York: Charles Scribner's Sons, 1977), 225.

27 John S. Wilson, "Satchmo Plays King Oliver," *DownBeat,* 10 November 1960, 33–34.

28 "Round Up," *Jet,* 22 October 1959, 28–29.

29 Louis Armstrong, as told to David Duchs, "Daddy, How the Country Has Changed!," *Ebony,* May 1961, 88.

30 "Louis and New Orleans," *DownBeat,* 7 January 1960.

31 "Satchmo Blasted in New Orleans," unidentified newspaper clipping, November 1959–January 1960, IJS.

CHAPTER FOURTEEN

1 Stanley Dance, *The World of Earl Hines* (New York: Charles Scribner's Sons, 1977), 226.

2 Barney Bigard and Barry Martyn, *With Louis and the Duke: The Autobiography of a Jazz Clarinetist* (New York: Oxford University Press, 1986), 133.

3 Bill Coss and Herb Snitzer, "On the Road with Louis Armstrong," *Metronome,* December 1960, 13.

4 Louis Armstrong, letter to Joe Glaser, 17 May 1960, 1997-29, Louis Armstrong House Museum.

5 Dan Morgenstern, e-mail to the author, 1 April 2010. Morgenstern's mention of "Mister Glaser" is a reference to how Armstrong always addressed his manager. Some have assumed that this was akin to a servant calling his boss "Mister," but to Louis it was simply a sign of respect. In a conversation with George Avakian in 1953, Armstrong vented about his previous manager Johnny Collins. Collins got drunk and during a verbal altercation called Armstrong a "nigger." In relating the story in 1953, Armstrong demonstrated how he had lost all respect for Collins. "You know what I told him? He come to apologize," Armstrong said. "I said, 'You're a rotten sonofabitch anyway. I've always respected you.' I've never called him 'Johnny Collins.' Right now, I've never called Joe Glaser 'Joe Glaser'—[it's] 'Mister.' I say [to Collins], 'You lost my fucking respect for you when you did that. Not that I've never been called "nigger" before. But from you?' "

6 Mike Baillie, liner notes to *Louis Armstrong and the Dukes of Dixieland, Vol. 2* (Blue Moon BMCD 3073, 1997), 4.

7 Rich Matteson, speaking on "Louis Armstrong—Play for Someone You Love (clinic)," a YouTube video, http://www.youtube.com/watch?v=dNKlmRPPGNs.

8 Humphrey Lyttelton, *Satchmo: The Story of Louis Armstrong,* 10-part BBC radio series broadcast in 1971. Tapes courtesy of David Ostwald.

9 Judith Robinson, "The Swingin' Persuader: Satch Swings to Africa over an Ocean of Pepsi," *Toronto Telegram,* 20 September 1960.

10 "Satchmo Aids College," Reuters item, 8 September 1960, IJS.

11 Max Jones, "Louis Looks In," *Melody Maker,* 15 October 1960.

12 "Satchmo Is Real Cool About S. Africa Ban," Reuters story, *New York Post,* 12 October 1960.

13 "Pepsi in Africa," October 1960, IJS.

14 "They Don't Dig Satchmo," *Toronto Telegram,* 19 October 1960, IJS.

15 Scrapbook 1987.3.39, Louis Armstrong House Museum.

16 *The Mike Douglas Show,* aired 27 May 1970.

17 "Ambassador Satchmo," *Long Branch Record,* 12 November 1960. The same editorial appeared as "He's Doing What Comes Naturally" in the *Wisconsin Rapids Tribune,* 18 November 1960.

18 Gilbert Millstein, "Africa Harks to Satch's Horn," *New York Times Magazine,* 20 November 1960, 71.

19 Ibid., 71.

20 Ibid., 76.

21 Max Jones, "With Louis and Duke in Paris," *Melody Maker,* 7 January 1961.

22 Danny Barcelona, interview with the author, 7 January 2005.

23 "Singer Middleton Stricken in Africa," *Jet,* 16 February 1961, 15.

24 Louis Armstrong, letter to Joe Glaser, February 1961, reproduced in *Jazz,* a catalog of
     jazz-related items auctioned by Guernsey's, New York City, 2005.

25 Bigard, *With Louis and the Duke,* 109.

26 Tape 1987.3.5, Louis Armstrong House Museum.

27 "Satchmo Says He Won't Hire Another Female Singer," *Jet,* 6 April 1961, 59.

28 Dan Morgenstern, liner notes to *The California Concerts* (Decca GRD-4-613, 1992), 11.

29 Louis Armstrong, letter to Joe Glaser, February 1961, reproduced in *Jazz.*

30 Jack O'Brian, "Carter to Play Louis Armstrong," *Sarasota Journal,* 17 August 1981, 7.

31 Joe Glaser, letter to Louis Armstrong, 24 July 1961, 2008.1.119, Louis Armstrong House
     Museum.

32 Stuart Nicholson, *Reminiscing in Tempo* (Boston: Northeastern University Press, 1999),
     328–329.

33 Bigard, *With Louis and the Duke,* 133.

34 Joe Darensbourg and Peter Vacher, *Jazz Odyssey: The Autobiography of Joe Darensbourg*
     (Baton Rouge: Louisiana State University Press, 1987), 16–17.

35 Ibid., 161–162.

36 Ibid., 162–163.

37 Barry Martyn, interview with Joe Darensbourg, 1984, JOHP.

38 Darensbourg and Vacher, *Jazz Odyssey,* 162.

39 Ibid., 165.

40 Ibid.

41 Ibid.

42 Ibid.

43 The popular young rhythm-and-blues singer LaVern Baker was an early candidate who
     even got as far as sharing an engagement with Armstrong at Basin Street East, the two
     bringing down the house on "That's My Desire." Armstrong offered Baker the regular
     position as female vocalist in the All Stars, but she was too busy forming a nightclub act
     of her own. (Joe Glaser would book her for the next few years.)

44 Jewel Brown, interview with the author, 15 September 2006.

45 Ibid.

46 Louis Armstrong, Voice of America interview, July 1956. Courtesy of David Ostwald.

47 Dan Morgenstern, interview with the author, 19 April 2004.

48 Bill Kirchner, interview with Cozy Cole, 1980, JOHP.

49 Phil Person, e-mail to the author, 5 November 2008.

50 Jack Bradley, interview with the author, 13 October 2007.

51 Chip Stern, liner notes to *The Real Ambassadors* (Columbia/Legacy CD 57663, 1994), 7.

52 "The Dave Brubeck–Columbia Records Story." Insert, Columbia/Legacy's various Bru-
     beck releases, 1998.

53 Tape 1987.3.191, Louis Armstrong House Museum.

54 Stern, liner notes to *The Real Ambassadors,* 6.

55 Jack Bradley, "Armstrong-Brubeck Recording Dates," unpublished notes on the *Real*

Ambassadors sessions, located in scrapbook "Louis 1960–1962," Jack Bradley Collection, 2008.2.3, Louis Armstrong House Museum.

56 Stern, liner notes to *The Real Ambassadors,* 5.

57 Bradley interview.

58 Bradley, "Armstrong-Brubeck Recording Dates."

59 *Joachim-Ernst Behrendt Presents Satchmo* (Jazz Door DVD, JD 11017, 2005).

60 "The Real Ambassadors," script, Jack Bradley Collection, 2008.3.518, Louis Armstrong House Museum.

61 Interview with Dave Brubeck for *Jazz: A Film by Ken Burns,* taken from the PBS Web site, http://www.pbs.org/jazz/about/pdfs/Brubeck.pdf.

62 Dave Brubeck, liner notes to *The Real Ambassadors,* 5.

63 Leonard Feather, "Satchmo—Then and Now," *International Musicians,* January 1962.

64 Brubeck, liner notes to *The Real Ambassadors,* 9.

65 Feather, "Satchmo—Then and Now."

66 Leonard Feather, "The Real Louis Armstrong," *DownBeat,* 1 March 1962, 23.

67 Feather, "Satchmo—Then And Now."

68 "Roundabout," *Coda,* August 1962, 6.

69 Darensbourg and Vacher, *Jazz Odyssey,* 165.

70 Brown interview.

71 Feather, "The Real Louis Armstrong," 23.

72 Darensbourg and Vacher, *Jazz Odyssey,* 167.

73 Brown interview.

74 Private tape made with George Avakian, 24 October 1953. Courtesy of David Ostwald.

75 Darensbourg and Vacher, *Jazz Odyssey,* 167, 169.

76 Ibid., 180.

77 Danny Barcelona, interview with the author, 9 January 2005.

78 Jack Bradley, transcription of an unpublished interview with Richard Shaw, Jack Bradley Collection, 2005.1.2186, Louis Armstrong House Museum.

79 Ibid.

CHAPTER FIFTEEN

1 Danny Barcelona, interview with the author, 7 January 2005.

2 Tape 1987.3.679, Louis Armstrong House Museum.

3 Arvell Shaw, interview for *Jazz: A Film by Ken Burns,* taken from the PBS Web site, http://www.pbs.org/jazz/about/about_transcripts.htm.

4 "Hello, Dolly!," 1987.13.371, Louis Armstrong House Museum.

5 Terry Teachout, *Pops: A Life of Louis Armstrong* (Boston: Houghton Mifflin Harcourt, 2009), 343.

6 Barry Martyn, interview with Joe Darensbourg, 1984, JOHP.

7 James Lincoln Collier, *Louis Armstrong: An American Genius* (New York: Oxford University Press, 1983), 322.

8 Barcelona interview.

9 Martyn, interview with Joe Darensbourg.

10 Geoffrey C. Ward and Ken Burns, *Jazz: A History of America's Music* (New York: Alfred A. Knopf, 2000), 436.

11 Joe Darensbourg and Peter Vacher, *Jazz Odyssey: The Autobiography of Joe Darensbourg* (Baton Rouge: Louisiana State University Press, 1987), 183.

12 Ward and Burns, *Jazz,* 436.

13 Barcelona interview.

14 Louis Armstrong, radio interview on *Be My Guest* (BBC, London, 2 July 1968). Courtesy of Jos Willems.

15 Darensbourg and Vacher, *Jazz Odyssey,* 183.

16 Patricia Willard, interview with Trummy Young, 1976, JOHP.

17 Dan Morgenstern, interview with the author,

18 John Norris, "Trummy Young: An Interview," *Coda,* August 1973, 9.

19 Tape 1987.3.345, Louis Armstrong House Museum.

20 Ron Welburn, interview with Russell "Big Chief" Moore, JOHP.

21 Ibid.

22 Jewel Brown, interview with the author, 15 September 2006.

23 Ibid., 132.

24 Ibid., 133.

25 Les Tomkins, "Playing with King Oliver Was Still the Real High-Spot," *Crescendo,* July 1965, 20–22.

26 Gary Giddins, *Satchmo* (New York: Doubleday, 1988), 191.

27 John S. Wilson, "Still The Champ," *New York Times,* 21 June 1964.

28 Patrick Scott, "Hello Louis! Satchmo Is Still Glowing at 64," *Toronto Globe,* July 30, 1964.

29 Barry Hale, "Dolly's the Ditty As Satchmo Sings," *Toronto Telegram,* July 30, 1964.

30 Brown interview.

31 Charles Sanders, "Louis Armstrong: The Reluctant Millionaire," *Ebony,* November 1964, 138.

32 Ibid., 144–146.

33 Ibid., 146.

34 Sanders, "Louis Armstrong," 138.

35 Jack Bradley, transcription of an unpublished interview with Richard Shaw, Jack Bradley Collection, 2005.1.2186, Louis Armstrong House Museum.

36 Jimmy Breslin, "A Normal Day with Joe Glaser," *New York Herald Tribune,* 15 November 1964, 24.

37 Darensbourg and Vacher, *Jazz Odyssey,* 184.

38 Ibid., 168.

39 Joe Muranyi, interview with the author, 26 October 2006.

40 Hugh Mulligan, "Satchmo Thrives on Steady Grind," Associated Press story, *Toronto Globe and Mail,* 4 August 1964.

41 Hugh Mulligan, August 23, 1964.

42 Mulligan, "Satchmo Thrives."

43 Breslin, "A Normal Day," 56.

44 Barcelona interview.

CHAPTER SIXTEEN

1   Dan Morgenstern, interview with the author, 19 April 2004.

2   Ron Welburn, interview with Russell "Big Chief" Moore, 1980, JOHP.

3 Morgenstern interview.
4 Ibid.
5 Arvell Shaw, interview for *Jazz: A Film by Ken Burns,* http://www.pbs.org/jazz/about/about_transcripts.htm.
6 "Louis Armstrong Scores Beating of Selma Negroes," Associated Press article, *New York Times,* 11 March 1965, 11.
7 "Armstrong Speaks Out on Racial Injustice," *DownBeat,* 22 April 1965, 14–15.
8 "Louis Armstrong Is Mum on Rights in East Berlin," United Press International article, *Baltimore Afro-American,* 23 March 1965, 6.
9 "Louis Armstrong in der DDR (Kulturzeit) oder: 'Nein, keine Waffen!' " YouTube video, http://www.youtube.com/watch?v=S0ozytbobWY.
10 Karlheinz Drechsel, liner notes to *Louis Armstrong: The Legendary Berlin Concert* (Jazz Point JP 1062, 2000), 5–6.
11 Ibid., 6.
12 Ibid., 5.
13 Joe Glaser, letter to George T. Simon, 24 December 1964, 2005-15, Louis Armstrong House Museum.
14 Buddy Catlett, interview with the author, 26 October 2006.
15 Susan Kastner, "Satchmo: Hits His Highest Note at 65," *Toronto Daily Star,* 17 July 1965.
16 Dan Morgenstern, "Yesterday, Today and Tomorrow: An Interview with Louis Armstrong," *DownBeat,* 15 July 1965, 18.
17 Patrick Scott, "An Ominous Streak Shows Up in Satchmo," *Toronto Globe and Mail,* 24 July 1965.
18 Patrick Scott, "Louis Armstrong: Prisoner of Fame," *Toronto Globe and Mail,* 7 August 1965.
19 Patrick Scott, "The Offstage Satchmo," *Globe Magazine,* 7 August 1965.
20 James Bacon, " 'Satchmo' Plans to Retire; He Just Can't Find Day Off," Associated Press story, *Fort Lauderdale News,* 6 October 1965.
21 Patrick Scott, "The Hot Miss Lil," *Globe Magazine,* 18 September 1965.
22 Patrick Scott, "The Crux of Satchmo's Dilemma," *Toronto Globe and Mail,* 16 October 1965.
23 Ibid.
24 "Louis Armstrong, 65, Hailed by Teen-Agers," United Press International story, *New York Times,* 5 July 1965, 9.
25 Louis Armstrong, letter to Lucille Armstrong, 24 September 1965, Louis Armstrong House Museum.
26 Louis Armstrong, letter to Lucille Armstrong, 31 September 1965, Louis Armstrong House Museum.
27 Jewel Brown, interview with the author, 15 September 2006.
28 Buddy Catlett, interview with the author, 26 October 2006.
29 Ruby Braff, taped conversation with Jack Bradley, 31 December 1991, 2005.1.2295, Jack Bradley Collection, Louis Armstrong House Museum.
30 *Time* magazine photo caption, 12 November 1965. Later in 1965, Armstrong appeared with Davis on the television game show *I've Got a Secret,* playing a duet with him on

"When the Saints Go Marchin' In," a sad and painful performance, as Davis hadn't played trumpet in decades, only to be handed one on live national TV.

31 Howard Thompson, "Screen: *This Property Is Condemned*," *New York Times*, 4 August 1966, 24.

32 Braff, taped conversation with Jack Bradley.

33 Geoffrey C. Ward and Ken Burns, *Jazz: A History of America's Music* (New York: Alfred A. Knopf, 2000), 397.

34 Catlett interview.

35 Jewel Brown, interview with the author, 15 September 2006.

36 Ibid.

37 "Billy Kyle, 53, Pianist Dies; Was with Louis Armstrong," *New York Times*, 24 February 1966, 19.

38 Brown interview.

39 Danny Barcelona, interview with the author, 9 January 2005.

40 Richard Meryman, "Louis Armstrong; An Authentic American Genius," *Life*, 11 April 1966, 112. Interestingly, when Meryman's interview was expanded and published by the Eakins Press in 1971, the author restored a line Armstrong spoke about Glaser immediately after this quote: "But sometimes, he went a little far out too."

41 Ibid., 114.

42 Ibid., 116.

43 Ibid., 95–96.

44 Ibid., 104.

45 Richard Meryman, *Louis Armstrong: A Self-Portrait* (New York: Eakins Press, 1971), 47–48.

46 Ibid., 46–47.

47 Jack Bradley, letter to "John," 21 March 1967, 2008.1.206, Jack Bradley Collection, Louis Armstrong House Museum.

48 Barcelona interview.

49 Robert Wahls, "Happy Birthday, Satchmo!," 3 July 1966, IJS.

50 Ed Berger, e-mail to the author, 18 February 2006.

CHAPTER SEVENTEEN

1 More on the history of Brunswick Records can be found at the very informative Web site http://www.brunswickrecords.com/history.htm.

2 Louis Armstrong, letter to Karlheinz Drechsel, 10 April 1967, 2008.1.30, Louis Armstrong House Museum.

3 Dan Morgenstern, interview with the author, 17 April 2004.

4 Buddy Catlett, interview with the author, 26 October 2006.

5 Larry King, "Everybody's Louie," *Harper's*, November 1967, 64.

6 Joe Muranyi, interview with the author, 26 October 2006.

7 Ibid.

8 Ibid.

9 Ibid.

10 King, "Everybody's Louie," 66.

11 Ibid., 63.

12 Ibid., 67.

13 Muranyi interview.

14 Humphrey Lyttelton, *Satchmo: The Story of Louis Armstrong,* 10-part BBC radio series broadcast in 1971. Tapes courtesy of David Ostwald.

15 Bob Thiele, as told to Bob Golden, *What a Wonderful World: A Lifetime of Recordings* (New York: Oxford University Press, 1995), 3.

16 Joe Muranyi, conversation with the author, 20 February 2008.

17 Louis Armstrong, radio interview on *Be My Guest,* BBC, London, 2 July 1968. Courtesy of Jos Willems.

18 Thiele, *What a Wonderful World,* 4.

19 Ibid., 4–5.

20 Ibid., 5. What Thiele doesn't mention in his book is the small fact that the session wasn't over yet after "What a Wonderful World" was recorded: the studio musicians and choir left and the All Stars took to the microphone to record two more songs. These peppy numbers must have satisfied Newton's appetite, but Thiele never mentions them. The first is 100 percent in the "Dolly" mode, another Broadway show tune, "Hellzapoppin'," complete with another banjoist on hand in Art Ryerson. But the flip side is a wonderful "Cabaret," honed to perfection after a full year of performing it live. Armstrong's trumpet shows no limitations, and the whole band sounds in top form. This version of "Cabaret" is joy personified, another testament that Armstrong's trumpet still had the power to surprise at such a late stage in the game.

21 "Louis Armstrong Is Ill," Associated Press story, *New York Times,* 26 September 1967, 52.

22 Louis Armstrong, letter to Slim Evans, 14 September 1967, 2008.1.32, Louis Armstrong House Museum.

23 Muranyi interview.

24 He even quoted the entire text of the song in a private letter to a Marine stationed in Vietnam, also in 1967. This letter is reprinted in full as "Letter to L/CPL. Villec (1967)," in *Louis Armstrong in His Own Words,* ed. Thomas Brothers (Oxford: Oxford University Press, 1999), 169–172.

25 Danny Barcelona, interview with the author, 9 January 2005.

26 Muranyi interview.

27 Ibid.

28 John S. Wilson, "Home Town Hails Armstrong," *New York Times,* 20 May 1968.

29 Max Jones and John Chilton, *Louis: The Louis Armstrong Story, 1900–1971* (Boston: Little, Brown and Company, 1971), 186.

30 Muranyi interview.

31 Steve Voce, "It Don't Mean a Thing: Hello Skinny," *Jazz Journal,* September 1968, 14.

32 Peter Harris, "Louis: The Best Show in Town," May 1968, IJS.

CHAPTER EIGHTEEN

1 James Lincoln Collier, *Louis Armstrong: An American Genius* (New York: Oxford University Press, 1983), 328.

2 "Dieting and Hard Work Bad Mixture for Satch," *DownBeat,* 31 October 1968, 1.

3 Louis Armstrong, letter to unknown recipients ("Good Evening Folks"), 1997-1.2, Louis Armstrong House Museum.

4 Collier, *Louis Armstrong,* 328.

5 Jim Tagalakis, "Louie in Concert: A Sight to Behold," *Lynn Daily Evening Item,* 7 July 1971, 10.

6 Collier, *Louis Armstrong,* 329. In his 2003 memoir, *Myself Among Others: A Life in Music* (New York: Da Capo Press), jazz impresario George Wein wrote about a 1970 conversation with Armstrong in which the trumpet player bitterly aired his resentment of his former manager. According to Wein, Armstrong told the story about going to see Glaser in a wheelchair, but instead of being shaken, he told Glaser, "I'll bury you, you mother-fucker." This is the exact opposite of every surviving tale of Armstrong and Glaser's relationship. Lucille, not really one of Glaser's biggest supporters, told the wheelchair story. Perhaps after a year and in another state of depression, Armstrong lashed out, but I feel that at the time of their mutual illnesses in 1969, Armstrong was devastated by Glaser's condition. Armstrong might have grown disillusioned with Associated Booking after Glaser's death. In a letter to friend Gösta Hägglof, Armstrong told him that Lucille was now his personal manager. Perhaps he didn't like his treatment by Associated Booking and angrily took it out on Glaser. Louis Armstrong, letter to Gösta Hägglof, 10 February 1971. 2011.1.4, Louis Armstrong Museum.

7 Louis Armstrong, letter to Little Brother Montgomery, 29 July 1969, 2010.6.1, Louis Armstrong House Museum. Truthfully, Glaser lost a big part of ABC way back in 1962 when he received a visit from an old associate, Sidney Korshak, the man the FBI once referred to as "the most powerful lawyer in the world." Korshak always had ties to the mob, and back in the 1920s he personally helped Glaser avoid jail time when he was arrested—twice—for beating women. Ernie Anderson heard the story from an unnamed Broadway press agent, who told it this way: "A guy from Chicago came into his office. 'I'm your new partner,' he told [Glaser]. Joe recognized this character from the old days on the South Side. He knew instantly that either he did what he was told or he died." After years of bullying people to get his way, Glaser had finally met his match. The "guy from Chicago" was Korshak, and according to Dennis McDougal, "By 1962, Glaser had ended all pretense of heading Associated Booking, formally sign-ing over all 'voting rights, dominion and control' to Korshak." Korshak might have taken control of the agency, but he definitely stayed hidden in the background. Jerry Heller wrote about his "two bosses" at ABC, Glaser and Korshak, but said, "I worked at Associated for months before I was aware of Sidney Korshak's presence. That was always Korshak's MO. He was the figurative man behind the curtain." It's not even known if Armstrong knew of Korshak's presence. Glaser always personally ran Arm-strong's career and remained the public face of Associated Booking. When he died, "Korshak officially took charge of the agency," according to McDougal. If he did, this was strictly a behind-the-scenes operation, as Glaser's will named Oscar Cohen as the new president of Associated Booking, with Dave Gold serving as vice-president and treasurer. Information also from Jerry Heller with Gil Reavill, *Ruthless* (New York: Simon and Schuster, 2007), 222–223, and Dennis McDougal, *The Last Mogul: Lew Wasserman, MCA, and the Hidden History of Hollywood* (New York: Da Capo Press, 2001), 141.

8   Ernie Anderson, "Louis Armstrong & Joe Glaser, Part 2: The All Stars," *Storyville* 161, 1 March 1995, 179.

9   Collier, *Louis Armstrong,* 330.

10 Anderson, "Joe Glaser & Louis Armstrong, Part 2," 179.

11 *The Dick Cavett Show,* 22 February 1971.

12 Louis Armstrong, "Louis Armstrong + the Jewish Family in New Orleans, La., the Year of 1907," in *Louis Armstrong in His Own Words,* ed. Thomas Brothers (Oxford: Oxford University Press, 1999), 6.

13 Gerald Early, " 'And I Will Sing of Joy and Pain for You': Louis Armstrong and the Great Jazz Tradition," *Tuxedo Junction: Essays on American Culture* (New York: Ecco Press, 1989), 295–296.

14 Armstrong, "Louis Armstrong + The Jewish Family," 8.

15 Ibid., 8–10.

16 "Potpourri," *DownBeat,* 17 April 1969, 15.

17 Albin Krebs, "Louis (Satchmo) Armstrong, the Jazz Trumpeter and Singer, Is Dead Here at 71," *New York Times,* 7 July 1971.

18 Tape 1987.3.387, Louis Armstrong House Museum.

19 Mark Schienbaum, "The Cats and Kids Fete Satch on His 69th Birthday," *Chicago Daily Defender,* 3 July 1969, 15.

20 *Nobody Does It Better,* 1998 television documentary, http://video.google.com/videoplay?docid=5340476382338057770.

21 *The Wonderful World of Louis Armstrong,* directed by John Akomfrah, (WinStar B00005B20K, 1999).

22 Louis Armstrong, "Good-Bye to All of You," in *Louis Armstrong in His Own Words,* 190.

23 Al Aronowitz, "Pop's Last Birthday Bash," *The Blacklisted Journalist,* 1 July 1996, http://www.blacklistedjournalist.com/Column11.htm.

24 Ian Dove, "Seen and Heard," *Coda,* August 1970, 44–45.

25 Ralph J. Gleason, "Rhythm Section: Everybody Loves Pops," *New York Post,* 30 June 1970.

26 Israel Shenker, " 'Just Plain Old Satchmo' Turns 70 Sweetly," *New York Times,* 4 July 1970.

27 An inadvertently humorous moment occurred when Armstrong had to make the long walk to the center of the stage . . . without knowing his wireless microphone was on! "Oh, you dog, you!" Armstrong exclaimed. "Sonofa—goddamn, this a long fucking walk! This is a long goddamn walk. Goddamn! Goddammit! Jesus Christ!" Once he arrived at the microphone with Carmichael, Armstrong asked to tell a joke and immediately told his favorite bawdy "hamburger" joke, breaking up the audience and starting the evening in a rambunctious mood. "I'm so glad to be here, I'm hamming it up," Armstrong told the audience.

28 *Jazz: A Film by Ken Burns,* episode 10, "A Masterpiece by Midnight."

29 Tape 1987.3.424, Louis Armstrong House Museum.

CHAPTER NINETEEN

1   Iain Calder, "2 Years After Doctors Said He Might Never Play in Public Again . . . Louis Armstrong and His Golden Trumpet Make Triumphant Comeback," *National*

Enquirer, undated clipping, Jack Bradley Collection, 2008.5.39, Louis Armstrong House Museum.

2 Joe Muranyi, interview with the author, 25 October 2006.

3 Eddie Adams, "Death Stopped the Trumpet's Will but the Smile of Satch Will Live On," *Florence* Times, 7 July 1971, 18.

4 Calder, "2 Years After."

5 Leonard Feather, *From Satchmo to Miles* (New York: Da Capo Press, 1987), 38.

6 Dan Morgenstern, interview with the author, 19 April 2004.

7 Muranyi interview.

8 Morgenstern interview.

9 Humphrey Lyttelton, *Last Chorus: An Autobiographical Medley* (London: JR Books, 2008), 175.

10 Ibid., 176.

11 Louis Armstrong, letter to Dr. Gary Zucker, 30 December 1971, 1996-7.2, Louis Armstrong House Museum.

12 Laurence Bergreen, *Louis Armstrong: An Extravagant Life* (New York: Broadway Books, 1997), 492.

13 Tape 1987.3.571, Louis Armstrong House Museum.

14 Tape 1987.3.486, Louis Armstrong House Museum.

15 John S. Wilson, "Louis Armstrong Takes to Horn in His Comeback at the Waldorf," *New York Times,* 7 March 1971, 60.

16 James Lincoln Collier, *Louis Armstrong: An American Genius* (New York: Oxford University Press, 1983), 331–332.

17 *Laughin' Louis: A Film Portrait of Louis Armstrong,* 1984.

18 Richard Meryman, "Satchmo, the greatest of all, is gone," *Life,* 16 July 1971, 70–71.

19 *Laughin' Louis.*

20 Ibid.

21 Earl Wilson, "It Happened Last Night," *Sarasota Herald-Tribune,* 8 March 1971, 10.

22 Phoebe Jacobs, conversation with the author, 31 August 2010.

23 In Patrick Scott's 1965 *Globe Magazine* account of a day with Armstrong, he recounts Armstrong wearing a pair of knee-high support hose made by Jobst and saying, "Can't get by without 'em since I had the phlebitis."

24 Arvell Shaw, *The Wonderful World of Louis Armstrong,* directed by Peter Davis and Terry Henebery (KAY Video Jazz, 1981). Courtesy of Håkan Forsberg.

25 Eddie Adams, " 'Satchmo' Appeared to Sense Hotel Date Was Last," *Toledo Blade,* 11 July 1971, 43.

26 Ibid.

27 Danny Barcelona, interview with the author, 9 January 2005.

28 Muranyi interview.

29 Adams, " 'Satchmo' Appeared to Sense."

30 Miriam Sandford, "Louis Armstrong: Ich lebe! Nur Trompete darf ich noch nicht spielen" [I Live! Only I can't play the trumpet yet], *Jasmin,* 16 July 1971. English translation at Louis Armstrong House Museum, 1987.6.234.

31 "Satchmo in Good Spirits," United Press International story, *Chicago Daily Defender,* 20 April 1971, 5.

32 Sandford, "Louis Armstrong: Ich lebe!"

33 Ibid.

34 Ibid.

35 Bernard Rabin, "Satchmo Can't Annoy Next-Door Neighbor," *New York Daily News,* 27 May 1971.

36 Michael Cogswell, *Louis Armstrong: The Offstage Story of Satchmo* (Portland: Collectors Press, 2003), 46.

37 Howard E. Fischer, *Jazz Exposé: The New York Jazz Museum and the Power Struggle That Destroyed It* (Nashville: Sundog, 2004), 26. There are some who believe that Milne is a different location than the Waif's Home and that Armstrong never attended it. But Armstrong himself never believed this, telling George Avakian as early as on a private tape recorded in 1953 that the Colored Waif's Home he went to was now called Milne.

38 Louis Armstrong, letter to Slim Evans, 30 May 1971, 2008.1.33, Louis Armstrong House Museum.

39 Sandford, "Louis Armstrong: Ich lebe!"

40 Marc H. Miller, "Louis Armstrong: A Portrait Record," in *Louis Armstrong: A Cultural Legacy,* ed. Marc H. Miller (Seattle: University of Washington Press, 1994), 213, 216.

41 Gary Giddins, *Satchmo* (New York: Doubleday, 1988), 206–210. Armstrong dated it 1970 but clearly meant 1971, since he had only one tracheotomy and that was in 1971.

42 Patricia E. Davis, " 'I'm One Old Cat You Just Can't Kill,' " *Sunday Bulletin,* 4 July 1971, 3.

43 "Old Cat That You Just Can't Kill," *Beaver County Times,* 6 July 1971, B14.

44 Ross Gilligan, "Satchmo Says He's Not Ready for Retirement," *Miami News,* 26 June 1971, 8A.

45 "Back Smiling—Jazz Great Louis 'Satchmo' Armstrong," *New York Times,* 25 June 1971.

46 Mary Campbell, "Satchmo Still Wailing Away at 70," *Sarasota Herald-Tribune,* 5 July 1970, 13.

47 Peter McLaughlin and William Reel, "A Eulogy for Louis: He Loved Everyone," *New York Daily News,* 7 July 1971.

48 Collier, *Louis Armstrong,* 332.

49 John Birks (Dizzy) Gillespie, "Louis Armstrong, 1900–1971," *New York Times,* 7 July 1971.

50 Albin Krebs, "Louis Armstrong, Jazz Trumpeter and Singer, Dies," *New York Times,* 7 July 1971.

51 "New Orleans Not Final Resting Place for Satchmo; Some Disappointed," *Jet,* 22 July 1971, 57.

52 Scrapbook 1987.8.72, Louis Armstrong House Museum.

53 Roy Wilkins, "Armstrong Set the Example," *Los Angeles Times,* 16 July 1971.

54 Cordell Thompson and Phyl Garland, "Satchmo's Funeral 'White and Dead' in New York but 'Black, Alive and Swinging' in New Orleans," *Jet,* 29 July 1971, 58.

55 Muranyi interview.

56 David Bradbury, *Armstrong* (London: Haus Publishing, 2003), 134.

57 Thompson and Garland, "Satchmo's Funeral," 62.

58 John S. Wilson, "Armstrong Was Root Source of Jazz," *New York Times,* 7 July 1971.

59 Craig McGregor, "Armstrong: 'His Tragedy Is One We All Share,' " *New York Times,* 8 August 1971.

60 Gerald Early, " 'And I Will Sing of Joy and Pain for You': Louis Armstrong and the

Great Jazz Tradition," *Tuxedo Junction: Essays on American Culture* (New York: Ecco Press, 1989), 291-292.

61　"Roses for Satchmo," *DownBeat,* 9 July 1970, 17, 19.

62　Gilbert Millstein, "The Most Un-Average Cat," liner notes to *Satchmo: A Musical Autobiography* (Decca DXM-155, 1957).

Index

TEXTUAL PERMISSIONS

Grateful acknowledgment is made to the following for permission to reprint previously published material:

Beinstock Publishing Company: Excerpts from "Boy from New Orleans" by Bob Thiele, Ruth Roberts, and Bill Katz. Reprinted by permission of Bienstock Publishing Company.

The Globe and Mail: Excerpts from four articles by Patrick Scott: "The Crux of Satchmo's Dilemma" (October 16, 1965), "An Ominous Streak Shows up in Satchmo" (July 24, 1965), "Satchmo Shows He Can Still Pack the House" (February 25, 1958), and "Louis Armstrong: Prisoner of Fame" (August 7, 1965). Reprinted by permission of *The Globe and Mail*.

Jazzpoint Records: Excerpts from the liner notes by Karlheinz Drechsel to the Jazzpoint Records CD *Louis Armstrong: The Legendary Berlin Concert*. Reprinted by permission of Jazzpoint Records.

New Pittsburgh Courier: Excerpts from "Armstrong Indignant over Race Ban Story—Says He Loves Race" (July 28, 1956) and "Satchmo Tells Off Ike" (September 28, 1957). Reprinted by permission of the *New Pittsburgh Courier*.

frontispiece
Photograph by Jack Bradley; the Jack Bradley Collection, Louis Armstrong House Museum

FIRST INSERT

page 1
Louis with Big Sid Catlett and Jack Teagarden: Courtesy of the Louis Armstrong House Museum
Louis and Joe Glaser: Photograph by Bill Mark; courtesy of the Louis Armstrong House Museum

page 2
Louis as King of the Zulus: Courtesy of the Louis Armstrong House Museum
The All Stars in Brussels: Courtesy of the Louis Armstrong House Museum

page 3
Louis and Lucille, Rome: Courtesy of the Louis Armstrong House Museum
Publicity photo for March of Dimes benefit: Courtesy of the Louis Armstrong House Museum

page 4
Louis recording, 1954: The Jack Bradley Collection, Louis Armstrong House Museum
Louis and Velma Middleton: The Jack Bradley Collection, Louis Armstrong House Museum
Louis with Lotte Lenya: The Jack Bradley Collection, Louis Armstrong House Museum

page 5
Louis in Chicago: Photo by Milan Schijatschky; courtesy of the Louis Armstrong House Museum
Louis, Swiss Kriss box, and unidentified fan: Courtesy of the Louis Armstrong House Museum

page 6

Edmond Hall, Louis, and Trummy Young in the Gold Coast: Courtesy of the Louis
    Armstrong House Museum

page 7

Louis at a school in Hinsdale, Illinois: Photo by Milan Schijatschky, courtesy of the Louis
    Armstrong House Museum

Louis in performance: Photo by Milan Schijatschky; from the personal collection of Milan
    Schijatschky

page 8

Louis with Danny Barcelona: Courtesy of the Louis Armstrong House Museum

Louis with nun: Courtesy of the Louis Armstrong House Museum

SECOND INSERT

page 1

Louis in Rome, 1959: Courtesy of the Louis Armstrong House Museum

page 2

Louis performing in West Africa, 1960: Courtesy of the Louis Armstrong House Museum

Louis and the Great Sphinx: Courtesy of the Louis Armstrong House Museum

page 3

Louis with Dave Brubeck: Photograph by Jack Bradley; the Jack Bradley Collection, Louis
    Armstrong House Museum

Louis flanked by Jerry Herman and Dave Kappin: Photograph by Jack Bradley; the Jack
    Bradley Collection, Louis Armstrong House Museum

Louis filming a Suzy Cute commercial: The Jack Bradley Collection, Louis Armstrong
    House Museum

page 4

Louis backstage in Denmark: Courtesy of the Louis Armstrong House Museum

Louis in Prague: Courtesy of the Louis Armstrong House Museum

page 5

Louis with Bob Thiele: Photograph by Jack Bradley; the Jack Bradley Collection, Louis
    Armstrong House Museum

Central Park photo shoot for *Louis "Country and Western" Armstrong*: Photograph by Jack
    Bradley; the Jack Bradley Collection, Louis Armstrong House Museum

page 6

Louis with his reel-to-reel tape collection: Courtesy of the Louis Armstrong House
    Museum

Louis with children in Corona, Queens: Courtesy of the Louis Armstrong House Museum

FRANK
The Voice
by James Kaplan

Frank Sinatra was the best-known entertainer of the twentieth century—infinitely charismatic, lionized and notorious in equal measure. But despite his mammoth fame, Sinatra the man has remained an enigma. Now James Kaplan brings deeper insight than ever before to the complex psyche and turbulent life behind that incomparable voice, from Sinatra's humble beginning in Hoboken to his fall from grace and Oscar-winning return in *From Here to Eternity*. Here at last is the biographer who makes the reader feel what it was really like to be Frank Sinatra—as man, as musician, as tortured genius.

Music/Biography

BENEATH THE UNDERDOG
His Words as Composed by Mingus
by Charles Mingus

Bass player extraordinaire Charles Mingus, who died in 1979, is one of the essential composers in the history of jazz, and *Beneath the Underdog*, his celebrated, wild, funny, demonic, anguished, shocking, and profoundly moving memoir, is the greatest autobiography ever written by a jazz musician. It tells of his God-haunted childhood in Watts during the 1920s and 1930s; his outcast adolescent years; his apprenticeship, not only with jazzmen but also with pimps, hookers, junkies and hoodlums; and his golden years in New York City with such legendary figures as Duke Ellington, Lionel Hampton, Miles Davis, Charlie Parker, and Dizzy Gillespie. Here is Mingus in his own words, from shabby roadhouses to fabulous estates, from the psychiatric wards of Bellevue to words of mysticism and solitude, but for all his travels never straying too far, always returning to the music.

Music/Autobiography

BOB DYLAN IN AMERICA

by Sean Wilentz

Sean Wilentz discovered Bob Dylan's music as a teenager growing up in Greenwich Village. Now, almost half a century later, he revisits Dylan's work with the skills of an eminent American historian as well as the passion of a fan. Beginning with Dylan's explosion onto the scene in 1961, Wilentz follows the emerging artist as he develops a body of work unique in America's cultural history. Using his unprecedented access to studio tapes, recording notes, and rare photographs, he places Dylan's music in the context of its time and offers a stunning critical appreciation of Dylan both as a songwriter and performer.

Biography

VINTAGE BOOKS & ANCHOR BOOKS
Available at your local bookstore, or visit
www.randomhouse.com